Heidegger, Coping, and Cognitive Science

Heidegger, Coping, and Cognitive Science

Essays in Honor of Hubert L. Dreyfus, Volume 2

edited by Mark A. Wrathall and Jeff Malpas

The MIT Press
Cambridge, Massachusetts
London, England

This book was set in New Baskerville by Best-set Typesetter Ltd., Hong Kong, and printed and bound in the United States of America

Library of Congress Cataloging-in-Publication Data

Heidegger, coping, and cognitive science: essays in honor of Hubert L. Dreyfus / edited by Mark A. Wrathall and Jeff Malpas.
    p. cm.
  Includes bibliographical references and index.
  ISBN 0-262-23207-3 (v. 1 : alk. paper)—ISBN 0-262-73127-4
(v. 1 : pbk. : alk. paper)
—ISBN 0-262-23208-1 (v. 2 : alk. paper)—ISBN 0-262-73128-2
(v. 2 : pbk. : alk. paper)
    1. Dreyfus, Hubert L.   2. Heidegger, Martin, 1889-1976—Influence.
3. Philosophy, European.   4. Philosophy, American—20th century.
5. Computers.   6. Cognitive science.   7. Dreyfus, Hubert L.—Influence.
I. Dreyfus, Hubert L.   II. Wrathall, Mark A.   III. Malpas, J. E.

B945. D764 H45 2000
193—dc21

                                                              99-056942

Contents

Foreword

Terry Winograd

My first exposure to Hubert Dreyfus was in the form of a memo written in 1968 by my graduate research advisor, Seymour Papert, at the MIT Artificial Intelligence Laboratory. It was titled "The Artificial Intelligence of Hubert L. Dreyfus: A Budget of Fallacies."[1] As the title suggests, the memo was not favorable to Dreyfus. Papert took him to task at length on a number of technical issues and on his reading of previous work in the field. Looking back today, I find it interesting to see how much of the discussion centered on the question of whether computers could play chess. If we take into account only the arguments that were made twenty years ago and the results of the Deep Blue/Kasparov matches of 1997, we might well come away thinking that Dreyfus was wrong. Computers can indeed play world-championship-level chess, and they do so not through any new philosophical insights, but simply through assiduous engineering within the standard paradigms of computation.

On the other hand, in the intervening three decades we have witnessed confirmation of Dreyfus's prediction that artificial intelligence and cognitive science would fail to live up to most of the high expectations of the early practitioners (both in the practical sphere and as a body of solid scientific theory). While this does not constitute a proof of the impossibility of artificial intelligence, it does imply that the problems are much deeper than the original researchers anticipated.

But the argument over the possibility of chess and of artificial intelligence in general is narrow when it focuses on categorizing activities into those that computers can do and those that computers cannot do. In fact, the very idea of trying to prove what computers cannot do is a decidedly computer-like perspective. Dreyfus may well have been wrong in some of his specific interpretations about how computers operate and what they can possibly do, but he has made a major contribution to computing and cognitive science. This contribution is not in the form of mechanisms and proofs, but in opening up a new horizon of questioning: creating a clearing in which new concerns appear and old questions are reformulated.

It would be an exaggeration to claim that the challenges posed by Dreyfus have been taken to heart by most AI researchers or cognitive scientists, even today. There are large chasms between the world of phenomenology and the world of symbolic programming. But there has been a steady undercurrent of re-evaluation and new thinking, even leading to a dissertation in that same MIT AI lab twenty years later that opens chapter 1 with: "Everyday life is almost wholly routine, an intricate dance between someone who is trying to get something done and a fundamentally benign world that is continually shaped by the bustle of human activity . . . A great deal is known about the nature of human activity. . . . Among the foundational works in this tradition were . . . : Heidegger's account of everyday routine activities."[2]

My own work in computer science was greatly influenced by conversations with Dreyfus over a period of many years, as reflected in my 1986 book with Fernando Flores[3] and in a complete shift of research direction, away from artificial intelligence toward a phenomenologically informed perspective on human-computer interaction. In a broader sense, we see an influence of Dreyfus's critiques of symbol manipulation in the growth of research on "nonsymbolic" or "emergent" approaches to cognition, such as neural networks.[4]

The question of what, if any, scientific approaches will succeed in achieving humanlike competence in significant application domains is still very much open. The ultimate assessment will of course be in the future (perhaps the far future) when scholars look back at twentieth-century achievements and fantasies with the hindsight that will help distinguish between the two. What is clear, though, is that Dreyfus has made a deep contribution to the creation of a culture of reflection—of questioning the deep premises—that informs and shapes computing and cognitive research.

Dreyfus has also played a key role as the primary introducer and interpreter of Martin Heidegger to the computer and technical world. It is not a great exaggeration to say that discussions of Heidegger within that world are really discussions of Dreyfus's exposition of Heidegger, both in his books about artificial intelligence and in his commentary on Heidegger's *Being and Time*.[5] This is certainly true of the book I wrote with Flores, which in turn was the first introduction to Heidegger for many people in computer and cognitive science.

As the papers in this volume indicate, Hubert Dreyfus has inspired a generation of thinkers about philosophy and practicality. He has provided both a standard for interpretation and a starting point from which to explore the implications of phenomenology for our understanding of computers and cognition. This book is not a capstone to his work, but a beginning of new explorations, inspired by his example of applying deep philosophical analysis to the concerns of our modern technological world.

Acknowledgments

The editors would like to give special thanks to Geneviève Dreyfus, without whom this volume would never have appeared, as well as to Larry Cohen at The MIT Press. Preparation of the volumes was completed while Jeff Malpas was a Humboldt Research Fellow at the University of Heidelberg. A number of students at Brigham Young University have assisted in the preparation of this manuscript, including Charle Allen, Julie Carter, Krista Halverson, Jodi Harranek, Kimberly Hicken, Heidi Poulson, Sarah Stewart, Marissa Turley, Megan Wilding, and Julie Murdock.

Introduction

Mark A. Wrathall and Jeff Malpas

In any conversation with Hubert Dreyfus it quickly becomes apparent that he has a rare sort of intellectual curiosity—one motivated not by fields of study or traditionally defined problem areas but by issues that confront him in the course of his life, in his encounter with the world around him. This trait has not only led him to research and write on a variety of topics somewhat removed from the discipline of philosophy, but has made his philosophical work a source of inspiration to a broad range of nonphilosophers.

Volume 1 of this Festschrift includes essays that engage with philosophers, notably Heidegger, in the so-called continental tradition, in order to pay tribute to Dreyfus's influence on the transmission and understanding of the work of these philosophers. But in addition to making an exegetical contribution to philosophy, Dreyfus's encounter with thinkers such as Heidegger and Merleau-Ponty provided the basis for the critique of artificial intelligence that first brought Dreyfus to the attention, not merely of the philosophical community, but of a wider public. Computing and artificial intelligence are not the only area where Dreyfus's research has been driven by his phenomenologically based intuitions. In his research with Stuart Dreyfus on skillful coping in activities as varied as chess-playing and driving, for instance, one finds Dreyfus working out of the same sort of phenomenological sense of the world that seems to have inspired, in very different ways, Heidegger's account of equipmentality and Merleau-Ponty's analysis of embodied responsiveness.

Dreyfus's phenomenology of skillful coping has buttressed his critique of artificial intelligence by providing an argument for the nonrepresentational nature of the background familiarity that makes intentional action possible. And it has also provided a productive basis for addressing problems in fields as diverse as ethics, business, and psychology.

The present volume consists of papers by scholars who have been influenced by Dreyfus's readiness to apply the insights of phenomenology to a variety of issues. Inasmuch as the papers draw, whether explicitly or implicitly, on Dreyfus's engagement with continental philosophy, the volume represents a broadening and continuation of, rather than a break with, the discussions in volume 1. But here Dreyfus's reading of philosophers such as Heidegger forms the background to issues in intentionality, skillful coping, and embodiment.

Part I of this volume addresses the phenomenologically based analysis of practices that is at the foundation of much of Dreyfus's work. Joseph Rouse, David Stern, Theodore R. Schatzki, John Searle, Mark A. Wrathall, and Charles Taylor all comment on issues raised by Dreyfus's account of skillful coping. Rouse complicates Dreyfus's distinction between practical coping on the one hand, and explicit articulation and theoretical understanding on the other, arguing for the assimilation of explicit articulation and theoretical reflection to the general model of skillful comportment. Schatzki develops a feature of Dreyfus's critique of Cartesian theories of mental states, arguing that folk-psychological attribution of beliefs, desires, and so forth, can and should be understood in a way compatible with Dreyfus's phenomenological critique of models in which having a mental state implies thematic awareness. Both Stern and Searle address Dreyfus's claims about the kind of analysis that can be given of practical comportment. Stern focuses on the idea that skillful coping resists any formal analysis and explores a number of arguments that support this claim. Searle, like Rouse, points to certain explicit forms of skillful coping (such as writing philosophical papers) in order to challenge Dreyfus's antirepresentationalist account of intentionality, and he argues that all skillful coping necessarily involves intentional mental activity. Searle also argues that Dreyfus's phenomenology of skillful coping fails to take appropriate account of the consciousness involved in and the logical structure of skillful coping. Wrathall's paper explores the relation between Searle's and Dreyfus's versions of the "background" in the context of a discussion of Heidegger's notion of disclosure. Charles Taylor concludes this part of the volume by examining the antifoundationalist consequences of emphasizing the importance of embodied, skillful coping in our understanding of human existence. At the same time, Taylor insists that there is more to historical change than a mere drift of practices.

Part II explores the continuing relevance of Dreyfus's phenomenological critique of contemporary forms of Cartesianism. Daniel Andler reviews the Dreyfusian influence on both artificial intelligence and contemporary movements in cognitive science such as the "new contextualists." Both Andler's paper and the paper by Sean D. Kelly respond to criticisms of Dreyfus's use of phenomenology in working on issues concerning intentionality and the mind—criticisms such as those posed by Searle's paper. Kelly argues that phenomenology ought to play a role in the cognitive sciences, likening the relationship between phenomenology and brain science to that of data and model. He illustrates this relationship in the context of skillful motor behaviors. Harry Collins explores the substantive limits of Dreyfus's critiques of artificial intelligence, arguing that Dreyfus fails adequately to consider different kinds of knowledge and different kinds of embodiment. The consequence is, Collins contends, that while Dreyfus correctly identifies things computers cannot do, he is not of much assistance in determining what can be done with computers. Finally, Albert Borgmann offers a diagnosis of the consequences and limits of the disembodiment made possible by computer-mediated multiuser domains.

The last part of the book presents several representative examples of the sort of work Dreyfus's "applied philosophy" has inspired. Dreyfus credits Charles Spinosa with pointing out to him that his best work has always been guided by a phenomenological sense for the everyday phenomena underlying the philosophical ideas in question. Spinosa's paper attempts to do just this by describing the sort of contemporary experience that illuminates Heidegger's account of the divine. This, in turn, allows Spinosa to offer a nonmystical account

Mark A. Wrathall and Jeff Malpas

of what it would mean for us to make room for an experience of living gods in our contemporary, disenchanted world. Robert C. Solomon draws on Dreyfus's work to elaborate an account of trust which understands it as a shared and transformative practice, rather than as either a mental or psychological state on the one hand, or as a sociological fact on the other. George Downing extends Dreyfus's account of expert coping to understand the role of the body in our experience of emotion. Fernando Flores employs a Dreyfusian understanding of practical being-in-the-world to reinterpret business practices, and outlines some of the consequences for business theory of this reinterpretation. Finally, Patricia Benner explores the consequences for nursing theory and practice of Dreyfus's interpretation of Heidegger's account of care as the structure of everyday practical engagement with the world; she also uses Dreyfus's interpretation of Heidegger's account of technology to criticize the growing dominance of techno-medicine.

I

Coping and Intentionality

1

Coping and Its Contrasts[1]

Joseph Rouse

Hubert Dreyfus is best known for his influential interpretations of Heidegger, Husserl, Merleau-Ponty, and Foucault, and for his detailed, phenomenologically based criticisms of artificial intelligence research and cognitivist philosophies of mind. These two projects come together in Dreyfus's phenomenological articulation of embodied, practical coping with one's surroundings as a fundamental mode of intentionality. Dreyfus claims that a philosophical explication should begin with the intentional directedness of such practical skillfulness, as more basic than the forms of directedness familiar from other accounts of intentionality. While he thereby makes common cause with non-naturalistic approaches to explicating intentionality, Dreyfus crucially differentiates his account from the familiar interpretivist, mentalist, and social-normative non-naturalisms.

In this chapter, I endorse Dreyfus's claim to the distinctiveness and importance of the intentionality of practical coping. I also argue, however, that Dreyfus's efforts to differentiate coping from other modes of intentionality concede too much to some of the philosophical programs that he criticizes. Dreyfus introduces the distinctive intentionality of practical coping by contrasting it to explicit, linguistic representation, to theoretical understanding (especially in the natural sciences and mathematics) and to accountability to social norms. For Dreyfus, practical coping can neither be made fully explicit nor can it be adequately explicated theoretically. While he does recognize the social normativity of everyday practical coping, he insists that its social character is dispensable for a philosophical account of intentional comportment. Linguistic representation, theoretical explanation, and social normativity are, he claims, distinct and important modes of intentional comportment, but they must be understood as phenomenologically founded upon practical coping.

I propose a reinterpretation of these three contrasts. What Dreyfus's work shows is not an irreducible difference between practical coping and explicit articulation, theoretical understanding, or social normativity, but rather the inadequacy of the received accounts of language, theory, and social norms which make possible the contrasts that set the stage for his account of coping. These contrasts were undoubtedly rhetorically important in introducing the distinctive features of Dreyfus's account, but they should be surpassed in order to appreciate fully its philosophical significance.

I   Coping with Intentionality

In this section, I shall explicate Dreyfus's account of the intentionality of practical coping without foregrounding his insistence upon its tacit, atheoretical, and asocial character. The contrasts to explicit interpretation, theoretical understanding, and social normativity then stand out as subsequent, debatable claims about the scope of practical intentionality rather than as constitutive contrasts that express its distinctive character as an intentional directedness.

By "practical coping," Dreyfus means to indicate the mostly smooth and unobtrusive responsiveness to circumstances that enables human beings to get around in the world. Its scope extends from mundane activities like using utensils to eat, walking across uneven terrain, or sitting and working at a desk, to the extraordinary mastery exhibited in competitive athletic performances or grandmaster chess. Tools figure prominently in these coping activities. Often we competently deal with a wide range of equipment as the background to more thematic performances: while holding a conversation, we unobtrusively adjust ourselves to a chair, the lighting, or the movements of others in the room; in writing a letter, we deftly wield the pen, hold the paper, lean on the desk, take a sip of coffee, and so forth.

The intentionality of practical coping is a directedness of bodies rather than minds. Dreyfus emphasizes bodily coordination and orientation toward the task at hand, as one hammers a nail, sits in a chair, drives to the grocery, or exchanges pleasantries at a party. Here a body is not an object with fixed boundaries, but the practical unification of coordinated activity. Mastery of a tool allows its incorporation within the field of one's bodily comportment; the difference between smooth competence and clumsy ineptness reflects the degree of bodily assimilation of the tool. Merleau-Ponty's example of a blind person's cane, or a myopic's eyeglasses, display relatively permanent extensions of the bodily field, but pens, chopsticks, automobiles, or wheelchairs (not to mention clothes) can be temporarily assimilated onto the near side of one's practical comportment toward the world. Bodies, one might say, are *geared* toward the world.

Such practical comportment is directed toward an actual situation. Three points are figured in this formulation. First, practical intentional comportment is not mediated by mental representations, a sensory manifold, tacit rules, or other forms of intentional content abstractable from the material setting of what one is doing. Practical coping instead discloses things themselves freed from intentional intermediaries. Second, these "things" are not discrete objects, but an interconnected setting organized around one's practical concerns. A fast-breaking basketball player is directed not just toward the ball she dribbles, but also toward the basket, the defenders, the teammates trailing the play or setting up on the wing, the cacophony of the crowd; or rather, to none of these things separately but toward the game in all its complexly articulated interrelatedness. Third, practical comportment is not a self-contained sequence of movements, but a flexible responsiveness to a situation as it unfolds. The situation is thus not a determinate arrangement of objects but the setting of some possible comportments. Some ways of responding to the situation are "called for," while others are out of place. These are not, however, a denumerable set of "actual" possibilities in hand, but the portent of some indeterminately "possible" ones.

This situational character of practical coping is an analogue to other intentional manifestations in a particular aspect or under a description. Intentional directedness traditionally has a sense, a particular "way" in which its object is manifest. Dreyfus takes this aspectual character of practical coping to be neither an "objective" characteristic of the things manifested, nor a definite projection or anticipation by an agent, but rather an intra-active[2] configuration of solicited activity and possible resistance and accord.

> In everyday absorbed coping, . . . when one's situation deviates from some optimal body-environment relationship, one's movement takes one close to that optimal form and thereby relieves the "tension" of the deviation. One's body is solicited by the situation to get into the right relation to it. . . . Our activity is completely geared into the demands of the situation.[3]

The situation is significant, and configured as a field of relevance, at least for the body that is set to respond appropriately.

The intra-activity of this manifestation reinforces Dreyfus's insistence that practical coping takes us directly to the things themselves. We can think in the absence of what is thought about, without losing the sense of our thoughts. To dribble in the absence of the basketball, however, is merely to pretend to dribble (or to *fail* to dribble). The activity is entirely different if there is no actual pattern of resistance and affordance to what one does, for practical coping is a responsiveness to such patterns. It is directed toward the actual environment, not toward some merely possible state of affairs. Thus, unlike familiar accounts of mental or linguistic intentionality, practical coping cannot *coherently* express its sense of a non-existent object. Such coping activities can indeed fail to engage their surroundings effectively. When that happens, however, intentional comportment at least momentarily falls apart. In reaching for a light switch that isn't there, or stepping toward the landing one stair too soon, I thrash or stumble, failing for the moment to get a coherent grip on anything without some adjustment. Unsuccessful moves are not senseless, but their sense is not even successfully expressed, let alone fulfilled.

This feature of the intentionality of practical comportment highlights Dreyfus's conjoining of two points that have often been conceived in opposition to one another. Practical comportment is a thoroughly *material* responsiveness to a material world. The hand that gently conforms itself to the contours of a teacup in a well-balanced grasp, the softball player who tracks the incoming fly ball and the tagging runner at third as she sets herself to catch and throw home in a single fluid response, or the conversationalist whose stance, expressions, gestures, and tones register and respond to the expressive posture of her interlocutor are bodily engagements with a material configuration of the world. Yet these are also *meaningfully* configured situations. For the softball player, the looping fly and the tagging runner stand out as salient, while the airplane passing overhead and the brawl in the stands behind third base recede into indeterminate background, even though the airplane and the brawl may be bigger, louder, and more "dramatic," than the ball and the runner along similar sight lines. The meaningfulness of bodily responsiveness to situations becomes obtrusive when a philosophical or psychological analysis omits it. Thus, Dreyfus tellingly objected to attempts to reduce situations to "merely" physical juxtapositions of things:

[AI researcher John] McCarthy seems to assume that ["being at home"] is the same thing as being in my house, that is, that it is a physical state. But I can be at home and be in the backyard, that is, not physically in my house at all. I can also be physically in my house and not be at home; for example, if I own the house but have not yet moved my furniture in. Being at home is a human situation.[4]

There "is" nothing there in the situation besides its material constituents, but the situation is a meaningful configuration of those constituents. As Dreyfus put it, "the meaningful objects embedded in their context of references among which we live are not a model of the world, . . . *they are the world itself.*"[5]

What "configures" a situation is the possibility of intelligible response to it by a being to whom the situation and its outcome *matter*. A situation is thus organized as a field of possible activity with something at stake. Dreyfus's Heideggerian account of situatedness structurally resembles Kant's conception of agency as the "end" of a practical stance toward the world as "means." Human beings are that "for-the-sake-of-which" a situation is meaningfully oriented; its constituents are "in-order-to" realize some possible way of being a "for-the-sake-of-which." The stakes in a situation, however, are not some more or less definite end, but a way of being: an open-ended practical grasp of how to make one's way in the world *as* a teacher, a gay man, a politically engaged citizen, a parent, a Presbyterian, a tough SOB, etc. Such ways of being are not definite plans of action directed toward the achievement of specific ends, but an ongoing integration of one's activities within a coherent "practice."[6] Moreover, wielding relevant equipment and interacting with other practitioners is not an indifferently instrumental taking up of various discrete "means" to chosen ends, but a referentially interrelated in-order-to-for-the-sake-of complex which sustains the intelligibility of its "component" practices and equipment.

The normativity that marks practical coping as genuinely intentional might thus seem pragmatic *instead of* alethic, marked by success or failure in dealing with circumstances and fulfilling various roles, rather than correct representation. Successful coping, however, is not the fulfillment of prespecifiable success conditions, but instead the maintenance and development of one's belonging to a practice through a flexible responsiveness to circumstances (think of successfully riding a bicycle across changing terrain). It would be better, therefore, to blur any such contrast between practical success and alethic disclosure. Not only does Dreyfus follow Heidegger in seeing practical coping as a kind of revealing; he explicitly denies any sharp contrast between acting and perceiving. Perceiving is neither a passive registration nor an intellectual synthesis, but is itself a kind of coping activity. Seeing a moving object, hearing spoken words, tasting a liquid, or feeling a texture requires an appropriate bodily set and a coordinated exploratory movement. Likewise, sustained activities involve a perceptive attentiveness to relevant circumstances, what Heidegger calls a "circumspective" (*umsichtig*) concern. Hence, pragmatic success and alethic disclosure should be understood to belong together.

We can now see an additional reason why a situation is not identical to a "merely" physical juxtaposition of objects. The situations that call for practical coping are constitutively temporal. The intentional directedness of an embodied agent does not just extend spatially beyond itself toward the object of its concerns. It is also a temporal directedness ahead toward the possible activities that would sustain its way of being. Such a situated directedness toward intelligible possibilities does not exist apart from actual configurations of equipment that can engage extant bodily repertoires of responsiveness, repertoires that must themselves be maintained and developed over time. A situation thereby incorporates a history; the present situation is both the *outcome* of a history embedded within it, and a solicitation toward and portent of possible futures.

This "historical" dimension of practical coping is perhaps most evident in the disciplining of bodies. Bodily repertoires for coping with surroundings are "produced by a specific technology of manipulation and formation."[7] Both the pervasive normalization of "das Man" and the bodily disciplines described by Foucault are ways in which bodily capacities are shaped and refined by physical surroundings and other bodily responses. These capacities are not produced by habitual repetition of movements, however, but by constraining and redirecting a body's active exploratory coping with its surroundings. Bodies are the assimilation of past practice refocused toward future possibilities; their capacities are neither causally imposed from without nor freely generated from within, but instead mark the ongoing intra-active configuration of a bodily field of activity. Bodies are situated within fields of power relations, without thereby becoming disempowered.

Recognition of the role of Foucauldian disciplines in shaping practical coping capacities might mistakenly suggest that the body as meaningful practical repertoire could be assembled from meaningless motions. After all, Foucault described techniques for the analysis and reconstruction of movements, "a breakdown of the total gesture into two parallel series: that of the parts of the body to be used . . . and that of the parts of the object manipulated . . . then the two sets of parts are correlated together according to a number of simple gestures [in] canonical succession."[8] Yet Dreyfus has repeatedly emphasized that such reconstructions cannot take full effect until the reconstructed sequence has been assimilated into a smooth bodily flow that revises and continues to adapt the initially practiced routines. The body that proceeds step by step in specified movements is the incompetent, inflexible body. The steps from learning to mastery shed the initially specified cues and patterns in favor of a fluid, adaptive responsiveness to meaningfully configured circumstances.

To recapitulate briefly, practical coping is "intentional" in two crucial respects. First, it is directed toward a situation *under an aspect*, which is constituted by the interrelations between *how* one comports oneself toward it, and what that comportment is *for*. How one reaches for, grasps, lifts, and tilts a cup gets its coherence from the cup's being for-sipping-from, and from the ways coffee-drinking belongs to a larger field of activity. Second, its directedness is *normative*: it can succeed or fail. Yet coping diverges from familiar renditions of intentionality in several crucial ways. It involves no psychological or semantic intermediaries, not even tacitly predetermined success conditions (which are instead flexible and openended). Nor is the body an intermediary, but is instead the intentional directedness itself: one does not form one's hand into a cup shape and move it to a presumed cup-location; one's hand reaches for and adjusts to the cup itself. Coping is thus always directed toward actual possibilities rather than a possible actuality. Its success is not the fulfillment of some determinately projected end, but an ongoing accommodation to what is afforded by circumstances. Failure, in turn, is not the expression of an unfulfilled sense, but an unconsummated expressiveness. One partially loses a grip on one's surroundings, without thereby getting hold of a setting that does not happen to exist. Finally, while bodily comportment is complex, it is not compositional: its "constituents" are not separable component movements, but merely distinguishable moments of a unified whole. Indeed, while one often acquires coping skills by practicing discrete component movements, their residual discreteness marks a possible failure of intentionality; they succeed only when transformed by assimilation into a relatively fluid unity.

II   Intentional Contrasts to Coping

Dreyfus has long argued that the intentionality of practical coping is distinct from and irreducible to other modes of intentional directedness. In particular, he takes the explicit articulation of propositional content, theoretical understanding, and social normativity to be distinct forms of intentional directedness that co-exist with practical coping (although possibly "founded" upon it). In this section, I shall briefly describe the contrasts that Dreyfus articulates between these various modes of intentional directedness.

Dreyfus's contrast between practical coping and explicit articulation is subtle and complex. First, it would be wrong to say that practical coping involves a "tacit" understanding embedded in skillful dealings with things. That would mistakenly suggest that skills are already propositionally contentful, even though their content is not explicitly spoken or kept in mind. Dreyfus insists instead that skillful coping does not have even tacit propositional content. Beliefs, desires, and other propositional attitudes are not appropriately attributed as background to coping skills; instead, Dreyfus argues that propositional attitudes are only intelligible against a background of nonpropositional comportments.

Dreyfus then distinguishes two successive levels of explication of coping skills (three, if one includes theoretical explication, discussed below).[9] At the first level,

the as-structure goes from being hidden in the understanding to being contextually explicit. We can, for example, notice that our hammer is too heavy, and ask for another one. Language is thus used in a shared context that is already meaningful, and gets its meaning by fitting into and contributing to this meaningful whole.[10]

A second level of explication occurs when contextual explication is not just attended to, but actually *expressed* linguistically. Thus,

in pointing out the characteristic of the hammer that needs attention I can "take a step back" from the immediate activity and attribute a "predicate" ("too heavy") to the hammer as "subject." This singles out the hammer and selects the difficulty of the hammering from a lot of other characteristics.[11]

Dreyfus's contrast of practical coping to explicit interpretation thus cannot be identified as a contrast between prediscursive and discursive intentionality. Language use can emerge at every level that Dreyfus identifies. Practical coping can *employ* language, as when one "communicates without wasting words"; it can take place *through* language use, as when one smoothly sustains the rhythm and flow of a conversation; and it can even be exhibited *in* one's ability to speak, as the articulate native speaker who "inhabits" a language differs from both language learners and less articulate speakers who struggle to find the right words (all of whom differ from those who confront a language as a code to be deciphered).

In the end, I think, the important contrast for Dreyfus is not between practical coping and the use of language, but between coping and propositional contentfulness. For one thing, Dreyfus is often less concerned with the content of assertions than with that of mental states. He explicitly distinguishes the intentionality of practical coping from "that of a mind with content directed toward objects"; the latter only arises

when ongoing coping is held up [and] we have to act deliberately. . . . If a doorknob we ordinarily use transparently sticks, we find ourselves *believing* the doorknob should turn, *trying* to turn it, *desiring* that it should turn, *expecting* the door to open, etc.[12]

The most crucial contrast between coping and (mental or linguistic) content, however, turns out to be the possibility of intentional comportment in the absence of its object.

In general, I can't exercise a skill except in conjunction with the appropriate equipment. On this most basic coping level, it turns out one cannot separate the intentional state from what satisfies it.[13]

Not surprisingly, Dreyfus believes that one can coherently express thoughts or claims about absent things; he only insists that such contentful expression differs from the ways we cope with our surroundings in everyday practice, and indeed depends upon everyday coping to sustain its contentfulness.

Dreyfus sees a more fundamental contrast to everyday practical coping exemplified in theoretical understanding. "Theory", for Dreyfus, primarily has the Platonic sense of *theoria*, of wonder and disengagement from practical involvement, but he also regards scientific theories as the intentional realization of such an attitude. In regarding things "theoretically," Dreyfus claims, we suspend the practical, contextual interrelations through which we encounter and understand our everyday situation. In so doing, we uncover an alternative way to be a thing.

Occurrent beings are revealed when *Dasein* takes a detached attitude toward things and decontextualizes them. Then things show up as independent of human purposes and even as independent of human existence.[14]

Such theoretical disclosure can also be understood as a third level of making things explicit. Ordinary assertions express what we attend to in contextual explication, but they do so in ways that still depend upon practical contextual cues for their sense. Indexical expressions would be the most obvious examples of contextually dependent expressions, but Dreyfus also highlights Heidegger's example, "The hammer is too heavy." The transition to theorizing is twofold: it involves detaching one's interactions and assertions from their specific contextual involvements, and recontextualizing them within the systematic relationships expressed in theories. Dreyfus takes these recontextualizations to be either purely formal systems of rules, or systems of causal relationships. In the end, the latter probably reduce to formal systems, however, since he seems to equate causal powers with what is disclosed by causal laws governing natural kinds, and the formal interrelations among such laws.

Dreyfus acknowledges that even theoretical science has practical involvements, both the "skills and instruments [that] decontextualize things and their properties"[15] and the mastery of the theoretical systems within which they are recontextualized. The intended contrast between practical coping and theoretical explication is thereby illuminated, however. Dreyfus asserts that "natural science, like any mode of existence, cannot make entirely explicit its projections, i.e., the basic assumptions and practical background skills in which the scientists dwell."[16] But what could it mean to make *anything* "entirely explicit"? Dreyfus seems to take theories to be deductively closed formal systems. A fully explicit system would then be one that was not only capable of expressing every property of every object in its domain, but was also capable of expressing how to apply its own concepts and rules. That is not possible, because no rule or concept can determine its own correct application. Dreyfus asks us to imagine, however, a system that leaves out *only* the "assumptions and background skills" that specify the correct application of its own concepts. If these assumptions and skills were not themselves part of the object domain of the theory, then there might be a sense in which it could give (at least in principle) a "fully explicit" representation of its object domain.

This conception of the telos of theoretical understanding would explain why Dreyfus has so long insisted that the human sciences do not provide appropriate domains for theorizing at all. In the human sciences, he argues, the assumptions and background skills for the employment of concepts are themselves part of the *object* domain of a science. Thus, an anthropological account of gift-giving practices cannot just apply its own rules for distinguishing "gifts" from "exchanges" and "insults," for the practices that sustain such distinctions for the gift-givers are themselves part of the anthropologist's domain of inquiry. Since these practices themselves involve flexible coping skills, Dreyfus argues, they do not admit of the kind of closure and relative completeness attainable in some of the natural sciences.

Social normativity has only emerged recently as a contrast to Dreyfus's account of the intentionality of practical coping. Initially, Dreyfus foregrounded the social dimension of practical intentionality. The in-order-to-for-the-sake-of structure in which everyday coping practices are significant is only sustained by a conformist institution and enforcement of norms. As distinctively social-normative accounts of intentionality have become more prominent, however, Dreyfus has begun to see an important difference in emphasis.[17] The most basic *intentional* relation in practical coping, he now argues, is between a body and its environs:

[T]he most basic level of intentionality requires only individual pragmatic activity. The normative dimension of intentionality derives not from social propriety nor from truth conditions but from action-based success and failure.[18]

The larger complex of significance-relations in which such individual activity acquires its stakes must be understood to presuppose bodily coping skills. Indeed, in the end, Dreyfus assimilates the contrast between bodily coping and social normativity to the more basic contrast between practical coping and the *explicit* articulation of propositional content: "Public norms only become constitutive at the linguistic level, and language, itself, is built upon the significance-structure revealed by skilled activity."[19]

III   Overcoming the Contrasts

The principal target of my criticisms in this section is not Dreyfus's account of the intentionality of coping, but the opposing conceptions of explicit articulation, theoretical understanding, and social norms that inform the contrasts discussed above. I begin with explicit articulation in language, an especially interesting case because Dreyfus himself recognizes some of the limitations in that supposed contrast.

Dreyfus's core claim about language is that the understanding embodied in ongoing practical coping with one's surroundings cannot be made fully explicit in words. But what is it to make something explicit in words? Dreyfus's critical engagement with artificial intelligence research offers an initially plausible operational specification: a capacity is explicitly articulable if one could write a program that would enable a computer to simulate that capacity effectively.[20] Certainly this conception of making something explicit has played a crucial formative role in Dreyfus's own work. An irony of this specification, however, is that in the light of Dreyfus's critique of AI, a primary example of a skillful coping capacity that cannot be made explicit is the ability to make something explicit. The conversational understanding and use of natural language has proven substantially intractable to formal, computational explication.

Why shouldn't explicit articulation in words then be regarded as exemplifying, rather than contrasting to, practical coping as a mode of intentionality? Dreyfus's own insistence on the irreducible practical/perceptual hearing of words rather than noises, and his recognition that articulate native speakers of a language exhibit a practical mastery comparable to other coping skills, strongly support this suggestion. Comparison to primarily "intellectual" skills such as chess mastery reinforces it. A competent chess player does not run through a large inventory of possible moves, but instead dwells within a configuration of the board fraught with significant possibilities. Similarly, a competent speaker does not run through a large inventory of possible expressions, but dwells within a richly configured field of articulative possibilities. Both chess master and speaker leave out of consideration a mass of legal moves and grammatical expressions that do not arise as relevant to the situation at hand. A situation calls for certain things to be said just as a chess position calls for some particular moves. If anything, explicit articulation is *more* dependent upon its sonorous or graphical material realization and stylized expressiveness than is chess play.

Making things explicit would then turn out to be the skillful use of words and sentences as equipment for coping with one's surroundings. Putting things in words would be a no more direct or immediate way of understanding them than would any other form of practical coping. Perhaps it is less so; language is among those tools that, once assimilated, reside permanently on the near side of our embodied engagement with the world. Physicist-philosopher Niels Bohr usefully captured the consequences of this closeness at hand: "We are suspended in language in such a way that we cannot say what is up and what is down."[21] In any case, the intelligibility of the alleged contrast between a fully transparently explicit articulation and the partial opacity of skillful coping depends upon a mysterious conception of articulation as possession of a "magic language of the mind whose terms directly and necessarily express Fregean senses."[22] Neither words nor thoughts could be direct, complete, and transparent expressions of an ideal "content." The absence of intrinsic limits to what can be expressed in words would no longer be troubling, however, once words have been divested of such magical transcendence.

Dreyfus would nevertheless likely reject a conception of explicit articulation as *entirely* a situated, practical coping with words and sentences as equipment for signifying. The principal reason for his reluctance to accept discourse as fully belonging to coping practices is that one can coherently talk about things in their absence. We have already seen how practical coping skills fall apart in the absence of their intended setting. One can, by contrast, sensibly talk at some length about unicorns, the Big Bang, even prime numbers larger than two, and machine translation. We need, therefore, to reconsider this capacity to speak about absent things.

The classic Fregean or Husserlian account of this capacity is that such talk expresses an ideal "sense," grasp of which then enables one to determine whether any extant things fulfill that sense. The problem is that such representationalist accounts of meaning leave mostly opaque what it is to articulate or understand a sense, and how one's expressions determine one sense rather than another.[23] Dreyfus responds in two stages. First, he insists that much of everyday discourse is not detached from its referential significance, but is instead contextually situated amidst ongoing coping practices. Second, even when assertions are decontextualized, he follows Heidegger in recognizing that they still take us directly to things, not to mental or linguistic intermediaries. Yet he crucially qualifies this recognition:

Everyday truth is possible because assertions are a special sort of equipment. They can be used to point not only to states of affairs that are right in front of us in the situation but to states of affairs behind us, like the picture's being crooked, and even to states of affairs that are somewhere else or have not yet occurred.[24]

This "special" character of assertions is, alas, left just as opaque as the direct mental grasp or linguistic expression of a sense. The most that Dreyfus suggests to explicate this special functional capacity is that while such assertions still remain globally dependent upon a background of coping practices, their representation of absent things is mediated by significations and the words that accrue to them.[25]

A different approach to linguistic meaning offers an attractive way to assimilate asserting more fully within Dreyfus's own account of practical coping. Recall first that coping practices extend the intentional directedness of bodies into the world, at the far side of one's equipment. The driver proximally attends to the turn in the road, not the rotational angle of the steering wheel; the jump shooter attends to the rim, not her wrist action or her grip on the ball. Language use is likewise directed toward its surroundings, and *like any other form of practical comportment*, its coherence depends upon sustaining a practical hold upon *actual* circumstances. This is the point of Davidson's principle of charity and Brandom's insistence that semantic articulation *requires* objective accountability.[26] Only if an overall pattern of utterances can be coherently connected to actual circumstances (in Davidson's terms, interpreted as mostly truthful) can they have *semantic* significance. A jump shooter can miss, and a speaker can utter falsehoods or use nonreferring terms. But the shooter cannot miss too badly too often without thereby dissolving the intelligibility of her actions as playing basketball, and the speaker likewise cannot be too badly in error too often without failing to be a speaker. Like other practical coping activities, the sense of asserting falls apart unless it sustains a substantially "correct" hold on its actual circumstances.

What sustains the illusion that assertions are a "special" kind of equipment is the *wordiness* of the world. Basketball, carpentry, or driving are intelligible practices only within appropriately prepared settings that contain all or most of the right equipment (including other persons with the right sort of skills and self-interpretations). The same is true of asserting and other discursive practices, except that the appropriate equipment has so thoroughly pervaded our world that speaking is only rarely radically out of place. Moreover, the complex and nested interrelations of discursive practices enable many assertions to function primarily in relation to other assertions. It might seem that language use then becomes quite remote from ordinary things, until one recalls that words and their expressively combined utterance are themselves among the most pervasive of ordinary things. Words do not exist alongside one's surrounding environment as a parallel space of re-presentation; they are a thoroughly intertwined part of our surroundings, and a mastery of their use is integral to ongoing bodily coping practices.

The familiarity and pervasiveness of words then suggests a misplaced analogy. A relevant practical analogue to speaking of absent things might seem to be something like hammering in the absence of nails; the "special" character of asserting would then be manifest in contrasting the familiarity of the former to the absurdity of the latter. Hammers, however, "refer" not just to nails, but to the entire referential context of carpentry; similarly, assertions refer not just to their truth conditions narrowly construed, but to the whole setting in which such an assertion would be significant. In using a hammer, the context "withdraws" from attention to enable a focus upon the task at hand. The same is true for assertions, except that since the task at hand in asserting is typically to "point out" or make salient some aspect of the world, the apparent locality and transparency of its referentiality seems heightened. Once we understand that assertions also function through a practical grasp of their whole "context," however, we see the mistake. An appropriate analogue to speaking of absent things would instead be interlinked equipment that enables one to "act at a distance," as the mediation of other words does. The relevant analogue to speaking falsely would be hammering in the wrong place or at the wrong angle, not hammering in the absence of nails or boards. If there is a discursive analogue to the latter, it would be utterances that "make no sense," failing altogether to connect to their circumstances.

Undoing the contrast between practical coping and explicit articulation may nevertheless then seem to heighten the contrast between coping and theoretical reflection. To see why, consider first that the philosophical approach to language sketched in the preceding paragraphs would ground semantics in pragmatics rather than in any formal structure discernable within everyday uses of words. Words acquire expressive significance through their ongoing use as part of a larger pattern of significant practical dealings with one's surroundings.[27] Yet it is manifestly possible to stand back from those everyday dealings and work out abstract, formal structures roughly exemplified in ongoing discursive practices. Even if such practices themselves are not realized through formal manipulations, their reconstruction as formal theoretical structures might mark a striking contrast to the intentionality of everyday coping. Indeed, Dreyfus seems to regard logic and formal semantics as a paradigm case of a theoretical reformulation of "data" decontextualized from ordinary coping practices.[28]

As with explicit articulation, we therefore need to ask more carefully what it is to understand something "theoretically." The contrast between coping and making explicit turned out to rely on an inappropriate conception of what it is to express something in words. Might the same be true of the alleged contrast between coping and theorizing?

Joseph Rouse

Dreyfus's contrast depends upon a threefold conception of theorizing. Theories are treated as formal structures (either uninterpreted axiomatic calculi or model-theoretic systems), theory-entry as decontextualization of "data," and theoretical understanding as disengaged "wonder." Space constraints prevent a direct strategy of arguing against the adequacy of each of these points in turn, although I note that philosophers of science have long abandoned anything resembling Dreyfus's conception of scientific data as decontextualized, while an attitude of disengaged wonder seems seriously to misconstrue the phenomenology of scientific theorizing. I shall instead suggest an alternative interpretation of theorizing that assimilates it to the intentionality of practical coping.

On this account, theories are tools that enable new ways of dealing with a variety of concrete situations.[29] They are typically worked out as groups of models for how to apply theoretical terms or techniques, exemplified by the standard calculational models for classical dynamics, quantum mechanics or population genetics, or the descriptive models of Darwinian adaptation. Learning a theory is learning how to apply or adapt its models to various situations, and how to perform characteristic operations upon or within these models: until the most advanced level of scientific education, the principal mode of theory acquisition is problem-solving exercises. The domain of a theory is determined not by universally quantified application of abstractly specifiable predicates, but by the open-ended practical applicability of the available and conceivable models that articulate it.[30]

Theories on this conception are not the intermediary of a novel mode of intentionality, but are instead a familiar kind of practical equipment. Their analogues are maps, diagrams, pictures, physical models, laboratory experiments,[31] computer simulations, and other equipment which enables people to engage with their surroundings more effectively by connecting them to a constructed setting which can be dealt with in different ways. Like reading a map and connecting it to situationally relevant landmarks, using a theory involves not a disengaged observation of decontextualized data, but a situated attentiveness to aspects of one's situation that are significant both for mapping/theorizing practices and for the purposes one is employing the map/theory. Developing a theory, like mapmaking, involves an intercalated practical grasp and working out of possibilities both within the "world" of maps and the world mapped. Theories, like maps, pictures, and models, can evoke amazement for their compactness, richness, elegance, simplicity, or power, but their use and development are more like practical immersion in a task at hand than the contemplative wonder envisaged by Aristotle.

The illusion that theories are relatively self-enclosed formal systems has multiple sources, including the philosophical tradition whose commitment to the distinctive status of *theoria* Dreyfus has only partially challenged. Its primary basis, however, is the richness and complexity of some prominent theoretical practices such that a relatively autonomous engagement in theorizing becomes intelligible. In cases like formal logic, mathematical physics or population genetics, and much of mathematics itself, theoretical practices have developed their own "internal" issues and stakes, such that substantial effort is sometimes needed to sustain significant connections between "theoretically" interesting achievements and issues, and other practical contexts from which those concerns once emerged. Peter Galison's discussion of the emergence of "trading zones" among experimental physicists, theorists, and engineers, which elicit analogues to the pidgin and creole languages that emerge at the interfaces of cultural practices, both highlights this point, and forcefully resists any conception of theory as a radically different mode of intentional directedness.[32]

A related basis for imagining theory as different in kind from practical comportment is the emergence of meta-theory: consistency and completeness proofs in logic, nonconstructive proofs that an equation has a solution, cladistic and pheneticist taxonomic theories, or the Gettier puzzle may seem especially remote from everyday practical concerns with argument, calculation, classification, or knowledge claims. Yet these are just further examples of theoretical practices with their own issues and stakes; their distance from "everyday" practice is no more surprising than that cartography raises issues quite remote from the concerns of those who only want to travel reliably from point A to point B. Brandom shows how even formal logic and semantics, which seemed initially to reinforce a distinction between practical engagement and theoretical reflection, are best regarded as a pragmatic extension of everyday discursive practices.[33]

Having proposed the assimilation of explicit articulation and theoretical reflection within Dreyfus's conception of the bodily intentionality of practical coping skills, I now turn to the third contrast. Should we still follow Dreyfus in distinguishing the intentional directedness of individually embodied agents from the emergence of *social* norms? In the other cases, Dreyfus criticized the philosophical *priority* often ascribed to explicit representation and theoretical disengagement as they have been traditionally conceived; I proposed going further, to reject altogether these traditional conceptions of theorizing and making explicit. Similarly, I suggest that we abandon the *conception* of social normativity that Dreyfus treats as derivative from practical coping skills. When we do so, we can better understand how such skills are irreducibly "social."

Social norms are typically invoked to understand how intentional directedness is accountable to authoritative standards. One's own standards will not do, for their authority can always be evaded by revising the standards. The normative accountability of individual performances might seem to be preserved, however, by understanding them as subject to the authority of the *communities* in which they participate.[34] Such views encounter formidable obstacles: they purchase the accountability of individual thought and action at the price of placing community practices beyond criticism; they make changes in communities or their norms rationally unintelligible; and the "shared norms" or "community consensus" whose authority they invoke generally do not exist outside of philosophers' and social theorists' imagination.[35] Dreyfus thus rightly rejects "the constitutive role of shared social norms [for] original intentionality."[36]

Yet it will also not do to locate the normativity of practical coping in the success or failure of individual activity. Philosophers who ground intentionality upon pragmatic success usually construe "success" naturalistically, for example, in evolutionary terms. Dreyfus seems to want a more proximate (and nonnaturalistic!) criterion of success, such as driving a nail or avoiding an obstacle. Yet why regard these as *successes*, rather than as failures to keep the nail out or to hit the target? One might try to answer such questions holistically, but that will not sustain the normative autonomy of individual action. Not only are the proximate "goals" of individual coping practices so closely intertwined with the practices and commitments of others that they resist identifications of practical goals as "mine" or "yours" (as Dreyfus himself convincingly shows!).[37] The normativity of such holistic interpretation of practical coping skills also thereby becomes unintelligible; what constrains the *interpretation* of hammering as nail-driving rather than as unsuccessful nail-obstruction?

The problem is instead with the construal of the "social" dimension of intentionality as a relation between individual agents and supraindividual "communities," what Brandom (1994) now rejects as an "I/We" conception of sociality. The social character of everyday coping is not a matter of subordination to a community, but of intra-action with other agents whom we *recognize* in practice as intentionally directed toward a shared *world* (*not* shared norms or beliefs about that world).[38] Through such intra-action and recognition, understanding and articulation acquire their intentional directedness as *aspectual* and *accountable*—an "understanding" of the world is only meaningful if there are alternatives, and the possibility of being mistaken. Yet this constitutive recognition of the partiality and accountability of one's practical grasp of the world does *not* require the postulation of a "sovereign" standpoint that could adjudicate once and for all what success or truth would consist in.[39] The ineliminably social character of being-in-the-world is not a relationship to some supra-individual entity within the world, but is instead how the world has a hold on us through our intra-action with "others," such that there is something at stake in ongoing coping with one's surroundings. There is much more to be said about *how* it is that such stakes arise and "bind" us, but the recognition of one's engagement with and accountability to "others" must surely be a noncontingent aspect of any adequate account.

In the end, these challenges to Dreyfus's proposed contrasts between practical coping and explicit articulation, theoretical understanding, and accountability to "social" norms should not be regarded as criticisms of his philosophical project. If I am right, the core commitments of Dreyfus's phenomenological conception of the intentionality of practical coping constitute an even more radical and, I believe, successful challenge to the philosophical tradition than he himself has ever been willing to acknowledge. In the world we inhabit, there are no magic languages, no decontextualizing theories, and no supraindividual consensus communities.

Coping with Others with Folk Psychology

Theodore R. Schatzki

Hubert Dreyfus's explorations of the role, scope, and significance of background skills in human activity are well-known to students of human life. Basing his descriptions in the work of the phenomenologists Martin Heidegger and Maurice Merleau-Ponty, Dreyfus has astutely and decisively demonstrated the impossibility of treating such skills in any purely computational or formalized fashion. He has further contended that this impossibility, inter alia, undermines dominant paradigms in cognitive science, renders unlikely a successful social science modeled on its natural science counterpart, and promotes particularistic ethics over rule-based alternatives. At times, Dreyfus has suggestively called these background skills "coping skills." This appellation makes explicit that these skills usually enable human beings to deal more or less successfully with the things, events, and situations encountered in day-to-day life— and to do so without having overtly to think about and figure out what to do.

The examples on which Dreyfus focuses are generally of people coping with the things around them, not of people coping with other persons. When he discusses, for example, chess, driving a car, and pattern recognition, he focuses on the situations and arrangements of things with which actors deal, rather than on the people who appear in these arrangements and situations. Dreyfus does not deny the significance of people's dealings with others, but he does not pay much attention to this phenomenon.

Theodore R. Schatzki

This essay brings other people onto center stage, juxtaposing Dreyfus's account of skills and human activity with certain pervasive acts of speaking and thinking by means of which actors "cope" with their fellows. I argue that Dreyfus's account contravenes these common linguistic practices, but that reconciling the account with the practices transforms the account in a way that also strengthens it.

This essay cannot examine all aspects of people's coping with one another. Not only is coping a multi-faceted phenomena, but people are too. The type of coping explored in the present essay is described at the beginning of section II. As for people, that aspect of people of present interest is agency. By "agency" I mean doing. My comments, accordingly, focus on coping with what others do and why. Although coping with agency does not exhaust coping with other people, this nominally narrower focus is nevertheless quite broad in scope and significance. The pervasive anti-"Cartesianism" in contemporary studies of mind and action has done away with mind as space, stage, or thing. (The quotes around "Cartesianism" acknowledge that views commonly bearing this label might not correctly be attributed to Descartes.) Filling the conceptual and investigative gap opened by this rejection has been human activity. The widespread construal of mental states as entities with which—essentially—action is explained, the thesis that mind and action form a single realm, and the rechristening of psychology as "behavioral science" all testify to this transformation. Dreyfus is a strong proponent of this change in focus. He writes, for instance, that the self is "a pattern of public comportment," a "subpattern of social practices."[2] A similar emphasis is present in Heidegger, whose phenomenology has played so important a role in Dreyfus's thinking. According to Heidegger, people, in their daily lives, encounter others primarily in what they do.[3] Coping with others is thus first, and for the most part, a matter of coping with agents.

I Dreyfus on Agency

Before examining coping, it is best to examine the phenomenon coped with. Dreyfus's account of agency is organized around a distinction between *deliberate* and *nondeliberate* activity. By "deliberate activity" he means activity to which an actor pays attention as he or she carries it out (72). An example of such activity is playing the piano attentively—thinking about what one is doing as one moves one's hand and depresses the keys. By contrast, nondeliberate activity is activity that a person carries out without paying attention to what she is doing. A skilled pianist, for example, plays her instrument without thinking about her actions,[4] instead immersing herself in the music or in some other matter or concern. Dreyfus emphasizes that a rather large share of daily activity is nondeliberate. Skillful activity such as playing the piano, habitual activity such as brushing one's teeth, casual unthinking activity such as rolling over in bed, and spontaneous and emotionally laden activity such as fidgeting are all usually nondeliberate.[5] He further claims—memorably—that deliberate action typically occurs in response to some sort of "breakdown" in ongoing absorbed coping.

The distinction between deliberate and nondeliberate activity is to be distinguished from two other distinctions that are prominent in philosophical accounts of human activity: intentional/unintentional and voluntary/involuntary. An action is intentional, roughly, when a person carries it out knowingly and on purpose—when the action is something that the actor aims to perform. Corresponding to this, an unintentional action is one that the actor performs unknowingly or not on purpose. A voluntary action, meanwhile, is one, roughly, over which its performer has control, where "to have control" means that if the actor had so chosen, she could have desisted from carrying it out. An involuntary action, accordingly, is one over which its perpetrator has no control.

Although these definitions call for refinement, and do not eliminate difficult cases, they suffice to distinguish these two contrasts from that between deliberate and nondeliberate activity. Indeed, the latter dichotomy cuts across the other two. All deliberate actions are intentional, as are many—but not all—nondeliberate ones (e.g., the skilled pianist's playing versus tapping one's fingers nervously). It is debatable, however, whether all deliberate actions are voluntary. If "being in control" is construed as the actor not being subject to

Theodore R. Schatzki

coercion (by other people or by force of social circumstance), the difficulties are palpable (e.g., a mass suicide of cult members). Even if "being in control" is construed as involving no reference to any circumstance outside the (possibly prosthetically or instrumentally enhanced) body of the agent, cases of involuntary deliberate action are still conceivable (e.g., an addict's consumption of cocaine). Moreover, the way the performance of one action (e.g., shouting "Fire!" in a crowded theater) can count, in its circumstances, as the performance of another (e.g., causing a riot) guarantees that some nondeliberate actions are involuntary (depending on the character of the original performance). Bodily reflex actions offer a different sort of example here.

Paying attention, knowledgeable purposiveness, and control constitute three distinct and gradational dimensions of human activity. I mention this because intentionality and voluntariness are the dimensions that generally receive most attention in contemporary, as well as previous, accounts of agency. Dreyfus, following Heidegger, Merleau-Ponty, and the very early Sartre, focuses on a dimension mostly overlooked or at least largely uncommented upon in traditional accounts. Although the existence of this dimension is beyond doubt, exactly what its existence implies is open to question.

According to Dreyfus, what follows is that different accounts of the determination of action pertain to the two sorts of activity. The determination of nondeliberate activity is the province of coping skills: nondeliberate activity is an absorbed coping that results from the exercise of an actor's skills for dealing with the phenomena she encounters.

We are all masters in our everyday world. Consider the experience of entering a familiar type of room . . . [O]ur feeling for how rooms normally behave, a skill for dealing with them that we have developed by crawling and walking around many rooms, gives us a sense of relevance. We are skilled at not coping with the dust, unless we are janitors, and not paying attention to whether the windows are open or closed, unless it is hot, in which case we know how to do what is appropriate. Our expertise in dealing with rooms determines from moment to moment both what we cope with by using and what we cope with by ignoring. . . . This global familiarity maps our past experience of the room onto our current activity, so that what is appropriate on each occasion is experienced as perceptually salient or simply elicits what needs to be done.[6]

The above suggests that the exercise of skills requires a structured intelligibility. Drawing on Heidegger's account of involvement (*Bewandtnis*), Dreyfus contends that nondeliberate activity is informed/ordered by orientations toward ends that determine it as the activity it is. To illustrate the point, he uses the example of nondeliberately writing on the board with chalk during a class in order to draw a chart, as a step toward explaining Heidegger, and for the sake of being a good teacher.[7] These "in order tos," "toward whichs," and "for the sake ofs"—in more conventional terms, purposes, tasks, and ends[8]—orient his activity in the sense of structuring what he is up to: in conjunction with the current situation, they specify that writing on the board *makes sense*—that is, is the appropriate and needed thing (given the situation and the purposes and ends involved). They determine, in other words, what might be called the *practical intelligibility* that informs nondeliberate activity.

When people act nondeliberately and are thus exercising their skills, they simply, without paying attention to what they are doing, do what makes sense to them. What makes sense to them to do is structured, moreover, by their orientations toward certain ends. Another way of putting this is to say that, barring breakdown, when a person skilled in a given arena of life acts in that arena, she simply does what, given the situation, makes teleological sense to her without having to think about it or pay attention to what she is doing. Skills, consequently, are not structureless capacities that lie behind the specific activities by reference to which they are defined. Rather, they are teleologically structured familiarities, readinesses, and knowhows that underlie indefinitely flexible initiative and response.[9]

Dreyfus stresses that although a person pursues purposes, tasks, and ends when acting nondeliberately, she is neither explicitly aware of them nor are they present in the form of some "mental representation." As Dreyfus likes to put it, action can be purposive without the actor having a purpose in mind. This entails that when acting nondeliberately, it is not just that the actor gives no attention to what she is doing; she also gives no attention to, and more generally is not explicitly aware of, what she is up to and why. She is not explicitly aware, in other words, of the teleological structuring of the practical intelligibility informing her activity. In an article on Searle, for example, Dreyfus characterizes nondeliberate action as action "in which there is no representation of the goal."[10] Beyond what a person is doing and why, the not paying attention that defines nondeliberate activity seems also—though this is not entirely clear—to pertain to features of the surrounding perceptual environment that are immediately relevant to what one is doing.[11]

When, on the other hand, people act deliberately, they pay attention to their activity. Explicit awareness, absent in nondeliberate action, here makes its appearance. According to Dreyfus, moreover, deliberate action occurs when absorbed skillful coping is no longer possible. A prominent sort of case here is that of breakdown—the experience of ongoing coping running into trouble. When a piano string or the chalk breaks, or when the pianist forgets the score or the teacher's identity is challenged by an inquisitive student, the actor suddenly becomes explicitly aware of her activity—the instruments she was using, what she was doing, what she was trying to accomplish, or that for which she was doing it. If this explicit awareness accompanies what she goes on to do, she acts deliberately.

It so happens, furthermore, that explicit awareness is, on Dreyfus's understanding, one of two defining characteristics of mental or intentional states. Dreyfus claims, consequently, that in breakdown situations, there emerges a "mind with content directed toward objects."[12] "[I]f the doorknob sticks, we find ourselves deliberately *trying* to turn the doorknob, *desiring* that it turn, *expecting* the door to open, etc. (This, of course, does not imply that we were trying, desiring, expecting, etc. all along.)"[13] More generally, "mental content arises whenever the situation requires deliberate attention."[14] *Only* then, in fact, does the subject-object polarity that distinguishes mentality emerge. Hence, a deliberate actor is directed toward her activity through mental states. Dreyfus's two favorite examples of such states are self-referential experiences that accompany activity, as when one tries to do something (his analysis of

Searlean intentions in action), and beliefs and desires that combine to generate actions (a view of action attributed to Davidson). It is important to add that, on Dreyfus's account, mental states exist and play the role they do vis-à-vis deliberate action, only against the background of the skills whose exercise is the basis for nondeliberate action.

Deliberate activity, however, is not distinguished only by the presence of mental states. Such mental states cause deliberate actions—more precisely, Dreyfus writes, they cause the bodily movements in which these actions consist. When the doorknob sticks, one's focused efforts to move it are caused by the desire to open it in conjunction with the belief that greater force will accomplish this, and repeated attempts are guided by the intention in action to budge it. As indicated, moreover, the content of each of these mental states—what one is up to, how things work, what needs to be done—is explicit to the actor. Hence, not only does deliberate action differ from its nondeliberate cousin by virtue of actors, paying attention to their activity; whereas nondeliberate action rests on the exercise of skills, deliberate action is caused by mental states (where mental states are causally efficacious states of being explicitly aware of something). As a result, when someone deliberately acts purposively, she has a purpose in mind, that is, she is explicitly aware of what she is out to accomplish (this purpose can be said to constitute the content of one of her desires).

This discussion makes clear that Dreyfus's account of agency centers, as befits the work of a phenomenologist, on a distinction between two kinds of awareness: thematic and nonthematic. A person is thematically aware of X in those cases where X is explicit to her. Such awareness, as Dreyfus emphasizes, is charged with subject-object polarity, since, when a person is thematically aware of X, not only is X present *as such* to her, it is also present as such *to* her. That is to say, when a person is explicitly aware of X, she is also cognizant that she is aware of it, that is, that she is the subject of the awareness. And this implies, as Kant made clear, that the fact, that someone is explicitly aware of X (is the subject of explicit awareness), can itself always become thematic to the person involved in a further moment of explicit awareness. This, then, is why Dreyfus argues that the subject-object split—and mind—arises only with deliberate action. Only here does there occur the thematic awareness that is at once self-awareness.

By contrast, when acting nondeliberately a person is nonthematically aware of her activity. Nonthematic awareness is a grasp of something that is not explicit *qua* grasped. The lack of any overtly present object entails that there is nothing *to* which something is present as such. As a result, in being nonthematically aware of X, a person is not cognizant that she is aware of it—there does not occur the sort of self-consciousness, and hence the subject-object split, that is characteristic of thematic awareness. When, therefore, a person acts nondeliberately and is nonthematically aware of her activity, no "mind with content directed toward object" occurs. There is only concerned skillful absorption in the world. This does not entail that a person cannot become thematically aware of something of which she was earlier nonthematically aware. But it does imply that the person understands herself as a subject only once this transformation occurs.[15]

Dreyfus argues, following Heidegger, that thematic awareness presupposes its nonthematic kin, and he adds that it is possible to conceive of a society that never displayed thematic consciousness, that is, a society whose members never acted deliberately or entertained explicit plans or goals.[16] What concerns me in the present situation, however, is Dreyfus's claim that thematic awareness is a feature of deliberate action alone. It is clear that because acting deliberately involves paying attention, it encompasses thematic awareness. But it seems to me phenomenologically the case that an actor is always thematically aware of something or other. The something can be, for instance, a bodily sensation, an instrument one is using, an action one is performing, something in the perceptual environment, one's mood, another's action or claim, the topic of a conversation, what one is up to, why one is up to it, a past event, a future task, an intellectual quandary, or the content of a fantasy. What's more, one can be thematically aware of such things in a variety of ways, for instance, by feeling, perceiving, noticing, imagining, attending to, conceiving of, thinking about, and keeping them in mind. When acting nondeliberately, the sorts of things of which a person is thematically aware typically include bodily sensations, perceived objects and events, past incidents, future scenarios, and conversational as well as intellectual themes. What the actor is not thematically aware of is her activity. Hence, what marks the distinction between deliberate and nondeliberate activity is not the presence or absence of thematic awareness, but the occurrence or non-occurrence of thematic awareness of a particular multi-dimensional phenomenon: activity itself. Given Dreyfus's conception of mental states, it follows that mental states are not associated with deliberate action alone.

In this context, it is worth noting the ambiguous role that perception plays in Dreyfus's account. He acknowledges that the course of nondeliberate action is tied to people's perception of their surroundings. A running theme in his account of expertise, for instance, is that skillful coping, including nondeliberate acts of problem solving, is often a response to familiar perceptual gestalts. Indeed, it is fair to say that skillful coping and hence nondeliberate activity in general rest on a perceptual grasp of the environment, including specific features of it. Consider, for example, a skillful skier. In order to get to the bottom of the mountain, she might not need, when skiing, to pay attention to what she is doing or why. But as she skis down she still needs to scan approaching terrain, watch for obstacles, and look out for other skiers, in short, pay close attention to her surroundings. According to Dreyfus, moreover, the course of nondeliberate activity does not just rest on perception. In his critique of Searle, he describes the experience present in nondeliberate acting as "the experience of the causal connection between our perceptions of our internal and external situation and our bodily motion . . ."[17] Finally, Dreyfus sometimes characterizes perceptions as mental states.[18] At other times, perception is treated as Dasein's "openness onto the world that makes possible the derivative experience [i.e., mental state—TRS] of looking or trying to see."[19]

It is not clear to me how to sort out these pronouncements. The difference between thematic perceptual acts such as looking, observing, listening, feeling, tasting, and staring, and the Merleau-Pontyan conception of perception in general as the presence of the world to someone, is clear. But the acknowledged role of perceptions in

Theodore R. Schatzki

nondeliberate action introduces explicitness where none should be found. For instance, as the skier scans the terrain, watches for obstacles, and looks out for other skiers, she is explicitly aware of various things and performs particular maneuvers accordingly. According to Dreyfus's analysis of nondeliberate action, however, these maneuvers should not be guided by thematic perceptual acts. (Dreyfus nowhere, curiously, addresses the role of perceptual *attention* in nondeliberate action.) As already noted, since an agent is always thematically aware of something, nondeliberate action is always accompanied, minimally, by one "mental state." Whenever, moreover, an actor's attention focuses on matters in the surrounding environment immediately relevant to what she is doing (e.g., the terrain, or instruments she is reading, repairing, or testing[20]), it is no longer clear whether she is acting nondeliberately or not. What is clear is that her activity is "guided by" a mental state and thus determined in the manner Dreyfus contends is characteristic of deliberate action. If, consequently, such activity qualifies as nondeliberate action, the implication is that mental states can guide nondeliberate activity. If, on the other hand, such actions do not count as nondeliberate, the category of nondeliberate action will contain fewer actions than Dreyfus suggests.

II Coping with Agency

People cope with one another, as with anything else, by performing actions. The actions involved here include speech acts such as acts of ordering, informing, calling, reprimanding, asking, answering, and persuading that are directed toward others or based on familiarity with or knowledge of them. People also, of course, cope with others through the performance (and nonperformance) of acts other than speech acts. Such actions include hugging, smiling, pointing, handing over, moving aside, slowing down, and feigning. In addition to such overt actions, there occur what George Downing calls "bodily micropractices"—bodily doings, gestures, and positionings, often subconscious, that, among other things, establish interpersonal relations with particular affective tonalities (e.g., comforting or unnerving), negotiate emotional exchanges among people, and help train children in the bodily performance and management of their own emotional systems.[21] People cope with others, in addition, by performing nonverbal acts that manipulate or are directed at non-humans, for instance, lowering blinds or building fences around backyards.

The actions through which people cope with one another also express and constitute understandings of agency. Like coping, however, understanding is not a single phenomenon. *Qua* cognition, understanding agency is, inter alia, grasping what someone is doing, comprehending why he is doing it, imagining doing the same (if one were in the actor's shoes), successfully explaining any or all of this to another person, and fitting others' activities into some technical interpretive schema. One of the strengths of Dreyfus's emphasis on skillful coping is that understanding others can also be recognized as "getting along with them." Understanding another person is not just cognitively grasping something about her agency, but also successfully getting on with her in day-to-day life. Practical understanding of this sort likewise takes different forms. One form is responding to others' provocations and eccentricities so as to maintain civility, harmony, and good relations; another is participating continually and successfully in common or interlinked activities. People who manage these things can be said to understand one another, in one of the senses in which one says in German, *Sie verstehen sich.* Hence, the actions through which people cope with one another do not just express and constitute cognitive understandings of others, but also amount to practical understandings of them. Even if it were possible for people to live together without ever explicitly paying attention to each other, still this would not exclude their understanding one another.

The following discussion concentrates on one sort of understanding of agency, namely, the understanding that consists in characterizing others using the language of ordinary "mental states" or, as it is sometimes called, the vocabulary of "folk psychology." Examples of such language are "seeing," "being in pain," "fearing," "being happy," "being joyful," "hoping," "expecting," "intending," "believing," "wanting," and "thinking." The set of such expressions encompasses all the terms Dreyfus uses to designate what he collectively

Theodore R. Schatzki

calls "mental" (or "intentional") states. In line, however, with a thesis mentioned in passing at the beginning of this essay, namely, that mind/action is a single realm, I construe this language as embracing not only terms for mentality, such as those above, but terms for activity as well. For this reason, I shall refer to this language as "life-condition language" rather than as either "mental state language" or "folk psychology."[22] In any event, understanding others in the sense specified is a matter of fitting them into the conceptual scheme carried by the use of this vocabulary. Both people's grasp of what others (and themselves) do and why, and the results of their imaginative projections into the lives of others (that is, empathy) are typically formulated with life-condition vocabulary.

An important way through which people cope with one another is those acts of speaking and thinking about others with life-condition vocabulary that constitutes understandings of what others are doing and why. The most prominent speech acts involved here are describing, explaining, predicting, and questioning. Of course, the particular understanding formulated in such speech acts are also expressed in a wider range of actions through which people cope with others. This fact, however, will be set aside in the present context. I want, instead, and for reasons that will emerge shortly, to concentrate on the speech acts that are involved here. The prominence of these acts of speaking and thinking in daily life indicates that life-condition understandings of others are central to human coexistence.

I should first note that acts of description, explanation, prediction, questioning, and thinking about agency can also employ technical terminology drawn from the human sciences. This occurs when people carry on the practices of those sciences, as well as in other situations, as when a psychologist talks to her children using the language of her profession. I should also acknowledge that the migration of technical vocabulary (e.g., "repression") into more general usage would seem to threaten any idea that life-condition vocabulary is clearly bounded and defined. In general, however, whether specific terms are technical terms or belong to widespread practices of interpersonal understanding sorts itself out with the passage of time. Moreover, regardless of how much conceptual migration of the sort at issue occurs, a solid core of common mind/action terms that are clearly distinguishable from technical terms does persist. Indeed, all the terms for mind and action used in the present essay clearly fall into this core.

Acts of describing, explaining, predicting, questioning, and thinking about others can be nondeliberate or deliberate. As Wittgenstein has emphasized, uttering words can be part of nondeliberate activity ("reactions" in his terms). Dreyfus agrees: "Language is often used transparently in situations where there is no disturbance, such as when I say 'See you at six.' "[23] To speak nondeliberately is to speak not paying attention, first, to the words uttered, second, to what one is doing in uttering them (describing, explaining, etc.), and third, to why one is doing this. (To speak nondeliberately is thus at once to perform a nondeliberate speech act.) Correspondingly, a person speaks deliberately when she pays attention to her words, to what she is doing in uttering them, and/or to why she is doing this. The same distinctions apply to thinking. One can think about something, for instance, next week's ski trip, without paying attention to what one thinks, to one's act of thinking, or to why one is thinking. One can also, of course, pay attention to one or more of these items. This is usually what transpires, for example, when one sets oneself to pondering or thinking through something.

Although Dreyfus agrees that people can speak nondeliberately, he might want to resist the further claim that they can speak and think nondeliberately when describing, explaining, predicting, questioning, and thinking about others with life-condition terms. His perceptive phenomenological descriptions of activity reveal that much moment-to-moment activity is continuous absorbed coping, in which actors, without paying attention to their activity, successfully deal with things and situations and accomplish what they are up to. Similarly, one can plausibly surmise, continuous moment-to-moment dealing with other people can, and often does, amount to absorbed, skillful coping. It might seem, as a result, that people describe, explain, predict, question, and think about others' agency only when there occurs a disturbance or breakdown in absorbed skillful coping with

Theodore R. Schatzki

them. For as long as one is coping skillfully with others, there is no need to engage in these acts. Hence, it might seem that, although language can be used nondeliberately, describing and explaining others (and all the other speech acts that can be involved here) are always deliberate acts.

Breakdowns in human interaction and in the intermeshing of activity can certainly occasion deliberate acts of explaining, questioning, and thinking about other people. Recall, however, the definition of the distinction between deliberate and nondeliberate acts as this applies to the use of language. It is a division of such acts into those in which the actor does, and those in which she does not, pay attention to the language used, what is being done with this language, and why. Only a small number of acts of describing and explaining others with life-condition expressions are deliberate in this sense. On occasions when it is unclear what to say about someone or what one says is guided by explicit perceptual scrutiny or observation of others, such acts might be deliberate. In the majority of cases, however, one simply describes or explains without thinking about it or paying attention to one's words, what one is doing, and why. What is true is that a person typically per-forms these acts *in response to* something she has observed, learned about, or experienced at the hands of other people. This does not entail, however, that the acts are deliberate. It does not even entail that a disturbance or breakdown has occurred in absorbed coping.

Now, a key fact about both deliberate and nondeliberate acts of describing, explaining, and thinking about others with life-condition vocabulary is that such acts are directed toward deliberate and nondeliberate activity alike. If one person asks a second what a third is doing, the second's response will draw on the same set of action terms regardless of whether the activity involved is deliberate or nondeliberate. If the questioner goes on to ask why the third person is doing whatever she is doing, the stock of vocabulary the second person will draw on is again unaffected by the deliberate or nondeliberate character of the activity. The real distinction between deliberate and nondeliberate action does not subtend the application to activity of two distinct conceptual schemes coordinate with the division. Indeed, the terms "deliberate" and "nondeliberate" (and the distinction between them) belong to the single set of English life-condition expressions. I might add that investigators of human life, when engaged in scientific practice, can speak deliberately or non-deliberately using technical vocabulary. The mix depends on such factors as their proficiency with the vocabulary, with whom they are conversing, and the degree of anomaly or deviancy of the subjects studied.

As already discussed above, however, Dreyfus claims that different accounts of determination apply to nondeliberate and deliberate activity and that the life-conditions designated by such terms as "belief," "desire," and "intention" accompany deliberate action alone. An incongruity thus arises between his phenomenological account of activity and our dispersed practices of using these terms in speaking and thinking about one another. (In claiming this, I am assuming that when a characterization of someone formulated with life-condition terms is true, the conditions designated by the terms used obtain with respect to the person concerned.) In this situation, I believe Dreyfus has no choice but to contest the cogency of common linguistic practices—the widespread application of life-condition terms to nondeliberate action must be illegitimate. And although he does not put matters in exactly this way, he does, in fact, challenge the cogency of such practices:

> Likewise, we cannot assume, as traditional philosophers from Aristotle to Davidson and Searle have done, that, simply because our concept of action requires that an action be explainable in terms of beliefs and desires, when we don't find conscious beliefs and desires causing our actions, we are justified in postulating them in our explanations.[24]

Yet this is exactly what people regularly do when employing life-condition terms to explain and describe (and so on) one another's nondeliberate actions. As this quotation suggests, however, Dreyfus is happy to cede "our ordinary concept of action" to theorists such as Davidson and Searle—who apply the life-condition scheme to deliberate and nondeliberate actions alike. This concept, he implies, is a concept of really deliberate action alone.[25] Consequently, it is improperly applied to the phenomenon of nondeliberate action. It follows that the ordinary use of the life-condition vocabulary is often illegitimate and ill-founded.

Post-Wittgensteinian philosophers have become sensitive to ask for a reason why when a thinker challenges common ways of speaking. It is important, in this context, to distinguish challenges to widespread beliefs from challenges to ways of talking. With respect to life-condition discourse, this difference is one between challenges to people's "commonsense" beliefs about such conditions and challenges to their actual use of life-condition language. Wittgenstein challenged certain pervasive "Cartesian" beliefs about these conditions through investigations of the use of the terms involved. Eliminative materialists have challenged the mental (but not action) component of life-condition vocabulary on the grounds that the theory of human beings informing its use is inadequate. Dreyfus challenges the use of this same mental vocabulary, in his case, its application to a prominent class of activity.

Dreyfus's challenge rests on a combination of good phenomenology and a mistaken understanding of life-conditions and life-condition vocabulary. Dreyfus is certainly right, phenomenologically, that much human activity proceeds largely in the absence of thematic awareness. I write "largely" because, as already noted, barring unusual circumstances people are always thematically aware of something or other, even if the somethings of which they are aware have no direct bearing on their activity. Nonetheless, Dreyfus is importantly correct that in many cases action is unreflective, meaning that people neither think explicitly about what to do before acting nor consciously monitor their activity as it occurs.

According to Dreyfus, however, mental life-conditions are causally-effective states in which something is explicit to someone. Both causal efficacy and explicitness are characteristics that modern thought has widely attributed to mentality. Neither attribution, however, stands up to careful scrutiny of what is going on when people use life-condition expressions in talking and thinking about one another (including themselves). There is no better investigation of the issues at stake here than the one found in Wittgenstein's late, post-*Philosophical Investigations* remarks on mentality. Although it is well beyond this essay to discuss these remarks,[26] two salient findings about the use of mental condition terms should be mentioned.

First, as is well-known from Wittgenstein's discussions elsewhere, not all uses of mental condition vocabulary amount to attributions of mental conditions. As Wittgenstein documents in *On Certainty*, for instance, the expression "belief" is used to carry off a range of acts and accomplishments, including assuring someone that something is the case, stressing the speaker's less than full certainty, indicating that something can be relied on, and attributing the condition of belief to someone (including oneself). Second, what is going on when someone describes, explains, and questions people (including herself) using life-condition terms is—to state matters inclusively and perfunctorily—that she is articulating or asking about how things stand or are going for them in the course of their continuing existences through concrete situations in relation to specific people, things, and events.[27] An attribution of joy, for instance, articulates a bodily expressed, infusive countenance that permeates both a person's approach to things and the ways those things grab that person. An attribution of belief, meanwhile, articulates how things stand with someone with respect to something or other. Being in the conditions thereby attributed, that is, being joyful and believing, is things standing and going for people in certain ways.

It follows from these findings that mental conditions are not causally effective states (at least not in the sense of efficient causality). Being in these conditions—things standing and going in certain ways—does not govern activity by causing it. Rather, orders activity by determining what makes sense to people to do. For instance, suppose that it is because someone is joyful after learning of a peace treaty, believes that others are likely to celebrate, and wants to join in, that she heads for the square in the center of the city. In this example, the supposition is that, because things stand and are going for her in the ways that are articulated by saying that she is joyful and believes and wants these things, it makes sense to her to act thus. I should mention that, *pace* Robert Brandom's recent remarks on Wittgenstein, practical intelligibility and its determination is not a normative phenomenon in the sense of rational "oughtness" or appropriateness.[28] What makes sense to someone to do, need not be what it is rationally appropriate to do, although on many occasions the action that is singled out coincides with the counsels of rationality.[29] Indeed, practical intelligibility lies on the *causal* side of Brandom's normative-causal divide—although this only means, to speak with Aristotle, that it is akin to formal and not efficient causality. In any event, what makes clear that the obtaining of certain life-conditions does indeed order activity in the above way is the fact that attributions of mental conditions explain activity by putting into words that which determines the intelligibility informing it, that is, by putting into words that by virtue of which certain actions make sense to people. In the example cited above, to specify that mention of joy, belief, and want explain the would-be celebrator's action is to specify that mention of them formulates why this action makes sense to her, that is, puts into words how things stand and are going such that this action makes sense. It is not to specify that mention of them accomplishes this by picking out discrete states that, in combination, "cause" (that is, bring about) the action.

A person need not, moreover, be explicitly aware of how things stand and are going for her. Formulated in terms of life-condition talk, this means that neither life-conditions nor their contents need be explicit to the people with respect to which they obtain. The would-be celebrator, for instance, need not be thematically aware—at any particular moment—of the joining-in that she wants or of her wanting it, of the likelihood of others celebrating in which she believes or of the fact that she believes it. She is, of course, explicitly aware of the signing of the treaty that prompts her joy and desire for celebration, since it is upon learning of this that she heads downtown. Furthermore and most importantly, it is not crucial, in order for an actor's being in this or that mental condition to determine, for example, practical intelligibility, that the actor be thematically aware of how things stand and are going for her. What is crucial is how things do, in fact, stand and are going and how this determines what makes sense to her to do. How things stand and are going for people is a dimension of human life that constantly informs and orders their activities regardless of the extent to which they are thematically aware of it.

Pace Dreyfus, then, mental conditions are not (efficient) causally-effective thematic states. The obtaining of some such condition is things standing and going in a particular way for someone. Regardless, moreover, of how much of themselves and their surroundings people are explicitly aware, people act as they do because of how things stand and are going for them. This is what is indicated by the descriptive, explanatory, predictive, and interrogatory application of mental life vocabulary to deliberate and nondeliberate activity alike. Hence, when people act nondeliberately, all sorts of mental conditions can obtain with respect to them.

Once Dreyfus's mistaken conception of the conditions at issue here is set aside, common practices of, for instance, describing and explaining people using life-condition vocabularies and phenomenological observations about the paucity of thematic awareness in acting, are incompatible. This is because, to state matters baldly, the role of life-condition terms in describing, explaining, questioning, predicting, and thinking about others (and oneself) is not to mark, give back, or articulate the phenomenon of thematic awareness and its significance—the conditions that these terms designate are not denizens of consciousness. I stress, moreover, that this reconciliation between common practices and phenomenological description does not depend on the particular account of life-condition vocabulary that was extracted from Wittgenstein's texts in the discussion above. Any analysis of life-condition or folk-psychological terminology that does not in general require, of the conditions this terminology designates (1) that they or their contents must be explicit to the people in them and (2) that they be defined by their causal powers, is in a position to effect this reconciliation.[30]

Although familiar linguistic practices do not jibe with Dreyfus's nonphenomenological conception of mental states, his phenomenological analysis of skills does, I believe, apply to these practices. The point here is that skills govern the *use* of this language in the way that Dreyfus claims they govern nondeliberate agency. Indeed, children quickly become "expert" users of this vocabulary in the sense that is proper to level five on the Dreyfus five-level skill story.[31] How they become experts, however, is a controversial empirical matter about which nothing further can be said in the present discussion. I should add that my reconciliation of linguistic practices and phenomenological description does not give succor to the cognitive theories that Dreyfus's account of skills opposes. How things "stand" and are "going" for people are not sorts of phenomena that cognitive science can exploit.

III Conclusion

I want to mention two conclusions that follow from the above reflections. The first is that a certain irony attaches to Dreyfus's account of agency. Dreyfus's impressive delineation of a skillful nondeliberate dimension of human activity hangs together with his desire, nurtured through close readings of Heidegger and Merleau-Ponty, to move beyond the "Cartesian" centering of human existence on a self-illuminating realm of consciousness. Phenomenological description reveals that people are often not thematically conscious of their activity and that they become thematically conscious only when absorbed skillful coping is no longer possible. Given the centuries old association of mind and mental states with consciousness and conscious states, it is plausible to argue, on this basis, that mind, mental states, and subject are present only in deliberate action. What's more, since nondeliberate action is not mediated or guided by mental states, something else, lacking the overt content of such states, must govern it. Skills, or knowhow, step forward as the missing element.

Moreover, given the interest in overcoming "Cartesianism," the persuasiveness of the thesis that there is a skill-governed directedness toward the world devoid of subjects and mental states is only increased when it is shown that the deliberate, or subject/object, mode of "being-in (the world)" presupposes such directedness. In addition, Dreyfus argues that the deliberate mode of directedness has a form of elaboration, called "pure contemplation," in which entities, including humans, are encountered as objects, that is, are understood to instantiate that general category of being called "occurrentness" (*Vorhandenheit*). Since this is precisely the sort of being that subjects and mental states possess, the thesis that the subject/object mode of being-in is grounded in the absorbed coping mode explains at once how "Cartesianism" emerges and why it misconstrues human activity. The idea of skilled nondeliberate action is not just phenomenologically persuasive, but also philosophically consequential.

However, in characterizing the deliberate/nondeliberate distinction in terms of mental states, and not just in terms of consciousness and awareness, Dreyfus has not fully carried out the anti-"Cartesian" program. Indeed, what he has done is to accept a "Cartesian" interpretation of mind and to utilize phenomenological description to limit the scope of that interpretation. The "Cartesianism" of the interpretation lies less in the ascription of causal powers to mental states than in the thesis that the objects of mental states are explicit, that is, in the thesis that mental states are conscious states. This latter claim is clearest in those places where Dreyfus treats consciousness, thematic awareness, and mentality as equivalent notions.[32] Consciousness and thematic awareness are indeed the phenomena that a non-"Cartesian" account of human life must displace from center stage. But mind need not be displaced along with them. Descartes and his successors did not invent the notion of mind; and non-"Cartesian" accounts of mind, of the conditions designated by mental life-condition vocabulary, certainly exist. So moving beyond "Cartesianism" *also* means moving beyond "Cartesian" conceptions of mind that assimilate it to consciousness and treat mental states as conscious states. (Moving beyond such conceptions means, in addition, moving beyond the conception of mind as space, substance, or apparatus.) The irony in Dreyfus's account of agency, then, is that he understands perfectly well what going beyond "Cartesianism" entails— "Heidegger's attempt to break out of the tradition is focused in his attempt to get beyond the subject/object distinction in all domains, including action."[33] But Dreyfus himself does not carry through this aim in all domains. In particular, he does not seek to transcend the subject/object distinction in the realm of mentality—even though his characterization of perception as Dasein's openness to the world evinces an understanding of what this could look like. As discussed above, a Wittgensteinian way out is to construe mentality as how things stand and are going for people, a dimension of existence that is formulated in life-condition language (and that is expressed in activity more generally).

The second conclusion is that Dreyfus's account of the determination of agency requires modification. People do not believe, intend, fear, hope, perceive, and so on *only* when acting deliberately. *Whenever* a person acts, various life-conditions obtain, and this determines (i.e., specifies) what she does. Although Dreyfus is importantly correct that thematic intentionality occurs against the background of transparent coping, it is equally true that the obtaining of mental conditions orders nondeliberate activity.

Despite appearances, this latter claim is compatible with Dreyfus's conception of skills. As discussed in section I, when people exercise their skills in acting nondeliberately, they do what makes sense to them to do. What makes sense to them is determined, moreover, teleologically. In section II it was suggested that attributing mental conditions to people puts into words that which determines the intelligibility informing their activity. Part of what it is for particular such conditions to obtain is, in other words, for particular actions to make sense in particular situations. Hence, an aspect of the phenomenon of nondeliberate activity as Dreyfus describes it (the determination of what makes sense) amounts to particular mental conditions obtaining for people, which is itself a state of affairs articulated using life-condition expressions. As already indicated, however, life-conditions are attributed to actors not just when they act deliberately, but also when they act nondeliberately. This implies that *in both cases* people do what makes sense to them and that, in both cases, what makes sense depends on how things stand and are going for them. Indeed, the only difference between acting deliberately and nondeliberately in this regard is that thematic consciousness plays a much more prominent role in the former, that is, in the case of deliberate action, people are much more thematically aware of what determines intelligibility. Thus, a phenomenon that Dreyfus ascribes to nondeliberate action alone, namely, doing what makes sense, is in fact a property of all actions; and the obtaining of life-conditions, which Dreyfus restricts to deliberate activity, in fact orders all activity. The obtaining of mental conditions *is* what determines (that is, specifies) practical intelligibility. Hence, all human activity *at once* rests on the exercise of skills and is ordered by the obtaining of certain mental conditions. Life-condition talk is not an alternative, but complementary, to skill talk.

It follows that the distinction between nondeliberate and deliberate action is not terribly consequential. This distinction is simply one between those actions that involve little and, in the limit, no explicit awareness and those that involve more. Nothing in the realm of determination and explanation, beyond the amount of thematic awareness in play, turns on this difference. That much human activity is nondeliberate is a striking fact whose significance Dreyfus more than anyone else has clarified. His conception of background skills is important and far-reaching. In fact, since it applies to deliberate as well as nondeliberate action, it reaches further than he claims. At the same time, it displaces folk-psychology only when the latter is misconstrued in a "Cartesian" manner. Coping with others is a matter of coping with actors who generally pay little attention to the matters determining what makes sense to them to do. Their doing this, one might say, is a key aspect of what it is to be a skilled actor.

3

Practices, Practical Holism, and Background Practices

David Stern

I   Beginning with Practices

"Begin with practices."[1] The importance of beginning with practices
is a theme that runs through much of Hubert Dreyfus's work on
Heidegger, cognitive science, and artificial intelligence. Beginning
with practices can help us to see how phenomena as diverse as consciousness, intentionality, rule-following, knowledge, and representation presuppose skills, habits, and customs, and so cannot be made
fully explicit. Drawing on Heidegger, Merleau-Ponty, Bourdieu, Foucault, and Wittgenstein, he has argued that these phenomena involve
a practical dimension that cannot be formally analyzed, and consequently cannot be used as autonomous points of departure in our
attempts to understand ourselves and our world. The principal aim
of this paper is to critically examine Dreyfus's notion of a practice
and his arguments for the primacy of practice. Why should we begin
with practices, and how does this lead to the conclusion that it is
impossible to give a formal analysis of our practical abilities?

Stephen Turner's *The Social Theory of Practices*, a recent critique of
the turn toward practices, provides a helpful point of departure. The
book begins with two exemplary quotations, the first from Wittgenstein's *On Certainty*, the second by Dreyfus:

"But I did not get my picture of the world by satisfying myself of its correctness; nor do I have it because I am satisfied of its correctness. No: it is the
inherited background against which I distinguish between true and false."

"Heidegger argues that . . . even when people act deliberately, and so have beliefs, plans, follow rules, etc., their minds cannot be directed toward something except on a background of shared social practices."

Practices, it would appear, are the vanishing-point of twentieth-century philosophy. The major philosophical achievements of the century are now widely interpreted as assertions about practices, even though they were not originally couched in this language.[2]

After observing that the notion of practice has its origins in the domain of social theory, Turner observes that it has recently become extremely widespread, not only in philosophy, but also in fields as diverse as literary criticism, feminist scholarship, rhetorical analysis, studies of the discourse of science, artificial intelligence, and anthropology. Yet it is extremely difficult to bring that vanishing point into focus:

But the concept is deeply elusive. What are "practices"? What is being referred to, for example, by Wittgenstein's phrase "the inherited background against which I distinguish between true and false"? What are "tacit pictures of the world"? These are not everyday objects. And they are given additional, mysterious properties—they are said to be "shared," or "social." How seriously should we take this language? Are there really objectifiable things that we should think of as being shared or inherited? Or are these merely figures of speech? And if so, why should we be willing to accept them as part of the explanation of anything as central as truth or intentionality? What do they stand for that enables them to play this kind of central role in our thought?[3]

In this opening passage, Turner already hints at a dilemma that is elaborated in the pages that follow: either practices are substantial, shared objects whose nature needs to be clarified, or they are insubstantial, nothing more than "figures of speech." However, the accounts of practice he considers presuppose that practices are mental entities which explain community members' common patterns of action and are socially transmitted. He goes on to argue that the notion of a practice as a "shared possession" is incoherent, "causally ludicrous." For a shared practice must "be transmitted from person to person. But no account of the acquisition of practices that makes sense causally supports the idea that the same internal thing, the same practice, is reproduced in another person."[4] Turner is surely right that if we conceive of practices as akin to tacit beliefs—

hidden, inner objects, that are causally responsible for our behavior—then the very notion of a social theory of practice is ludicrous, and there are insuperable difficulties in understanding how the very same thing can be passed on from one person to another.

Rather than following Turner's recommendation that we reject the notion of practice in favor of talk of "habits," patterns of behavior that do not presuppose a concealed, causally efficacious object, we would do better to ask whether there is a way of conceiving of practices that avoids these liabilities. Both Heidegger and Wittgenstein, two of the most important influences on Dreyfus's conception of practice, were deeply critical of philosophers who postulate inner objects in order to explain what we say and do. Indeed, Turner's objections to conceiving of practices as hidden inner objects have striking affinities with Wittgenstein's critique of the notion of inner mental objects.

II Theoretical Holism and Practical Holism

Dreyfus follows Heidegger and Wittgenstein in conceiving of practices as a matter of publicly accessible action, patterns of saying and doing; like them, he is deeply opposed to conceiving of them in terms of mysterious inner objects. Toward the beginning of his book on *Being and Time* he gives a summary of his reasons for thinking that social practices cannot be understood as objects, or as a belief system implicit in the minds of individual subjects. Dreyfus reads Heidegger as arguing that our shared agreement in our practices, our *"pretheoretical* understanding of being"[5] cannot be set out as a belief system because it does not consist of beliefs at all:

There are no beliefs to get clear about; there are only skills and practices. These practices do not arise from beliefs, rules, or principles, and so there is nothing to make explicit or spell out. We can only give an interpretation of the interpretation already in the practices. . . . [A]n explication of our understanding of being can never be complete because we dwell in it—that is, it is so pervasive as to be both nearest to us and farthest away—and also because there are no beliefs to get clear about.[6]

There is an excellent exposition of the nature of these commitments, and their implications for a conception of practice in "Holism

David Stern

and Hermeneutics," a paper written some ten years earlier. There Dreyfus introduces a contrast between two kinds of holism: theoretical holism, the view that all understanding is a matter of interpreting between theories, and practical holism, the view that while understanding "involves explicit beliefs and hypotheses, these can only be meaningful in specific contexts and against a background of shared practices."[7] Quine's views about interpretation are his chosen example of theoretical holism; Heidegger's hermeneutics in *Being and Time* his principal example of practical holism:

> The Quinean *theoretical* circle results from what Heidegger calls *Vorsicht*, i.e., from the fact that all verification takes place within a theory, and that there is no way out of the circle of holistic hypotheses and evidence. The Heideggerian *hermeneutic* circle, on the other hand, says that this whole theoretical activity of framing and confirming hypotheses takes place not only on the background of explicit or implicit assumptions but also on a background of practices (the *Vorhabe*) which need not—and indeed cannot—be included as specific presuppositions of the theory, yet already define what could count as a confirmation. Thus all our knowledge, even our attempt to know the background, is always already shaped by what might be called our implicit ontology, an "ontology" which is in our practices as ways of behaving towards things and people, not in our minds as background assumptions which we happen to be taking for granted.[8]

> According to the ontological hermeneutics of both Heidegger and Wittgenstein, when we understand another culture we come to share its *know-how and discriminations* rather than arriving at agreement concerning which *assumptions and beliefs* are true. This coordination comes about not by making a translation, or cracking a code, but by prolonged everyday interaction; the result is not a commensuration of theories but what Heidegger calls "finding a footing" and Wittgenstein refers to as "finding one's way about."[9]

This practical background is not an agreement in beliefs, but in ways of acting and speaking. As Wittgenstein puts it, "What people *say* is true and false; and they agree in the *language*. That is not agreement in opinions, but in form of life."[10] Without these shared skills, communication would be impossible. The theoretical holist will reply that even if such a background is necessary,

> one will be able to analyze that background in terms of further mental states. Insofar as background practices contain knowledge, they must be based on

implicit beliefs; insofar as they are skills, they must be generated by tacit rules. This leads to the notion of a holistic network of intentional states, a tacit belief system, that is supposed to underlie every aspect of orderly human activity, even everyday background practices.[11]

In turn, the practical holist will respond that it is a mistake to assume that there must be a theory lying behind our practices, to postulate tacit belief whenever explicit beliefs cannot be found:

> *What makes up the background is not beliefs*, either explicit or implicit, but habits and customs, embodied in the sort of subtle skills which we exhibit in our everyday interaction with things and people. . . . While one may, indeed, on reflection treat aspects of the background as specific beliefs, as for example beliefs about how far to stand from people, these ways of acting were not learned as beliefs and it is not as beliefs that they function causally in our behaviour. We just do what we have been trained to do. Moreover, as practices, they have a flexibility which is lost when they are converted into propositional knowledge.[12]

Clearly, a great deal depends on just how one conceives of skills in this connection, and Dreyfus pursues a number of complementary expository strategies in explaining his conception of skills. One is to appeal to the accounts offered by other philosophers who have given skills a fundamental role; in the context from which the passage I have quoted is taken, Dreyfus glosses the "subtle skills" in question as Foucault's "micropractices," connecting this with Wittgenstein's dictum that it is "our acting, which lies at the bottom of the language-game"[13] and shortly afterward draws on Heidegger's notion of "primordial understanding"[14] as a way of discussing the role of practice as a noncognitive precondition of understanding. Indeed, one can read much of *Being-in-the-World*, Dreyfus's commentary on Division I of *Being and Time*, in just this way. A complementary strategy, particularly helpful with an audience unfamiliar with these philosophers, and thus particularly prominent in *What Computers Still Can't Do* is to make use of striking examples of skills. Swimming, cycling, and skiing are all favored examples of motor skills; chess, the prime example of an intellectual skill; and conversational competence, the preferred example of a social skill. Each example has its own strengths, but the microskills involved in fluidly conducting a conversation are particularly relevant here, as they can serve to illustrate just how much familiarity with a culture is needed before one can be counted as a competent conversationalist. Such skills embody an interpretation of an entire culture:

And just as we can learn to swim without consciously or unconsciously acquiring a theory of swimming, we acquire these social background practices by being brought up in them, not by forming beliefs and learning rules. A specific example of such a social skill is the conversational competence involved in standing the correct distance from another member of the culture depending on whether the other person is male or female, old or young, and whether the conversation involves business, courtship, friendship, etc. More generally, and more importantly, such skills embody a whole cultural interpretation of what it means to be a human being, what a material object is, and, in general, what counts as real. This is why Heidegger in *Being and Time* calls this cultural self-interpretation embodied in our practices "primordial truth."[15]

But before we look more closely at arguments that draw on specific examples of social skills it will be helpful to consider an even more direct strategy: saying what practices are, and why they matter.

III What Are Practices?

Here it will be helpful to turn to a position paper published at the same time as the Heidegger book, which starts by addressing precisely these concerns about the nature of practice:

Begin with practices, not with consciousness. What are practices? What is in the practices? How do they fit together? What is our relation to them?[16]

The paragraphs that follow provide telegraphic summaries of his replies to each of these four questions. The answer to the first reads:

1. Practices are *social skills*. By *skills* I mean to capture two aspects of the practices. (1) Skills are not based on representations—that is, on beliefs or rules—nor can they be analyzed in terms of, or generated by, formal structures. They are passed on by society through individuals without necessarily passing through consciousness (Foucault, Bourdieu.) (2) Skills have rich interconnections so that modifications of any part of the system of skills will modify the others.

By *social* skills, I mean that there is a convergence of skills, that is, everyone does things roughly the same way. If there are deviations, they are not coerced and coopted. People just naturally conform to what everyone does.

Social practices are what one does. If you thematize that, you get the idea of *norms*, although the people who are acting them out do not think of their practices as norms. Modern norms have a special character Foucault calls *normalization*. Norms seem to be based on truth—there is a right way of doing things. Norms are not merely what one does, but what one *ought* to do. This is not a necessary aspect of the structure of social skills; it is an aspect of the structure of *modern* social skills.[17]

Notice that the very first part of the answer already takes for granted the conclusion of the argument that will be the focus of this paper: "Skills are not based on representations—that is, on beliefs or rules— nor can they be analyzed in terms of, or generated by, formal structures." The remainder of this passage sketches an argument for this conclusion. The point is not simply that skills are not usually taught by means of explicit instructions or rules; but that as a matter of fact, many skills cannot be acquired in this way. Instead, they are "passed on," as Dreyfus puts it here: one learns "what one does" by means of conformism: "People just naturally conform to what everyone does." The second paragraph, on the social character of skills, argues that while skills cannot be approached individualistically, the social dimension to skillful activity may simply be a matter of conformism, and so does not presuppose a grasp of norms—what one does in a given situation—and normativity—what one ought to do. Instead, norms and normativity, arise out of, and depend on, a more primitive circumstance: people tend to converge on doing things in roughly the same way. However, this emphasis on the training of behavior is only part of the story, for socialization into a set of practices amounts to nothing less than an understanding of existence, an understanding that we embody. This leads up to the subject of some of the subsequent questions Dreyfus sets himself, from which it emerges that this conception of practice has extremely far-reaching philosophical implications:

2. What is in the practices? In social practices there is an understanding of what it is to be a person, what it is to be an object, what it is to be an institution, and these all fit together and are an understanding of what it is to be.

4. What is our relation to the practices? That is, in fact, the wrong way to ask the question, since it suggests that there is us, and then there are

practices. Rather, we *are* the practices. They set up a *Spielraum* of possibilities of action for us, and this space of possibilities is not something that we have a relation to, but something *embodied* in us. "We are the world existing," Heidegger would say. . . . This idea that we are a clearing or opening is my interpretation of the self as transcendence, or better, as transcending.[18]

We can put aside Dreyfus's third question about practices—how do they fit together?—until later, for it is a question about the extent to which practices share a common structure, a question that is best considered once the outlines of the overall approach are clearer.[19] The following passage condenses the train of thought we have just been considering still further, summarizing the argument I have just outlined into a few terse and deceptively simple sentences:

To explain our actions and rules, humans must eventually fall back on everyday practices and simply say, "This is what one does." In the final analysis, all intelligent behavior must hark back to our sense of what we *are*. We can never explicitly formulate this in clear-cut rules and facts; therefore, we cannot program computers to possess that kind of know-how.[20]

Given the richness of the conception of everyday practice Dreyfus is working with, talking of harking "back to what we *are*," while not in itself misleading, certainly takes a great deal for granted for so much depends on how one understands the appeal to "what we *are*." One way of spelling out this notion that there is only so much to be said by way of explaining why we do what we do, is to be found in passages in Wittgenstein's *Investigations* that echo many of these concerns:

The common behaviour of mankind is the system of reference by means of which we interpret an unknown language.

—How do I explain the meaning of "regular," "uniform," "same," to anyone?—I shall explain these words to someone who, say, only speaks French by means of the corresponding French words. But if a person has not yet got the *concepts*, I shall teach him to use the words by means of *examples* and by *practice*.—And when I do this I do not communicate less to him than I know myself.

How can he *know* how he is to continue a pattern by himself—whatever instruction you give him?—Well, how do I know?—If that means "Have I reasons?" the answer is: my reasons will soon give out. And then I shall act, without reasons.

"How am I able to obey a rule?"—, if this is not a question about causes, then it is about the justification for my following the rule in the way that I do.

If I have exhausted the justifications I have reached bedrock, and my spade is turned. Then I am inclined to say: "This is simply what I do."[21]

But here, if not before, one wants to ask: why have we "reached bedrock"? Why can't we explicitly formulate what we ordinarily take for granted and teach by means of examples of practice? Dreyfus, like the Heidegger of *Being and Time*, and unlike the Wittgenstein of the *Philosophical Investigations*, does not think that we must come to a full stop at this point, that even when the reasons a competent speaker can supply have come to an end, there is still more that can be said. In particular, we need an explanation as to why skills can't be taught by means of explicit instructions or rules, and instead must be "passed on . . . through individuals." To appeal to "what we are" or to say "this is simply what I do" is not so much an argument as a placeholder for one, to presume that it has already been shown. In what follows, we will consider a number of different ways of defending this claim.

IV Why Can't Background Practices Be Made Completely Explicit?

"Hermeneutics and Holism" proposes two principal reasons for concluding that our background practices cannot be spelled out in a theory:

1. the background is so pervasive that we cannot make it an object of analysis
2. the practices involve skills[22]

The background is "pervasive" because of its intimate role in every aspect of our lives; as Dreyfus puts it in a Heideggerian turn of phrase quoted at the beginning of section II, we "dwell" in it. It is difficult to find a way of putting this point without recourse to a simile: background practices are like water to a fish, or the light we see by, or the vantage point from which we see, so near to us and for that very reason furthest away, that we are unable to get at a critical distance from them. However, Dreyfus immediately goes on to qualify his endorsement of the first line of argument by saying that it presupposes the second, for "if it were merely the pervasiveness of one's own background which made it inaccessible to theory, it could be made the object of theoretical analysis by another culture, or, perhaps, another stage of one's own culture."[23] Indeed, once one qualifies the argument in this way it is unclear how much force, if any, it has left, for the qualification opens up the possibility that we ourselves might arrive at a stage in our development where we are sufficiently distant from a background we once took for granted that we are able to make it completely explicit. After all, if the only reason the background cannot be made fully explicit were that in any act of understanding one always has to take something for granted, then the argument would be no better than trying to show that one cannot see everything because one always has to look from somewhere, and one cannot see the place that one looks from.

This problem does seem to affect the following attempt by Charles Taylor to show that the idea that one can make the background completely explicit is "incoherent in principle":

There must always be a context from which we are attending if we are to understand the experience of a being [with engaged agency]. So bringing to articulation still supposes a background. . . . We do some of it now, so why not, bit by bit, do all of it eventually? But if we treat it as a standing condition of intelligibility, from which we have to attend . . . then the incoherence of this notion becomes clear. . . . [The background] can be made explicit, because we aren't completely unaware of it. But the expliciting itself supposes a background. The very fashion in which we operate as engaged agents within such a background makes the prospect of total expliciting incoherent.[24]

The "pervasiveness" argument, while important for the light it casts on the role of background practices in our lives, cannnot, by itself, show as much as Taylor believes. And even if it succeeds in showing that it is in principle not possible to articulate everything, it does not show that there is anything, that is, in principle, impossible to articulate. This leads us back to the second train of argument: that the background cannot be spelled out in a theory because the practices involve skills.

As we saw in section II, the standard theoretical holist strategy in responding to practical holism is to treat practices as a system of beliefs, to be analyzed in terms of constituent beliefs. The point of the turn to skills in Dreyfus's second train of argument is that they are not intentional states and so lack the sort of content that would be explicated by such an analysis. One of the morals of Dreyfus's detailed discussion of specific skills is to get us to see that they play a very different role in our lives to beliefs—to attempt to assimilate them to explicit propositional attitudes would be to misrepresent both the way in which they are learned, and their role in our actions. To put the point in Rylean terms, know-how is not reducible to knowledge that. Here, it is helpful to consider familiar examples of skillful activity which do not lend themselves to a formal analysis:

Most of us know how to ride a bicycle. Does that mean we can formulate specific rules to teach someone else how to do it? How would we explain the difference between the feeling of falling over and the sense of being slightly off-balance when turning? And do we really know, until the situation occurs, just what we would do in response to a certain wobbly feeling? No, we don't. Most of us are able to ride a bicycle because we possess something called "know-how," which we have acquired from practice and sometimes painful experience. That know-how is not accessible to us in the form of facts and rules. If it were, we would say we "know that" certain rules produce proficient bicycle riding.

There are innumerable other aspects of daily life that cannot be reduced to "knowing that." Such experiences involve "knowing how." For example, we know how to carry on an appropriate conversation with family, friends, and strangers in a wide variety of contexts—in the office, at a party, and on the street.[25]

Here, bicycle riding figures as an example of a motor skill, something we know how to do, but are unable to provide a procedural specification of how to do it. At the end of this passage, a parallel point is made for a social skill: knowing how to carry on a conversation. The boundaries between the two kinds of skills are not, perhaps, as clear as one might think at first. For a beginner, bicycle riding is primarily a matter of physical coordination, but later on, learning to ride in traffic can be as much a social skill as conducting a conversation; and many of our bodily movements in an ordinary conversation are as unreflective as the ones involved in balancing a bicycle.

David Stern

However that may be, both cases are examples of a knack for doing something, a know-how, that cannot be articulated entirely in assertions. But how much comfort can we draw from the fact that this knowledge is "not accessible to us in the form of facts and rules"? Two different, albeit related claims, seem to be packed in here. First, there is a phenomenological point: we don't, at least for the most part, experience our knowledge of how to ride a bicycle, or carry on an appropriate conversation, as a matter of explicitly formulating rules. Even though one might from time to time say such things as "lean to the side you want to steer toward" or "don't dominate the conversation," this is only the tip of the iceberg. Even these explicit instructions depend on a grasp of how one goes about leaning a bike into a curve, or what counts as dominating the conversation, and often we will be altogether at a loss as to how to put what we've done into words. Second, but closely related, is a technical point: as a matter of fact, despite our best efforts, we have not been able to provide formal analyses of such skills.

At this point, the theoretical holist will argue that there must be a tacit set of rules, or procedures, lying behind our ability to ride, or converse, and the phenomenological and technical difficulties raised in the previous paragraph only show that the rules in question are unconscious, or very difficult to specify, not that they do not exist. That such rules have not been found, either in consciousness, or in research to date, does not show that they cannot be found. But this leads to two further problems. On the one hand, if one tries to give an analysis in terms of the kind of rules that a person might actually follow,

then the cognitivist will either have to admit a skill for applying these rules, or face an infinite regress. Or, if he says that one doesn't need a rule or skill for applying a rule, one simply does what the rule requires, . . . why not just accept that one simply does what the situation requires, without recourse to rules at all?[26]

On the other hand, if the theoretical holist tries to replace everyday rules with formal nonmental rules, of the kind found in computer modeling, the problem arises of specifying the basic elements that the rule would operate on:

A formal rule must be represented as a sequence of operations. But there seem to be no basic movements or ideas to serve as the elements over which such rules would have to operate. Even though bodily skills, for example, are sometimes learned by following rules which dictate a sequence of simple movements, when the performer becomes proficient the simple movements are left behind and a single unified, flexible, purposive pattern of behaviour is all that remains. . . . No one has the slightest idea how to construct formal rules for the skills involved in swimming or speaking a language, let alone the skills embodying our understanding of what being means. It seems that the background of practices does not consist in a belief system, a system of rules, or in formalized procedures; indeed, it seems the background does not consist in representations at all.[27]

A further, related point, is that even if we can give a formal specification of how to proceed, it will be incapable of handling new and different cases, or of showing creativity in responding to unexpected circumstances. Practices are more flexible than beliefs; a real expert faced with an unexpected challenge, a case quite unlike an ordinary or routine one, will be able to respond creatively and imaginatively when a routine response would be inadequate or inappropriate. The ability to respond creatively to a challenging case is a distinctive difference between a human expert and an "expert system." A final, rather different, reason for holding that skills cannot be made explicit is that there are certain social skills, primarily those involved in the maintenance of repressive and oppressive social structures, which would break down if articulated and thematized self-consciously. This is a theme that is prominent in the work of Foucault and Bourdieu, but which receives surprisingly little attention in Dreyfus's work, perhaps because this inexpressibility is always specific to a particular culture, and he is primarily interested in reasons why certain skills cannot be made explicit under any circumstances.

Up to this point, we have primarily considered the negative implications of the claim that practices involve skills, reasons why an attempt to make them fully explicit cannot succeed. This is the principal concern of *What Computers Still Can't Do* and *Mind Over Machine*. But there is also a more positive way of approaching the claim in question: one can take it as an invitation to provide a portrayal of the role of skills in our lives, and this approach is prominent in *Being-in-the-World*'s interpretation of disclosure, the fore-structure of interpretation, and sense. Skillful activity is holistic, connected with other skills and ways of living, and so acquiring skills is a matter of being socialized into a social world.

One of the most important morals that emerges from Dreyfus's Heideggerian work on skillful activity is that it would be a mistake to think of it as a matter of endorsing practice over theory, for background skills, our familiarity with the world, are equally a precondition of both theoretical and practical activity:

[W]henever we are revealing entities by using or contemplating them, we must simultaneously be exercising a general skilled grasp of our circumstances. It is this background orienting that makes everyday coping possible. . . . Our general background coping, our familiarity with the world, what Heidegger calls originary transcendence, turns out to be what Heidegger means by our understanding of being. . . . And Heidegger is explicit that this understanding of being is more basic than either practice or theory:

"In whatever way we conceive of knowing, it is . . . *a comportment toward beings*. . . . But all practical-technical commerce with beings is also a comportment toward beings. . . . In all comportment toward beings—whether it is specifically cognitive, which is most frequently called theoretical, or whether it is practical-technical—an understanding of being is already involved. For a being can be encountered by us *as* a being only in the light of the understanding of being. . . ."[28]

It is the discovery of the primacy of this understanding of being, not of the primacy of practical activity, that Heidegger rightly holds to be his unique contribution to Western philosophy.[29]

V Conclusion

Perhaps the most difficult question raised by this account of "our general background coping, our familiarity with the world" is the following: what is the identity of the "we" that is under discussion here? In other words, *whose* practices are we talking about? Does such an approach presuppose a specific community or group as its subject matter? Should the "we" be contrasted with the "we" of other groups, or does it refer quite universally, to any person whatsoever? Is there just one understanding of being, or are there many?

The Heidegger of *Basic Problems* takes it for granted that his subject matter is *the* understanding of being, not *an* understanding of being.

Later, Heidegger was to think of "comportment toward beings" as the understanding shared by the West, or "those cultures that have excelled at the skill of history-making," and it is this approach that Dreyfus, Spinosa, and Flores have taken as their point of departure in *Disclosing New Worlds*.[30]

Because "we *are* the practices,"[31] this question about the nature of the subject of Dreyfus's account, the "we," is at the same time a question about the nature of its object, the practices. This brings us back to the third of Dreyfus's four questions that were posed at the beginning of section III, namely "How do they fit together?"

> 3. How do the practices fit together? This question raises other questions: How *totalized* are they? Does everything fit together, or only parts? How do you characterize the parts that do fit together, and the aspects that are left out? Do practices, for example, fit together like elements in a formal system, or do they fit together at varying distances from paradigm cases, with overlapping similarities, or are there other models for how they fit together?[32]

Notice that unlike his other three questions, this one leads him to a number of further questions, rather than a definite answer. At the 1997 NEH Institute on Practices, Dreyfus approached the issues surrounding the primacy of practice, and the nature of practices, in a similar way, but looking at different accounts of how practices change over time, rather than their identity at a single time. He began by giving a summary of the conception of skills and background practices that we have surveyed in the last three sections. This led to a discussion of different conceptions of the ways in which skills can change and develop: do they become more specialized and stable, articulating goods that are internal to the practice, or are later developments discontinuous with previous ways of acting? Turning to the question of the ethico-political consequences of beginning with practices, he mapped out five competing views about how practices change over time, and the extent to which practices are unified or dispersed, integrated or disseminatory, and argued that each has substantive ethical and political implications. Briefly, the views he set out can be summed up as follows.[33]

(1) Stability. (Wittgenstein, Bourdieu) The practices are relatively stable and resist change. Change may be initiated by innovators, or

be the result of "drift," but there is no inherent tendency in the practices for this to happen. The consequence is either a conservative acceptance of the status quo or revolutionary prescription of change.

(2) Articulation. (Hegel, Merleau-Ponty) The practices have a telos of clarity and coherence, and become increasingly more refined as our skills develop. This leads to political progressivism and whiggish history, albeit with the recognition that the path to progress will not always lead in that direction.

(3) Appropriative Gathering, Ereignis. (Dreyfus's reading of later Heidegger) When practices run into anomalies, we make an originating leap, drawing on marginal or neighboring practices and so revising our cultural style. This supports those who can best bring about such change within a liberal democratic society, such as entrepreneurs, political associations, charismatic leaders, and culture figures.

(4) Dissemination, Différance. (Derrida) There are many equally appropriate ways of acting, and each new situation calls for a leap in the dark. The consequence is a sensitivity to difference, to loosen the hold of past norms on present and future action, and to become aware of the leaps we make rather than covering them up with whiggish history.

(5) Problematization. (Foucault) Practices develop in such a way that contradictory actions are felt to be appropriate. Attempts to fix these problems lead to further resistance. This leads to a hyperactive pessimism: showing the contingency of what appears to be necessary and engaging in resistance to established order.

This is a rich and suggestive set of connections between theories of practice and ethico-political commitments. However, I would prefer to end on a note of caution. First, it may be a mistake to think that we need to give a single uniform answer to such questions about how practices develop. Isn't a pluralism which acknowledges that some practices aim at ever greater complexity and subtlety, while others break apart into conflicting tendencies, much more plausible? Rather than having to decide between these accounts, it may be that all of them have their own domain of applicability. Second, it is far from clear that any such account of practices must have determinate ethico-political implications; much depends on the context in which any particular conception of practice is taken up. Heidegger's conception of practice has been taken to support a wide range of very different political agendas, for instance. Even if we can agree to begin with practices, I have my doubts as to whether that will determine where we end up.

4

The Limits of Phenomenology

John R. Searle

This article will be mostly a commentary on Dreyfus's discussion of Heidegger.[1] Dreyfus has probably done more than any other English-speaking commentator to make the work of Heidegger intelligible to English-speaking philosophers. Most philosophers in the Anglo-American tradition seem to think that Heidegger was an obscurantist muddlehead at best or an unregenerate Nazi at worst. Dreyfus has usefully attempted to state many of Heidegger's views in a language which is, for the most part, intelligible to English-speaking philosophers. For this, we are all in his debt.

One of his rhetorical strategies in his Heidegger book is to contrast my views unfavorably with Heidegger's. However, he persistently misstates my views, and I believe his misunderstandings are not accidental. Dreyfus has real difficulty in understanding my position, because he thinks I am trying and somehow failing to do phenomenology. He seems to think that the analysis of intentionality must somehow be phenomenological and he also seems to think that there are only two possible general approaches to intentionality, the Husserlian and the Heideggerian. Since I am clearly not like Heidegger, he supposes my view must be like Husserl's. I am sure he has read my work, but he seems to think that he already understands it a priori, or rather perhaps I should say he *always already* understands it. One thing his discussion reveals is that the activity of logical analysis, in which I am partly engaged, is fundamentally different from phenomenology, as he describes it. Phenomenology is, at best,

John Searle

the first step but only the first step in logical analysis. In developing the Heideggerian position which he endorses, I think he reveals inadvertently the limitations of the phenomenological method in philosophy. For phenomenology how things seem to an agent, "letting something show itself" (32), is crucially important; but for logical analysis it is only the first step.

I must say immediately that I have not read enough of the works of Husserl, Heidegger, or phenomenology generally to have an intelligent opinion about what they actually say. When I say "Heidegger," I mean "Heidegger-as-described-by-Dreyfus," and ditto for "Husserl" and "phenomenology."

This article will consist of four parts. First (the most boring part), I will correct some (not all) of the major misunderstandings of my work. Second, I will criticize the Heidegger-Dreyfus account of skillful coping because I think it is incoherent. Third, I will try to show the endemic weaknesses of the phenomenological method, as they practice it. Finally I will try to contrast my method for examining these issues, with phenomenology, as Dreyfus describes it.

Because some of my effort will be in correcting misunderstandings, it is important that I not misunderstand Dreyfus. He has kindly agreed to check every interpretation to see that he is not misquoted or misrepresented. He holds, or at least at the time of original publication did hold, all of the views I attribute to him.

I

An early example of Dreyfus's systematic misunderstanding is his claim that I think of intentionality as a relation between "a self contained subject with mental content (the inner) and an independent object (the outer)" (5). Dreyfus also calls this the "subject-object" conception of intentionality(105). It ought to worry him that I never use expressions like "self contained subject" (in fact, I am not quite sure what it means); nor do I characterize my own views as the "subject-object conception," and it ought to worry him further that I explicitly expressed objections to the metaphors of inner and outer. The views he describes are not my views, and indeed are inconsistent with my position. On my view the key to understanding intentionality is the *conditions of satisfaction* which are determined by the contents of intentional states, and the Background of capacities that enables intentionality to function. You would never get an understanding of these central principles from Dreyfus's parody of my views. Nor would you get the idea that on my view phenomenology does not necessarily reveal either the conditions of satisfaction or the Background.

In another misrepresentation, when describing my conception of the Background, Dreyfus says: Searle's only alternatives are either "subjective intentionality" or "objective muscle machinery" (103). But, of course, the Background is neither subjective intentionality nor objective muscle machinery. Dreyfus goes on to say that my two categories are mind and body. Since I have spent many years of my life trying to overcome the dualism of mind and body, that is an amazingly false claim for him to make.

The list goes on: in another striking example of misunderstanding, Dreyfus says that on my view, whenever I take it that I am seeing a house or that I am reaching for the salt, I am performing a sort of mental interpretation. This is not even remotely like my view. For me, literal cases of acts of interpretation are rather rare, and they are certainly not in general features of reaching for the salt or recognizing a house. Again he says that "according to Husserl and Searle" whenever there is an intentional relation there must be an "ego doing the taking."[2] I never use expressions like "ego doing the taking" and frankly I have no idea what Dreyfus is referring to. He says, "I must represent to myself that my bodily movement is meant to bring about a specific state of affairs," and this he describes as "active meaning-giving."[3] Such conceptions are foreign to my way of thinking, and the whole notion of "representing things to myself" is really quite different from the conception I have of intentional states as mental representations, as we will see later.

Dreyfus says, "On Searle's analysis, all acting is accompanied by an experience of acting" (56). This is doubly wrong. First, I explicitly deny that all actions require experiences of acting.[4] But second, when they do occur such experiences are not an "accompaniment." This is an important point and I will say more about it later. Again, he says that according to Searle, "When we don't find conscious beliefs and desires causing our actions, we are justified in postulating them in our explanations" (86). I make no such claim, indeed I explicitly deny that all actions are preceded by prior intentional states.

Yet another instance where Dreyfus misunderstands my view is the following. He says, "Heidegger, as we have seen, would also reject John Searle's claim that even where there is no desire we must *have in mind* conditions of satisfaction" (93, my emphasis). That "have in mind" is strictly Dreyfus's invention and it is not surprising that he gives no page reference. He goes on: "Phenomenological examination confirms that in a wide variety of situations human beings relate to the world in an organized purposive manner without *the constant accompaniment* of representational states which specify what the action is aimed at accomplishing" (93, my emphasis). Examples are skillful activity, like skiing or playing the piano. etc.

The dead giveaway that his critique rests on a radical misrepresentation of my view is in this criticism: "Activity can be *purposive* without the actor *having in mind* [my emphasis] a *purpose*" (93). Quite so. But why does he think that on my view the purposiveness must be something the actor "has in mind"?

These misrepresentations about "constant accompaniments," "having in mind," and "mental representations" are important misunderstandings and, indeed, I believe they are the key to seeing both what is wrong with Dreyfus's account of my views and with his own Heideggerian theory. He thinks that when I say that an intentional state is a representation of its conditions of satisfaction, I think of the representation as a kind of thing one "has in mind," as a "constant accompaniment" of my activities. He thinks this because he supposes that if representations exist, they must exist phenomenologically. But that is not remotely like my view. Representation for me is not an ontological, much less a phenomenological, category, but a functional category. As I said at the beginning of *Intentionality*, "There is nothing ontological about my use of the notion of 'representation'. It is just a shorthand for this constellation of logical notions borrowed from the theory of speech acts."[5]

When I am trying to do something, the representation is not something in addition to the trying, a constant accompaniment, rather the trying (what I call the intention in action) just is a representation (in my sense) of what I am up to, because it determines what counts as success or failure. Dreyfus persistently states that on my view, the intention in action causes the action. But that is not my view. On my view, the intention in action is part of the action. It is the intentional part of the action, it is that fact about the action that makes the action intentional. I will say more about this point later.

In short, Dreyfus is trying to read me as if I were a phenomenologist, and then given the options in phenomenology he tries to read me as if I were Husserl, and then he reads Husserl's theory of action as postulating a set of higher order mental representations as a "constant accompaniment" to all intentional behavior. Because Dreyfus thinks that I am trying and somehow failing to do phenomenology, his misunderstandings are systematic. When I speak of "representation," "conditions of satisfaction," "causal self-referentiality," and "intentions in action" he thinks I am talking about the phenomenology of agents. I am not. I am talking about the logical structure of intentional phenomena, and the logical structure does not typically lie on the surface, it is not typically discoverable by mere phenomenology.

Dreyfus, by the way, constantly criticizes Husserl's theory of action and says how much it is like mine. But he never quotes any passages from Husserl's alleged works on the theory of action. It would be nice to see Husserl's original theory of action. I am so ignorant that I did not even know that Husserl had a well-developed general theory of action. In which of his many books did he develop it? Sometimes Dreyfus talks as if Husserl *would have had* or *might have had* views like mine. Can it be that he is inventing a theory of action (mine) to attribute to Husserl? I have to say that if that is what Dreyfus is claiming then it seems to me less than fully responsible. One cannot say of another author what he would have said or might have said, one should only discuss what he actually did say.

It is, as I warned the reader it would be, boring to just give a list of misinterpretations of my views. The interest of the list derives from the fact that it reveals the distinction between two ways of doing philosophy and Dreyfus is so wedded to phenomenology that he literally is unable to see that I am not doing phenomenology. I am engaged, among other things, in logical analysis and that enterprise is quite different from phenomenology. His misunderstanding is as if somebody thought Russell's theory of descriptions made the claim that anybody who says "The King of France is bald" must "have in mind" the existential quantifier as a "constant accompaniment." Russell analyzed the truth conditions of sentences, and in that enterprise, the phenomenology of speakers is largely, though not entirely, irrelevant. I extend the methods of logical analysis beyond sentences and speech acts to analyze the conditions of satisfaction of beliefs, desires, intentions, perceptual experiences, and intentional actions; and to that enterprise phenomenology is largely, though not entirely, irrelevant. But you will not uncover the logical structure of these phenomena if you do not go beyond phenomenology. The problem with Heideggerian phenomenology, as we will see later, is not so much its falsity but its superficiality and irrelevance.

As I said, this last misunderstanding, that intentionality is a "constant accompaniment" that one "has in mind," is perhaps the key to Dreyfus's whole book, so I want to use it as a lead-in to the more important part of the discussion. A main theme in this book is to contrast my theory, according to which intentional contents play a causal role in producing bodily movements and other conditions of satisfaction, with Heidegger's theory according to which there are no such contents, except in a few odd cases. Dreyfus, in short, repeatedly contrasts "skillful coping" with intentional behavior. Here is a representative passage.

John Searle, like Bourdieu, argues that formal and causal accounts in the social sciences must fail, but he, like Husserl, holds that the problem is that intentional mental states play a causal role in human behavior and so must be taken account of in any science of human beings. But since, as Heidegger and Bourdieu emphasize, much of human behavior could and does take place as ongoing skillful coping without the need for mental states (i.e., beliefs, desires, intentions, etc.), intentional causation does not seem to be the right place to start to look for an essential limit on prediction in the human sciences. What is crucial is that, even when no intentional states are involved, what human beings pick out as specific sorts of objects depends on background skills that are not representable. (205)

I believe there are a number of things wrong with this passage. I do not claim that causal analyses in the social sciences must fail. On the contrary, I insist that intentional causation is the right analytical tool for understanding social phenomena. I do not reject formal accounts. On the contrary, I regard formal, mathematical economics as one of the great intellectual achievements of the social sciences in the twentieth century. I will say more about this passage later, but for the present I want to zero in on its central claim. What this passage emphasizes, along with many others, is the contrast between "ongoing skillful coping" behavior, and behavior that "involves" mental states, and the general claim is that normal behavior does not involve any mental states at all. The objection to it is the obvious one: ongoing skillful behavior "always already" involves mental states in the only sense that matters: such behavior can succeed or fail, and the conditions of success and failure are internal to the behavior in question. To an exploration of that idea, I now turn.

II

Anyone who reads Dreyfus would get the impression that he must spend an awful lot of time playing basketball and tennis, and above all, hammering nails. But, since I know him as a colleague in Berkeley, I can say that most of his waking hours are devoted to reading, writing, talking, and lecturing on philosophy and other matters. Now this is of some importance, because, for Dreyfus, almost all of his "ongoing, skillful coping" is linguistic. Indeed the passage I just quoted in the preceding section is a typical example of Dreyfus engaged in ongoing skillful coping. So let us try to apply Dreyfus's account of skillful coping to this paradigm example, where skillful coping is manifested in the very statement of the theory of skillful coping. According to Dreyfus we are supposed to accept that when he wrote this passage, and presumably also when he rewrote, edited, and proofread it, he *had no mental states whatever: no "beliefs, desires, intentions, etc."* Frankly, I find the idea out of the question. I believe that when Dreyfus wrote the passage, he did so *intentionally*, that is, he intended to write that very passage. Furthermore I think he wrote the passage in the "*belief*" that it was true and with a "*desire*" to say the things he said. Mental states like belief, desire, and intention are so "involved" in the production of this passage that if he had not had them he would not have written the passage at all. Worse yet, I believe that all of this skillful coping was conscious.

Can he really want us to accept that in his ongoing skillful behavior of writing this passage there were no beliefs, desires, intentions, etc., involved? It looks to me like a paradigm case of intentional mental behavior. Seldom in the history of philosophy can a view have been presented that seems so self refuting. Far from contrasting behavior which is skillful coping with intentional behavior, his own example of skillful coping in language exemplifies intentional behavior, and because it consisted in the performance of speech acts, his skillful coping expresses beliefs, desires, and intentions.

So, what is going on here? How can Dreyfus's theory be so at variance with his practice? I think the explanation is the one I suggested before. He thinks that if mental states are "involved" they must be involved phenomenologically as a "constant accompaniment." His picture is that the skillful coping is like a soprano singing and the mental states are like a piano accompaniment, and he cannot for the life of him figure out why I seem to be saying that no soprano can sing without a piano accompaniment. This explains the stilted vocabulary in which he tries to state my views. He says "I *must represent to myself* that my bodily movement is *meant* to bring about a state of affairs."[6] If that means anything, it must mean that I have higher order thoughts that are a constant accompaniment to my intentional acts. But that is not my view. Sometimes the soprano just (intentionally) sings.

Well, one might say, it is unfair to take a linguistic example. Perhaps Dreyfus did not mean for us to consider speech acts as a form of skillful coping. Perhaps they are an exceptional case, and he only meant "skillful coping" to cover the prelinguistic cases. The problem with that way out is that almost all human behavior, certainly the sorts of examples he gives, are linguistically permeated. There is no way you can play basketball or tennis without the activity being linguistically loaded. To begin with, in such activities the players have to be constantly performing speech acts to each other, and there are lots of other symbolic components. For example, the basketball player has to know the score, he has to know which team he is on, he has to know which play is being run, whether they are in zone or man-to-man defense, how much time is left on the shot clock, how much time in the game, how many time-outs left, and so on. All of this knowledge is part of the player's "skillful coping" and it is all in various ways linguistic.

My own work on intentionality grew directly out of my work on speech acts so I was never tempted to the view that you could examine intentionality while totally ignoring language.

With all this in mind let us look at what Dreyfus says about such things as playing tennis or basketball. Here is what it is like to be Dreyfus's tennis player: "We not only feel that our motion was caused by the perceived conditions, but also that it was caused in such a way that it is constrained to reduce a sense of deviation from some satisfactory gestalt. Now we can add that *the nature of that satisfactory gestalt is in no way represented.*"[7]

I think any clinician would say that Dreyfus describes a deaf mute tennis player who also seems to be suffering a bilateral lesion of the hippocampus that prevents him from having any overall sense of the game. Consider the contrast between Dreyfus's tennis player and real life. Suppose in a real-life situation the tennis player has just blown the match and the coach asks him, "What the hell happened?" Now what does he say? Does he say, "Coach, it's not my fault. I did not cause anything, rather my motions were caused by the perceived conditions, and those conditions failed to reduce the sense of deviation from some satisfactory gestalt, where the nature of that satisfactory gestalt was in no way represented"?

Or does he say something like this: "Coach, I was hitting the ground strokes short because I got really tired in the fifth set. And when I started to lose my concentration, I couldn't get my first serves in"? The problem with Dreyfus's example is not that it is false; rather it is beside the point, because it fails to capture the level at which tennis players (as well as basketball players, carpenters, and philosophers) are consciously trying to do something when they engage in "skillful coping." The tennis player is above all trying to win, and he is trying to win by—for example—hitting harder serves and hitting his ground strokes closer to the base line. All of this is intentional, all of it *involves* "beliefs, desires, intentions, etc.," and all of this is left out of Dreyfus's account.

Since this is an important issue between Dreyfus and me, let me state what I think goes on in the mind of a typical tournament tennis player. A typical competitive tennis player has the following sorts of intentional contents: first of all, he and his coach have to get together to decide which matches he should enter. This produces endless discussion. No intentional contents? Finally they decide on a certain match and he is entered. More intentionality. There are also endless debates about how to get to the tournament, which car, who is going to drive, etc. Again, the tournament tennis player is very interested in the opponent he is paired against and he and the coach will plan his tennis strategy very carefully. All of this planning, from beginning to end, is loaded with intentionality, right up to the extreme nervousness and anxiety with which he approaches the match. Now we are actually in the match. What does Dreyfus describe? According to him the tennis player's experience is this: "I am simply letting myself be moved by the gestalt tensions I experience on the court."

Here is what I think is more likely to be the sort of thing that is going through his mind: "I am supposed to be able to beat this guy but I am now behind two games in the second set. He is ahead five to three in the second set with me serving and the score is forty/thirty. I had better get this shot in, because I do not want to go to deuce in this game." All of this he thinks "in a flash" without having to think each—or even any—word.[8] But these are the sort of thoughts going through his head when he lunges for the ball. The idea that he is passively "letting himself be moved" seems to me, frankly, out of the question as a description of what it is actually like to engage in any serious competitive activity. A serious competitive activity is filled with intentionality down to the ground.

I think Dreyfus would insist that even where there are all these intentional phenomena, still there must be a lot of micro practices that are more "primordial." He is rather vague when it comes to spelling them out, but let us mention some. The tennis player has to be able to hold the racket and move about the court. When he talks he has to be able to move his mouth and tongue. Unless he engaged in these practices he could not talk and play tennis.

I think there is an important point here, but the phenomenological method is unable to state it. The point is: all intentional activity goes on against a Background of (abilities. Those abilities make the practices possible, and the practices are not something separate from the intentional phenomena, rather they are the way that the intentional phenomena are carried out. For example, in order to try to hit the ball harder I have to be able to hold the racket and swing it, in order to write this article I have to be able to move my fingers over the keyboard. The two essential points are, first, that intentionality rises to the level of the Background ability; and second, it reaches to the bottom of that ability in its exercise. For example, my intention in action (what I am trying to do) is to hit the ball close to the baseline, but in so doing my subsidiary movements are done intentionally, even though they are not at the level of what I am trying to do. All of this is explained in detail in *Intentionality*. Dreyfus rejects the analysis, but he nowhere answers the arguments.

I believe that Dreyfus's account of skillful coping is inadequate and that the contrast he makes between intentional behavior and skillful coping is wrong, because skillful coping is intentional behavior right down to the ground. Since if I am right, the mistake is obvious, what accounts for it?

Three things:

First, as I mentioned, he thinks that intentionality, if it exists in skillful behavior, must exist phenomenologically as an accompaniment, as a second level of thought processes in addition to the actions, the piano accompaniment to the real singing. But that is a misunderstanding. I do not drive to my office and give a lecture and then in addition have a set of second-level thoughts about driving and lecturing, rather the driving and lecturing are precisely the form that my intentionality takes. All of his talk about "mental representations" is based on this mistake.

The simplest proof that there exist conscious experiences of acting as part of actions in addition to bodily movements is to contrast the normal case, where, for example, I consciously and intentionally raise my arm, with the Penfield cases. Penfield could cause the bodily movement in his brain-damaged patients by stimulating the relevant portions of the motor cortex with a micro-electrode. Now in both the normal case and the Penfield case the bodily movement is the same. So, what is the difference? It seems to me there is an obvious difference between the experience of doing something (what I call the experience of acting) and just observing the same bodily movements as something that happens to one.

The introduction of consciousness leads to the next point. A second source of the error is his failure to come to terms with consciousness. Is skillful coping supposed to be essentially conscious or not? In *Being-in-the-World*, Dreyfus seems to be saying that Dasein need not be conscious, that consciousness does not matter to Dasein. But that cannot be right. Except in a few really weird epileptic cases, all skillful coping requires consciousness. You can only cope skillfully if you are conscious of what you are doing. In subsequent writings he concedes this point. But the concession has enormous logical implications. Suppose he concedes the following: in order to give a lecture, drive to my office, or play a set of tennis I have to be conscious and the consciousness is an essential part of these activities. But then, wherever there is consciousness, there must be some content to the consciousness. And in all these cases, the content determines the conditions of success and failure in what I am trying to do. That is, I do not give my lecture and in addition have consciousness as a musical background, rather the content of the conscious intentionality determines the content of the lecture. Also there may be a whole lot of different levels of consciousness. While I am consciously driving to my office, I may be also consciously planning my lecture. Once you concede that consciousness is essential to skillful coping behavior you have conceded that there is an intentional content to the behavior, because the consciousness is the bearer of that content. It is not an "accompaniment," it is an essential part of the actions. That is, the conscious content determines what counts as succeeding or failing in the behavior in question. It determines what I call the conditions of satisfaction. And this does not of course imply that the conditions of satisfaction are phenomenologically explicit in the conscious state. For example, it takes a lot of analysis to get to the causal self-referentiality of certain conscious mental phenomena, a point to which I now turn.

In a major misinterpretation, Dreyfus writes, "[in] everyday skillful coping, there is awareness but no self-awareness. That is, there is no self-referential experience of acting as this is understood by Searle (and would have been understood by Husserl)" (67). This passage equates self-awareness with self-referentiality and thus reveals the confusion between phenomenology and logical analysis that I have been calling attention to. The self-referentiality of the experience of acting has nothing to do with the phenomenology of self-awareness. Self-referentiality is a purely logical feature having to do with the relationship between the intentional state and its conditions of satisfaction. The fact that Dreyfus thinks self-referentiality implies self-awareness reveals that he has totally misunderstood the theory I am advancing. Any animal capable of intentional action and perception has causally self-referential intentional states. But self-awareness is very sophisticated and probably confined to primates and other higher mammals. There is certainly no connection between self-referentiality and self-awareness. Furthermore, the use of the term "awareness" here and the contrast between awareness and self-awareness reveals Dreyfus's problem about consciousness. Normally awareness implies consciousness. But if so, then we are confronted with the problems that I have been calling attention to. If skillful coping, as he says, requires awareness, and awareness is consciousness, and consciousness in such cases always has intentional content, then Dreyfus's claim that skillful coping does not have intentionality reduces to self-contradiction.

A third source of the mistake is that the method, the "phenomenological" method, at least as practiced by Dreyfus's version of Husserl and Heidegger, is inadequate. It is bankrupt because it can only tell us how things seem at a certain level of seeming and does not give a logical analysis of the phenomena. I want to develop this idea in more detail in the next section.

I can summarize my objections to Dreyfus's account of "skillful coping" as follows:

The actual account that he gives of skillful coping is so vague that you cannot quite tell what he has in mind. But as soon as you spell

John Searle

it out in detail, you see that it must be false. So, let's spell it out in some detail. Suppose I am engaged in a kind of skillful coping, such as doing my physical exercises. I am doing my push-ups, running in place, etc. Notice that this is such skillful coping for me that I am able to do these things while thinking about something else. I can be doing these things while thinking about philosophical problems at the same time. These exercises need not be at the center of my attention when I do them. I mention this because it is typical of many of Dreyfus's examples of skillful coping that you are able to do one thing and because you are so skillful at it, you can think about something else at the same time.

Now let us ask about this skillful coping at exercising.

1. First, is it intentional?
The answer to that question is obviously yes. So we then have to ask the next question:

2. What fact about it makes it intentional?
Before we answer that question, let us go to the next point:

3. Was the agent conscious while engaged in skillful coping?
And the answer to that question is obviously yes. But that leads to our step four:

4. Whenever there is consciousness, there must be some content to the consciousness.[9]

Now these two lines of investigation, points one and two on intentionality and points three and four on consciousness, come together at exactly this point. The content of the consciousness and the fact that corresponds to the attribution of intention come together exactly, because it is the content of the consciousness that determines that I am doing these physical exercises intentionally. I am, for example, consciously trying to do my push-ups and I will succeed or fail in my intention depending on whether I do, in fact, do my push-ups. And that amounts to saying that it is part of the content of my consciousness that I will succeed under some conditions, and fail under others. But exactly that point is what I mean when I say the activity has *conditions of satisfaction*. The conscious experience of trying or acting determines or represents the conditions of satisfaction. Now, Dreyfus has much trouble with this concept of "representation," so let me say, as I said in the texts that he criticizes, that the word is inessential to my account. The representation is not an *accompaniment* to the conscious coping, it just is the intentional part of the coping.

Frankly, I do not see how anyone could deny any of the above. Heidegger and Dreyfus appear to be denying it. But Dreyfus denies it by first supposing that the view is committed to some sort of extra "mental representations" in his sense, that is, as a constant accompaniment of the activity. But as we have seen that is entirely alien to my way of thinking of these things. And second, he then proceeds to describe how it seems to the agent, at such a low level of the agent's consciousness, that we are unable to get at the actual conditions of satisfaction; we are unable to get at what the agent is trying to do. It is because the description is given at such a low level, that we get all these puzzling remarks about how it seems to Larry Bird, etc. I want to say for the most part those are irrelevant. How it seems to the agent at that level is only of preliminary interest. It is only of interest to us insofar as it enables us to get at the essential point, namely, what are the conditions of satisfaction? Under what conditions does the agent's intentional content, whether conscious or unconscious, succeed or fail?

I said above that Dreyfus's account of skillful coping was incoherent. I can now state exactly what the incoherence is: on the one hand he wants to maintain that ongoing skillful behavior does not involve any mental component. But on the other hand, whenever we try to give an account of any ongoing skillful behavior, we will see that it invariably contains a mental component, and this comes out in various ways in his talk of "awareness," or in my terminology, "conditions of satisfaction." He tries to cover up this inconsistency by supposing that any awareness sufficient to determine conditions of satisfaction would have to be second level. It would have to be "self-awareness." But that is inconsistent both with the facts and with my account of the facts.

John Searle

III

I think Dreyfus's book dramatically illustrates the weakness of the phemomenological method, at least as practiced by him and Heidegger. Because I have only a limited amount of space I will confine myself to three sorts of examples.

1. *Using this method, many of the most important questions in philosophy and science cannot even be stated.*

For example, in linguistics and philosophy of language, the central question is about the relations of sound and meaning. It is just a plain fact (call it fact 1) that when I utter a sentence I make an acoustic blast. It is also a plain fact that I perform a speech act (fact 2). How does fact 1 relate to fact 2? How do I get from the physics to the semantics? Dreyfus thinks that because we phenomenologically experience the sounds as meaningful there can be no problem. "So if we stick close to the phenomenon we dissolve the Husserl/Searle problem of how to give meaning to mere noises" (268). But the phenomenology does not dissolve the problem at all, it simply refuses to face it. Granted that phenomenologically we experience the sound as a speech act, the question remains: what is the relation between the sound and the speech act? Phenomenology not only misses the point, but in Dreyfus's case it makes it impossible to see the point. He assumes that the question is about phenomenology, and thus thinks that when there is no phenomenological question, there is no question. But fact 1 and fact 2 remain as plain facts regardless of the phenomenology. This example is only one of many where phenomenology is systematically blind. The blindness extends to all of institutional reality—money, property, marriage, government, etc.

2. *Where it can see the questions, Heideggerian phenomenology typically gives systematically false answers.*

This can be best illustrated with the following sort of example. When I drive to work in the morning, I drive on the right-hand side of the road. Why? What is the causal explanation for my driving on the right-hand side of the road as opposed to, say, the left-hand side of the road or in the middle of the road? Here are two possible answers.

1. I am unconsciously following the rule, "Drive on the right-hand side of the road,"

2. My behavior is just a habitual case of skillful coping. I have become a skillful driver, and, as a skillful driver in the United States, I just automatically drive on the right.

Now, I take it, Dreyfus thinks that the first of these answers is phenomenologically wrong and the second answer, Heidegger's, is correct; and that one is forced to choose between them. I think a moment's reflection is sufficient to show that both answers are right. They are not inconsistent answers to the same question, but consistent answers to two different questions. As a matter of how it typically seems to me on the spot "phenomenologically," the second answer is clearly right. When I drive to the campus I almost never think about the traffic laws. Unless there is some obstacle in the way, such as a hole in the road or a parked car, I routinely drive on the right-hand side of the road without even thinking about it. But the first answer is also obviously right. The reason that I have acquired the habit is that I have a general policy of driving on the right in order to obey the law. I would never have acquired this particular habit if I did not know the rules of the road or if I lived in England. Notice that the first claim meets all of the conditions for a true causal attribution. Consider the counterfactual conditions: If the law had never been that way in the first place, I would never have driven the way I do. If the law changes, I will change my behavior. If asked to explain my behavior, I will appeal to the traffic laws. If I had not known the law, I would not have behaved the way I did. And so on. In other writings,[10] I have pointed out that my Background habits, dispositions, and abilities evolve the way they do because of the rules, even though when I exercise those abilities, I do not have to think about the rules. The behavior is sensitive to the rules even though the rules are not part of my consciousness then and there.

So it can be both the case that I follow the rule unconsciously in such a way that the rule plays a causal role in the production of my behavior and also that I do not consciously think about the rule at all as I drive to work. But the phenomenology cannot get at both of these truths. The point I am making is fairly obvious but the reason for making it is to illustrate that Dreyfus's method prevents him from seeing it. Phenomenology, as he describes it, can only describe how things seem to us at a certain very low level of seeming (reducing gestalt imbalances, etc.) and cannot get at the *logical* structure of what is happening. What is true of driving is true of most forms of skillful coping: brushing my teeth, paying my taxes, playing tennis, and giving my lectures. In all these cases there are different levels of intentionality, and a description of the lowest level of how it seems to the agent phenomenologically is unable to capture all of these levels. You will never understand my tooth brushing behavior if you think it is all about removing gestalt imbalances, and not about preventing cavities.

3. *There is a systematic ambiguity in Heidegger's philosophy between phenomenology and ontology; this produces inconsistencies.*

Both in conversation with me and in the text Dreyfus maintains that he and Heidegger are complete realists about the real world as described by science and common sense. No relativism. But then he says things like the following: "The Greeks stood in awe of the gods their practices revealed, and we have to *discover* the elementary particles—we do not construct them" (264). But the Greek practices did not "reveal" any gods because there never were any. There is no way that the Greek practices can reveal gods when there are none to reveal. One might as well say that children's practices at Christmastime "reveal" Santa Claus. The Greeks *thought* that Zeus and Co. existed, just as small children believe that Santa Claus exists, but— does one really have to say this?—in both cases they are mistaken. I have been to Mt. Olympus. I think Dreyfus would like to say that the Greek gods were revealed within their practices—in fact he does say that, but it is both false and inconsistent with his other views. And the "practices" are no help in rectifying the falsehood and the inconsistency. You cannot have it both ways. You cannot be a complete realist about science and the real world and then say things that are inconsistent with that realism. You cannot say, as he does, (261) "science cannot be a theory of *ultimate* reality." Physics, chemistry, cosmology, etc. are precisely sciences of "ultimate" reality. If they fail as such, they fail, period. You cannot accept that they succeed and then deny that success.

Dreyfus tries to cover this inconsistency over with remarks like the following: "It follows from Heidegger's account that several incompatible lexicons can be true, i.e., reveal how things are in themselves" (279). He even talks about "incompatible realities" (280). But strictly speaking lexicons (much less realities) are never compatible or incompatible, true or false; only statements, etc., made within vocabularies provided by lexicons can be compatible or incompatible, true or false. And two incompatible statements cannot both be true. He gives no examples to show how incompatible statements might both be true, but rather speculates that Aristotelian final causes might turn out to be more "revealing." But that is no help. If Aristotelian final causes exist than the theories that say they do not exist are just plain false. To repeat, you cannot have it both ways.

IV

My enterprise in analyzing intentionality is totally different from that of Husserl and Heidegger, and I want to end this discussion by explaining that difference, because many of Dreyfus's misunderstandings come from a failure to appreciate it.

From my point of view both Husserl and Heidegger are traditional epistemologists engaged in a foundationalist enterprise. Husserl is trying to find the conditions of knowledge and certainty, Heidegger is trying to find the conditions of intelligibility, and they both use the methods of phenomenology. In my theory of intentionality, I have no such aims and no such methods. I am engaged in a large number of projects, one of which can be reasonably thought of as logical analysis in the sense in which Russell, Tarski, Frege, Austin, and my own earlier work on speech acts exemplify logical analysis. I start with certain facts as we know them: the universe consists entirely of physical particles in fields of force ("ultimate reality") and these are usually organized into systems. Some systems on our little planet are made of organic compounds. These carbon-based systems are the products of biological evolution by way of natural selection. Some of them are alive and have nervous systems. Some of these nervous systems have consciousness and intentionality. And one species at least has even evolved language.

Now my question is, from a logical point of view, how do language and intentionality work to determine truth conditions and other conditions of satisfaction? How do they work as natural, and above all biological, phenomena? A sane philosophy *starts* with atomic theory and evolutionary biology and with the fact that we are identical with our living bodies, and goes from there. And do not say that these are just "scientific" truths, rather they are just plain facts. To say they are scientific truths is to suggest that there might be some other kind of truth, equally good, but inconsistent with these. But science is the name of the methods for discovering truths, and once discovered, truths are just plain true. For example, if God exists then that is a fact like any other. It is a mistake to think that it is a fact in some ontological domain, a *religious* fact, as opposed to a *scientific* fact. If God and electrons both exist then those are just facts in the real world.

You begin with the fact that we are embodied brains, and that there is a sheer physical boundary, our skins, between our bodies and the rest of the world, that we are identical with our bodies, and that our consciousness and other intentional phenomena are concrete features of the physical world located inside our brains. Philosophy starts with the facts of physics, chemistry, biology, and neurobiology. There is no going behind these facts to try to find something more "primordial." Now, with this in mind, what are we to say about Husserl and Heidegger? Well, as far as I can tell from Dreyfus, they do not have anything to say about neurobiology or chemistry or physics. They seem to think it is important to know how things seem to the agent. The difference between them, then, from my point of view, becomes quite trivial. Husserl thinks that intentionality is a subject/object relation between a transcendental subject and an intentional object. Heidegger thinks that there is no such distinction, that there is only the skillful coping of Dasein, with Befindlichkeit and Geworfenheit also to be found and thrown in. But, from my point of view, both of these are more or less irrelevant to getting an adequate theory of the logical structure of the intentionality of biological brains encased in biological bodies.

Uncovering this logical structure simply cannot be done by phenomenology. For example, in criticizing my views Dreyfus likes to cite the naive, introspective reports by Larry Bird, the basketball player, and by mountain climbers. It seems to Larry Bird and to the mountain climbers that they are just responding to the environment, that they cannot even make a distinction between themselves and the environment. But, so what? What question is that supposed to be an answer to? We know for a fact that their bodies (hence themselves) are distinct from the environment. There are no axons in the basketball or the mountain. The only question that I can think of, that it is an answer to, is the question: how does it seem phenomenologically to the agent when he is engaged in some normal ongoing, skillful coping activity? But now, because such data are useful only at the very beginning of the investigation, why would we care how it seems to the agent? I think Dreyfus has no answer to this except to say that he has no research project in intentionality beyond that question. Phenomenology is in large part precisely about that question. Once that question is answered he has nothing more to say about the intentionality of the phenomena.

One of the great lessons of philosophy in the past century is that logical structure typically does not lie on the surface of how things seem. The theory of descriptions, the theory of speech acts and the theory of intentionality are all examples of how you start with how things seem, but then have to dig deeper to get at the real underlying structure.

Some of Dreyfus's comments border on mystification. So, for example, in the passage I quoted above, he says, "Background skills . . . are not representable" (205). But what can that possibly mean? Anything at all is representable. Indeed, he just represented the background skills by referring to them as "background skills." What he must mean in this case is that the background skills do not *consist in* representations. But so what? Very few things in the world consist in representations, but that does not mean they are not representable. This mistake is more than just a slip. It is not just that he meant to say "do not consist in representations," and put in "are not representable" by mistake; rather I think there is a deep confusion about the conditions of possibility of our practices. The conditions of possibility of our practices are that we are conscious neuro-biological animals. Our species has developed through evolution, and we are now genetically and culturally endowed with certain coping abilities. There is no reason whatever why we cannot investigate these coping abilities and their neuro-biological basis. The deep confusion in the phenomenological method, as described by Dreyfus, is that it cannot start with the most basic facts of atomic physics and evolutionary biology. He feels he has to start with the ongoing skillful capacities of Dasein. "There are independent real things, objective space and time, and assertions can agree with the way things are in themselves—but these realities and the detached stance from which they are revealed cannot account for the meaningful practices in which we dwell" (281). But why not? There is no reason why an examination of the facts cannot account for "the meaningful practices in which we dwell." Dreyfus and Heidegger think that because the investigation presupposes the practices that therefore the practices cannot be investigated. But that is a fallacy. Just as we use the eye to study the eye, language to study language, the brain to study the brain, etc. so we can use the practices to study the practices, and indeed we can, as I do, use the Background to study the Background.

V

Dreyfus has made many valuable contributions to philosophy. One thinks of his powerful criticisms of traditional artificial intelligence, for example. In my view, his work is at its best when he speaks with his own voice. I think we should be grateful that he has tried to expound the work of philosophers who are less clear headed and less talented than he, but much as we may value these expository efforts, I hope in the coming years he will not neglect his own considerable gifts.[11]

Background Practices, Capacities, and Heideggerian Disclosure

Mark A. Wrathall

Hubert Dreyfus and John Searle have both argued that intentional states can only have a content against a non-intentional or pre-intentional background. Despite striking similarities in their respective descriptions of and arguments for the background, their accounts of the workings of the background are, in the final analysis, very different. The difference is most pronounced when comparing their explanation of what the background is. For Searle, the background is a "neuronal structure" capable of generating intentional states—hence, his preferred description of the background as a set of capacities. For Dreyfus, on the other hand, the background is a set of practices, skills, and activities. Corresponding to, or rather, responsible for their differing accounts of the nature of the background are different conceptions of how the background is meant to explain intentional states. The explanatory function of the background is, I contend, the most significant source of disagreement between Searle and Dreyfus in their otherwise very similar accounts of the pre-intentional background.

In this chapter, I begin by briefly reviewing some differences between Searle's and Dreyfus's backgrounds—differences which, incidentally, have resulted in Searle and Dreyfus often speaking past each other on the subject of the background. I will then show how Dreyfus's misunderstanding of what Searle's background is meant to do results in his criticism of Searle missing the mark. I conclude by arguing, however, that a redirected reading of disclosure in

Heidegger—a concept Dreyfus misleadingly glosses as "background coping"—allows us to see a genuine shortcoming in Searle's background.

I Background Practices

Following Heidegger, Wittgenstein, and Merleau-Ponty, and anticipating Searle's argument for the background, Dreyfus argued already in *What Computers Can't Do* that intentionality is only possible against the background of a pre-intentional set of bodily skills, a meaningfully ordered world (or situation), and nonrepresentable human purposes and needs.[1] This background, Dreyfus argued, simply cannot be analyzed in terms of representable facts and rules:

> In explaining our actions we must always sooner or later fall back on our everyday practices and simply say "this is what we do" or "that's what it is to be a human being." Thus, in the last analysis, all intelligibility and all intelligent behavior must be traced back to our sense of what we *are*, which is, according to this argument, necessarily, on pain of regress, something we can never explicitly *know*.[2]

But the unknowability of the background does not mean that we can say nothing about it at all. Indeed, in the introduction to his Heidegger commentary, Dreyfus claims that Heidegger should be understood in *Being and Time* as laying out the "elaborate structure" of the background to everyday intentional comportment.[3]

The job of the background in the Dreyfus/Heidegger account is to "enable[] us to make sense of things"; background practices "provide the conditions necessary for people to pick out objects, to understand themselves as subjects, and, generally, to make sense of the world and of their lives" (4). They do this both by allowing objects to show up to us as already meaningful, and by articulating the ways in which things show up as meaningful. Dreyfus's argument for the background, it must be remembered, was developed as a response to a cognitivist model of the mind. According to that model, the mind's relation to the world, and ability to make sense of itself and the world around it, is understood as a matter of information processing. The world is taken to consist in independent elements which impinge on the mind in the form of sensory data and which, in and of themselves, have no meaning for a human subject. The mind is taken to function by representing the independent elements of the world and then processing those representations or bits of information in order to arrive at a meaningfully structured world. Dreyfus, in general, treats cognitivism as a special case of the view of mind and world which has prevailed since Descartes:

In Descartes's ontology the ultimate building blocks of the universe are the elements of nature (*naturas simplices*) understood by natural science. But one could also try to account for everything in terms of sense data, monads, or, as in Husserl, relations among the "predicate senses" corresponding to relations among the primitive features of the world to which these basic elements purport to refer. Heidegger presumably has this last stage of the atomistic, rationalist tradition in mind when he speaks of understanding the world in terms of "a system of relations" "first posited in 'an act of thinking'" . . . . This Husserlian project culminates in recent attempts to understand the world and the objects in it as a complex combination of features, and the mind as containing symbolic representations of these features and rules or programs representing their relationships. (108)

There are two crucial failings of the cognitivist model, however—failings which lead Dreyfus to posit a non-intentional background of practices. First, Dreyfus points out, its description of our encountering the world as a set of meaningless, atomistic elements is phenomenologically unsupported: "Things are not encountered as isolated occurrent entities to which we attach isolated function predicates. . . . [N]othing is intelligible to us unless it first shows up as already integrated into our world, fitting into our coping practices" (114–115). In short, it is only in quite unusual circumstances that we are able to see things as "occurrent entities."

Of course, what makes the cognitivist approach attractive is that it appeals to our sense that the universe, as it is in itself, is not meaningfully ordered in terms of human beliefs and concerns. If we are to accept Dreyfus's phenomenology, and reject the idea that the universe is made meaningful by a mental process, we need some alternative account of how it is that things can be encountered by us as already meaningful. Dreyfus's answer, as the quotes above indicate, is to see natural entities as being meaningfully "integrated" into our world by a background of "coping practices."

Mark A. Wrathall

The second failing of the cognitivist model, and perhaps the more profound, is its inability to explain how a rule-governed processing of bits of atomistic information can arrive at anything which approximates our understanding of the world. This argument applies even if one rejects Dreyfus's phenomenology of everyday experience; one might argue that the phenomenology simply overlooks the information processing because it occurs at a subconscious level. Of course we experience the world as already meaningful, the cognitivist might say, but this is only possible because our minds have made it meaningful. Dreyfus's response, in both *What Computers Can't Do* and *Being-in-the-World,* is to point to the holistic and skillful articulation of our understanding of the world. The holism of our understanding of things makes it difficult to see how any rule-governed approach to constructing what we know could capture even the simplest forms of understanding. Dreyfus illustrates this point with the example of a table:

> [J]ust adding to the representation of a table the fact that it is to eat at or sit at barely scratches the surface of its involvement with other equipment and for-the-sake-of-whichs that define what it is to be a table. Such function predicates would not be sufficient to enable a person from traditional Japan to cope with our kind of tables or even fully understand Western stories where tables played their normal part. All the propositions spelling out tableness would have ceteris paribus conditions, and so would those conditions, etc. (117)

In addition, Dreyfus points to the "argument from skills." When we try to capture the content of what we know about the world, we find that much of that knowledge consists simply in our skills for getting around the world—that is, our "readiness to deal with what normally shows up" in a given situation. If we are to treat the mind as processing bits of information, we would have to treat these skills as rules for responding to meaningless elements we encounter in the world. In addition, human skills respond not just to objects but to situations, so we would need to add rules trying to define different situations and the way in which the situation alters our skills for responding to things in the situation. But this approach pushes us into an infinite regress, for the application of rules itself depends on skills for applying rules. If we try to capture *those* skills in terms of the application of further rules, then . . . . The mistake, of course, is to treat our understanding of the equipmental whole and our ability to respond to it as rule governed. Dreyfus explains: "Since our familiarity does not consist in a vast body of rules and facts, but rather consists of dispositions to respond to situations in appropriate ways, there is no body of commonsense knowledge to formalize. The task [of formalizing skills as rules] is not infinite but hopelessly misguided" (117–118). In the place of mental rules, Dreyfus concludes, we need to see intentional activity as grounded in a background of practices which simply dispose us to act as it is appropriate to act.

In sum, the background of practices in Dreyfus's interpretation of Heidegger explains how things in our world show up as meaningful and how we are able to act intelligibly. Things are given meaning according to the ways they are integrated into our practices. And we are able to act because our background practices dispose us to responding in a certain way to the things and people we encounter in our going about in the world.

Dreyfus reads Heidegger as distinguishing two levels of background practices—practices for coping with particular things or items of equipment, and practices for coping with whole contexts of equipment. The idea seems to be, at a certain level, quite commonsensical. Of course, one cannot cope with particular items of equipment unless one has a "general skilled grasp of our circumstances" in which those particular items of equipment have their place (105). Dreyfus provides a nice example of how this is meant to work:

For example, when I enter a room I normally cope with whatever is there. What enables me to do this is not a set of beliefs about rooms, nor a rule for dealing with rooms in general and what they contain; it is a sense of how rooms normally behave, a skill for dealing with them, that I have developed by crawling and walking around many rooms. Such familiarity involves not only acting but also not acting. In dealing with rooms I am skilled at not coping with the dust, unless I am a janitor, and not paying attention to whether the windows are opened or closed, unless it is hot, in which case I know how to do what is appropriate. My competence for dealing with rooms determines both what I will cope with by using it, and what I will cope with by ignoring it, while being ready to use it should the appropriate occasion arise.[4]

Heidegger, according to Dreyfus, thus sees the need to posit a background against which specific local coping is possible—that is, a background which "permits particular coping activities to show up as possible in the current world" (186). This background coping, or disclosure, grounds discovery by letting us bring our skillful ability to use particular pieces of equipment into play by "being ready in particular circumstances to respond appropriately to whatever might normally come along" (103).

At the same time, Dreyfus takes pains to point out that background coping is essentially the same as specific coping:

> But, on the other hand, originary transcendence (being-in-the-world, disclosure) is not something radically different from ontic transcending (transparent coping with specific things, discovering); rather, it *is the same sort of coping* functioning as the holistic background for all purposive comportment. . . . One needs to be finding one's way about in the world in order to use equipment, but finding one's way about is just more coping. Any specific activity of coping takes place on the background of more general coping. Being-in-the-world is, indeed, ontologically prior—in Heidegger's special sense, *a priori*—as the ontological condition of the possibility of specific activities, yet being-in-the-world is just more skilled activity. (106–107)

On Dreyfus's Heideggerian account, then, human intentional comportment is primarily a matter of skillfully acting and responding to particular things in the world around us on the basis of our mastery of the situation within which things are encountered. Background coping (or disclosing) makes possible transparent coping with particular things (or discovering) by letting us focus, so to speak, on what is relevant and appropriate to do in the circumstances. Finally, the background of coping (that is, disclosing + discovering) makes possible particular thematic states, with a determinate content, because only on the basis of this background familiarity with things and a world is it possible to be directed toward things in such a way that our intentional states have a determinate content. Dreyfus's background, in short, "explains" intentional states by explaining what sort of activity is necessary to give those states the particular content that they have.

It is precisely the distinction between "directed coping" and "background coping," Dreyfus claims, which gives Heidegger's account of the background a crucial advantage over Searle's notion of background capacities. But before we can review Dreyfus's argument for this claim, we need to take a look at Searle's account of the background.

II Background Capacities

In its most carefully developed form, Searle's hypothesis of the background is as follows:

All conscious intentionality—all thought, perception, understanding, etc.–determines conditions of satisfaction only relative to a set of capacities that are not and could not be part of that very conscious state. The actual content by itself is insufficient to determine the conditions of satisfaction.[5]

It seems, at first blush, as if Searle offers the same kind of explanation of a background condition for intentional states as Dreyfus —that is, it looks like Searle too wants to know how particular intentional states get their content (in Searle's jargon, how they determine conditions of satisfaction). And Searle often uses Dreyfusian terms in describing the background capacities which determine conditions of satisfaction. Capacities are frequently explained, for instance, as "abilities to engage in certain practices, know how, ways of doing things, etc."[6]

What's more, in arguing for the background, Searle, like Dreyfus, makes reference to the threat of regress which follows from the holism of intentional states, or from positing rules to be applied in grasping intentional states. One reason for believing that there must be a background, Searle argues, is that the content and the conditions of satisfaction of an intentional state can only be articulated by reference to other intentional states. But when we try to specify what is included and excluded in the content as a set of propositions, we find ourselves with an infinite task. Searle illustrates this point nicely by alluding to the difficulties involved in interpreting even the simplest utterance:

I wish to say that there is a *radical* underdetermination of what is said by the literal meaning of the sentence. There is nothing in the literal meaning of the sentence "She gave him her key and he opened the door" to block the interpretation, He opened the door with her key by bashing the door down with the key; the key weighed two hundred pounds and was in the shape of an axe. Or, he swallowed both the door and the key and he inserted the key in the lock by the peristaltic contraction of his gut. . . . [T]he point is that the only thing that blocks those interpretations is not the semantic content but simply the fact that you have a certain sort of knowledge about how the world works, you have a certain set of abilities for coping with the world, and those abilities are not and could not be included as part of the literal meaning of the sentence.[7]

The problem is perfectly generalizable to other intentional states. The point is, if we were to try to specify in terms of other intentional states what exactly is ruled in and ruled out by the content of a given intentional state, we could go on forever listing things. And if we try to understand the application of intentional content to the world as rule governed, we get ourselves into an infinite regress. The background is meant to put an end to the regress and the infinite process of specifying the content of our intentional states. Or rather, it stops the process before it even starts.

It is important to see that the problem does not just arise when we are trying to interpret the meanings or actions of others (although that is perhaps the easiest situation in which to see it). Of course, we do not interpret ourselves in the same way we sometimes interpret others. But still, we need to be able to say how we get directed toward things in the world under a determinate description. One might tell a story which is analogous to the interpretation story—that we have within us rules which determine under what aspects we are directed toward the world around us. But if we go this route, we will need rules to determine the rules, but then rules for the application of those rules, and so on. Once again, we find ourselves forced to posit an infinite set of rules to explain something which we do not perform by following rules—we just do it. Both Dreyfus's Heidegger and Searle put an end to the regress by reference to a nonrepresentational, non-rule-governed background.

As I have already noted, Searle often speaks of the background in terms of practices. For instance, he presents the following argument to show how background practices are necessary in order for our utterances to have meaning:

There are perfectly ordinary sentences of English and other natural languages that are uninterpretable. We understand all the meanings of the words, but we do not understand the sentence. So, for example, if you hear a sentence "Sally cut the mountain," "Bill cut the sun," "Joe cut the lake," or "Sam cut the building," you will be puzzled as to what these sentences could mean. If somebody gave you an order, "Go cut that mountain," you really would not know what to do. It would be easy to invent a Background practice that would fix a literal interpretation of each of these sentences, but without such a practice, we do not know how to apply the literal meaning of the sentence.[8]

In other words, for our intentional states about cutting to have content—to determine conditions of satisfaction—Searle argues, we must have background practices for the relevant kinds of cutting.

It thus seems puzzling, at least from the Dreyfusian perspective, when Searle says that talk about a background of practices and skills is just shorthand for a neurophysiological structure which causes our intentional states. In fact, speaking of nonrepresentational *capacities* is introduced precisely to avoid, so far as possible, an explanation of the background on the level of practices, assumptions, skills, and so forth: "By capacities I mean abilities, dispositions, tendencies, and causal structures generally. It is important to see that when we talk about the Background we are talking about a certain category of neurophysiological causation. Because we do not know how these structures function at a neurophysiological level, we are forced to describe them at a much higher level."[9]

Searle's background of capacities explains intentional states by showing how they can determine conditions of satisfaction without having to work through some sort of computation functioning at the intentional level. To understand language, for instance, we do not need to perform an act of interpretation; we instead have an "immediate, normal, instantaneous understanding of utterances" (at least for languages in which we are fluent).[10] Likewise, intentional action is generally not a matter of applying rules in order to do something, we just do it: "For many institutions, particularly after I have become expert at operating within the institution, I just know what to do. I know what the appropriate behavior is, without reference to the rules."[11] On this point, of course, Searle and Dreyfus are in agreement.

Mark A. Wrathall

But Searle, unlike Dreyfus, wants to use the background to explain no more than this "just doing" intentional acts or "just having" intentional content. To reconstruct Searle's argument somewhat, the threat of regress shows that our intentional states cannot determine conditions of satisfaction by means of some sort of computation or rule-based process. It is thus a logical condition of intentional states that, at least much of the time, they be sufficient to determine intentional content without explicitly appealing to any other intentional states. The background fulfills this logical condition by supplying us with a mechanism which generates intentional states directly. Now practices, activities, skills, as well as lots of facts about the world contribute to the determining of conditions of satisfaction, but only mediately. These things work by causing in us a neurophysiological state, and it is the neurophysiological state against which intentional states determine their conditions of satisfaction:

[W]hat I have been calling the Background is indeed derived from the entire congeries of relations which each biological-social being has to the world around itself. Without my biological constitution, and without the set of social relations in which I am embedded, I could not have the Background that I have. *But all of these relations, biological, social, physical, all this embeddedness, is only relevant to the production of the Background because of the effects that it has on me, specifically the effects that it has on my mind-brain.*[12]

Precisely this is meant when Searle insists that the background must be mental: because the background is the capacity to generate intentional states, even though this capacity is created by our interactions with other people and things in our world, it could be the way it is without that world.

Indeed, from Searle's perspective, the background of practices that Dreyfus appeals to cannot explain our being in an intentional state because the fact that I characteristically do things in such and such a manner—say, my practice of driving on the right-hand side of the road—does not account for my now believing a particular thing—like, "I am driving on the wrong side of the road." I can have all the skills necessary for driving, I can have been taught all the rules of the road, etc., and still, without reference to some causal mechanism to produce in me that belief with its conditions of satisfaction, no reference to practices, skills, and activities will explain my being in that state.

III Dreyfus's Critique of Searle's Background Capacities

We are now in a position to review Dreyfus's critique of Searle's version of the background in order to see how it fares. I should note first that there is, arising from Dreyfus's background of skillful coping practices, one disagreement between Dreyfus and Searle that I intend to leave aside. As we have seen, Dreyfus agrees with Searle that when we are in a "thematic" intentional state—that is, an intentional state with a propositional content and determinate conditions of satisfaction—our being in that state is made possible by background practices. Dreyfus and Searle disagree, however, on the extent to which our ability to act intentionally requires, in every instance, a representational content and determinate conditions of satisfaction.[13] I hope to avoid this controversy in order to focus on Dreyfus's claim that Searle's background is inadequate as a description of the conditions necessary to intentionality.

In particular, I want to explore two specific ways in which, according to Dreyfus, the Dreyfus/Heidegger background is superior to the Searle background in accounting for intentional comportment. Before looking at what I think is the more interesting objection— that Searle's background is unable to account for what Heidegger calls "disclosure"—let me address quickly Dreyfus's claim that Searle is mistaken in arguing that the background is mental. Dreyfus explains:

The basic difference between Heidegger's and Searle's accounts of intentionality is that for Heidegger the relation of mental contents to objects (ontic transcendence) presupposes a mode of being (originary transcendence) that is not a relation at all, whereas Searle takes as basic the relation between mental content and things, holding that, in some sense, even the background, though not a belief system, is still mental. (347, n.8)

Dreyfus does not elaborate on this objection, although one can get a sense for it. If Searle, in saying that the background is mental, meant that it functions in the same way as mental states like beliefs, desires, etc., then it would surely be a mistake. The background is not, even on Searle's own account, the sort of thing which could stand in a representational relationship with the world around us. But, as we have seen, in calling it "mental," Searle does not mean to say that it has the same structure as more familiar mental states; he means that our disposition to be in a particular intentional state is internal to us in the sense of being a neurophysiological feature of us. Searle grants that, as a matter of fact, our background "capacities" rely on habits, practices, skills, and the state of our environing world. But the structure which generates our intentional states is specifiable, on his view, without reference to the habits, practices, skills, and things which make it the structure it is:

> *That* I have a certain set of Intentional states and *that* I have a Background do not logically require that I be in fact in certain relations to the world around me, even though I could not, as a matter of empirical fact, have the Background that I do have without a specific biological history and a specific set of social relations to other people and physical relations to natural objects and artifacts.[14]

In order to argue that the background is not mental in this sense, one would need to show that it cannot be specifiable merely in terms of neurophysiological structures.

Since Dreyfus does not offer such an argument, I will move on to his second objection to Searle's version of the background. According to Dreyfus, Searle lacks a sense for what Heidegger calls "disclosure" or what Dreyfus calls "background coping." As a consequence, Dreyfus claims, Searle's account is unable to do justice to the phenomenology of being in a world:

> In response, then, to Husserl and Searle and their exclusive concern with subject/object intentionality, Heidegger points out that in order to reveal beings by using or contemplating them, we must simultaneously be exercising a general skilled grasp of our circumstances. Even if there were an experience of effort or acting accompanying specific acts of hammering (which Heidegger does not find in his experience) there would seem to be no place for an experience of acting with its conditions of satisfaction accompanying the background orienting, balancing, etc., which, as being-in-the-world, makes using specific things possible. It is hard to make sense of what a Husserlian/Searlean intentionalistic account of being-in-the-world

would be. Searle would seem to have to make the implausible claim that one's being-in-the-world, which is "not conscious and intended" . . . , is still somehow caused and guided by intentions in action. To avoid this claim, Searle thinks of the background not as constant coping, but merely as a capacity. But the notion of a capacity leaves out the activity of disclosing—precisely what leads Heidegger to think of the background as an originary kind of intentionality. (105)

The argument seems to be, then, that a condition of any particular intentional act is an ability to intentionally cope with the world as a whole, and particular sub-worlds within that world. Because for Searle all intentional action is guided by a representational content, and because "background coping"—our "general skilled grasp of our circumstances"—could not possibly have such a representational content, it seems that Searle is unable to account for "background coping."

In contrast, Dreyfus claims, Heidegger does provide an account of background coping, or disclosure which is distinct from any specific intentional activity. In particular, Dreyfus explains, his sense for background coping is what allows Heidegger to account for disclosing in terms of the care structure: "Precisely because the care-structure, which we shall later see is the structure of disclosedness, stays in the background, philosophers like Husserl and Searle overlook it in their account of mental states" (105).

But if it is true that background coping or disclosing is just more coping activity, like our skillful ability to use particular pieces of equipment, it is not clear just what this account adds to Searle's background (other than, perhaps, identifying a new feature of the topography of the background). Here is the problem. On Searle's account, our background capacities cause us to just do what we do when it is appropriate to do it. When we speak, we do not have to take cognizance of the setting in which we are speaking, and make a conscious decision what we should say. We just immediately speak. Likewise, when eating in a restaurant, we cope with the context of a restaurant simply by doing appropriate things with menus, waiters, bills, and our food. It adds nothing to these foreground forms of activity to say there is also a generalized activity directed toward the room as a whole. In short, Searle has available a ready response to

Dreyfus: what more is there to coping with the world, he might ask, than just doing a particular activity which is appropriate given that background? Our ability to "just do it" is precisely what Searle means with his notion of background capacities which, unlike other intentional acts, are not a matter of having representative content. And these background capacities are, as Searle freely admits, nonrepresentational. If that is the case, and Dreyfus cannot give any positive account of what is involved in background coping beyond simply acting, then it is not clear that Heidegger's account of disclosive comportment adds anything at all to Searle's account of background capacities.

I think, however, that Heidegger's account of disclosure *does* add something which cannot be accounted for on Searle's version of background capacities. The problem with Dreyfus's account stems, I believe, from a false step on his part—namely, the claim that disclosure is just more skilled activity. In the section that follows, I hope to demonstrate that this constitutes a misunderstanding of Heidegger's account of disclosure. This in turn will allow me to say what it is that Heidegger contributes to our understanding of the background. I should emphasize the actual areas of disagreement between the interpretation of Heidegger I am offering here and Dreyfus's interpretation are minor. Indeed, I follow Dreyfus's general account of the disclosedness of the world in terms of the care-structure. I agree that this structure is the background on the basis of which we are able to engage with particular things in particular circumstances. Where I disagree is in seeing disclosing as an activity on par with our using particular items of equipment. Although my focus here is not Heidegger exegesis, it is worth pointing out a few features of Heidegger's discussion of disclosure which I take as demonstrating my claim that disclosing is not an activity.

V Heideggerian Disclosure

There are three main considerations which persuade me that Heidegger never intended disclosing to be understood as the activity of coping with general circumstances. First, I find the distinction Dreyfus draws between discovering and disclosing unsupported by Heidegger's actual use of these terms. According to Dreyfus, discovery and disclosure are both kinds of active coping, differentiated only by the fact that disclosing copes with a whole context while discovering copes with a particular thing. But this cannot be the difference because discovery itself is a kind of coping with a whole context. The discoveredness of things, according to Heidegger, consists in their having a place within an equipmental whole: "An entity is discovered when it has been assigned or referred to something, and referred as that entity which it is."[15] The meaning of things is thus a function of the relation the thing has within a whole directed sphere of interrelated things and practices. As a result, while Heidegger does frequently mention the discovery of some specific intraworldly entity, the more fundamental analysis of discovery is concerned with the uncovering of a totality of equipment. Before "any 'individual' item of equipment shows itself," Heidegger writes, "a totality of equipment has already been discovered."[16] This is because, as Heidegger argues, things are constituted by their "involvements" with other things and human practices. If so, it follows that "an involvement is itself discovered only on the basis of the prior discovery of a totality of involvements."[17] It also follows that Dreyfus cannot be right in saying that the differentiating feature of disclosing is coping with a whole context, because such coping is already part of discovery.

The second reason that persuades me that Heidegger does not understand disclosing as an activity of coping is that Heidegger believes we disclose even, or perhaps most authentically, in cases of breakdown—that is, in cases where active coping ceases. For Dreyfus, the paradigmatic case of disclosing is a condition where a whole situation is seamlessly available to us on the basis of our knowing our way around the world. "We are masters of our world," Dreyfus explains, "constantly effortlessly ready to do what is appropriate."[18] But the paradigm case of disclosure for Heidegger is found in moods like anxiety. "Being-anxious discloses," Heidegger tells us, "primordially and directly, the world as world." He explains:

It is not the case, say, that the world first gets thought of by deliberating about it, just by itself, without regard for the entities within-the-world, and that, in the face of this world, anxiety then arises; what is rather the case is that the world as world is disclosed first and foremost by anxiety, as a mode of state-of-mind.[19]

Mark A. Wrathall

As Dreyfus's account of anxiety illustrates beautifully, a defining characteristic of anxiety is that in it we are unable to cope at all. In anxiety, Dreyfus explains, "Instead of Dasein's transparently pressing into the future using some equipment towards some end, absorption simply ceases" (179). The consequence is clear; either Heidegger is not consistent in his use of the notion of disclosing, or disclosure is something other than transparent background coping.

The final reason for rejecting Dreyfus's view of disclosing as a kind of activity or kind of comportment is the simple fact that he never uses the phrases "disclosing comportment" or "activity of disclosing." Instead, disclosing is described in terms of opening and making available, or attuning and disposing. When an active verb is used, it is generally something which suggests a kind of "temporalizing." Of course, explaining what these ideas might mean is the next obvious task.

In what follows, I should note that my analysis in general reconverges with Dreyfus's. On a more charitable reading than I have offered so far, one would note that when Dreyfus says that disclosure is "*the same sort of coping* [as discovery] functioning as the holistic background for all purposive comportment" (106), he cannot mean that we use the world in the same way we employ objects in the world. He cannot mean this, because he knows that the world in Heidegger's sense is not an object we can manipulate or put to use. We thus cannot cope with the world in just the same way that we cope with things in the world, like ballpoint pens and hammers. Instead, when Dreyfus says that background "coping" is "functioning as the holistic background for all purposive comportment," he means simply that insofar as a world is disclosed, we are poised or ready for certain actions, and unready for others. The only reason for making an issue of Dreyfus's gloss of disclosing as an activity is to bring home the point that such an interpretation runs the risk of missing Heidegger's response to Searle's neuronal version of the background. The remaining task is to provide some positive indication of what Heidegger means by disclosing, and how the idea of disclosing brings something to the explanation of the background of intentionality that Searle's description of the background in terms of capacities for generating intentional states lacks.

The first things to remark are the similarities between Searle's and Heidegger's views. Of course when Searle describes the background as a capacity, he does not mean a *mere* capacity, that is, a hypothetical ability to do something. There is a sense in which I have the capacity to speak Latin, but it would take an awful lot of work for me to realize this capacity. As Searle himself explains, he means to identify a certain subclass of capacities which are ready, in the right circumstances, to be activated: "By capacities I mean abilities, dispositions, tendencies."[20] Disclosure for Heidegger is meant to point to the same sort of abilities to activate coping skills—abilities pointed to by explaining our understanding in terms of a "disclosive ability-to-be [seinkönnen]," or noting the way mood "attunes" or "disposes" us toward certain possibilities within the world. For both Heidegger and Searle, then, the background functions as a kind of capacity for certain responses within the world. Activities, even transparent coping activities, are not the most fundamental kind of background to intentional states, but are themselves possible only on the basis of such a background.

The objection Heidegger would make to Searle's background, then, is not that Searle describes the background as a capacity. Instead, the objection is that describing it as a *neuronal* capacity is the wrong level of description for capturing what is uniquely human about intentional states. Intentional states are, Heidegger argues, temporal. It is only against a temporal background that an activity is recognizable as a *human* activity. But the temporal background of intentional states and acts can neither be captured in terms of intentional content, nor can it be accounted for by positing a physical capacity to have an intentional content.

In §68(b) of *Being and Time*, Heidegger takes up the problem of, as the title of §68 puts it, "The Temporality of Disclosedness in General." The purpose of §68, in other words, is to demonstrate how each of the structural moments of the disclosedness of a world—understanding, disposedness [befindlichkeit], and falling, together articulated by discourse[21]—are opened up temporally. If this can be done, Heidegger explains, the result will be to "show that temporality constitutes the disclosedness of the 'there'," for "In the disclosedness of the 'there' the world is disclosed along with it."[22] The strategy Heidegger pursues is to show how, "*except on the basis of temporality*," none of the structural moments of disclosedness is possible.[23]

For instance, Heidegger demonstrates the temporally disclosive nature of mood by reminding us that the world which is disclosed in anxiety is "one in which entities can be freed only in the character of having no involvement."[24] This does not mean for Heidegger, that, in anxiety, the things around us show up as meaningless. As Dreyfus explains, "The world does not cease to be a referential whole. . . . Rather, the world collapses away from the anxious Dasein; it withdraws. No possibilities solicit Dasein" (179). In other words, we no longer find ourselves able to act intentionally, or if we do, it is only with great effort. This, in turn, makes it impossible to live a life, to carry out a meaningful course of activity. As Heidegger notes, the sort of world disclosed by anxiety is one with a uniquely temporal character—namely, it is a world in which it is impossible to "project[] oneself upon a potentiality-for-Being which belongs to existence and which is founded primarily upon one's objects of concern."[25] That is, in anxiety it is impossible to futurally project because anxiety "brings one back to the pure 'that-it-is' of one's ownmost individualized thrownness."[26] The point is that anxiety cannot be fully captured by the intentional content of our beliefs about the things around us—that is in fact unchanged. Nor can it be captured by the fact that we do not happen to be using them. Rather, the disturbing feature of anxiety lies in part in the fact that, when anxious, one is unable to cope with particular things, even though one's background understanding of how to cope with them is unchanged, and the reason one is unable to cope is that one finds oneself in a paralyzing relation to one's habits and practices—as a result of seeing them as radically ungrounded. To make sense of this experience, it will take more than an account of thematic intentional comportment plus the capacity to have intentional content. It will take in addition some explanation of how we are directed temporally, but not quite intentionally (i.e., without a determinate content which determines conditions of satisfaction) within a world.[27]

It is important to note, in the context of this example, that the objection is not that Searle fails to account for the effect of moods on intentional states. Indeed Searle, in language uncannily echoing Heidegger and Dreyfus, accepts that "mood provides the tone or color that characterizes the whole of a conscious state. . . . It seems to me it is characteristic of normal human conscious life that we are always in some mood or other, and that this mood pervades all of our conscious forms of intentionality, even though it is not itself, or need not itself be, intentional."[28] Searle could readily grant that mood sometimes affects the conditions of satisfaction of an intentional state or act (as when one reads a sign to stave off boredom rather than to get directions). Likewise, he could accommodate the effects of mood in terms of his story of background capacities. In the case of Heideggerian anxiety, he might say that mood is manifest as a change in background capacities. A possible explanation of anxiety in terms of intentional contents and modes would be to say, for instance, that whereas before my capacities would have generated in me both the belief that I should answer a ringing phone and the intention to answer a ringing phone, I now have capacities which generate the belief but not the corresponding intention.[29] But without reference to our temporal stand in the world, one misunderstands fundamentally the intentional comportment which results from being enveloped in such a mood. When seized by anxiety, it is not just that I am not disposed to answer the ringing phone, but that I am not disposed to answer the phone *because* my world no longer has a grasp on me. I am no longer able to project forward into possibilities for realizing my identity, nor am I any longer transparently taken up into my normal course of activities. Nor is it right to understand the phenomenon of mood as a subjective coloring or tone added to intentional contents, unless it is recognized how the coloring or tone itself opens up certain possibilities for action and closes off others. But to see this is to see mood itself, and not just its neurophysiological realization, as part of the background which disposes one to some intentional states and undisposes one to others.

The same sort of temporal analysis applies not just to mood, but to the understanding—to our knowing how to do things, knowing what is appropriate, necessary, what makes sense.[30] According to Heidegger, a background temporalizing of the understanding opens up an existential space for particular actions. To put the point somewhat differently, a given intentional action is constituted as what it is not just by the conditions of satisfaction of the action itself (which can be specified independently of the role the action plays in the life of the agent), but also by the way the action refers forward to future possibilities for action. For instance, my drawing a chart on the chalkboard this morning had conditions of satisfaction determined by my intention of, for instance, communicating a point to the people sitting in the room. But the action was not just a communicative action; it was part of my being a teacher, and affected by the students being students. Thus, the action looked beyond the communicative intention toward a "future" realization of an identity which is not itself the object of an intention I hold. As Heidegger would put it, in acting, Dasein always "maintain[s] itself in an existentiell possibility."[31] Every act is marked by the place it holds in the "ability-to-be" which we have projected for ourselves. This temporal dimension of intentional action is, consequently, neither an action itself, nor is it captured by pointing vaguely to some physical capacity to generate intentional states. Instead, it stands as a background orientation to the world—an orientation which does not merely determine the conditions of satisfaction of particular actions, but also is essential to understanding them as the actions that they are.

For Heidegger, then, if one were to say what disclosing consists in, one might say it consists in temporalizing. It is temporalizing which opens up a world. But temporalizing is not an activity like swinging a hammer or writing a letter, nor is it simply a capacity. It is more like a readiness for or disposedness to act in certain kinds of ways. In this way, Heidegger's view is importantly different from Searle's. Within our set of abilities, tendencies, and capacities, there will be some capacities which will be primed or ready according to the temporal structure of the situation. The distinction between a readiness and a capacity is not the same distinction as that between what I earlier called a "mere" capacity and an ability. To see this point, imagine someone fluent in both German and English, but who has never had any exposure to Latin. We might say of this person that she has a (mere) capacity to understand Latin, but is able to understand German and English. In addition, when in the United States, she will ordinarily be ready to hear English, but not German. Indeed, if someone began speaking German to her, it might actually take a moment before she understood what was being said. My claim is, in short, that Heidegger's concept of disclosure is meant to demonstrate how our active response to things and people in the world around us is made possible by a readiness for the things which ordinarily shows up in the world. Searle does not draw a strong distinction between abilities and readiness. But Heidegger believes that if we want to understand what ordinarily generates intentional states, it is the readinesses, not the abilities, which are determinative.

The idea of temporalizing thus highlights the sense in which Searle's notion of the background misses out on the worldliness of the world. In particular, it shows that the idea of a capacity to just have an intentional state cannot do justice to the way in which intentional states are constituted not just by their conditions of satisfaction, but also their place in a temporal existence. This is because it takes more than intentional states—intentional contents with modes, or conditions of satisfaction with directions of fit—to characterize fully the nature of an intentional action. The temporal structures are not themselves thematic intentional states. As a result, it will not explain an action to say that there is a non-intentional capacity which generates intentional states. In addition, one needs to point to the temporally embedded character of human existence—a character which cannot be explained in terms of neurophysiological structures.

Searle, I should note, has already anticipated this objection, and argued that the background generates intentional contents with a "narrative shape," that is to say, it structures "sequences of events" into a coherent narrative. He explains:

I not only perceive things as houses, cars, and people but I also possess certain scenarios of expectation that enable me to cope with the people and objects in my environment; and these include a set of categories for how houses, cars, and people interact, or how things proceed when I walk into a restaurant, or what happens when I shop in a supermarket, for example. More grandly, people have a series of expectations about bigger categories in their life, such as the category of falling in love, or getting married and raising a family, or going to a university and getting a degree.[32]

All that is, of course, right. The problem is seeing how it fits into Searle's framework of neuronal capacities which generate

Mark A. Wrathall

intentional states. Searle agrees that the "scenarios of expectation" cannot be captured as a set of intentional states. But having granted that, he ought also to recognize that it is my background sense of what it is to be a college professor, not the neurophysiological capacity to do the things college professors do, that gives my activities a "narrative structure." Describing the physical realization of the background is, even if scientifically accurate, the wrong level of description for understanding intentional states and acts.[33]

6

What's Wrong with Foundationalism?: Knowledge, Agency, and World

Charles Taylor

I

Antifoundationalism seems the received wisdom of our time. Almost everyone seems to agree that the great enterprise of Descartes, to build up certain knowledge from undeniable building blocks, is misconceived. Everyone from Quine to Heidegger, passing through various post-modernists, seems ready to sign on to this.

And yet this wide agreement hides yawning gaps in outlook. There is in fact more than one antifoundationalist argument; and the different approaches start from quite different basic ideas, and generate very different conclusions, and quite divergent anthropological and political consequences. Moreover, the different ways of conceiving the common antifoundationalist thesis account for most of the other major differences in outlook. Understanding antifoundationalism as they do, these thinkers each look at crucial notions of the others as betraying a grievous lack of understanding of the common antifoundationalist point.

Thus for me, talk of brains in vats smacks of the Cartesian dark ages, and I react to this part of John Searle's position as still insufficiently liberated from what we have both identified as a mistake. I am sure he has equally complimentary things to say about my position.

Rorty and I have an analogous debate going, in which each accuses the other of continued thraldom to Cartesianism.[1]

In this chapter, I want to explore some of the issues at stake in this intra-mural debate of contemporary philosophy, conscious as I am of the immense contribution which Hubert Dreyfus has made in this area. I am thinking especially of his critique of artificial intelligence[2]; and of his commentaries on Heidegger.[3] But I do not want to implicate him directly in the polemics I may engage in in the ensuing discussion.

I will start by reviewing some of the antifoundationalist arguments that seem right to me, and then move from these into some other major issues.

Cartesian-Lockean foundationalism breaks down because the certainty-producing argument would have to proceed from establishing elements (whatever else is true, I am SURE that: red, here, now) to grounding wholes; but you cannot isolate elements in the way you would have to for this to work. In other words, a certain holism gets in the way. But buyer beware! Holisms come in practically as many flavors as Baskin-Robbins ice cream, and this one is NOT the Quine-Davidson holism. That is a holism of verification, first of all; it reflects that propositions or claims cannot be verified singly. It is only derivatively a holism about meaning, insofar as attributions of meaning to terms in the observed agent's speech amount to claims which like most others cannot be verified singly, but only in packages with other claims. In other words, Quinean holism is a thesis which applies even after accepting the classical Cartesian-empiricist doctrine of the atomism of the input, as Quinean talk of "surface irradiations" and "occasion sentences" makes clear. But the holism I am invoking is more radical. It undercuts completely the atomism of the input. First, because the nature of any given element is determined by its "meaning" (Sinn, sens), which can only be defined by placing it in a larger whole. And even worse, because the larger whole is not just an aggregation of such elements.

To make this second point slightly clearer: the "elements" which could figure in a foundationalist reconstruction of knowledge are bits of explicit information (red, here, now; or "there's a rabbit" <"gavagai">). But the whole which allows these to have the sense they have is a "world," a locus of shared understanding organized by social practice. I notice the rabbit, because I pick it out against the stable background of those trees and this open space before them. Without having found my feet in the place, there could be no rabbit-sighting. If the whole stage on which the rabbit darts out were uncertain, say swirling around as it is when I am about to faint, there could be no registering of this explicit bit of information. But my having found my feet in this locus is not a matter of my having extra bits of explicit information—that is, it can never just consist in this, although other bits may be playing a role. It is an exercise of my ability to cope, something I have acquired as this bodily being brought up in this culture.

So "holism" in some form is a generally agreed thesis among antifoundationalists. All the trouble arises when each one of us spells out what seems obviously to follow from this; or makes clearer what seems evidently to be the nature of this holistic background. What seems evident to one seems wildly implausible to others.

My spelling-out involves something like this. Our ability to cope can be seen as incorporating an overall sense of ourselves and our world; which sense includes and is carried by a spectrum of rather different abilities: at one end, beliefs which we hold, which may or may not be "in our minds" at the moment; at the other, abilities to get around and deal intelligently with things. Intellectualism has made us see these as very different sites; but philosophy in our day has shown how closely akin they are, and how interlinked.

Heidegger has taught us to speak of our ability to get around as a kind of "understanding" of our world. And indeed, drawing a sharp line between this implicit grasp on things, and our formulated, explicit understanding is impossible. It is not only that any frontier is porous, that things explicitly formulated and understood can "sink down" into unarticulated know-how, in the way that Hubert and Stuart Dreyfus have shown us with learning[4]; and that our grasp on things can move as well in the other direction, as we articulate what was previously just lived out. It is also that any particular understanding of our situation blends explicit knowledge and unarticulated know-how.

I am informed that a tiger has escaped from the local zoo, and now as I walk through the wood behind my house, the recesses of the forest stand out for me differently, they take on a new valence, my environment now is traversed by new lines of force, in which the vectors of possible attack have an important place. My sense of this environment takes on a new shape, thanks to this new bit of information.

So the whole in which particular things are understood, bits of information taken in, is a sense of my world, carried in a plurality of media: formulated thoughts, things never even raised as a question, but taken as a framework in which the formulated thoughts have the sense they do (e.g., the never questioned overall shape of things, which keeps me from even entertaining such weird conjectures as that the world started five minutes ago, or that it suddenly stops beyond my door), the understanding implicit in various abilities to cope. Like in the multimedia world of our culture, although some parts of our grasp of things clearly fit one medium rather than others (my knowing Weber's theory of capitalism, my being able to ride a bicycle), in fact the boundaries between media are very fuzzy, and many of the most important understandings are multimedia events, as when I stroll through the potentially tiger-infested wood. Moreover, in virtue of the holism which reigns here, every bit of my understanding draws on the whole, and is in this indirect way multimedia.

Maybe I am still saying things with which all antifoundationalists agree. But very soon, I come to further inferences where we part ways. For instance, it seems to me that this picture of the background rules out what one might call a representational or mediational picture of our grasp of the world. There are many different versions, but the central idea in this picture is that all our understanding of the world is ultimately mediated knowledge. That is, it is knowledge which comes through something "inner," within ourselves, or produced by the mind. This means that we can understand our grasp of the world as something which is, in principle, separable from what it is a grasp of.

This separation was obviously central to the original Cartesian thrust which we are all trying to turn back and deconstruct. On one side, there were the bits of putative information in the mind—ideas, impressions, sense-data; on the other, there was the "outside world" on which these claimed to inform us. The dualism can later take other, more sophisticated forms. Representations can be reconceived, no longer as "ideas," but as sentences, in keeping with the linguistic turn, as we see with Quine. Or the dualism itself can be fundamentally reconcentualized, as with Kant. Instead of being defined in terms of original and copy, it is seen on the model of form and content, mould and filling.

In all these forms there is something which can be defined as inner, as our contribution to knowing, and which can be distinguished from what is out there. Hence the continuance of skeptical questions, or their transforms: maybe the world does not really conform to the representation? Or maybe we will come across others whose moulds are irreducibly different from ours, with whom we shall therefore be unable to establish any common standards of truth? This underlies much facile relativism in our day.

But a reflection on our whole multimedia grasp of things ought to put paid to this dualism once and for all. If we stare at the medium of explicit belief, then the separation can seem plausible. My beliefs about the moon can be held, even actualized in my present thinking, even if the moon is not now visible; perhaps even though it does not exist, if it turns out to be a fiction. But the grasp of things involved in my ability to move around and manipulate objects cannot be divided up like that. Because unlike moon-beliefs, this ability cannot be actualized in the absence of the objects it operates on. My ability to throw baseballs cannot be exercised in the absence of baseballs. My ability to get around this city and this house, comes out only in getting around this city and this house.

We might be tempted to say: it does not exist in my mind, like my theoretical beliefs, in my "head," but in the ability to move which I have in my whole body. But that understates the embedding. The locus here is the ability to move-in-this-environment. It exists not just in my body, but in my body-walking-the-streets. Similarly, my ability to be charming or seductive exists not in my body and voice, but in body-voice-in-conversation-with-interlocutor.

A strong temptation to place these abilities just in the body comes from the supposition that a proper neurophysiological account of the capacities can be given which would place them there. But once one really escapes Cartesian dualism, this ceases to be so self-evident.

This ought to ruin altogether the representational construal. Our grasp of things is not something which is in us, over against the world;

it lies in the way we are in contact with the world, in our being-in-the-world (Heidegger), or being-to-the-world (Merleau-Ponty). That is why a global doubt about the existence of things (does the world exist?), which can seem quite sensible on the representational construal, shows itself up as incoherent once you have really taken the antifoundational turn. I can wonder whether some of my ways of dealing with the world distort things for me: my distance perception is skewed, my too great involvement with this issue or group is blinding me to the bigger picture, my obsession with my image is keeping me from seeing what is really important. But all these doubts can only arise against the background of the world as the all-englobing locus of my involvements. I cannot seriously doubt this without dissolving the very definition of my original worry which only made sense against this background.[5]

Here we come to a serious parting of the ways. Some people think that what we are really against is just foundationalism, that is, the attempt to offer a convincing construction of knowledge "from the ground up." They think you can show this to be impossible on Quinean holist grounds, or on grounds closer to older skeptical arguments. But they are willing to leave in place what I am calling representationalism, that is an account of the agent's knowledge which is distinct from the world.

For others (here I include myself), the exciting thing about deconstructing Cartesianism is the relegation of this picture of the "subject." The idea is deeply wrong that you can give a state description of the agent without any reference to his/her world (or a description of the world qua world without saying a lot about the agent).

II

Someone who takes my position stands in what I want to call an unproblematic realism. Our formulations of reality may involve blind spots and distortions. We may, for instance, be badly misrepresenting the life of another people. But these formulations do not exhaust our grip on reality. We are also in contact with our world though being in it, with the other, through being before her, we are active in the first, and have to deal with, or communicate with the second. And so we can be challenged by reality, or by the other; it can dawn on us that something does not fit, that we are not getting something important; and this can be the beginning of a process of revision. In the intercultural case, this can lead to a fusion of horizons—although this sense of challenge can also be blocked by relations of unequal power, as the long, tragic history of colonial empires illustrates.

Unproblematic realism allows that our representations may (but alas, are not forced to) change to accommodate reality, that is, in the direction of truth. On another level, it means that our whole way of life, representations and practices, may change in response to perceived goods, and in this it differs sharply from a widespread contemporary outlook of ethical nonrealism, nourished by a hermeneutic of suspicion, and made fashionable by "postmodernism." I would like now to unpack this issue by examining further what the conception of the agent in the world means for our moral, social, and political lives.

The multimedia nature of our grasp of the world means that we cannot understand the contribution of our practices on their own. Bourdieu's "habitus" sounds like an example of a level of practice which functions on its own, free of more explicit "theoretical" formulations. For instance, we train our youth to stand respectfully before their elders, to bow at appropriate moments, not to raise their voices, to use certain forms of address. In all this, they learn to respect, even revere their parents and elders. Or women are trained always to look at the ground in the company of men, never to look them straight in the face, etc., hence to assume a subordinate position, and not to challenge them.

But learning this kind of habitus is not just a matter of learning certain movements. It is learning certain social meanings through such training. Thus, the kids would not have learned if they did not get the point that certain appropriate feelings and attitudes go along with this demeanor, that certain value judgements are consonant with their way of acting and others not. Thus, if I as a young person am filled with contempt for my elders even as I conform, I recognize right off that this is something I must hide, that I am in fact dissimulating as I bow, that there is some conflict within me as I go on conforming to the norms, that I am an inner rebel.

Another way of seeing this point is that I do not conform just by making movements of a certain neutral description. The movements are meant to embody respect. That is why there are ways of carrying them through in such a perfunctory or even jaunty way, that I am actually being cheeky, and hence violating the norm.

So the habitus here is a medium of access to a social world with its constitutive meanings. And there are other modes of access, including: "theoretical" statements about older people, that they are worthy of respect, and why; including: symbols and recognized symbolic connections, headdresses of elders, rituals they engage in, etc; including stories people tell, legends, cautionary tales, etc. All of these interpenetrate and mutually affect each other. The kind of respect I feel, as a well-brought-up boy, will be deeply colored by that story of an exemplary elder, and the love and admiration his children showed him, which deeply impressed me as a child, by some striking formulations of the idea that men grow wiser, by some saintly figure I met when I was a mere kid.

A deep question arises here, which I raise without being able to resolve. The question arises against the background of another major thesis, which I also present without arguing. This is to the effect that it is language in some suitably broad sense which makes it possible for us to have the human meanings we have—moral, political, aesthetic, religious. But of course, this must take language in a broad enough sense to include those bodily practices which reflect and embody these meanings, such as the bowing of our youth mentioned above. Meaning is embedded in the whole gamut of media, in declarative speech, in story, in symbol, in rules, and in habitus. The question is whether this plurality of media is essential to our having the meanings we do; whether there could just be habituated action without related stories, rules, symbols, philosophies, and theologies. My hunch is that the answer here is no. Habitus requires symbols and formulations in declarative speech.

But whatever is true about the limits of possibility here, it is clear that we in fact live through a wide gamut of media; that the respect for elders we learn in our comportment is also cast in symbol, story, injunction, moral theory.

Now this seems to me to mean something for the way our practices shape our lives, the way they change in history, the way this change, or resistance to change, can figure in our moral and political striving; and what it indicates is at variance with a widely held cluster of theories and discourses about practices, which emanate in large part from the great "post-modern" thinkers, especially Derrida and Foucault.

These two, while very different on all sorts of scores, nevertheless seem to me to come together in this, that they offer us a picture of our practices changing in history—and hence of our lives being reshaped—without reference to the other media. It is as though the practices change on their own, expand, contract, alter, displace themselves, without reference to the human meanings which they encode, and which receive fuller articulation in the symbols, stories, definitions of good, etc. with which they communicate and stand in relations of mutual definition.

Something like this seems to be implied in Derrida's notion of dissemination, where practices undergo change in face of the contingent flow of events. And Foucault's account of the development of the practices of discipline, for instance, in *Surveiller et Punir*, seems to portray them as just growing, without offering any explanation in terms of their meaning.

This is not to say that these writers are blind to the human meanings involved here because they can see how a new set of practices can make new goods hegemonic. Modern disciplines spawned a world in which people admire self-control, long-term instrumental planning, unwavering consistency of character, etc. If these theorists ignored *this* connection, their accounts would lack the relevance and interest that they undoubtedly have for us. But curiously, while they are aware of the *results* in terms of meaning, they seem to want to deny meaning any *causal* role in bringing the fateful changes about. As though the relation of mutual definition were not a two-way street.

Now, of course, there *is* just drift in practices. Anything structured analogously to language, with a *langue* dimension and a *parole* dimension, is subject to undirected change over time; since the langue is only kept alive through repeated acts of parole, and these are open to endless variation. And, of course, there *are* changes in practice unmotivated by the meanings that these practices embody. We know all too well how some practices can be marginalized as an unintended and usually unforseen side effect of other changes. Lots of people valued the local grocery store, where they know you, and you can chat with the owner and keep up on the local news even as you stock up for the weekend; you did not intend to put it out of business, but the supermarket was just so handy and cheap; you could save all that time, and money, and get the whole shopping done in time to get home for your favorite TV show.

But drift and invisible hand change occur in a field in which the direction of events is also motivated massively by the meanings which are important to people, however confused the meaning and ill considered the action. Real historical change is a rich brew in which all these things are going on at the same time, and it is utterly misleading to abstract one dimension, let alone to write large books explaining the crucial transitions to modernity from out of this single dimension.

One can sense here a reaction to an equal and opposite error, one that would see the great fateful changes of modernity, for instance, as all *planned*. One day humans woke up and decided to be free, autonomous, rational, and so they set about remaking themselves. According to the outlook which emerges out of the disciplinary culture, this is a flattering picture; these historical agents, our ancestors, show exactly those traits of self-control, long-range instrumental action, consistency of character that we admire. This is the essence of the Whig account of history; we project back on our great predecessors, of the Renaissance and Reformation, a proto-version of nineteenth-century liberalism. Freedom has been broadening down from precedent to precedent. All the confusion, cross-purposes, disastrous and unforseen consequences, as well as accident, drift, etc., are ironed out.

Drift or "just happened" accounts are the dialectical negations of Whig explanations. The latter see history as totally transparent to meaning, unfolding like a well-executed plan. The former reply by negating intention altogether. They belong together as equal and opposite distortions. And, I believe, they also share some very deep background assumptions; they are equally incapable of envisaging finite meaningful action in history; and this in turn is linked to a totalistic view of autonomy; what might be called the "Fichte disease."

I would like now to try to illustrate these points by looking at an example. Among the practices which were more or less wiped out during the rise of disciplinary modernity were those of Carnival. This seems still alive and well in Rio. But whatever we think of this contemporary form, and other vestigial examples, like Fasching, it is clear that practices of this kind were rife throughout Europe up till the sixteenth century, and then were widely done away with, or withered. Even countries which did not make much of Mardi Gras, like England and northern Europe, had a host of similar festivals, like Lords of Misrule, or Boy Bishops.

An important feature of all these was "the world turned upside down." For a while, there was a ludic interval, in which people played out a condition of reversal of the usual order. Fools and commoners ruled, boys were bishops, licence and disorder, even mock violence, were in, and virtue, sobriety, etc., were mocked.

These festivals are fascinating because their human meaning was at once very powerfully felt in them—people threw themselves into these feasts with gusto—and yet also enigmatic. The enigma is particularly strong for us moderns, in that the festivals were not putting forward an alternative to the established order, in anything like the sense we understand in modern politics, that is, presenting an antithetical order of things which might replace the prevailing dispensation. The mockery was enframed by an understanding that betters, superiors, virtue, ecclesial charisma, etc. ought to rule; the humor was in that sense not ultimately serious.

Natalie Davis had argued for an origin of these feasts of the urban setting in the villages, where there was recognized licence for the class of young unmarried males to indulge in mockery and mayhem, like the charivari. But as she points out, this mockery was exercised very much in support of the ruling moral values.[6]

And yet, for all this acceptance of order, plainly something else showed through the display and the laughter, some deeply felt longings, at variance with this order. What was going on? I do not know, but I will just present a few of the ideas which have been put forward to lay out some alternatives.

Even at the time, the theory was put forward that people needed this as a safety valve. The weight of virtue and good order was so heavy, and so much steam built up under this suppression of instinct, that there had to be periodic blow-outs if the whole system were not to fly apart. Of course, they did not think in terms of steam at the time, but a French cleric expressed the point clearly in the technology of the day.

We do these things in jest and not in earnest, as the ancient custom is, so that once a year the foolishness innate in us can come out and evaporate. Don't wine skins and barrels burst open very often if the air-hole is not opened from time to time? We too are old barrels . . .[7]

Also at the time, and more since, people have related these festivals to the Roman Saturnalia. There seems no good ground to trace a real historical connection, but the supposition that something similar is resurfacing here is perfectly acceptable in principle. The thinking behind this parallel draws on theories about the Saturnalia, and other similar festivals (e.g., the Aztec renewals of the world). The idea is that the intuition underlying these is that order binds a primitive chaos, which is both its enemy but also the source of all energy, including that of order. The binding has to capture that energy, and in the supreme moments of founding it does this. But the years of routine crush this force and drain it; so that order itself can only survive through periodic renewal, in which the forces of chaos are first unleashed anew, and then brought into a new founding of order. Or something like this; it is hard to get it entirely clear.

Then, of course, there is Bakhtin, who brings out the utopian strain in laughter. Laughter as the solvent of all boundaries; the body which connects us to everyone and everything; these are celebrated in Carnival. A kind of carnal Parousia is adumbrated.[8]

Victor Turner proposes another theory. The order we are mocking is important but not ultimate; what is ultimate is the community it serves; and this community is fundamentally egalitarian; it includes everyone. Yet we cannot do away with the order. So we periodically renew it, rededicate it, return it to its original meaning, by suspending it in the name of the community, which is fundamentally, ultimately of equals, and which underlies it.[9]

I have laid all these out because whatever the merits of each one, they point up an important feature of the world in which these festivals occurred. It incorporates some sense of the complementarity, the mutual necessity of opposites, that is, of states which are antithetical, cannot be lived at the same time. Of course, we all live this at some level: we work for x hours, relax for y hours, sleep for z hours. But what is unsettling to the modern mind is that the complementarity behind Carnival exists on the moral or spiritual level. We are not just dealing with a de facto incompatibility, like that of sleeping and watching television at the same time. We are dealing with things which are enjoined and those condemned, with the licit and illicit, order and chaos. All the above accounts have this in common, that they postulate a world, and underlying this perhaps a cosmos, in which order needs chaos, in which we have to give place to contradictory principles.

Time in this world cannot be the "homogeneous, empty time" which Benjamin makes central to modernity. To try to live it this way is to court disaster. Time is kairotic; that is, the time line encounters kairotic knots, moments whose nature and placing calls for reversal, followed by others demanding rededication, and others still which approach Parousia: Shrove Tuesday, Lent, Easter.

The enigma of Carnival thus has a shape, that of this necessary alternation, or of a kairotic time. Thus, while it is true that Carnival as a practice is less multimedia than, say, the Mass, or the Joyeuse Entrée of the King, because while these latter are lavishly theorized in theology and doctrines of kingship, it remains mute on this level; nevertheless we cannot understand it just on the level of practice, as though it related to no explicit articulations at all. On the contrary, it relates very much to the awesome realities of Eucharist and kingship, with all their elaborate and learned explications; it is precisely these among others which it parodies and mocks. For a while, a prescribed period, it decenters these; penetrating the enigma would be to say why.

Now an important consequence of the rise of the disciplinary culture from the sixteenth century on was the suppression of this kind of festival. The élites which took the lead in introducing this new culture, actuated either by Reform, in its Catholic of Protestant variants, or by neo-Stoic ideals, began to find these feasts repugnant. They awakened a profound unease. These élites, which had previously participated along with everybody else, first withdrew, then moved to suppress these practices.

National government, city governments, church authorities, or some combination of them, came down hard on certain elements of popular culture: charivaris, Carnival, feasts of "misrule," dancing in church. What had previously been seen as normal, which everybody had been prepared to participate in, now seemed utterly condemnable, and also, in one sense, profondly disturbing.

Erasmus condemned the Carnival he saw in Siena in 1509 as "unchristian," and that on two grounds: first, it contained "traces of ancient paganism"; and second, "the people over-indulge in licence".[10] The Elizabethan Puritan, Philip Stubbes, attacked "the horrible vice of pestiferous dancing," which led to "filthy groping and unclean handling" and so became "an introduction to whoredom, a preparative to wantonnesse, a provocative of uncleanness, and an introit to all kinds of lewdness."[11]

Now as Burke points out, churchmen had been criticizing these aspects of popular culture for centuries.[12] What is new is (a) that the religious attack is intensified because of the new worries about the place of the sacred; and (b) that the ideal of civility, and its norms of orderliness, polish, and refinement have alienated the leading classes from these practices.

Civility by itself would have led to what Burke calls the "withdrawal of the upper classes" from popular culture.

In 1500 . . . popular culture was everyone's culture; a second culture for the educated, and the only culture for everyone else. By 1800, however, in most parts of Europe, the clergy, the nobility, the merchants, the professional men—and their wives—had abandoned popular culture to the lower classes, from whom they were now separated, as never before, by profound differences in world view.[13]

Civility meant that in the sixteenth century:

The nobles were adopting more "polished" manners, a new and more self-conscious style of behaviour, modelled on the courtesy-book, of which the most famous was Castiglione's *Courtier*. Noblemen were learning to exercise self-control, to behave with a studied nonchalance, to cultivate a sense of style, and to move in a dignified manner as if engaging in a formal dance. Treatises on dancing also multiplied and court dancing diverged from country dancing. Noblemen stopped eating in great dining halls with their retainers and withdrew into separate dining rooms (not to mention "drawing rooms," that is "withdrawing rooms"). They stopped wrestling with their peasants, as they used to do in Lombardy, and they stopped killing bulls in public, as they used to do in Spain. The nobleman learned to speak and write "correctly," according to formal rules, and to avoid technical terms and dialect words used by craftsmen and peasants.[14]

By itself, the ideal of civility would have been sufficient to bring about this withdrawal, which actually came in the eighteenth century to distance itself as well from elements of traditional piety, as too "enthusiatic." But interwoven with religious reform and the neo-Stoic vision, it went beyond withdrawal into attempts to suppress and remake the culture of the people; attempts like that of Maximilian of Bavaria, whose program of reform in the early seventeenth century forbade, inter alia: magic, masquerades, short dresses, mixed bathing, fortune-telling, excessive eating and drinking, and "shameful" language at weddings.[15]

How are we to understand this often forcible remaking? On one level, to be sure, some practices displaced others; those of discipline did away with these forms of "licence." But this move was powerfully motivated by new visions of goodness and order, however confused, and in some respects contradictory they might have been. We cannot cut things into neat periods; this alternative vision had been building up during the later Middle Ages. In some ways, its seeds are even to be found in Charlemagne; and certainly one of its points of departure is the Hildebrandine reform of the eleventh century.

The original idea is what Arquillière calls "political Augustinianism." This is slightly unfair to Augustine, as Arquillière admits.[16] But the basic terms were drawn from him, so we will let him take the rap for the sake of simplicity. The fullness of justice, which for Augustine must include giving to God his due, cannot be expected in this world. Sinners will abound until the end. But a regime can be envisaged in which people are subordinated to rule which models itself on full justice. If kingly power really follows the injunctions of those speaking with the authority of God's will (the hierarchy of the Church), then an order can be established in which those truly good will rule, and the bad will be forced to conform.[17]

The idea begins to arise of a world here and now in which no compromises need to be made with any alternative principle. The promise of the Parousia, that God will be all in all, can be realized here, albeit in the reduced form which requires constraint. The drive of Christian reform from this point onward tends to take this direction: the mass of the faithful must be made over to come as close as possible to the minority of dedicated Christians. Foucault was right, that the decision of the Fourth Lateran Council in 1215, prescribing one-on-one confession for the entire laity, was part of this project of making over.

Gradually, a new understanding of the world and time begins to gain ground, according to which the complementarity of order and chaos is no longer necessary. Conceding a place to this chaos is no longer a necessary alternation, going with the kairotic shape of time, but an unnecessary concession to that which we are trying to extirpate, a compromise with evil. And so the voices critical of these elements of popular culture become more and more frequent, and reach a deafening chorus among élites in the sixteenth and seventeenth centuries.

There is a long story here; but very shortly put, we can see that this new understanding of world and time, orginally arising within a Christian outlook, is taken over by secular variants; we might better say, gradually slips over more and more in a secular direction, starting perhaps with the neo-Stoicism of Justus Lipsius. Indeed, we might say that it helps to constitute the modern secular outlook, of which "homogeneous, empty time" is a crucial constituent. And along with this come new uncompromising conceptions of order: order in our lives; and social order.

Among other things, modern versions of this latter are much less tolerant of violence and social disorder than earlier variants. The sixteenth century sees the taming of the unruly military aristocracy, and its domestication in court service, court attendance, or estate management. The eighteenth century begins to see the taming of the general population. Riots, peasant rebellions, social disorders begin to become rarer in northwest Europe. Until we reach the rather high standards of nonviolence which most Atlantic societies expect in their domestic life. (In this, as in other respects, the United States is a curious throwback to an earlier epoch.)

And growing through all this development, partly driving it, partly strengthened by it, is a growing sense of our *ability* to put this kind of order in our lives. This confidence is at the heart of the various programs of discipline, both individual and social, religious, economic and political, which begin to make us over from the sixteenth to the seventeenth centuries. This confidence is consubstantial with the belief that we do not have to compromise, that we do not need complementarity, that the erecting of order does not need to acknowledge limits in any opposing principle of chaos. And because of this, this drive to order is both offended and rendered insecure by the traditional festivals of reversal. It cannot stomach the "world turned upside down."

IV

This is very much our story; I mean that of us moderns. I hope it is clear how caricatural it would be to understand it just as a drift of practices; or as consisting in the unexplained fact that certain practices just came to dominate. There are reasons, and they have been partly articulated.

And yet it is far from being a Whig story as well. It is full of its own enigmas (what really draws people in this model of root and branch reform?), confusions, its surprises, and unwilled consequences (after all, what started out as a great enterprise in Christian perfection helped to create the culture of secularism and unbelief), its combination with other contingent circumstances to produce the unprecedented (e.g., capitalism); and one could go on.

All this says something complex about the place and importance of articulation. On one side, we can see reason to believe that it can be destructive. For instance, the particular way in which Carnival opened a space of complementarity with the established order depended very much on the non-said; or if you like on an ambiguous, even enigmatic language of humor, parody, mockery, where a complex message was played out rather than declaratively formulated. And perhaps this balance of celebrating the alternative while ultimately endorsing the existing could never be properly formulated in declarative prose. So the people who were declaratively articulate about it back then were either its enemies (the whole damn thing is pagan), or its ambiguous friends (like the French cleric with his "air-hole" explanation, which really hides away the deeper reasons for complementarity).

But once we have embarked on this destructive articulation, once we are engaged in a hermeneutic of discredit, like Erasmus and Stubbes and others, if you feel (as I do) that something terribly important was lost in this suppression, you have no recourse but to engage in a counter-hermeneutic. You have to try to reinterpet this whole passage of our history, in order to begin to discern what possibilities it leaves for us.

In other words, articulation may not only serve greater refinement, and the drawing of more subtle distinctions. That may be a good in some cases, but it may also be useless, or even corrosive, as I would argue it would have been for Carnival in its heyday. But articulation may also serve another purpose, not where we want to unpack what is involved in a practice about which we feel unproblematically positive, but rather where we experience a profound conflict about our practices, or else they conflict with each other. Here what we are looking for is not refinement of our existing way of being, but a way out of the impasse in which we find ourselves. We articulate in order to become clearer about our options, to see what recourse is open to us.

At this very general level, where we speak of defining options, the work of Foucault is a clear and impressive example of this kind of thinking. He was making a "history of the present" just in this sense, that his reading of the rise of modernity was meant to open possibilities for us which would have remained invisible without it. My complaint is not with this general goal, but with the idea that a path-opening reading can be other than a hermeneutic here; that it can be helpful to read the rise of modern disciplinary society without any reference to its motivation in visions of the good or the just or the holy, and hence without reference to the articulations of these with which its path is strewn. Not that these may not be confused, and often self-deluded. On the contrary, our task is undoubtedly to correct them. But we have to start by identifying them if we are to do this.

What did Foucault think he was doing, giving a history of the present which forewent any reading of the meaning of the past? Because he did not just do this in a fit of absence of mind. There is an implicit anthropology, a sense of the human predicament here. Visions of the good, or the just, or the holy, will seem to you ultimately irrelevant, if you see the good of human life as not situated in any of these. Now in a way we could say that this is incoherent, because any view of the human good is a view of the good. But if we do not quibble about words, we can see a point here.

If you see the good of human life purely in some version of radical autonomy or freedom, then any vision of the trans-human good, be it organic, cosmic, social, or religious, will seem, at best, irrelevant, and probably also threatening. Foucault operated on one such version, the goal of self-making, which rather late on he situated in an aesthetic register, the self as a work of art.[18]

Because of this, Foucault was profoundly uninterested in any conception of good order. There is none such. There is, in particular, no solution to the social problem of a good order. The good is all in the register of individual autonomy; and while some structures will plainly be more oppressive and destructive than others, all must be regarded with suspicion and met with resistance.[19]

In this regard, Foucault, for all his great originality, was representative of a widespread modern phenomenon: the tremendous power of theories of radical freedom on one hand, and their affinity for formal, or content-free thinking on the other. This is especially evident in the ethical field. Formal theories of ethics, which derive the right from some procedure, by this very act detach it from any substantive notion of the good. Kant's is the most famous theory of this form, but he is in his own way repeating a very general structure; this we can see also in, say, Rousseau's theory of the general will; or in earlier contract theory, where what matters for legitimacy is not the good society substantively defined, but rather meeting the procedural requirements of consent.

Charles Taylor

The appeal of this move into the formal register is evident. Among other things, by unhooking the right from any substantive good, it allows us to affirm that the central ethical issue is autonomy itself. Not what you will, but how you will is what matters; and the how is defined to secure autonomy (so that you obey only yourself—Rousseau; or the self-given law—Kant).

Foucault, however distant from Kant, reedits something like this structure in a post-Nietzschean register. Autonomy now commands not formal thinking, in the sense of some rigorous procedure. But it does command prescinding from the content, from the passionately felt meanings which help drive historical change. Practices come and go, expand and contract, in a self-contained universe, shorn of their hermeneutic horizon; their only relevance being the way they refract power, that is, how they either frustrate or abet self-making.

Needless to say, the affinities of Derridean thought with its own kind of formalism, the content-free generation of change, is evident enough in such key terms as "différance" and "dissemination."

But if this is what underlies the difference in Foucault's reading of history from the one I propose here, if it comes down to the affinity for radical freedom and formal thinking, then we are once more back in the neighborhood of modern epistemology. For both representationalism and radical freedom involve drawing a sharp line between self and world; which is why so many of the major thinkers in each of these traditions are the same: Descartes, Locke, Kant. It is the conception of agency as in the world which has tried to restore a sense of our embedding in body, world, and society. It once again appears that how you refute foundationalism makes a fateful difference to how you think on a crucial range of contemporary philosophical questions.

II

Computers and Cognitive Science

7

Context and Background: Dreyfus and Cognitive Science

Daniel Andler

In Hubert Dreyfus's critique of artificial intelligence,[1] considerable importance is given to the matter of context—used here as a blanket term covering an immense and possibly heterogeneous phenomenon, which includes situation, background, circumstances, occasion, and possibly more. Perhaps the best way to point to context in this most general sense is to proceed dialectically, and take as a first approximation context to be whatever is revealed as an obstacle whenever one attempts to account for mental dynamics on the formal model of a combinatorial game over families of interchangeable, fixed, self-standing—context-free as it were—elements. Dreyfus has argued persuasively that the human mind always "operates," if that is the right word, within a setting which permeates whatever it is it operates on.

Dreyfus's thought on these matters was shaped during the years when artificial intelligence (AI) was at the height of early hopes and initial successes. This was also a period during which what was to become known as "cognitive science" was little more than a ray of light falling on psychology and linguistics from the rising sun of AI.[2] Neuroscience was scarcely visible. Philosophy of mind as we know it today was confined to a small, exclusively philosophical circle, and philosophy of language was only beginning to enter the "cognitive turn." The whole field has by now undergone a sweeping reconfiguration, as well as an enormous development. On one hand, AI is no longer a central subdiscipline in cognitive science, and it has been

Daniel Andler

thoroughly transformed by the advances of neurocomputing; it is now "good old-fashioned artificial intelligence" (GOFAI[3]) which has become scarcely visible from the standpoint of mainstream cognitive science. On the other hand, philosophy of mind and philosophy of language have all but fused into one single branch of philosophy of which a major trend has become a partner in the cognitive enterprise.

Despite the changes, Dreyfus's analysis of AI not only continues to be relevant as a critical tool for evaluating the field of AI as it has evolved—as he himself has shown in the third edition of *What Computers Can't Do*, in the book with his brother Stuart Dreyfus[4] and in various papers, and as the present volume proves—but it also raises crucial issues for cognitive science today. However, on this second front the situation is far less clear, and the present essay aims at showing, on a modest scale, what sort of clarification is required. The reasons this is not an entirely straightforward matter are twofold.

There is, first, the general question of the relation between Dreyfus's work and cognitive science. Less attention than what might have been expected has been paid by either side to the other. This could be the effect of one of two opposite causes.

On Dreyfus's part, it could be seen as the consequence of his belief that his main arguments apply, *mutatis mutandis*, to most of cognitive science, and therefore need not be spelled out at length, at least not by him. That belief in turn could be supported by either one of two arguments. On the side of the analysis, Dreyfus could claim that his diagnosis of AI is but the outcome of a much more general assessment of the whole Western philosophical tradition, and that cognitive science, for the most part, to the extent where it resists straightforward reduction to, or absorption by, neuroscience, is directly inspired by that tradition and therefore falls under the same critique. On the side of the object of the analysis, Dreyfus could be tempted to say that cognitive science is really, as Collins saw it in the early days, just AI pursued by more diverse means.[5] It would not even be necessary, then, to take the long route through the philosophical tradition.

Alternatively, Dreyfus could decline the responsibility of assessing cognitive science as a whole, and insist on being read as aiming solely at a certain paradigm,[6] of which AI is an immediate, literal application, and which could, and probably has, informed parts of cognitive science, without taking a stand on the extent to which the actual commitments of today's cognitive science relate to that paradigm.

Symmetrically, cognitive science may regard the Dreyfusian critique of AI as either too sweeping, and thus overshooting the mark, or too restricted to be of concern. If Dreyfus—so might cognitive scientists reason—thinks of his arguments as militating against the very idea of cognitive science,[7] he must be wrong; if on the other hand he takes them to apply only to AI, why should we feel concerned?

The second reason why it is no easy matter to assess the mutual relevance of the Dreyfusian analysis of context to cognitive science and vice versa is that there has been a considerable evolution in the way philosophers of language and of mind have been thinking of content and context. In the last fifteen years or so, several important research programs have been launched which are all predicated on one or another form of contextualist assumption—the assumption, or perhaps the observation, that context is a crucial and ineliminable aspect of intentionality. These programs have reached a degree of sophistication and depth which makes proposals offered in the GOFAI framework look simplistic or obsolete. It would thus be reasonable to expect the contributors to this recent current of thought, on one hand, and Dreyfus and his followers, on the other, to acknowledge one another's work: one camp would be praised as pioneers, the other would welcome the fulfillment of its predictions. But in fact there is—as far as I know—no sign of any awareness of the other group's existence. Why is that? Perhaps there is, appearances notwithstanding, little in common between the two—the issues may be distinct, and/or the inspirations which guide the analyses orthogonal. Perhaps philosophical styles and traditions make mutual understanding impossible. However it be, the question deserves to be asked.

The chapter has two aims. One is simply to lay out in the open what I take to be, in rough outline, on one hand Dreyfus's contribution to the general issue of context, and on the other what the new contextualism is about; space limitations prevent all historical and textual detail, but enough is provided I think to show, first that

Daniel Andler

Dreyfus has directly exerted some, insufficiently acknowledged, influence, but that common sources also have their share in whatever convergence there is, and second that there is a lot of divergence as well between the two enterprises. The other aim is to sketch some ways of reducing the gap, thus outlining the relevance of Dreyfus's work to some central issues in cognitive science, and conversely the possibility of bringing recent developments of cognitive science and philosophy of mind to bear on his theses.

I Dreyfus's Analysis of Context, Situation, and Background: A Bird's-Eye View

At first glance, context, background, situation, circumstances, and environment are so closely related and at once so loosely defined that one may wonder whether, appearances notwithstanding, they do not refer to one and the same phenomenon. On the other hand, it would certainly be wrong to defer to common, or philosophical, usage to distribute different contents to these notions as if there were a consensus on how to do it. The fact is that, as far as the terms go, common parlance is hopelessly fickle, while theorists in philosophy of language, philosophy of mind, artificial intelligence, and cognitive science have by no means agreed on a distribution of technical uses.

The three basic terms, in Dreyfus's vocabulary, are "context," "situation," and "background." Dreyfus employs "context" and "situation" as nouns standing by themselves, and they are entries—rich ones—in the index of *What Computers Can't Do*; while "background" does not usually stand alone, being often a constituent of the phrase "against the background of [e.g. practices]," or appearing in expressions such as "[contextual regularity is] the background of problem solving, language use, and other intelligent behavior" (271), and does not appear in the index of the book. Only when discussing, many years later, Searle's notion of Background (capital B) does Dreyfus treat "the background" as a noun phrase in subject position, and background as some sort of entity. However, the basic idea of the background, as it has come to be known following Searle's 1983 *Intentionality*, is fully present in Dreyfus's 1972 *What Computers Can't*

Do, and the grammatical difference reflects his well-developed view on the background phenomenon and what distinguishes it from the context and situation phenomena.

Context, for Dreyfus, is at root the setting (to use the vaguest possible word) in which humans encounter facts, utterances, problems, etc.; the essential feature of context is that it is not definable by rules nor readily representable in any way (in particular, it does not consist, on any given occasion, of a finite set of features, let alone pieces of information). The context phenomenon is a basic character of our cognitive or mental lives which consists in the fact that we are never (at least in natural circumstances) confronted with any task at all outside a context: there is no such thing as understanding a word, translating a sentence, solving a problem (however simple), deciding on the appropriate response to a demand, independently of some context in which the word, sentence, etc. has in fact appeared: for human beings, signs, demands, tasks *never* show up in isolation. Therefore whatever fixed meaning, rule, knowledge, representation, or information may be thought to be attached to a given sign, demand, task etc. in a proprietary way (as on the traditional view, the word "dog" is endowed with a fixed meaning consisting, for example, in a rule for determining the correct application of the word) has to be "mixed" in one way or another with "ingredients" coming from the context.

This view is conceptually[8] compatible with a position which Dreyfus actually rejects: AI of the traditional sort (GOFAI), as well as various schools in semantics and pragmatics, agree that "meaningful stimuli" or representations seldom come in isolation. The process of understanding or "processing" such stimuli, they believe, consists in determining the contribution of context, and this they conceive of as discovering the set of relevant aspects of the context, finding the appropriate representations of those aspects, and running a kind of inference on the set of premises consisting of the content or information attached to the meaningful stimulus by itself, together with the representations of the relevant features of the context.[9] Everyone agrees that this is a very difficult task, but the view is that it is actually performed by the human mind; therefore, the *context problem*, which I take to be the scientific problem of describing this process,[10] be it step by step in restricted families of cases, is a meaningful problem.

Let us call this view *moderate contextualism*. Moderate contextualism stands in contrast with a position which is even further away from Dreyfus's view, and which may be called *context eliminativism*. Contextual dependence, according to this other view, is a mere appearance, which a proper reanalysis of the task under consideration will simply eliminate: context-dependent processing, or processing of context-dependent items, are really nothing but "wild" varieties of context-free processing of context-free elements: it is all a matter of discovering the right elementary procedures and elements, which is naturally harder than in the case of laboratory-grown varieties (also known as toy problems).

As is well-known, Dreyfus attacked eliminativism in his 1972 book with such effectiveness that when, in the mid-eighties, the connectionists reappeared on the scene with the PDP paradigm,[11] one of their main arguments, on the performance end, was that connectionist nets were not only context-sensitive (which at least by that time all self-respecting GOFAI programs equally claimed to be), but that they were *naturally* so, which meant that they could deal with context without, in effect, eliminating it, in contrast, said the connectionists, with GOFAI programs.

PDP connectionists were in fact moderate contextualists, if not in theory, at least in practice, insofar as the context problem, which their models could conceivably solve, was the problem which moderate contextualism construes as the context problem. Because Dreyfus had not considered the possibility of moderate contextualism at first, probably due to the fact that the position he wanted to discredit was GOFAI's eliminativism, he welcomed PDP as a step in the right direction. However, he had already provided, in the 1972 book, arguments equally effective (or ineffective) against moderate contextualism as against eliminativism.

These arguments are those which appeal to the situation and to the background. Dreyfus does not in fact make a clear terminological distinction in the book, and it is only my decision as a commentator to use the label "situation" for one set of considerations, and the label "background" for another. In Dreyfus's mind, they go hand in hand, and I do not know how helpful he would regard my analytic attempt at peeling them apart.

Situation, as I propose to use the term, is *based* on objective features of the environment. However, as Dreyfus sees it, not only is it not represented, but that it is such that it cannot, in principle, be turned by a cognitive system (man, animal, or machine) into a bunch of representations with the help of which the system then determines the proper course of action. Now why is such a move impossible? Dreyfus advances two reasons. On one hand, a situation is *holistic*. Its (brute) elements do not exist independently of the context as a whole, or at least they do not carry an intrinsic significance: only the situation endows them with meaning and relevance. Therefore, it is not open to the system to evaluate the situation *on the basis of* its elements. On the other hand, the situation already includes the system's expectations and goals, so there is not even the possibility of first assessing, in whatever way, the (holistic) contribution of the environment, independently of the system's state, in order to determine the course of action as a function of environmental constraints and internal dispositions. What the environment contributes is, so to speak, laden with the system's views, somewhat in the way in which philosophers of science have come to recognize that observations are theory-laden, and even, since Kuhn, that the very meaning of observational terms depends on the theory within which they are deployed.

The phenomenon of situation per se does not actually spell the inevitable doom of moderate contextualism, although it remains to be shown exactly how situations would be handled in that framework. But context also carries or constitutes a background; and there perhaps lies a reason why context must evade any form of moderate contextualism, however sophisticated.

Let us consider again, in as simple a form as possible, the question which is being raised. A human being—or, more generally, a cognitive system—is, again and again, confronted with the problem of what to do next. Although the person or system may not think of its predicament as a problem, let us accept this description and construe it sufficiently broadly as to include, for example, the "problem" for Mary of how to give meaning, here and now, to an acoustic stream such as "Could you pass the salt?" The question being raised, again, is whether there exists a general method which Mary, or any creature or system, can apply to the "terms" of the problem in order to discover its "solution," a method which moreover could in principle be made fully explicit and be shown to consist of a sequence of simple, unproblematic, steps.

Context-eliminativism consists in postulating a positive answer. But as we have seen, arguments provided by moderate contextualists as well as Dreyfus have conclusively shown that there is no way the theorist can reparametrize the "phase space"[12] so that contextual clues disappear altogether. Further, as we have just seen, contrary to the hopes of the moderate contextualists, there is no way one can systematically infer the correct answer as a function of the occasion regarded as constituted by a *given* collection of *objective* features of the state of affairs obtaining at the time and location under consideration, features defined independently of the occasion (holism) and of the expectations of the creature (subjectivism). Still, why couldn't there be a mechanism which, given the expectations of the creature, and the objective totality of features of the physical setup on the occasion under consideration, would produce, for example, as a fixed point in the sense of (mathematical) functional analysis, a global solution made up of (interrelated) features of the physical setup, of the relevant aspects of the subjective take on the situation by the creature, and of the algorithm leading to the desired next step? Such would be the fond hope of a sophisticated moderate contextualist.

That hope is futile, according to Dreyfus, because context, on a given occasion, not only defines a situation, but also constitutes a background. The postulated mechanism would in effect treat the occasion as a type, and in order to subsume it under that type would tear it away from its singular spatiotemporal location. But why should we believe that such an extraction might be possible? This would require an absolute standpoint from which to conduct the operation. In turn, this absolute standpoint could be obtained only by emptying the occasion under consideration of *all* of its features. Indeed, the moderate contextualist's sophisticated strategy consists in distinguishing between the "ordinary" context, made up of local and localizable features of the occasion, what may be called the "proximal context" on one hand, and on the other, the "distal context" which includes all the rest.[13]

Dreyfus's immediate objection is that this is more than can fit in any *manageable* notion of context: it is too much to detach. The background which is present on any given concrete occasion is, in his words, "something like an ultimate context [. . .] the even broader situation—call it the human life-world."[14] What we have here is something like a logical argument, akin to the fact that the collection of all sets is too "large" to itself be a set. On that reading of the notion, there is *nothing* such as the background, rather the background is the *medium*, the Husserlian "outer horizon" or even perhaps the Jaspersian *Umgreifenden* ("the encompassing").

But Dreyfus has a second problem in mind, which he regards as even more serious. For him, background operates as an existential, rather than purely logical, precondition. In Wittgensteinian language, it is a (or *the*) human form of life: "The human world . . . is prestructured in terms of human purposes and concerns in such a way that what counts as an object or is significant about an object already is a function of, or embodies, that concern."[15] A biological counterpart might be von Uexküll's *Umwelt*. But Dreyfus's major references are Heidegger and Merleau-Ponty. The background, in the Heideggerian framework, is provided by a particular state, mode of being in which an involved human being (no mere creature) copes with a situation already fully endowed with meaning, and bearing within itself, so to speak, the entire equipment necessary for coping. On this reading then, the background is the condition of possibility for there to be anything at all of any significance to a being.

A rather different way of construing the background makes it a causal factor in the production of representations. Two options are available here. One is mentalistic, and is defended by John Searle in his book *Intentionality:* "The Background is a set of nonrepresentational mental capacities that enable all representing to take place."[16] In later works, however, he seems to generalize his notion of the Background, as witnessed by the following characterization: "Intentional phenomena . . . only function within a set of Background capacities which are not themselves intentional."[17] Among those

Daniel Andler

capacities are manners of doing, know-how, ways of comporting oneself in the human, in particular social, arena. But Background is no longer in Searle's revised picture, mentalistic in a literal sense: "[W]hen we talk about the Background we are talking about a certain category of neurophysiological causation."[18] The "capacities" (by which he means "abilities, dispositions, tendencies, and *causal structures generally*"[19]) involved need not have an exact description in the vocabulary of psychology; indeed, one should expect them usually *not* to have such a description, given that psychology as currently understood is intentionalistic, while Background is *defined* by Searle as composed of "nonintentional or preintentional capacities."[20]

Dreyfus, however, criticizes Searle for falling into the same trap as Husserl: they are both wrong to assume, he writes, "that . . . meaning must be brought into a meaningless universe, from outside as it were, by *meaning-giving minds*."[21] He charges both Husserl and Searle with holding on to the notion of a something in the head, a noema or a neurophysiological process, in which the essence of intentionality would lie.[22] Seen in this light, background only informs this process, shapes it to give it its specific content. Dreyfus rejects this view and wants to steer clear of both a logical and a psychologistic construal of the background.

For this he relies in part on Merleau-Ponty's idea of a bodily origin of meaning; on the view he defends, and which is becoming increasingly popular in cognitive science, action comes before reflection, and body before mind: "He [Merleau-Ponty] argues that it is the body which confers the meaning," writes Dreyfus.[23] The body is the seat of a learning process in virtue of which, according to the Dreyfus and Dreyfus model,[24] the logical world of context-free rules, which in many cases at least guide the beginner, is transformed into a set of generalized bodily habits or skills. This makes the background sound much more concrete and much less transcendental.

But Dreyfus emphatically does not want to reduce it to the neuroscientific description of the underpinning of a *psychological process*. Following Heidegger, Dreyfus denies the possibility of an intentional content disconnected from involved coping; at least, of *primary* intentional content; what does exist is derivative intentional content which is ontologically, and presumably ontogenetically, dependent on pretheoretic understanding; and which (I assume) would not conceivably arise in the absence of that very special social skill called language.

That this would be hard to accept should not surprise us, according to Dreyfus: the whole philosophical tradition has hidden it from our view. Producing a transparent account of background is surely beyond the purview of this chapter. For our purpose here, it may perhaps suffice to summarize the discussion thus: the background is no thing, not even a set of objective practices, corporal dispositions, acquired skills, or whatever; rather, it is what practices, corporal dispositions, acquired skills etc., jointly secrete in historical time and which makes significance possible (not logically, not in every possible world: in our human world).

II The New Contextualism

At a distance, it is fairly easy to discern a cluster of ideas which notwithstanding differences in disciplinary origin, motivation, content, fineness of grain, share an interest in contextual phenomena and a conviction that, very roughly, standard formalist approaches are unable to account for them. An additional trait which they share is contrastive: they all *look* very different from Dreyfus's ideas—which is one reason[25] why it is so tempting to think they deal with completely disjoint topics. The challenge is to bring to light the connections between what Dreyfus on one hand, and the new contextualists on the other, have in mind, without simply lumping them together under the common banner "We Take Context Seriously!"

The new contextualism forms a large domain straddling mostly the semantics/pragmatics province of linguistics—including computational models—philosophy of language, and, increasingly, philosophy of mind. Some new contextualists remain formalists, convinced however, precisely by the unsolvability of the context problem(s) in the classical framework, that new formalisms must be invented, or that formalism itself must undergo reform. At the other extreme, some draw their inspiration from Wittgenstein and have no interest in exploring any kind of formalistic or naturalistic research program. In between are those who are antiformalists but seek a reformed, nonfunctionalist, naturalism. What keeps the conversation going between them, despite their differences, is a shared Fregean culture, and a common starting point: the matter of meaning, and more specifically the coherence or applicability of the notion of literal meaning. While what gets in the way of a conversation between them and Dreyfus is the latter's starting point—the matter of intelligence and more specifically the coherence or applicability of the notion of mechanical intelligence—and on the cultural side the existential phenomenology from which he draws his deepest inspiration.

The idea that words have fixed, intrinsic, literal meanings is one of the most entrenched in philosophy, as well as common sense, and it retains its appeal even in the present context-aware atmosphere. One important dimension along which the new contextualists can be ordered is the degree to which they attempt to distance themselves from the thesis that *something like* literal meaning plays a role in the intentionality of words and of acts of linguistic communication. The leading figure in the moderate camp is David Kaplan. Kaplan's idea[26] is that what is intrinsically attached to a word is not a meaning in one or another traditional construal (intensional or extensional), but rather what he calls *character*, which is a function from contexts to contents. In other words, a word standing by itself does not in general directly point to anything at all, whether material or Platonic; instead, it requires a context of occurrence to do so. Kaplan's goal is to show that the word provides, or is constituted by, a set of rules which automatically take the occurrent context as input and outputs the content. Some words, according to Kaplan—he calls them pure indexicals—fit this scheme perfectly: there is a rule which, given an occurrence of the sentence "I am thirsty," provides the word "I" with its referent, *viz.* the speaker (in the simple case where the sentence has been uttered). Similar rules work for "here," "now," "today," and so forth. He contrasts these words with what he calls "demonstratives," whose content depends on both a (static, occurrent) context and on a *demonstration*, a particular event which accompanies the occurrence of the word: typically, "this" is accompanied by a pointing event.

This bare beginning of a sketch of Kaplan's line of thought will do for present purposes. The following questions can already be intelligibly raised: (1) Does Kaplan's scheme work in the most favorable case, that is, for pure indexicals? (2) What exactly is a demonstration? (3) Isn't there something to say about what a context is, and isn't it reasonable to ask, in view of Kaplan's goal to provide self-standing semantic rules? (4) Are all contextual effects, beyond indexicality and "demonstrativity," likely to yield to the same sort of treatment? In particular (5) To what extent is the semantic (properly linguistic) level sealed off from the pragmatic (*general* cognitive) level? If the latter somehow leaks into the former, how are we going to protect the objective context from the boundless influence of subjectivity? Or, in other words, what is going to protect us from the possibility that any given sentence can get to mean anything at all according to the participants' states of mind, even when linguistic conventions remain fixed? And thus finally (6) What if context comes first, in such a way that there can be no context-independent rule attached to words and strings of words which dictates what parameters need to be assigned values, and what aspects of contexts are to determine these values?

This chapter's aim is not to provide encyclopedic, let alone original, answers to these complex, interrelated questions: they motivate an extensive literature to which the reader is referred. Here they can help us set up a few landmarks on the territory.

A preliminary observation concerns the relevance of the problems raised by context for *linguistic* phenomena to the problems concerning *cognitive* phenomena. In interrogative form, what does Kaplan's line, for example, which is obviously part of the philosophy of *language*, have to do with the philosophy of *mind*? Well, the passage from language to thought is provided by the idea that the meaning of a declarative sentence is a proposition, and that propositions are the sort of entity which many of our mental states are relations to (attitudes toward); conversely, it seems natural to individuate many of our mental states by way of specific beliefs, the specification being provided by a declarative sentence. Seen in this light, there is a very close connection between the sentence "It's raining" and the thought or belief *that it is raining.*

This simple transfer principle immediately leads to problems such as the following. There are indexical sentences, are there correspondingly indexical thoughts? According to the classical Fregean framework, thoughts cannot be indexical: the completion of meaning works at the linguistic level, and the proposition labelled by the sentence is necessarily complete, self-standing. But this is not the case, as John Perry has convincingly shown[27]: there are thoughts, or propositions, which contain an ineliminable indexical element. The transfer principle applied in the reverse direction then raises a question for Kaplan's treatment of pure indexicals in sentences. But Perry's work also raises an interesting point for Dreyfus's analysis, as we will briefly indicate in Section III.

A related issue is whether all the "ingredients" of a thought are present in the sentence whose meaning it constitutes—can one think a thought which *involves* X without the thought including a thought *about* X? In the standard framework, the answer is no, but Perry again shows this to be mistaken[28]: some thoughts at least comprise elements which are not represented. And again this throws a new light on Dreyfus's take on the issue of representation.

Perry, and his co-author Jon Barwise, are fairly radical. Radicalism may also result from a certain way of examining questions (2) through (6) above. For example, the phrase "Jim's book" involves a "demonstration" not only of Jim (the hearer, reader, interpreter of the sentence must know which Jim is being referred to), but also of the relation indicated by the genitive.[29] The classical attitude treats the underdetermination as a form of polysemy: the interpreter has to choose, among the several meanings of the genitive, which one applies in the case under consideration: are we talking of the book Jim *owns*, or of the book Jim *is reading*? The trouble is that there simply is no finite list, and actually no list at all, of the relations which Jim may bear to the book: he may be giving it, stealing it, praising it, hating it, printing it, having wanted to write it for years, using it as a fly swatter, sitting on it to reach his plate, thinking about it obsessively, quoting from it, not being able to remember its title, denying it ever existed, and so on ad infinitum.

This is but one (especially interesting) case of what is referred to since Friedrich Waismann as the *open texture*[30] of natural language, and examples such as this are so familiar among the new contextualists that one sometimes marvels at how much delight seems to go into making up ever better and wilder variations in order to illustrate very similar points. Of course, the inspiration here is Wittgenstein, and the best representative of unabashed radicalism, as far as linguistic contextualism goes, is Charles Travis, the author of a book subtitled *Wittgenstein's Philosophy of Language*.[31] Travis's thesis is that the truth conditions of a sentence are *occasion dependent*. Whether it is the case or not that there is water in the refrigerator depends on the occasion in which the sentence is considered or uttered: is the topic drinkable water in an accessible container and in sizable quantity, or is it humidity rendering the refrigerator electrically permeable, or is it frost on the coils, or is it H_2O molecules in the cottage cheese?

Contrary to pure indexicals, polysemous words, lexicalized metaphors, anaphoras and the like, sentences such as "There is water in the refrigerator," or "York lies 25 miles northwest of Leeds," or "The table is covered with breadcrumbs" do not bear their incompleteness on their sleeves.[32] They contain no pointer to some element whose interpretation is both needed for an understanding of the sentence (or the fixation of its truth conditions) and requires searching the context, the circumstances of the occasion. It is the context which tells the interpreter which features of the sentence need contextual determination. Words, on that view, lose the leading role which is theirs in the traditional picture, and remains theirs in moderate forms of contextualism.

Yet another important feature of examples of this sort is that they can undergo an indefinite number of additions such that the truth conditions of the sentence (or the applicability of the predicate) under consideration, undergo a brutal change at every addition. This shows that there is no locality principle in virtue of which, given a sentence (or predicate), there is a prespecified list of aspects of the context which it is sufficient to consult in order to fix its truth conditions (or applicability). This is a form of holism which does not appeal to notions such as the sense of the situation, the practices of the community, the involvement in a form of life, in short, the background in one or another form, but is every bit as threatening to the formalist view.

Daniel Andler

Reference to Wittgenstein, as well as the general flavor of the examples in this literature, and also the passion for collecting these examples, these signs all point to two authors well known to the reader. One is Dreyfus, of course, the other is John Searle, who deserves a special mention here for his theoretical contribution of course, but also because of the likeness of some of his views to Dreyfus's. Very roughly, Searle uses context in the straightforward sense, at first, as an argument against the cognitivist view of the mental; he then generalizes his notion of context to background, and uses background as an argument against the intellectualist component of cognitivism; third (though not last chronologically), he argues against the informational/functionalist component of cognitivism. All of this is (very forcefully) written up in books and papers which appeared from the late seventies to the mid-nineties. But all this is present, couched in a different language and framed in a different setting, in Dreyfus's 1972 book. The paradox is that Dreyfus quotes Searle, in his later writings, while Searle hardly ever quotes Dreyfus.

Indeed, it sometimes seems as though Searle enacts his own Chinese Room thought experiment with *What Computers Can't Do* instead of the Chinese phrase book. It may well be that although the book does figure in the bibliography of *The Rediscovery of the Mind*, Searle has not read it. But he certainly has absorbed it through osmosis, which is less of a miracle than might appear to one who is not familiar with the lively exchanges on the topic of AI prompted by Dreyfus's arrival at Berkeley in 1969. During the twenty-odd years when Searle's philosophy of mind developed, a constant flux of students, teaching assistants, post-docs, fellows of the richly endowed Institute of Cognitive Science, gathered intellectual pollen from various teachers and dispersed it to everyone's benefit. The "critique of artificial reason" which made Dreyfus famous in some circles, and gives the book its subtitle, appeared in 1972 but was in the stage of intensive preparation in the years immediately preceding, and in particular was aired at a two-year seminar which many people attended and where well-known philosophers such as Charles Taylor gave talks. Chapter 9 of Searle's *Rediscovery*, published in 1992, is entitled "The Critique of Cognitive Reason," without a reference to Dreyfus's 1972 book (which appears, as was just mentioned, in the bibliography, but *stripped of its subtitle*). Similarly, Searle says at the beginning of chapter 8, that "[i]n the early 1970s [he] began investigating the phenomena that [he] later came to call 'the Background',"[33] and somewhere he writes that his theory is akin to no one else's except perhaps Bourdieu. But that investigation was actually started in the mid-1960s by Dreyfus, and essentially concluded by the early 1970s; the basic arguments, the basic features of "Background," the kinds of example,[34] all this was laid open in Dreyfus's 1972 book.[35]

There is a lesson in this, which has something to do with context in fact. What must have happened is that Searle was so caught up in his initial problem, which was what to make of Wittgenstein's attack on the Fregean ideas about meaning,[36] that he did not realize he was picking up ideas which Dreyfus was developing across the hall while thinking about the mind. As he admits, "[t]he thesis [that only against Background are conditions of satisfactions defined] was originally a claim about literal meaning (Searle 1978), but [he now] believe[s] what applies to literal meaning applies also to speaker's intended meaning, and indeed, to all forms of intentionality, whether linguistic or non-linguistic."[37] But this is a rediscovery of the mind as Dreyfus pictured it, in print, twenty years earlier.

Before leaving the new contextualism, a word should be said about an extreme form of radicalism within that current of thought. For thinkers such as Lawrence Barsalou, Douglas Hintzman or Ronald Langacker,[38] meanings vanish entirely from the theoretical horizon. They are replaced, essentially, by repertoires of cases, in other words, by *encyclopedic* information acquired through exposure. This is quite close to Dreyfus's idea (put to use by the PDP modellers) that an intelligent mind proceeds not by applying rules but calling forth from experience a collection of examples, applying an intuitive similarity metric, and finally dealing with the problem at hand in roughly the same way as with the experience closest to it.

One final remark may help in making out the level at which Dreyfus and the contextualists are converging. If they are right, a consequence of either view is that pure reflection plays a lesser role in mental life, in intelligent behavior, than the first cognitivists thought, and that what is no longer attributable to reflection must be borne either by the environment or by the mind itself, but then not in the form of representations. There may well be representations: some contextualists such as Searle tend to believe it, Dreyfus, or at least some of his radical followers, tend to doubt it, but at any rate they all argue in favor of a nonrepresentational ground on which mental life rests, either, somehow, directly, or via a representational process.

III Narrowing the Gap

Despite their overlap and similarities which should by now be evident, Dreyfus and the new contextualists are equally clearly not saying all of the same things. Not only do they have different theoretical goals, and thus focus on different aspects of the phenomenon, but they also differ in the way they cut things up. And quite likely they actually disagree on important points. To narrow the gap does not mean to make the positions appear to be close, but to lower their degree of incommensurability. In this final section, I will attempt to bring out features of the respective frameworks, with the hope of offering a clearer picture of the problem situation; besides, the issues raised are of interest in their own right.

It is a striking fact that mind and intelligence have very complex, and very different grammars. It is tempting for an outsider to think that Dreyfus and a typical contextualist such as Searle or Perry are simply not on to the same topic, one being concerned with intelligence, the other with mind. Insiders know better: grammar is misleading, they believe, and everyone is in fact after the same thing. The truth, I suggest, lies somewhere in between.

There are (at least) two reasons for the grammatical complexities. The first is that "intelligence"[39] is polysemous even within the present context: in one usage it is nearly synonymous with "mind" (as in "Newborns [or dogs] are intelligent," which means the same as "Newborns [or dogs] have minds"); in another, it is a graded property of something, mind, behavior, person, and even, though perhaps metaphorically, system, institution, machine . . . The second source of complexity lies in the ontology: mind is either regarded as a thing, or as a function. On the reified, Cartesian view, intelligence is an "accident" (in the Aristotelian sense) of the "essence" mind; it can still be either roughly co-extensional with mind (the nongraded sense) or belong to a mind to a lesser or greater degree. On the functional view, intelligence is either strictly synonymous with mind or denotes its graded quality.

The whole idea of Turing, in his famous paper in *Mind*, is to get rid of these perplexities by adopting a stance which one could call "grammatical behaviorism," and which may or may not, depending on further theoretical options, result from plain scientific behaviorism. Intelligent behavior on this view becomes the sole primitive notion, and mind and intelligence remain only as derivative notions, one with a built-in threshold (having a mind is equivalent to being above threshold) and one without (behavior can be intelligent to any degree from nil to infinity).

ιAI, which is Dreyfus's topic, is a form of behaviorism, directly bequeathed by Turing. But it brings in the mind through the back door: it postulates representations. Whether or not this is an inevitable consequence of the Turingian option is a difficult question which must be left for another occasion.[40] The crucial point for our purpose is that Dreyfus's main target is precisely that move. AI's original sin, for him, is not its behaviorism, it is its representationalism (its intellectualism). Dreyfus does not fault AI for being too behavioristic, but for being inconsistent in its behaviorism: it is not behavioristic all the way and in the right way, that is, in the way sketched by Heidegger and Merleau-Ponty. This is the deep reason[41] why the problem of AI is the right problem for Dreyfus to tackle, or rather why is it for him the right entry into the problem of mind. Although his ontology of mind remains mostly implicit, he is a radical anti-Cartesian, an eliminativist about the mind.

The new contextualists, on the other hand, have as their starting point not behavior but language. They are after *linguistic* understanding. Everybody knows since Chomsky's famous review of Skinner's book that language is the Achilles heel of (psychological) behaviorism. But Frege already had a Cartesian view of the mind, and so did Brentano (at least as contemporary analytic philosophers read him). Frege provides the framework for mainstream philosophy of language, and Brentano provides mainstream philosophy of mind with a definition of mind as bearer of representations. The new contextualists, by and large, belong squarely in that tradition.

Thus it is now plain that Dreyfus and the new contextualists, with different points of departure, meet on the topic of mind. It is equally plain that they deeply disagree: Dreyfus defends a sophisticated behaviorism, the new contextualists defend a sophisticated Cartesianism, or, to accommodate Searle's position, a sophisticated representationalism. The irony is that both camps use arguments from the phenomenology of context to show the inadequacy of the crude versions of their respective options: contextualists disprove simpleminded cognitivism, and Dreyfus disproves simple-minded behaviorism indirectly, by showing that cognitivism in any form is false for reasons which apply equally to behaviorism in the classical construal (cognitivism is indeed, seen from the right perspective, behaviorism pursued by novel means).

This way of putting the matter is an oversimplification however. As we have seen, among the new contextualists, while a majority lean toward naturalism,[42] a minority tend to oppose it. This is where radicalism matters: very radical contextualists side with Dreyfus against all of their less than fully radical colleagues. Or rather, they would side with him, presumably, if they cared, as he does, to disprove the possibility of the cognitivist enterprise. Moderate contextualists, however sophisticated, hold on to the hope of discovering a "calculus" of thought which would faithfully model contextual effects while lending itself to mechanization, by virtue of being a calculus in at least roughly the sense imagined by AI. This stance is exemplified in a particularly clear and coherent way by Sperber and Wilson's Relevance Theory.[43] While recognizing, and indeed illustrating by entertaining and convincing examples, the "open texture" of communication, they defend a mechanistic account of interpretation: According to them, a hearer retrieves, from among the indefinitely many possible interpretations of a speaker's utterance, the correct one, by (nonconsciously) observing a double-maximization principle: she goes for the most relevant at the cost of the least processing effort; and this works because the speaker is (nonconsciously) counting on her to follow this strategy. Clearly, the hearer's task is a very particular one as far as cognitive tasks go: retrieving a speaker's communicative intention, as I have argued elsewhere,[44] has a number of features which make it comparatively simple from the theoretical standpoint. But this is not the critical issue from a Dreyfusian perspective: what Dreyfus wants to know is whether anyone claims to have a theory *of* relevance. But Sperber and Wilson are quite clear about the scope of their theory: their "principle of relevance" does not define, quantify, or characterize in any way the relevance, for a hearer, of the informations she can potentially extract from an utterance by exploiting contextual clues. Such a task would be, they believe, hopelessly unconstrained. Their goal is to show how communication proceeds, in a given "landscape" of potential relevance: Relevance Theory is not a theory *of* relevance, but a theory of communication based on the idea that interpretation is inferential, that inference is permissive and therefore requires control, and that maximization of relevance subject to minimization of effort provides the necessary control principle.

Well then, it seems legitimate to ask whether the theory, beyond its obvious contribution to pragmatics, has a role to play in the overarching enterprise of naturalization of the mental. It is clearly meant to have. One should therefore expect the authors to hope that their theory would, in the fullness of time, hook onto a naturalistic account of relevance. Now sophisticated cognitive scientists do not take the failure of GOFAI's attempts at providing such an account as negative evidence against its possibility. But they are bound to pay attention to Fodor's arguments, in Part IV of *Modularity of Mind,* against the possibility of a science of "central processes"—in other words, a science of thought. Fodor bases his attack on, roughly, the consideration of context, and explicitly refers to Dreyfus in the penultimate paragraph of his book[45]: Fodor's general line can be characterized as an argument against the possibility of a theory *of* relevance. So that, while leaving untouched Relevance Theory, Fodor points to a severe potential limitation of its importance for cognitive science. One should therefore expect the authors of Relevance Theory to try and undermine Fodor's line. Indeed, Sperber mounts an attack against Fodor's "impossibility theorem for cognitive science" by questioning the irreducibly nonmodular character of central processes.[46] Although he does not claim to hold a solution to the problem of relevance, he argues that central processes are modular to a certain, and perhaps large, extent. In a certain way, Dreyfus could partly agree with Sperber's line: after all, as we have seen, he agrees that there is a nonrepresentational dimension of mind. But of course, the "joints" within the "central processes" are of a vastly different nature than Dreyfus's embodied skills and concerned coping. And Fodor's intuitions on the matter, which for once echo Dreyfus's, retain most of their appeal, despite Sperber's pleas for domain-specificity.

The reader may feel at this point that the story is told: Dreyfus believes that intelligence cannot be mechanized, or naturalized for that matter, while the new contextualists believe that literal meaning is not the centerpiece of linguistic theorizing; these concerns only partly overlap (that they do overlap is what I have been at pains to show), so that some agreement is possible, and actual to a small extent, and disagreement is possible, and actual to a large extent, but the opposition is too oblique to be resolved.

Yet this is perhaps not the end of the story. Each camp has its blindspot, and each has ideas which the other could profit from. There are several issues that are worth exploring. One is the self: Perry has shown that egocentric thoughts[47] must have a very particular, quite un-Fregean, structure if they must enter into an adequate account of action. This connects, on one hand, with the ontology of mind, and on the other with Dreyfus's account of the Merleau-Pontian conception of the centrality of the body in behavior. It is quite striking that traces of the primacy of the concrete, bodily ego should be found in the very structure of the simplest and ontogenetically earliest thoughts.

Another issue is Dreyfus's basic taxonomy of states of mind, inspired by his reading of Heidegger's *Being and Time* Division I. Thoughts about hammers, for example, come in two varieties according to the mode of the state of mind of which they are a part. In the involved mode, there is no concept or representation of the hammer as a separate object in objective space-time, with objective, intrinsic properties, although there is competent coping with the hammer and also, as Dreyfus came to see,[48] a form of awareness of the hammer. In the detached mode, the hammer-thought looks like a traditional representation, but it results from a rational reconstruction, it is not primitive or basic. The passage from one to the other mode occurs on the occasion of a breakdown (the hammer not fitting in the fluid, competent coping in which the subject is engaged). The question which can be raised, from the standpoint of the neurophysiology and neuropsychology of motor action[49] but also perhaps by re-examining its phenomenology, is whether every state does not include both a deliberative, detached, component, and an involved, automatic, component. This would not sit well with the thesis of the primacy of the involved mode of thinking. One place to look for further inspiration on this issue is developmental psychology: babies are not prone to deliberation, in the standard sense, yet they seem to display a highly differentiated, and systematically evolving, pattern of conceptual competence.[50]

This is not the time to pursue either of these issues. But enough has been said, I hope, to show that Dreyfus's critique of artificial intelligence, far from setting him apart from contemporary cognitive science, puts him and his followers in direct contact with it. As always, contact means risk for both sides, as well as potential for enrichment.

Grasping at Straws: Motor Intentionality and the Cognitive Science of Skilled Behavior

Sean D. Kelly

A drowning man will catch at a straw, the Proverb well says.
Richardson, *Clarissa*

Hubert Dreyfus has had a lot to say over the years about the inadequacies of traditional cognitive science. He is also, of course, one of the foremost commentators on the work of the founders of modern phenomenology—Martin Heidegger and Maurice Merleau-Ponty—not to mention a gifted phenomenologist himself. Anyone who knows Bert or his work will know that for him these two apparently disparate projects—one unabashedly empirical, the other paradigmatically philosophical—form two sides of the same coin. He calls this coin, in a pleasingly difficult phrase, "applied philosophy." Applied philosophy as Dreyfus practices it comes, characteristically, from the simple fount of common sense. It is predicated on the observation that if phenomenology tells us about the phenomena of human experience, its results ought to be relevant to the human sciences. This simple formula has led Dreyfus to explore areas of human science as diverse as nursing, management science, and artificial intelligence. But the very first problem he addressed—in his Ph.D. dissertation at Harvard—was the problem of perception. Although I do not intend to discuss the problem of perception per se in this chapter, I do want to think about a problem that is tightly connected with it—namely, the problem of determining the phenomenological features of certain skillful bodily actions. I will argue

Sean D. Kelly

that the phenomenology of these actions, as it is developed by Merleau-Ponty in *Phenomenology of Perception,* is inconsistent with the standard cognitive science models of them. Furthermore, certain neural network models of action, I will argue, are much better at accounting for these phenomenological data. In approaching the problem of bodily action this way, I intend this essay to be both a methodological and a substantive tribute to Dreyfus's work: it not only sits squarely within the methodological rubric of applied philosophy, it also returns to substantive problems that are related to perception, the problem that launched Dreyfus's philosophical career. Because this is a problem with which, in his equally valuable role as teacher, mentor, and advisor, he has helped me to launch my own, I hope that any contribution this chapter makes will be seen as a further tribute to him.

I   What Is Phenomenology and Why Should a Cognitive Scientist Care?

Phenomenology is essentially descriptive. Its goal is completely and accurately to describe the phenomena of human experience without the interference of metaphysical presuppositions inherited from psychological, scientific, historical, sociological, or other theoretical frameworks. Description is so central to the method of phenomenology that, as Heidegger says, the phrase "'descriptive phenomenology' . . . is at bottom tautological".[1] And yet, description is not as easy as it seems. This is because, metaphysical presuppositions being the tenacious creatures that they are, the phenomena of human experience tend to hide themselves: "Just because the phenomena are proximally and for the most part *not* given," Heidegger explains, "there is need for phenomenology."[2] To say that phenomenology is descriptive, then, is not in any way to minimize its difficulty or worth.

Some evidence for the value of a phenomenological approach to philosophy can be found in the fact that even traditional analytic philosophers, the sworn enemies of all things continental, sometimes endorse a descriptive—which is to say, broadly speaking, a phenomenological—methodology. The remarks of the later Wittgenstein, for instance, and the ordinary language philosophy of J. L. Austin are often mentioned in this regard. Both of these approaches have an important descriptive element to them, but a particularly interesting and little noticed ally of phenomenology can be found in the descriptive method that Strawson employs in his famous book *Individuals*.[3] The phenomenological preference for descriptive accuracy over systematic theoretical cogency is there reiterated by Strawson in his preference for what he calls "descriptive" over "revisionary" metaphysics: "Descriptive metaphysics is content to describe the actual structure of our thought about the world, revisionary metaphysics is concerned to produce a better structure."[4]

I mention Strawson here both because his sympathy for the descriptive approach may lend credence to the phenomenological approach, and also because the differences between these approaches can help better to characterize phenomenology. The major distinction between Strawson and the phenomenologists is that Strawson, as he says in the quote above, is concerned primarily with "*thought* about the world," while the phenomenologists believe that many of our most basic ways of relating intentionally to the world are precisely not in the form of having thoughts about it. Rather, perceiving and acting upon the objects in the world are more basic modes of intentionality, according to the phenomenologists, and these perceptions and actions have an intentional content that is, as Merleau-Ponty says, "pre-predicative."

I will say more about pre-predicative content later in the paper (Merleau-Ponty's idea of "motor intentionality" will play a central role there), but for the moment I will just mention that even this idea, or something like it, has shown up recently in the analytic world. Gareth Evans, a student of Strawson's, departs from his teacher when he advocates a "non-conceptual content" for perception, a kind of content that is strikingly similar to the pre-predicative content that Merleau-Ponty describes.[5] Without addressing here the relation between their work, I will simply remark that the advantage of phenomenology continues to be found in the depth of its commitment to descriptive accuracy without the interference of metaphysical presuppositions: even Evans is led to misdescribe the content of perceptual experience because of presuppositions he has about the content of the demonstrative thoughts it makes possible.[6]

Sean D. Kelly

What, then, is the descriptively complete and accurate account of perception and action that phenomenology endorses? One central aspect of it is certainly this: that any complete and accurate description of normal perceptual or behavioral phenomena leads to the denial of a private, inner subject who experiences a transcendant, outer world. In place of this roughly Cartesian picture, the phenomenologist holds that perceptual and behavioral phenomena take place in the context of what the psychologist J. J. Gibson calls the "organism-environment system"; in phenomenological terms they are attributed not to the Cartesian subject, but to "open heads upon the world" (Merleau-Ponty) or simply to "Dasein" (Heidegger). Very crudely what this means is that if I am having a perceptual experience of an apple, I cannot completely and accurately describe this experience without at least some reference to the very apple I am having an experience of. Because the apple and the experience of the apple are intertwined in this way, we would be misdescribing the perceptual phenomenon (equally, the content of the perceptual experience) if we said it was attributable to a completely independent, inner self.[7]

I do not intend to argue for this claim here, only to point out that it is at the center of any good phenomenological account of perception and action. And having said this, I want to point out further that, despite a prima facie difficulty, this denial of the Cartesian subject is in no way at odds with the possibility of a scientific, neurophysiological account of perceptual or behavioral phenomena. The prima facie difficulty is generated by the observation that, while the brain scientist explains perception and action in terms of the "inner" workings of the brain, the phenomenology of perception and action denies the existence of an "inner" self. But of course this apparent problem is based on a simple confusion between two different uses of the term "inner." There is an important difference between the inner, Cartesian, subject of experience, on the one hand, and the inner, physiological mechanism of experience, on the other. Even if the accurate description of perceptual and behavioral phenomena demands the denial of an inner, Cartesian, subject, it nevertheless remains the case that the intentional phenomena being described are realized in the physical substrate of the human body, with particular emphasis on the human brain. We must not confuse the phenomenological fact that the right description of our intentional relation to the world denies that we are private, inner subjects, with the scientific fact that this intentional relation is physically realized within the human organism.

Phenomenology and brain science, then, are not at odds with one another. This is a point that Merleau-Ponty is not always so clear about, but that Dreyfus has emphasized repeatedly in his work with the neurophysiologist Walter Freeman.[8] But if this is so, then what exactly is the right relation between phenomenology and brain science? I propose that the right relation between phenomenology and brain science is that of data to model: brain science is ultimately concerned with explaining the way the physical processes of the brain conspire to produce the phenomena of human experience; insofar as phenomenology devotes itself to the accurate description of these phenomena, it provides the most complete and accurate presentation of the data that ultimately must be accounted for by models of brain function. Thus, the phenomenological account of a given aspect of human behavior is meant to provide a description of those characteristics of the behavior which any physical explanation of it must be able to reproduce.

In this chapter, I intend to address a very special case of the interplay between phenomenology and brain or cognitive science. I will be concerned only with the kind of skillful motor behaviors that take place naturally in the context of environmental cues—behaviors such as grasping a doorknob in walking though a door, grasping a coffee mug to drink from it, or, as in Richardson's extreme case, grasping after a thin reed to prevent oneself from drowning. What all of these actions have in common is that they are not, in any strict sense, deliberate or reflective; rather, they are actions that are, as Gibson would say, "afforded" by the environment. Skillfully grasping an object, in the most natural and everyday cases, occurs in this unpremeditated mode. It is my contention that the phenomenology of these skillful grasping behaviors invalidates the standard assumptions made by the traditional cognitive science models of them.

Furthermore, although the classical models of skillful action fail to reproduce its phenomenology, I believe that certain neural network models can be interpreted as accurately reproducing at least some of the most important phenomenological characteristics of skillful grasping behavior. In particular, I will discuss briefly a model of limb movement to a target that has been developed by the neurologists Donald Borrett and Hon Kwan. By explaining this motor behavior in terms of network relaxation, their models can be interpreted as reproducing the central phenomenological characteristics of the understanding of place that is inherent in the skillful grasping of objects. Because these characteristics are realized in a model that is, at least in some general sense, neurophysiologically plausible, I believe that their account of skillful motor action goes some way toward meeting the dual constraints of neurophysiological plausibility and phenomenological accuracy that ought to guide all projects devoted to discovering the physical bases of human experience.

II Motor Intentional Behavior

The central feature of skillful motor behaviors, according to Merleau-Ponty, is that they are not accurately described in either an empiricist or an intellectualist vocabulary, but rather, "we have to create the concepts necessary to convey"[9] them. Neither the empiricist, who believes that skillful motor behavior is analyzable in terms of completely non-intentional elements like the reflex arc, nor the intellectualist (or modern day cognitivist), who believes that skillful motor behavior is analyzable in terms of completely rational cognitive processes, can account for all the essential phenomenological characteristics of this kind of behavior. The empiricist account fails because its purely mechanical vocabulary does not allow it to distinguish between mere reflex movements and directed, skillful motor actions. On the other hand, the cognitivist account fails because its purely cognitive vocabulary does not allow it to distinguish between unreflective motor actions like grasping an object, and deliberate, cognitive actions like pointing at one. I will develop the anticognitivist point later in the chapter, but for now I will simply note that because of the inability of either empiricism or cognitivism to explain them, Merleau-Ponty understands skillful motor actions like grasping an object to define a category of behavioral phenomenon that is between the mechanical and the cognitive. He calls this kind of phenomenon "motor intentionality":

We are brought to the recognition of something between movement as a third person process and thought as a representation of movement—something which is an anticipation of, or arrival at, the objective and is ensured by the body itself as a motor power, a "motor project" (*Bewegungsentwurf*), a "motor intentionality."[10]

The argument against the empiricist account of motor intentional behavior is simple and obvious. It is based on the observation that there is a clear phenomenological distinction between a reflex movement, such as the leg exhibits when struck just below the kneecap, and a directed, skillful action like grasping an object. The difference is that the grasping action has a certain kind of intentionality to it— it is directed toward the object to be grasped—while the reflex action does not. One way to convince yourself of this is to notice that the success or failure of the grasping act, unlike that of the reflex act, depends in part on whether or not the intended *object* was grasped. If I perform the very same physical movement but do not end up holding the intended object, then the grasping act has failed. The success or failure of the reflex act, on the other hand, depends entirely on the occurrence of the relevant muscular contractions. Because the empiricist is devoted to explaining all behavior in terms of the non-intentional reflex arc, she is incapable of accounting for the intentional component of motor intentional behaviors like grasping an object.

The argument against the cognitivist account of motor intentional behavior is more complicated. Roughly speaking, the idea is that the cognitivist cannot account for the motor component of motor intentional behavior. In the next section, I will show that Merleau-Ponty develops this criticism by focusing on the cognitivist assumption that all the features of motor intentional behavior "are fully developed and determinate",[11] while a complete and accurate phenomenological description requires rather that we "recognize the indeterminate as a positive phenomenon."[12] Motor intentional behavior is "prepredicative," according to Merleau-Ponty, precisely because it identifies the object it is directed toward in an indeterminate, provisional

Sean D. Kelly

manner. I will conclude the next section by arguing that neural network models, under an interpretation provided by Borrett and Kwan, have the capacity to mimic the kinds of indeterminacy that Merleau-Ponty sees as central to motor intentional behavior.

III The Phenomenology and Cognitive Science of Motor Intentional Behavior

One good way to determine the phenomenological characteristics of a behavior is to consider the behavioral pathologies that can occur. Toward this end, Merleau-Ponty considers a patient, Schneider by name, who is

unable to perform "abstract" movements with his eyes shut; movements, that is, which are not relevant to any actual situation, such as moving arms and legs to order, or bending and straightening a finger.[13]

On the other hand,

Even when his eyes are closed, the patient performs with extraordinary speed and precision the movements needed in living his life, provided that he is in the habit of performing them: he takes his handkerchief from his pocket and blows his nose, takes a match out of a box and lights a lamp.[14]

Among the abstract movements he is incapable of performing, Schneider is unable to describe the position of his body or head, and he is unable to point to a part of his body when asked to do so. On the other hand, among the "concrete" movements he is capable of performing, Schneider, like a normal subject, will quickly move his hand to the point on his body where a mosquito is stinging him. Thus, Merleau-Ponty argues, following Goldstein,[15] that in Schneider there is a

dissociation of the act of pointing from reactions of taking or grasping . . . It must therefore be concluded [given that Scheider is capable of the one but not the other] that "grasping" . . . is different from "pointing."[16]

Merleau-Ponty goes on to describe the phenomenological characteristics in terms of which grasping and pointing are distinct. It is these characteristics, which we will discuss in a moment, that must be accurately reproduced in any model of motor behavior. Before we develop the phenomenological distinction between pointing and grasping, though, let us look at the typical cognitivist account of grasping actions.

Traditional cognitivist theories of movement are incapable of distinguishing between pointing and grasping, since they explain the latter in terms of the former. Although Merleau-Ponty had already levelled this criticism against cognitivism in 1945,[17] as recently as 1992 it was considered a radical point to make:

We often do not differentiate between grasping and pointing when we generalize about how vision is used when generating limb movements. It is possible, that how individuals use vision may vary as a function of whether they are generating pointing or grasping movements, and that some principles of how vision is used during reaching and pointing is [sic] not generalizable to grasping.[18]

Why should cognitivist theories so adamantly refuse to distinguish between pointing and grasping behavior?

The answer has largely to do with the kinds of problems that motivate the relevant psychological research. Much of the psychological research on limb movement is organized around the well-studied phenomenon of speed-accuracy tradeoff.[19] The relation between the speed and the accuracy of a limb movement was first discussed by Woodworth in his now classic article "The Accuracy of Voluntary Movement"[20]; the general idea is that the faster you make a movement, the less likely it is that the movement will accurately reach its target, and conversely, the larger the target, the faster you can make the movement accurately. The general relation between speed and accuracy is described by Fitts's Law.[21] The theoretical question, according to the psychologists, is how to explain the generation of motor behavior in such a way as to account for the fact that there is a constant relation between speed and accuracy.[22]

All the theoretical explanations of this phenomenon share the basic assumption, due to Woodworth himself, that rapid movements involve two successive phases, which he called "initial adjustment" and "current control." The first of these is a gross movement of the relevant body part in the general direction of the target location; the second of these "corrects any errors made along the way, using sensory feedback to reach the target accurately."[23] The characteristic

Sean D. Kelly

explanation of these two phases is given by Woodworth using an example of what might be called a "calculative" movement:

If the reader desires a demonstration of the existence of the "later adjustments" which constitute the most evident part of the "current control," let him watch the movements made in bringing the point of his pencil to rest on a certain dot. He will notice that after the bulk of the movement has brought the pencil point near its goal, little extra movements are added serving to bring the point to its mark with any required degree of accuracy. . . . If now the reader will decrease the time allowed for the whole movement, he will find it more difficult, and finally impossible to make the little additions.[24]

Woodworth admits, though it is not widely remarked in the literature, that the "groping" characteristic of the current control phase is more evident in beginners and unskilled practitioners of a given task (he considers singing a note, playing a note on the violin, and performing a musical passage on the piano), but speculates that even for the virtuoso "the later adjustment is probably there, but it is made with perfect smoothness, and has by long and efficient practice attained the sureness and speed of a reflex."[25] This assumption, apparently made (in the absence of any scientific evidence) for the simple sake of theoretical cogency, has been maintained for nearly a century. The major debate in the psychological literature is not over whether there are two distinct phases of rapid movement, but over whether movement speed affects movement accuracy primarily by affecting the current-control or the initial adjustment phase.[26]

A typical and influential entry in this debate was offered by Crossman and Goodeve in the late 1960s, though it is still important today.[27] The linear feedback correction model of rapid movement that they developed is typical in that it uses sensory feedback during the current control phase to account for how the limb reaches its target accurately. On this model the actual position of the limb is continuously compared with the target position to produce an error measure which is reduced by means of a linear feedback mechanism. The faster the speed of the limb movement, the less accurate will be the comparison between limb and target position. The appeal of this model is taken to be the fact that it predicts the relation between movement speed and movement accuracy to be exactly that

described by Fitts's Law. The disadvantage, from the phenomenological point of view, is that because it takes for granted the general
assumption that all limb movement is comprised of two distinct
phases, the second of which is calculative in nature, it does not
have the resources to distinguish between pointing and grasping
behaviors.

What are the phenomenological characteristics of this distinction?
According to Merleau-Ponty, the central characteristic is that pointing and grasping are based on two different kinds of understanding
of place:

If I know where my nose is when it is a question of holding it, how can I not
know where it is when it is a matter of pointing to it? It is probably because
knowledge of where something is can be understood in a number of ways.[28]

Furthermore, the way in which we understand where something is
when we are grasping it *is capable of being experienced* independently
from the way in which we understand where something is when we
are pointing at it. Thus, far from its being the case that grasping
behavior can be explained on the model of pointing behavior (by
assuming that the understanding of an object's place with respect to
the limb is uniformly expressible in terms of an objectively determined distance function) it seems instead that the understanding
of place underlying the concrete, situational behavior of grasping is
of a distinct and independently experiencable kind altogether. As
Merleau-Ponty says, "Bodily space may be given to me in an intention to take hold without being given in an intention to know".[29] Presumably the case of Schneider provides evidence that this claim is
empirically true.

Further psychological evidence to this effect has recently been provided by the physiological psychologists Melvyn Goodale and David
Milner, in the case of the subject whom they call DF.[30] Like Goldstein's Schneider, DF is capable of very sophisticated differential
behavior when directing visuomotor actions toward an object; nevertheless, because of a profound disorder in perception she is incapable of identifying the very object qualities to which she is,
apparently, responding. In fact, there is a double dissociation here,
since patients with the disorder called optic ataxia appear to be able

Sean D. Kelly

to pick out objects by their qualities without being able to handle them. Goodale and Milner argue, on the basis of this evidence, that

the visual processing underlying "conscious" perceptual judgements must operate separately from that underlying the "automatic" visuomotor guidance of skilled actions of the hand and limb.[31]

In a series of articles over the last ten years, Goodale and Milner have hypothesized that the ventral and dorsal pathways for visual information, which have traditionally been interpreted as providing "what" and "where" information about an object, should instead be interpreted as providing "what" and "how" information.[32] The "what" information of the ventral pathway tells us about the object qualities traditionally associated with perception, while the "how" information of the dorsal pathway tells us how to respond to the object in a motor intentional manner. If the visual information from these two pathways is encoded differently, as Goodale and Milner suggest, then this would explain at the neural level Merleau-Ponty's phenomenological claim that we understand the place of an object differently when we are grasping it than when we are pointing at it.[33]

What are the phenomenological characteristics of these different kinds of understanding of place? In the case of pointing to an object, as in Woodworth's calculative pencil-pointing example, the place of the object is given "as a determination of the objective world."[34] That is to say, I understand the place of the dot on the paper as objective, determinate, and outside of myself. Since a representation of the place of an object by means of its three-dimensional coordinates in Cartesian space would reproduce these features, the idea of a current control phase in pointing behavior is at least phenomenologically viable, since the idea of comparing an external, visually identified, determinate, objective location in three-dimensional Cartesian space to an internal, kinaesthetically (or perceptually) identified, determinate, objective location in three-dimensional Cartesian space makes sense. Indeed, it is phenomenologically evident that something like this kind of comparison and calculation does take place in the pencil-pointing example.

On the other hand, in the case of grasping an object, the place of the object is not understood as outside of me in a distinct objective world: "There is no question of locating it in relation to axes of coordinates in objective space."[35] Rather,

there is a knowledge of place which is reducible to a sort of co-existence with that place, and which is not simply nothing, even though it cannot be conveyed in the form of a description or even pointed out without a word being spoken.[36]

The phenomenologist must attempt to give an accurate description of the features of this kind of understanding of place.

When I want to drink some coffee from my coffee mug in the morning, I simply grab the mug in a single, smooth, undifferentiated movement. As Merleau-Ponty says, "From the outset the grasping movement is magically at its completion."[37] This is different from pointing to the mug or even touching it without the intention to grab it. For instance, if in the act of grabbing for my coffee mug I am stopped and told to touch it with my forefinger instead, the movement takes on a radically different character: "[A grasping movement] can begin only by anticipating its end, since to disallow taking hold is sufficient to inhibit the action."[38]

The major difference between grasping and merely touching is that it is very difficult to touch the mug with my forefinger unless I have relatively extensive visual feedback, at least toward the end of the movement; as with the pencil-pointing example, I seem to be relatively sure of the general direction of the mug (initial adjustment), but actually to touch it I have to look (current control). On the other hand, if I want to grab the mug in order to drink from it, this act requires little visual feedback at all. In fact, my understanding of the place of the coffee mug when I intend to grasp it depends so little on visual feedback that if the mug is nearby in a place I have recently put it, I can even grab it with my eyes closed. Merely to touch it with my forefinger under these circumstances is much more difficult. Thus it seems that the central phenomenological characteristics of the understanding of place that underlies grasping behavior are that the place of the object is understood equally well and in the same manner at the beginning of the grasping motion as it is at the end, and that this understanding is dependent upon the intention *to grasp* the object, not just to point at it or locate it in space. For the kind of understanding of place that underlies grasping behavior, then, the current control phase of movement is inappropriate, since there is little or no sensory feedback in terms of which an external, visually identified, determinate, objective location can be compared to an internal, kinaesthetically (or perceptually) identified, determinate, objective location.

But how does a grasping action identify its object, if not by simply locating it objectively in space? To find the answer to this question, we can look to recent empirical work by Goodale, Jakobson, and Keillor.[39] These authors have shown that there are measurable qualitative differences between natural grasping movements directed at an actual object and "pantomimed" movements directed toward a remembered object. When an actual object is present to be grasped, there are certain characteristic actions that subjects are seen to perform in the act of reaching for the object. For instance, among other things subjects typically scale their hand opening for object size and form their grip to correspond to the shape of the object. In pantomimed actions, on the other hand, when there is no object present, although the subjects continue to scale their hand opening, their grip formation differs significantly from that seen in normal target-directed actions.

This empirical result is interesting because it gives us some sense of the ways in which, in normal situations, the grasping act identifies the object it is directed toward. In normal circumstances the act of grasping a coffee mug is from the start scaled and formed in such a way as to take into account a multiplicity of aspects of the mug including, among other things, its size, shape, orientation, weight, fragility, and contents. This scaling and forming of the hand in the act of grasping is a way of identifying the object, since we scale and form our hands in different ways depending upon the object we are trying to grasp. And it is a much more sophisticated way of identifying the object than merely picking out its location in space, since it is dependent on many more aspects of the object in question. But most importantly, it is a way of identifying the object that makes sense of the phenomenological claim that "[f]rom the outset the grasping movement is magically at its completion."[40] This is because the scaling and forming of the hand is a measurable component of the grasping action that begins with the very initiation of movement toward the object to be grasped.

I have suggested that the scaling and forming of the hand in grasping is a sophisticated way of being directed toward an object that is not merely a way of locating the object objectively in space. The understanding of the "place" of an object that is inherent in the grasping actions directed toward it is properly spelled out not in terms of the objective location of the object, but rather in terms of the scaling and forming of the hand and the movements of the arm that are required to perform the grasping act successfully. This motor intentional understanding of the object is precisely not the kind of cognitive identification of it in terms of its objective location that is inherent in the current control phase of the cognitivist models of skillful grasping actions.

Having identified some phenomenological aspects of the understanding of an object inherent in the motor intentional act of grasping, I want to go on briefly to suggest that a neural network model of action can reproduce some of the most important features of this way of identifying an object. On the conceptualization of movement generation suggested by Borrett and Kwan,[41] a movement is conceived as the behavioral correlate of the evolution or relaxation of a recurrent neural network toward a fixed point attractor. Thus, the initial conditions of the network represent the initial position of the limb, the relaxation of the network toward the attractor state represents the movement of the limb, and the final state of the network at the fixed point attractor represents the position of the limb at its desired endpoint. The most important aspect of this proposal is that, after the network has been trained, whenever it is given a set of appropriate initial conditions its output will evolve in a manner representative of movement to the endpoint with no moment-to-moment supervisory mechanisms required to oversee its evolution.

On this interpretation of the neural net model of limb movement, the movement of the limb from initial position to endpoint occurs without the sensory feedback loop for the current control phase of the movement that is required by models like that proposed by Crossman and Goodeve; in fact, the whole idea of a two-phase process has been scrapped. In particular, there is no locating in relation to axes of co-ordinates in objective space since there is no representation of the objective location of the object in the model, and there is no error correction by means of feedback since there are no supervisory mechanisms by means of which such correction could occur.[42] Instead, the understanding of place reproduced by this model is one in which, as with grasping movements, the initial generation of the movement contains its completion in it. The initial conditions of the model, like the initial intention to grasp, is sufficient to ensure, in normal circumstances, that the limb will reach the appropriate endpoint in the appropriate way. In this sense we can say that the neural net model of limb movement reproduces the central phenomenological features of grasping behavior since, as with grasping, the model is from the outset "magically at its completion."

IV Conclusion

Merleau-Ponty argues that the phenomenological analysis of action indicates the need for a category of behavior that is between the purely reflexive and the properly cognitive. He calls this category motor intentional behavior, and he takes the grasping of an object to be a canonical example of this type of behavior. When we grasp an object we are directing ourselves toward it, and therefore the action is intentional. But grasping actions do not identify the object they are directed toward in terms of any of the objective, determinate features it has. In particular, they do not identify it in terms of its objective location, the way a pointing action might. Rather, grasping actions identify their object in terms of the bodily movements required to grasp it successfully—movements such as the shaping and forming of the hands. These actions are provisional and indeterminate in the sense that they change and develop throughout the course of the movement, only completely conforming to the object at the moment the grasping action is complete. It is this indeterminacy that leads Merleau-Ponty to say that the grasping action identifies its object "pre-predicatively": it does not give the kind of information about the object that could be made into a descriptive sentence about it.

If this phenomenological account of motor intentional behavior is accurate, then it is an important resource for those attempting to develop scientific models of actions like grasping an object. As Dreyfus's applied philosophy suggests, the conclusions of phenomenology provide the data for scientific explanations of human phenomena. In the instance we have discussed, the phenomenology of motor intentional behavior highlights a simple fact: that scientific models of action should not attempt to assimilate the explanation of grasping to that of its more cognitive cousin, pointing. It seems that grasping at straws is not only a canonical type of motor intentional behavior, it is also the desperate act of a cognitivist program going under for the last time.[43]

9

Four Kinds of Knowledge, Two (or Maybe Three) Kinds of Embodiment, and the Question of Artificial Intelligence

H. M. Collins

I What Computers Can't Do

After a lot of people told me I must, I read Bert Dreyfus's *What Computers Can't Do* in 1983.[1] It gave me a nasty shock. Here was a book which said what I wanted to say, but much better than I could say it, based on a deeper knowledge of the technicalities of computing and, to make matters worse, doing it in style. All I was left to do was mutter "yes," "he's right," "that's it," "he's got it," "I wish I'd said that," "damn!" and so on.

At that time, having being an academic for only ten years or so, I assumed that the business of criticizing artificial intelligence was now over. It seemed to me that as soon as the computer people had a chance to read the book carefully, they would give up. But it is never like that. The computer people came up with what they thought were counter-arguments. Granted, the counter-arguments were superficial and uncomprehending of the major points, but any port will do in an academic storm. Typically, the critics isolated the surface illustrations in their responses. For example, "Dreyfus says that computers will never reach such and such a level at chess, but this chess computer has done well, so Dreyfus must be wrong." The crucial issue, of course, was about computers' inability to play chess in a humanlike way; if it turned out that chess was the sort of game in which unexpectedly small amounts of unhumanlike brute strength processing could produce a victory, it was chess that we were learning about, not computers.

Luckily for me, the fact that Dreyfus's arguments did not sweep all before them in the way they would in the academic world of our dreams, meant that the opportunity to do more work remained. Nevertheless, the difficulty of saying anything that was not already in, or immanent in, Dreyfus's book was not reduced. That is one reason I am honored to be invited to contribute to this festschrift; I hope it means I have managed to find something additional to say about the topic of *What Computers Can't Do*. Of course, even my criticisms of the book are themselves a tribute; twenty-five years after its publication the book is still providing the agenda; it fought the hard battles which opened up the territory. *What Computers Can't Do* is the crucial criticism of brute AI, and the intellectual explanation of how AI's ambitions were bound, sooner or later, to change. It was Dreyfus who did the big thing first, best, and most influentially.

II   What Computers Can't Do Can't Do

1   Two Spy Stories and Four Kinds of Knowledge

Let us start by asking how knowledge is transferred.[2] Consider a couple of lighthearted but revealing accounts. A comic strip in my possession concerns industrial espionage between firms that manufacture expert systems. One firm has gained a lead in the market by developing super expert systems and another firm employs a spy to find out how they do it. The spy breaks into the other firm only to discover that they are capturing human experts, removing their brains, slicing them thin, and inserting the slices into their top-selling model. (Capturing the spy, they remove and slice his brain, enabling them to offer a line of industrial espionage expert systems!)

Another good story—the premise of a TV film—involves knowledge being transferred from one brain to another via electrical signals. A Vietnam veteran has been brainwashed by the Chinese with the result that his brain has become uniquely receptive. When one of those colander-shaped metal bowls is inverted on his head, and joined via wires, amplifiers, and cathode ray displays to an identical bowl on the head of some expert, the veteran speedily acquires all the expert's knowledge. He is then in a position to pass himself off as, say, a virtuoso racing driver, or champion tennis player, or whatever. Once equipped with someone else's abilities, the CIA can use him as a spy.[3]

The "double-colander" model is attractive because it is the way that we transfer knowledge between computers. When one takes the knowledge from one computer and puts it in another, the second computer "becomes" identical to the first as far as its abilities are concerned. Abilities are transferred between computers in the form of electrical signals transmitted along wires or recorded on floppy disks. We give one computer the knowledge of another every day of the week—the crucial point being that the hardware is almost irrelevant. In this way, we can transfer "*symbol-type knowledge.*"

i *Embodied Knowledge*

If we think a little harder about the transfer of symbol-type knowledge as it might apply to humans, we begin to notice complications. Let us imagine our Vietnam veteran having his brain loaded with the knowledge of a champion tennis player. He goes to serve in his first match—Wham!—his arm falls off. He just does not have the bone structure or muscular development to serve that hard. And then, of course, there is the matter of the structure of the nerves between brain and arm, and the question of whether the brain of the champion tennis player contains tennis-playing knowledge which is appropriate for someone of the size and weight of the recipient. A good part of the champion tennis player's tennis-playing "knowledge" is, it turns out, contained in the champion tennis player's body.[4]

What we have above is a literalist version of what is called "the embodiment thesis." A stronger form suggests that the way we cut up the physical world around us is a function of the shape of all our bodies. Thus, what we recognize as, say, a "chair"—something notoriously undefinable—is a function of our height, weight, and the way our knees bend. Thus both the way we cut up the world, and our ability to recognize the cuts, are consequences of the shape of our bodies.

We now have the beginnings of a classification system; there are some types of knowledge/ability/skill that cannot be transferred simply by passing signals from one brain/computer to another. In these types of knowledge the "hardware" is important whereas there are other types of knowledge that can be transferred without worrying about hardware.

ii Embrained Knowledge

Some aspects of the abilities/skills of humans are contained in the body. Could it be that there are types of knowledge that have to do with the *brain's* physicalness rather than its computerness? Yes: certain of our cognitive abilities have to do with the physical setup of the brain. There is the matter of the way neurons are interconnected, but it may also have something to do with the brain as a piece of chemistry or a collection of solid shapes. Templates, or sieves, can sort physical objects of different shapes or sizes; perhaps the brain works like this, or like the working medium of analogue computers. Let us call this kind of knowledge "embrained." It is interesting to note that insofar as knowledge is embrained (especially if this knowledge were stored "holographically," to use another metaphor), the comic book story—about brains being cut up and inserted into expert systems—would be a better way of thinking about knowledge transfer than the double-colander model.

iii Encultured Knowledge

We now have knowledge in symbols, in the body, and in the physical matter of the brain. What about the social group? Going back to our Vietnam veteran, suppose it were Ken Rosewall's brain from which his tennis-playing knowledge had been siphoned. How would he cope with the new fiber-glass rackets and all the modern swearing, shouting, and grunting? Though the constitutive rules of tennis have remained the same over the last fifty years, the game has changed enormously. The right way to play tennis has to do with tennis-playing society as well as brains and bodies.

Natural languages are, of course, the paradigm example of bits of social knowledge. The right way to speak is the prerogative of the social group not the individual; those who do not remain in contact with the social group will soon cease to know how to speak properly. "To be or not to be, that is the question," on the face of it, a stultifyingly vacuous phrase, may be uttered without fear of ridicule on all sorts of occasions because of the cultural aura which surrounds Shakespeare, *Hamlet*, and all that. "What will it be then, my droogies?" may not be uttered safely, though it could have been for a short while after 1962. Let us agree for the sake of argument that when William Shakespeare and Anthony Burgess first wrote those phrases, their language-influencing ambitions were similar. That the first has become a lasting part of common speech and the second has not, has to do with the way literate society has gone.[5] One can see, then, that there is an "encultured" element to language and to other kinds of knowledge; it changes as society changes, it could not be said to exist without the existence of the social group that has it; it is located in society. Variation over time is, of course, only one element of social embeddedness.[6]

We now have four kinds of knowledge/abilities/skills:

1. Symbol-type knowledge (That is, knowledge that can be transferred without loss on floppy disks and so forth.)

2. Embodied knowledge

3. Embrained knowledge

4. Encultured knowledge

What Computers Can't Do showed that the early ambitions of AI researchers were based on the idea that all knowledge was of type 1, but that since this kind of knowledge is only a small part of human abilities, their ambitions would fail; this is the key insight. Where the book went wrong was to put too much stress in the early and subsequent arguments on knowledge types 2 and 3 and not enough on type 4.

2 The Artificial Intelligence Problem and Spell-checkers

Just like Dreyfus, I want to argue about what computers can and can't do and just like Dreyfus, I want to use, not abstract arguments alone, but examples. The simpler the example the better. Now, the "artificial intelligence problem" is like a hologram—the whole of it can be recognized in any of its parts, however small; let us establish this first.

To establish the point I will take a very small bit of the problem—spell-checking. Spell-checking, one might think, is hardly artificial intelligence at all, because it is merely a matter of comparing one list of typed words with another. Certainly the spell-checking problem has none of the horrendous difficulties of, say, speech transcription. The input for a spell-checker is constrained and filtered by a keyboard which forces writers to organize their input into strings chosen from one hundred or so discrete signals. In contrast, speech transcription, a typically "difficult" AI problem, starts with the need to separate out words from a continuous train of air vibrations without any natural separators, in which every speaker's input is markedly different. To a computer, the key strokes of one person are very much like the key strokes of another; but one person's spoken sounds, thought of as physical signals, are very different from those of another person even when they are saying what would be the same words if typed out. Likewise, the same sentence spoken at different times by the same person could look completely different if the waveform was represented on an oscilloscope. It is because spell-checkers appear so simple—and are so much a matter of manipulating ready-made symbols—that they are an excellent case for establishing that the AI problem has a holographic character.

Here is the AI problem as it appears for the spell-checker. Consider the following test-sentence for spell-checking:

My spell-checker will correct weerd processor but won't correct weird processor.

This sentence does contain the truth for current spell-checkers: since "weird" is spelled correctly, current spell-checkers will allow "weird processor" to pass without note, whereas "weerd processor" will be flagged or corrected.

To those who have not noticed the difficult problem of AI, this seems like a technical matter. One way to fix it is to make the dictionaries larger so that common pairings of words are also checked. A spell-checker using such an enlarged dictionary would notice that there was something wrong with "weird processor." But that is not the difficult problem. The difficult problem is that every word in the example is spelled exactly as I want it for the purpose of writing this passage, so a really "intelligent" spell-checker must flag nothing at all—neither weird processor nor weerd processor. To manage that—something that a human editor would accomplish without remark—the spell-checker would have to understand the meaning of the whole passage. And to understand the meaning of the whole passage, the spell-checker would have to be just as well-educated, and just as familiar with the English language, as you and I. Thus, the big problem for AI—such as is evident in the speech transcription—can be found even in as small and easy a job as spell-checking.

Interestingly, this analysis shows that the ability to spell-check or otherwise edit passages of typed text containing novel mistakes is a much better test of "machine intelligence" than any of the much-hyped but ill-understood versions of the "Turing test." For a Turing test to be really telling you something, one has to know whether the apparent conversational success could have been achieved by brute strength methods or by unconsciously overcharitable interpretations on the part of the judges. The approach put forward here puts the onus of interpretation onto the computer.[7]

There is an easier problem for AI, which is making machines that work satisfactorily. For chess-winning machines, that has almost been solved. For spell-checking it has been solved since, for example, WORD6's spell-checker came on the market. WORD6 does not try to correct the words, but merely flags those which do not match its dictionary. All the intelligent stuff—all the understanding of meanings, and recognition of context, and so forth—is left to the human, and that is a very good arrangement.

III Kinds of Knowledge Revisited

1 The "Social Embodiment Thesis," the "Individual Embodiment Thesis," and the "Minimal Embodiment Thesis"

With the artificial intelligence problem understood through the simple spell-checker example, let us work through the last three types of knowledge again. Wittgenstein said that if a lion could speak we would not understand it. More to the point in respect of this example, if a lion could speak, it still could not edit text. Take the example of text offered above. To edit it you have to understand it, and to understand it you have to know what a word processor is, and to know what a word processor is you have to know about typing. Now, lions, not having fingers, almost certainly would not have writing even if they had speech. Lions would almost certainly have an oral culture only because of the way their legs end. So the "form of life" of lions would include no concept of writing, no concept of typing, and no concept of word processing. Thus lions, even those who lived in speaking-lion society, would be nonstarters when it came to spell-checking sentences like the test sentence. Note that there is no reason to suppose that pigeons as we know them, with no oral culture, could not be trained to get it nearly as right as current computers, give and take a few quantitative measures; pigeons can do a lot of tasks without understanding them, just as computers can. And even nonspeaking lions, we might suppose, with enough training, and supplied with big foot-operated pedals, could do as well as pigeons. The question concerns the kind of spell-checking that *does* depend on understanding writing.

That lions could not spell-check the test sentence because of the way their legs end is an example of the "embodiment thesis": the conceptual structure of our world is, in part, a function of the way our bodies are arranged. But while this argument is sometimes correct, it confuses two quite distinct embodiment theses. There is what I will call the "social embodiment thesis" and the "individual embodiment thesis." Let us see how these theses apply to lions who can speak.

The social embodiment thesis is what, without knowing it, we have been describing above. We can be reasonably sure that a society made up of speaking lions would not understand word processors because their legs are different from our arms and hands. But what about a single lion? Suppose we kidnap a newborn speaking lion and give it to human parents to care for and raise. We know that the lion will not learn to type, and probably will not learn to write, but this cannot exclude it from understanding the concepts of typing, writing, and word processing unless we also want to say that a human with serious congenital malformations of the upper limbs will never understand typing, writing, and word processing. I do not know whether it is true or not, but I would certainly bet that there are those who cannot write because of such malformations who can still read and, therefore, can still edit. I would bet that there are those with such malformations who could understand the test sentence and who could edit it, in a way that no foreseeable spell-checker could.

In *What Computers Still Can't Do*, Dreyfus says:

Since it turns out that pattern recognition is a bodily skill basic to all intelligent behavior, the question of whether artificial intelligence is possible boils down to the question of whether there can be an artificial embodied agent. (250)

Editing the test sentence is a pattern recognition problem—pattern recognition is just another piece of the AI "hologram"—so Dreyfus is implying with the above claim that an artificially embodied agent would be needed to edit or do the equivalent of editing the test-sentence. What is more, he remarked earlier in the book:

What makes an object a *chair* is its function, and what makes possible its role as equipment for sitting is its place in a total practical context. This presupposes certain facts about human beings (fatigue, the way the body bends), and a network of other culturally determined equipment (tables, floors, lamps), and skills (eating, writing, going to conferences, giving lectures, etc.) (237)

At worst, this must be taken to imply that the test sentence for word processors could be edited only by one who had the proper limb ends. At best it means that the two kinds of embodiment thesis have not been separated in his argument. Whichever, it means that Dreyfus winds up making too strong a claim about the need for a machine which is to have an intelligence like ours to have a body like ours.

I do not think there is anything in the embodiment thesis to show that the congenitally physically challenged, speaking lions which have been brought up by humans, or gray stationary metal boxes could not have intelligence like ours. There is everything to show that *societies* of such entities would not have intelligences like ours, but that is another matter. The questions that have to be asked about individual entities are to do with their upbringing and linguistic socialization.

Having said all this, I discover that I do not believe it in its entirety. In particular, I do not believe that a stationary gray metal box could really become fully socialized just through linguistic interaction. Imagine a human who was subject to total sensory deprivation from birth except for conversational input and output—it is hard to imagine he or she becoming socially fluent. A gray stationary metal box with the right kind of brain would be much like such a sensorily deprived human. Here I am more or less agreeing with Dreyfus's response to my criticism of his version of the embodiment thesis; he says a body needs an inside and an outside, a sense of balance, the ability to move around obstacles, and so forth.[8] I have to agree that intelligences need enough of a body to have some sensory inputs or they would never make any sense of the conversations in which they were trying to take part. But this is a minimal requirement and it is important not to confuse it with the more ambitious claim that to be socialized you need to have a body that is similar in shape to the bodies of those that are socializing you. To repeat, it seems to me that shape of body is important for the collective embodiment thesis but not for the individual embodiment thesis. For the individual embodiment thesis the requirement is a minimal body with some sensory mechanisms. Lions and the congenitally physically challenged are well equipped in this respect. Thus the acceptable part of the individual embodiment thesis should really be called the "minimal embodiment thesis" thesis.

In sum, all an intelligence needs is enough of a body to be potentially socialized; it does not need the kind of body that will fit it to a particular kind of social fluency. Previous arguments, which seem to show that entities with radically different bodily forms cannot be socialized in the same way as humans, confuse the social embodiment thesis and the individual embodiment thesis.

2   The Embrainment Thesis

There is a claim, though I have never understood it fully, that the chemicals of which the brain is constituted are important. More substantial is the argument that the potential of an artificial brain depends crucially on the way its components are arranged. In a trivial sense, both of these claims must be correct. Thus, John Searle tells us that if a "brain" were made out of old tin cans it would be absurd to think it could work in the same way as a real brain—but this problem might simply arise out of the size of old tin cans. Obviously, a "chip" made out of a million or so old tin cans and their associated connections would be very large, very energy inefficient, and very unreliable compared to a chip with a million transistors etched on its surface. So the intelligent machine made out of old tin cans might be absurd, but no more absurd than Babbage's intelligent machine made out of thousands of brass gear-wheels; this kind of absurdity does not cut much philosophical ice. We are here sailing among the icebergs of necessary and sufficient. It may be necessary for an intelligent machine to be made of small, nonmechanical components, but this does not show that there is anything sufficient, or even anything necessary about any *particular* kind of small nonmechanical components. For example, there is nothing in the argument that makes us prefer wet components over dry ones.

But the argument for a certain kind of *arrangement* of small nonmechanical components is more content-filled and persuasive than this. The argument has come to have salience because of the development of so-called "neural nets." Neural nets, to use the anthropomorphic language of AI, are arrangements of components with some similarity to the arrangement of components in the brain. That is, they have artificial "neurones" linked to other artificial neurones, via links whose connectivity is affected by variable "weights." Certain neurones in one "layer" can cause more or fewer neurones in another layer to "fire," depending on how useful such firing has proved to be in the past. The whole neural net is presented with a task and initially its neurones are set to fire at random. But whenever a desired output is produced, some feedback is given to the system that encourages it to strengthen the connections that fired so as to produce the desired outcome. After many iterations, these systems can "learn" certain tasks involving discrimination and "pattern recognition." An example of their abilities that is often cited is the discrimination of objects on the sea bed, specifically, rocks and explosive mines. The nets, it is said, given sufficient training, can use visual and sonar information to tell the difference between rocks and mines.

The attractive thing about neural nets, which make Bert Dreyfus think they are something significantly new, is that the rules for the tasks the net learns never have to be made explicit. Nets have to be supplied only with varying degrees of reinforcement or discouragement depending on the promise of their current output and they will "work out the rules for themselves." One might even want to say that, like humans under a Wittgensteinian way of thinking, the nets do not use explicable rules at all. Or, as Dreyfus argues, that the rules that they do use are not functions of the objects for which we have names but some less explicable congeries of information.

Again, we have to separate the necessary from the sufficient. It is certainly true, as the Dreyfusian analysis reminds us, that human knowledge is not based on explicit rule following. Thus, if an intelligent computer is to have humanlike knowledge, it will be more like a neural net than a symbol manipulator, but it does not follow that a neural netlike machine moves us any significant distance toward humanlike abilities. Here we can draw on the analogy that Dreyfus used to such devastating effect in respect of GOFAI (Good Old Fashioned AI): neural nets may be like stepping from the floor onto a chair—they bring us nearer the moon—but a pile of chairs will not get us all the way.

One of Dreyfus's own examples is revealing of the limitations of neural nets. He explains that the army, faced with the problem of automating the task of seeing camouflaged tanks hidden in forests, trained a neural net on a set of images until it could discriminate faultlessly. Unfortunately, when it then moved on to a new set of images it failed. Only then was it realized that all the tank photographs in the original set were taken in one kind of weather, while all the nontank photographs were taken in another. The neural net had learned to distinguish weather not tanks!

I would argue that this neural net failed in the task because its training was so impoverished. Again, it had been trained like a pigeon—via stimulus and response—whereas humans are trained through socialization, which involves far richer mechanisms that we do not understand. Even human beings do not learn to discriminate properly if they are trained through a purely stimulus-response regime. Humans who are separated from human society until a late age exemplify the point—so would a human trained only in the same way as a neural net. Thus, the improvement over symbolic AI that neural nets represent is not actually in the direction of human-type non-rule-explication but is, rather, in the direction of pigeon-type non-rule-explication—which is not very exciting, and has not much to do with the later Wittgenstein's view of the world.

Going back to the rock-mine discriminator, the task may be doable by a machine so long as the circumstances remain limited, but what happens when the enemy starts to disguise mines as rocks? A human given the task would then start searching for all kinds of other cues, from the changing political environment, to the disposition of the enemy's forces within the particular battlefield. The rock-mine problem, as it is usually described, is the kind of dream problem— or micro-world—invented by generals fighting the last war. In the next war the problem will not take such a neat form and to deal with it, much more than local knowledge designed for a circumscribed task will be needed.[9] The rock-mine problem is, once again, congruent with the spell-checker problem. Given a circumscribed task, a neural net-based spell-checker could soon learn to spell. Given a world in which it is always possible to invent new sentences that require the whole context to be understood the neural net would not get far. To get as far as a human the net would have to be continually immersed in the social world in the way that a human is immersed, and be able to learn from it in the way that a human learns.

Neural net knowledge is, arguably, differently embrained from GOFAI knowledge but, since neural nets are no nearer to full socialization in human society than the top of a chair is nearer to the moon than the floor it stands on, it is hard to see what the fuss is about. A socializable machine will surely have to be able to use rules that it cannot explicate, but this does not mean that a machine that uses rules that it cannot explicate is anything like a socializable machine; a socializable machine will have to have a brain that is capable of allowing it to be socialized like a human but, as the next example shows, having a neural net as a brain is by no means a sufficient condition.

3 The "Socialness" Thesis

Let us now consider certain entities that fulfill every necessary condition of artificial intelligence so far discussed. The entities in question have superb bodies with full mobility and the developed ability to find their way around the world; they have brains with many more neurones than even the most ambitious silicon brain-builder dreams of; for what it is worth, their brains are made from the same kind of wetware as the brains of humans; they are self-programming, make use of rules they cannot explicate; and, finally, beyond anything we have discussed so far, many examples have been exposed to exactly the same training regime as young human beings. The entities are domestic dogs.

Domestic dogs show why all these features of artificially intelligent entities are not sufficient, because even when put together properly and placed in the right environment, dogs still cannot edit. We know that editing would not be included within the form of life of dog-society because of what is not on the end of their legs—fingers—but individual domestic dogs are given all the advantages that our imaginary individual speaking-lion was given: they are snatched from the cradle at or near birth and brought up in human families, many getting more love and attention than a fair proportion of human children. But something is still missing.

Dogs cannot even tidy up your room—a task for which they are admirably physically equipped. And this is because tidying the room means knowing what counts as dirty and what counts as clean, and what counts as in place and what counts as out of place. Distinguishing such things—like the test sentence for word processors—is another view of the AI-problem hologram; to know what counts one has to understand the whole context. "Rubbish" and "antique" are categories that continually shift both in time and space. Even something as ephemeral as the newspaper changes its value as the events it records change. Most issues of yesterday's newspaper are rubbish, but those recording momentous events, such as great victories or crimes, gain a sentimental value, or become memorabilia or collectors' items. To know which newspapers to dump and which to keep, the dog would have to be able to read the stories and to know what they meant in terms of what was going on in the world. Unlike our imaginary lion, the domestic dog does not come from speaking-dog society, it comes from ordinary dog society, and ordinary dogs have something missing in spite of what seem to be highly promising brains.

Unfortunately, what dogs have missing is something of a mystery. What dogs have missing is a bit like gravity was for Newton—a force whose influence was readily recognizable by its effects but whose content was "action at a distance." What dogs have missing is "social-ness." Socialness is the capacity of humans (and perhaps some other entities), which enables them to attain social fluency in one or more cultures.[10] (I say "perhaps some other entities" because the jury is still out in the case of chimpanzees and dolphins. We are still trying to work out if chimpanzees and dolphins have socialness by trying to teach them our culture and language.[11])

Socialness is a potential that is not always realized: feral children—those who have been separated from human society from birth until some later age, have, it seems, lost the capacity for social intercourse, though they must have had it at one stage and, presumably, all the physical components are still in place. Not all humans have their full share of socialness: persons with autism may not have as much poten-tial for acquiring forms of life as other humans. It may also be that the capacity to take part in a culture may be lost as a result of damage to the frontal lobes. The test of whether an entity has socialness is to expose it to a human culture—through the ordinary processes of socialization—and see whether social abilities are acquired. So far as I know, no artificially intelligent machine has even the beginnings of this capacity.

The question to ask about each new generation of potentially intel-ligent machines, then, is not whether they have robotic abilities—dogs have this but cannot edit. The question is not whether they have their artificial neurones arranged this way or that—dogs have a splen-did arrangement of neurones but cannot tidy. The question is not whether the brain is made of this kind of substance or that—dogs have splendid brain stuff, but cannot speak. The question is whether the new machines can be socialized. It does not matter whether they are stationary metal boxes; it does not matter how their neurones are arranged; and it does not matter what their "brains" are made of; if they cannot be socialized they will not be able to fix the test sentence for word processors and its equivalents. The potential to be socialized is what one needs to ask about in order to answer the big question of AI.

To answer smaller questions about AI—namely, what can computers do? one also needs to know about society. Dreyfus's great book remains great for telling us what computers can't do, but it never was very good at saying what they can do, because it was too concerned with cognitive matters and individuals and not concerned enough with interactions. The spell-checker on my WORD6 word processor is a terrific program because of the way it interacts with me—leaving me to do the hard bit while quietly doing all the mechanical stuff like looking up words in the dictionary. To know what computers *can* do one has to understand how the mechanizable and the non-mechanizable blend in ordinary human activity, and how this blend might change over time. This is not a trivial task. Furthermore, it is a task for the observer and analyst of human activity rather than the analyst of the brain or the mind.[12]

IV   Conclusion

What Computers Can't Do remains the classic critique of artificial intelligence. It showed that symbolic AI failed to encompass what was special about human accomplishments. I have argued, however, that the book placed too much emphasis on individual humans—their bodies and their brains—and insufficient emphasis on human society. An intelligence must have the right kind of brain, and the right kind of body to be socialized; we still have no idea how to design the former, while the latter leaves room for great variation in bodily form. The position developed within *What Computers Can't Do* and its successors overemphasizes the contribution of neural nets to brainlikeness and confuses *the individual embodiment thesis, the social embodiment thesis,* and *the minimal embodiment thesis.*

Because of its emphasis on action rather than interaction, *What Computers Can't Do* is also not very good at telling us what computers *can* do. It is not able to make good predictions about the way computers will develop as tools rather than mimics of human abilities. To correct the mistakes in emphasis, and to develop the critique into a more accurate predictor, we need to know more about how humans act within societies. We need to know when humans act like machines, and when they will be ready to act like machines even if they act like humans now. We need to know when and where humans will be ready to work in partnership with machines—supplying the social skills while the machines supply the brute strength. For these things we need a new theory of human action.

Such a new theory of human action would allow us to understand better the shifting patterns and manner of execution of various human competences. It would help us understand the manner and potential for the delegation of our competences to symbols, computers, and other machinery, as well as the moments when that potential is absent or undesirable. It would also help us see the ways in which machines are better than humans: it would show that many of the things that humans do, they do because they are unable to function in the machinelike way that they would prefer. We would notice, then, what humans are good at and what machines are good at, and how these competences meet in the changing pattern of human activity. The analysis of skill, knowledge, human abilities, or whatever one wants to call the sets of activities for which we use our minds and bodies, must start from a theory of action in society, not the abilities of the individuals.[13]

Semiartificial Intelligence

Albert Borgmann

The thesis that much of Hubert Dreyfus's work has revolved about is simple and direct. As the title of his classic 1967 paper has it, "Computers Must Have Bodies to be Intelligent." Dreyfus outlined some of the crucial reasons why this is so in 1967 already; hence the full title of his article reads "Why Computers Must Have. . . ." He has since provided a wealth of observations and arguments to bolster his thesis, and by now, as he has said in the most recent edition of his book on the subject, his position is no longer controversial but amounts to "a view of a bygone period of history."[1]

Though Dreyfus's thesis can now be regarded as established and there is closure on the issue, Dreyfus's work on artificial intelligence has always had and has to this day a wider and at least threefold significance. First, as the quotation above suggests, it constitutes a chapter in the history of ideas. It is a story with an exemplary protagonist and an enduring moral. Artificial intelligence as a goal and enterprise began with a plausible claim of bringing scientific light to one of the last dark corners of modern culture. What all these tenebrous regions have in common is a seemingly mysterious complexity, and the several kindred campaigns of enlightenment have names like cybernetics, information theory, catastrophe theory, systems theory, cellular automata or artificial life, neural nets, chaos theory, and complexity theory. Dreyfus had turned his attention to the apparently best defined and certainly most fascinating dark spot— human intelligence, and in his 1972 *What Computers Can't Do* gave a classic description of the characteristic pathology of these movements. They begin as grand programs based on some formal or scientific discipline. They furnish striking illustrations and first steps of their ambitious project. Then progress stalls. Instead of breakthroughs there is more and more tedium. At length the limited gains and insights are consolidated into more or less helpful additions to our store of knowledge.[2] The grand claims fall silent, ambition evaporates and is exhausted. Terra incognita remains what it was.[3]

Second, Dreyfus's work on artificial intelligence remains a significant contribution to philosophical anthropology. The contrast with computers and programs enabled Dreyfus to bring the human condition into uniquely clear relief. Dreyfus showed how integral the human body is to the way we take in the world, how our embodied needs organize a situation, and how our situation connects up with the world through an inexhaustible tissue of practices.

Third and most important, the fusion of the first two points of significance issues in a deep diagnosis and therapy of contemporary culture. It is not just scientific programs that aim at taking control of what look like superannuated fortresses of mystery and complexity. There is a tendency in the technological culture entire to be rid of regions beyond our domination and manipulation. Dreyfus in an exemplary way has shown that such a final victory is an illusion and that the consequence of the appropriate disillusionment need not be obscurantism or resignation but intelligent acceptance. The practices that constitute the backdrop of human life are inexhaustible, to be sure, but they are not unintelligible. We can illuminate, evaluate, and cultivate practices and make them conducive to being at home in the world.

A spirit of clarification and a sense of clarity pervade Dreyfus's work in artificial intelligence. But this clarity has lately been overtaken by a peculiar ambiguity that has arisen from the convergence of work in artificial intelligence with the culture of technology at large. Technology as a form of life does not refute its adversaries but attempts to circumvent and obviate them. Thus the ambiguity in question (I will call it virtual ambiguity) does not so much refute Dreyfus's position as it appears to make it irrelevant. On reflection it turns out, however, that Dreyfus's core insight helps us to dispel the ambiguity, and it does so when we transpose it from the descriptive to the moral key, from a finding to a norm.

Virtual ambiguity appears most clearly in Multi-User Domains. A MUD, so called, is a domain in cyberspace that is accessible via the keyboard and the screen of a computer connected to the Internet. The medium is typed messages. In a MUD one is free to stylize one's personality at will, and one engages other people, similarly stylized, in conversation. Sherry Turkle reports on a MUD that contains a housekeeping program, a bot, named Julia.[4] In addition to providing information about the MUD and keeping order, Julia can flirt and talk about hockey. "Julia is able," says Turkle, "to fool some of the people some of the time into thinking she is a human player."[5] One actual player by the name of Barry pursued Julia for over a month without realizing that she is a piece of software.

If after five minutes of questioning Julia leaves three out of ten of her suitors wondering whether she is a human being or not, she has passed the Turing test as originally stipulated by A. M. Turing.[6] Has Dreyfus been proven wrong after all? Julia does not converse on the strength of the deep syntactic and semantic grasp humans have of language. Rather she scours the surface of the messages she receives for clues that match a long list of largely precooked replies.[7] When all else fails, she can fall back on tricks of delay, humor, and sarcasm that mask breaks in the flow of her replies.

Julia has no body that could mark the center of a world. The material and moral coherence of a world discloses itself only to the profound sensibility of a mindful body and the endless reach of an embodied mind. Hence the world that appears in her language cracks and collapses when she misreads an ambiguous clue or cannot find a clue and gives a reply that fails to fit the imaginary context of her chatter. That context is in any case dependent on the principle of charity, the advance of credibility and coherence her conversation partners must provide to supply background, implicit detail, and solicitous interpretations of her remarks. We come by that principle easily and naturally so that even in metadiscourse Sherry Turkle and this author refer to Julia as "she" and would find it jarring to use the neuter pronoun. Not surprisingly, on those occasions when the principle is strained beyond belief, Julia at times gets out of her impasse by presuming heavily on her partner's sympathy. She comes out with a remark that covers symptoms of artificiality with a protest of bodily sensibility. Thus Julia distracts Barry from his suspicion that he is talking to software by telling him: "I have PMS today, Barry."[8]

Although human intelligence and embodiment are coextensive, there are distinct aspects of mind and body. The receptive and sensible side of intelligence, called *intellectus passivus* by the scholastics, is closer to the senses, the size, and the mobility of the body while the spontaneous and comprehending side of intelligence, the *intellectus agens*, is closer to the body's brain. These are sides of one continuum. But it makes sense to distinguish them because the former is more accessible than the latter. The more strictly cognitive dimension of human intelligence is known to us at the top and at the bottom. We can comprehend the cognitive accomplishments of the brain—mathematical proofs, scientific theories, empirical reports, etc.—and we understand the brain's biochemistry and physiology to a fair level of complexity. But how, and which, neurons accomplish something like the demonstration of the Pythagorean theorem is as yet utterly mysterious.

Thus the *intellectus agens* is evident in the capacities of human intelligence, in the kinds of problems it can solve. As Dreyfus makes clear, the core of the *intellectus agens* supervenes on the human body and therefore lies beyond simulation by way of hardware and software. Its boundaries are still being defined, however. When we learn that a certain kind of brute force computer science surpasses the best of human beings in playing chess or reading electrocardiograms, we learn something new about minds and computers.[9] Moreover, though simulation of the *intellectus agens* is impossible, some semblance can be produced under certain conditions, and advances in computer science and technology will make such semblances more deceptive.

It is otherwise with the *intellectus passivus*. The sensible and receptive side of intelligence is evident more in its location than its capacities. Embodied intelligence takes up space and time in the distinctive way that marks the standpoint of a situation and of a narrative. Since reality is a plenum, it leaves no empty slots that artificial intelligences could claim as their place and story. Capacities can be faked for a while, locations far less so. If Julia claimed she was a Wall Street lawyer who had a season ticket for the New York Rangers, a resolute and resourceful Barry could make a list of all Wall Street lawyers with the first name of Julia, obtain a list of the New York Rangers season ticket holders and look for a match. If he failed to find one and would press Julia for additional personal information, Julia's programmer would have to choose between obliging Barry with more red herrings or pulling Julia back behind a denser veil of ambiguity. At length Barry would find himself disillusioned in the former case, and frustrated in the latter.

Why is it, then, that Barry fails to notice Julia's lack of location till finally the deficiency of her capacities catches up with her to reveal her software identity? Entry into the cyberspace of a MUD encourages if it does not prescribe the forfeiting of one's location. Since one enters a MUD in a disembodied state one cannot import one's bodily location. One's tie to reality is loosened and one's standpoint fades into an indistinct background. Barry fails to notice Julia's groundlessness because he and she have met at a point they have reached from opposite directions. The insubstantial program, named Julia, has been given a half-intelligent pretense of a place in this world while the substantial Barry has so detached himself from his location in reality that his half-artificial intelligence has retained the mere penumbra of a place in the world. A semiartificial intelligence sees his reflection in an artificial semi-intelligence. The region where the two come to resemble one another is virtual ambiguity.

Traditionally, ambiguity has implied a corrective norm—clarity. Ambiguity has been an indication of imperfection. The symbolic ambiguity of texts, scores, or plans is resolved through realization, through an enlargement or enrichment of reality that is instructed by cultural information. The ambiguity of an actual situation is resolved through engagement with an existing reality, with the wilderness we are disagreed about, the urban life we are unsure of, or the people we do not understand. In either case, the resolution of ambiguity leads to clarity—the splendor of reality.

The ambiguity of a MUD, however, is at least at first thought to be a positive and in fact glamorous phenomenon. It promises to combine what in the real world is forever separate and antagonistic—unencumbered freedom and intense engagement. When reality begins to dissolve, so do our obligations and burdens. That detachment from reality (experienced as liberty) and ambiguity increase jointly is clear from the technical sense of ambiguity in information theory. Consider for illustration the community hospital in Bullfrog, Montana, where during the day four physicians are in attendance whose names happen to be Alfred, Alice, Alphonso, and Alexandra. One of them is as likely as another to be called to the emergency room by a jovial nurse who likes to tease his doctors and call them by nicknames and abbreviations, "Paging Doctor Fred," "Paging Doctor Sandy," and so on. One day the nurse needs to call Doctor Alphonso and says on the public address system: "Paging Doctor Alfie, paging Doctor Alfie." Whatever the intention, the signal is ambiguous. It could refer to Alfred as well as Alphonso and is only half as informative as, say, "Paging Doctor Fonz." Failing to get a prompt response, the nurse gets urgent and shouts, "Paging Doctor Al, Paging Doctor Al." Within the context of paging a physician at the hospital, this signal is entirely ambiguous and carries no information at all. In an unambiguous signal, there is a firm tie between information and reality. "Paging Doctor Alphonso" makes for a tight connection between the emergency room and the physician who is needed there. In "Paging Doctor Alfie" the bond has been loosened. It still conveys some information, viz., "The physician who is needed is not Alice or Alexandra; it is either Alfred or Alphonso." In "Paging Doctor Al" the connection, under the particular circumstances, has snapped. There is no information.

Similarly, to the extent that players in a MUD have no location in the world, what they say about themselves or to one another tells us little or nothing about reality. In that sense MUD language is uninformative. To the extent, however, that a MUD is a self-contained universe of discourse, it holds the promise of rich and exciting contents of its own. Release from the obligations of reality allows for the free play of imagination and desire. Thus a man of conventional cast in real life can explore in a MUD his feminine or homosexual side, his amorous dreams, his desire for power or acclaim and so enlarge and enrich the scope of his experience. And more than exploration is possible. A woman can shift her very center of gravity from reality to virtuality and feel most fully alive when she moves in virtual space. Virtual ambiguity seems to be a burst of fluorescence that dispels the darkness of ordinary life and reveals another more luminous reality.

Reflection shows, however, that virtual ambiguity, when accepted for what it is, renders virtual reality trivial, and, when pressed for its promise of engagement, evaporates. The truly gripping stories about the virtual reality of MUDs are accounts that chronicle not the enduring splendor of virtual ambiguity, but its painful dissolution. Of course ambiguity can be sustained if participants in a MUD engage in trivial exchanges. To lead a life of many and diverse roles is possible as long as only one of the roles truly matters. A married graduate student may live the life of a medical doctor on some MUD and pursue a courtship ending with a wedding on another. Such games are feasible as long as they are walled off from actual life and kept barren of real consequences. But if the student were to lead a really polymorphous life, he would be taken to court for practicing without a license and polygamy. The human body with all its heaviness and frailty marks the origin of the coordinate space we inhabit.

Sooner or later, the gravity of their bodily existence pulls MUD players through the veil of virtual ambiguity into the entanglements of ordinary life. Sometimes a player is cast out of his virtual seclusion when his wife discovers his amorous multiplicity. More often, players get impatient with the vacancy of virtuality and allow themselves to be drawn into reality. They set out to meet the enchanting MUD persona face to face. Or they try to satisfy their hunger for reality by devouring the promise of actuality that comes with a new MUD friendship. As soon as the thrill of novelty is gone and the specter of virtual vacuity rises, they move on, endlessly reenacting their quest for real engagement.

When players decide to leave the MUD in search of the real person who has a place in reality, a standpoint vis-à-vis the world, and the depth and gravity of an actual person, they are usually disappointed by the relative drabness and heaviness of the human being they encounter.[10] At the leading edge of technological culture, however, one kind of ambiguity is followed by another, virtual ambiguity by commodified ambiguity.

Albert Borgmann

Imagine Barry encounters Jackie in his MUD. Her glamorous cyberambiguity promises to open up into reality. She agrees to meet Barry at a restaurant in downtown Manhattan, and sure enough, there she sits at the appointed table, every bit as athletic and resplendent as advertised. Barry is delighted but soon wonders: how old is she? Definitely not in her twenties. So is she 35 or 45 or 55? How can he tell? In William Gibson's *Neuromancer*,[11] science fiction has provided for the possibility of more than the surgical tightening of skin and removal of fat and the sculpting of one's body through carefully administered training. One can select and acquire an entirely new body. It will exhibit in the flesh the grace and vigor that are stipulated in a MUD by mere words. This radical reshaping implies the liberation of one's body from all traces of one's ancestry, age, or frailty. Such unresolvable ambiguity of one's body amounts to an ontologically novel perfection. Yet it is one of the shrewd insights of Gibson's that this cannot be so. The novel's antihero, Case, encounters two men who

sat side by side on the couch, their arms crossed over tanned chests, identical gold chains slung around their necks. Case peered at them and saw that their youth was counterfeit, marked by a certain telltale corrugation at the knuckles, something the surgeons were unable to erase.[12]

In our less advanced world, there will be many more of these telltale remainders and reminders.[13] Thus the commodified beauty of surgically restyled men and women may leave us undecided between admiration for their money and boldness and pity for their wearing a deceptive shell. Commodified ambiguity, of course, is not restricted to human beings. Barry may have been wondering whether the flowers on the table were artificial or not, whether he should have sugar or Sweet 'n Lo and cream or creamer in his coffee, whether the chairs were covered with leather or plastic, etc. Human ambiguity is of course the most troubling and in the end the least sustainable. At length human frailty will overcome training regimens and cosmetics, the half-credible beauty of a face will yield to an incredible mask and finally to calamitously unnatural devastation. And then comes death, the defeat rather than the conclusion of a life. Not surprisingly, cyberspace casts its ambiguous glow over death, trying to wrest it from the dying person's incontinence, irritability, and incoherence and making it a sweetly shared experience.[14]

In the face of death, artificial intelligence seems to regain once more its original ambition, and in defiance of everything Dreyfus has said, it promises nothing less than immortality. The idea is again that the core of a person's personality is one's mental life and that the latter can be captured without remainder in some program. To this is added the prognostication that this program can in its entirety be transferred from one substrate to another, again and again, for ever and ever.[15]

There is no question, to be sure, that Dreyfus's thesis of the essential embodiment of human intelligence stands. But we are now in a position to see that we can deny though not refute the thesis by disembodying our intelligence in cyberspace and commodifying our bodies in reality. For a person who lives in these ways, the thesis that intelligence is essentially embodied and the body is the disclosure of how we are located in the world is no longer a description but the prediction of a dire truth that will implacably catch up with people when they age and die. Full embodiment is no longer the character of one's life but one's eventual fate of descending into the hell of senility and mortality.

The better alternative is to embrace Dreyfus's thesis as a norm to be lived: our body should neither be denied in cyberspace nor should it conceal the place and particularly the time we occupy in the world. "T[here] is a depth to love conferred by time," says Charles Taylor by way of an aside.[16] If we ponder the resonance this remark leaves us with, we come to see that there is a symmetry between the sensibility of the body and the depth of reality. That symmetry unfolds fully if we allow the body to gather in and exhibit its place and its time. Fidelity to place is difficult to achieve. The betrayal of time is hard to resist. Yet an ever-moving standpoint disturbs the context of things and practices and stunts the growth of a person. The flow of a life's narrative is arrested when we conceal our passage through time behind a mask of eternal vigor. Placelessness and timelessness are compatible with artificial intelligence. Human intelligence, so Dreyfus teaches us, is embodied. It must take place and have time if it is to be at home in the world.

III

"Applied Heidegger"

Heidegger on Living Gods

Charles Spinosa

Identifying the presence, or at least traces of the presence, of divinities plays an important role in Heidegger's later work. Their presence is crucial for living a non-nihilistic life, one where something has an authority worth making sacrifices for.[1] Hubert Dreyfus has helped us understand the sense in which, for Heidegger, works of art—what Dreyfus calls cultural paradigms—are gods.[2] In this essay, I will try to advance Dreyfus's work by drawing on Heidegger's account of the Greek daimons to show how Heidegger makes sense of the possibility of living gods in today's disenchanted world. I shall show that there are contemporary forms of religious and secular experience that accord with Heidegger's account of the presence of divinities and their traces. But we cannot make sense of these experiences with our minimal ontology of subjects and objects. We, therefore, need to add to our ontology "attuning," or the coming into an appropriate mood for making sense of things and people. Attuning is not mysterious; it gives us access to certain everyday phenomena that we would not want to live without but that our current ontology encourages us pass over.

In order to see what Heidegger understands by the divine and to make sense of attuning, I shall begin by distinguishing Heidegger's divine from that of Judeo-Christian religious experience, which philosophers usually take as their model. In the current philosophic world, the most influential phenomenological account of Judeo-Christian experience is the one developed by Rudolf Otto in his *The*

Idea of the Holy.[3] Like Heidegger, Otto holds that the rationalizing of religious experience in onto-theology has had the effect of producing a domesticated god of interest only to philosophers.[4] Also, both Heidegger and Otto recognize the difference between what Heidegger calls the ontological and ontic dimensions of life, which Otto calls the numinous and the natural. Generally, for both, the ontological or numinous is incommensurate with the ontic or natural that it makes possible. For Otto, as for the Heidegger of *Being and Time*, when the numinous or ontological is experienced, it is experienced as uncanny, as dreadful, as a *mysterium tremendum* (to use Otto's technical term) that gives one a sense of the insignificance of the ontic or the natural. Otto's religious phenomenology examines the nature of this dread. He admits that one must rely on analogy to natural states in order to articulate the numinous states with any precision, but it is a phenomenology of the incommensurable to which Otto is committed.[5]

Although Heidegger may have started thinking along similar—though secular—lines with his "*Grundbefindlichkeit*" *Angst*, by the 1930s, when he starts thinking of the *understanding of being* (which, following Dreyfus, is the style of a culture as necessarily incarnated by a gripping, living work of art or some other cultural being), he opens the possibility of relating oneself to the ontological in more ontic or normal ways. Heidegger's divine experiences are more worldly than those of the Judeo-Christian heritage. Heidegger shows that the Greeks' practices for seeing and dealing with the temple attuned in a specific way their practices for dealing with virtually everything else in their world.[6] Practices for dealing with the temple's luster determined how the Greeks saw the brightness of anything. The temple's solidity determined how they dealt with anything's solidity or fluidity. Even blades of grass were seen by the Greeks in terms attuned by their way of dealing with the temple. The Greeks, in Heidegger's account, experienced the divine when the temple worked to light up their world. Consequently, Heidegger's investigation of the experience of the divine among the Greeks leaves him mostly uninterested in the dreadful experiences of the other-worldly that Otto describes.

Since Heidegger approaches the experience of the divine in a more down-to-earth, even Nietzschean, way, he writes in a way that sounds both theistic and atheistic. Since attuning activity is the realm of the divine, Heidegger can write about gods with divine agency. And since attuning goes unthematized in modernity, Heidegger says that religious encounters are rare today because the gods have withdrawn themselves. He can also say, like Nietzsche, that such encounters are rare because our practices do not let us see attuning. We are the ones who are killing the gods and making ourselves nihilists. Since our practices are part of the problem, we can become part of the solution by recognizing attuning.

How does Heidegger think that we, in our disenchanted, hyper-reflective modern mode of being, can make sense of experiencing a living god rather than understand the experience as an hallucination? We can begin by drawing on Heidegger's claim in "The Origin of the Work of Art" that an entity that manifests and glamorizes the style of a people's practices will manifest for those people what they share and consequently be regarded as holding authority over their lives. Since such a cultural paradigm, whether it be a temple, sacred words, a sacrificial act, a constitution, or what not, manifests everything that is important to them as a people, it will be worth dying for. Since it creates and sustains their world, it will fill them with love, pride, respect, and devotion. In short, it will be adored as a god and in its power to grip be experienced as having a divine agency.

Let us now add those features of such a paradigm that would make the divine agency into a *personal* god. For Heidegger does not want us to think of the temple, the god within the temple, or other divine cultural paradigms as anything other than having a living agency. They have to be the kind of personal living divinities to whom man can reverently ask for guidance (most often in prayer), sacrifice to, fall on his knees before in awe, and play music and dance before.[7]

A living god would have to possess the power to affect our relation with nature, with our work, with others, and with ourselves. Such a god, moreover, would hold authority over us, not just because of its power, but because the god is sympathetic to our way of life, or, at least, our way of life when it is happening in its most exemplary form. And because the god uses its power in support of this way of life, the god elicits reverential behavior from us, much the way any living human authority figure elicits some degree of reverence. Most important, however, this god is one that we can speak and pray to, and who can answer back. The god is also a person in that he or she takes responsibility for his or her acts and feels that both the actions and the responsibility for them matter. Indeed, by virtue of acts and responsibility mattering, we also understand that this god has passions and moods roughly like our own. Because the god has a voice, moods, passions, and a sense of responsibility like our own, and so far as we experience voices, moods, and passions as coming from bodies, we experience the god as embodied. (From this it is not clear that a god must be gendered, but it is likely to be the case, since most bodies for us are gendered.)

Such a description is incompatible with our modern sensibilities. Indeed, it strongly suggests that gods are nothing more than anthropomorphic inventions. But we should remember when thinking about anthropomorphism that our pervasively skeptical sensibility is a relatively recent development. Experiences in which a god communicated in person with people were common among believers both before the Enlightenment *and after*. Nor were such experiences reserved for the sensitive minds of those destined for sainthood. As William James points out, many hardheaded people had religious experiences right through the nineteenth century, and, again, as James points out, science could say little to dissuade them from the so-called truth of such experiences.[8] For, first, such people based their beliefs on clear perceptual experiences that seemed to them no more hallucinatory than any scientist's data, and, second, the recurrence of such experiences meant that they were repeatable, though not at will.

That hardheaded people have long had perceptual encounters with gods does not mean that divine power is akin to the physical forces described by scientific laws. Just as, for Heidegger, being depends on man so does divine power. This condition, however, so long as man also depends on divine power, only diminishes onto-theological interpretations of the divine. The basic claim developed here is that gods give situations their particularly clear mood or attunement. As an example, Aphrodite's appearance would bring out the erotic aspects of a situation, or, better, reveal the situation as over-ridingly erotic. A modern being functioning as an erotic paradigm can have the same power that such a god had. In the late 1950s and early 1960s, for instance, Marilyn Monroe became the paradigm of feminine erotic appeal. At certain moments, she was able, like Aphrodite, to change the look and feel of a situation. She could bring people into sharpened affective states that enabled specific possibilities to appear and others to remain hidden. In this basic way, she was a goddess. Our subject-object ontology leads us to describe such situation-changing effects in psychological terms, but we shall see that such description misses crucial aspects of the phenomenon and that the vocabulary of divine effects makes better sense.

I Heidegger on the Greek Gods

To start with, we shall consider two passages on the preclassical gods from Heidegger's *Parmenides*. In the first, Heidegger explains why we no longer experience divinities or, as he calls them here, daimons.[9]

[T]he *daimon*, the self-showing ones, the pointing ones, are who they are and are the way they are *only* in the essential domain of disclosure and of the self-disclosing of being itself.[10]

We do not experience gods because we do not appreciate the experience of revealing or disclosing nowadays. Our web of social practice contains no powerful beings that act with divine power by showing us what sorts of things are intelligible. Our modern subjective or postmodern ironic practices distance us from such beings. We may sense, as Wittgenstein points out, that particular things have a feel or an attunement associated with them.[11] Wittgenstein usefully calls this a "field of force."[12] But we do not sense ourselves under the spell of one or another mood or way of being. Certainly, nothing clearly shows us this.

The contrast of our condition with the preclassical Greeks in awe of their temple makes this point clearer. The web of interrelated Greek practices for making things and people intelligible was incarnated in the temple. Thus, the temple did not do its work in isolation. Its way of making things intelligible pervaded all of Greek life just as Gospels and later the Gothic cathedral pervaded Christian life. The pervasive force of such paradigms was experienced by

Charles Spinosa

Christians as the holy spirit. The Greeks experienced it as daimons. Heidegger thinks of divinities or daimons as the ones who give things and situations their feel.

> What shines into beings [i.e. lights up beings], though can never be explained on the basis of beings nor constructed out of beings, is being itself. And being, shining into beings is *to daion—daimon*. Descending from being into beings and thus pointing into beings, are the *daiontes-daimones*. The "demons" . . . are not casual additions to beings, which man could bypass with no loss of his own essence and could leave aside. . . . In consequence of this inconspicuous unsurpassability, the *daimons* are more "demonic" than "demons" in the usual sense could ever be. The *daimons* are more essential than any being. They . . . determine every essential affective disposition from respect and joy to mourning and terror. Here, to be sure, these "affective dispositions" are not to be understood in the modern subjective sense as "psychic states" but are to be thought more originarily as . . . attunements.[13]

From this quotation, we see that gods, for Heidegger, have to do with the way things appear for us affectively, not with how material-physical things are caused to exist. The philosophical appropriation of the Christian God as a creator God had bound Him to material-physical causality and thus concealed the divine act of revealing or disclosing of how things and people matter in attunements or moods.[14]

Heidegger's point about attunement breaks down into two: (1) that gods are what lights up beings[15] and thereby, give these beings their look[16] and (2) that the look these gods give to things by looking at them is an affective one. Gods, we might say, give things the feel of their look.[17] But (1) what precisely does this mean; (2) how can we get from what gods do to what gods are; and (3) how do these claims provide us with the sense of seeing, talking to, and worshipping gods? I shall take up these questions in order.

II The Feel of a Look

The first question has to do not only with the particular effect of a god but also divine power generally. Heidegger tells us that a god *imparts* the *feel* of the look that something has. To get a sense of what he means by the *feel* of the look, let's turn to a simple example. If we look at our own nation's currency in one hand and another nation's currency in the other, we see something very curious. In one hand, we see something that *looks* valuable. In the other, we see something that looks like play money. We might try to tell ourselves that *really* we are having very similar visual experiences of paper, color, texture, shape, etc., and that we are *interpreting* the money in one hand with one subjective feeling and interpreting the money in the other hand with another. Or, we might try to say that we are *ascribing* the subjective feeling we have when we see either of the currencies to the currency itself as an objective feature. But when did the interpretation or ascription take place? Upon examination of the activity of looking at the money, it becomes clear that we experience neither ascription nor interpretation. If we are told, for instance, that our nation's money which we hold in our hand is counterfeit, we are still likely to see the money as valuable. Thus, we see the value despite our active ascription or interpretation. Indeed, to deal with our own money as just paper inscribed with certain markings requires development of specialized skills, like those of Treasury agents.

This example should help us recognize something beyond the normal phenomenological claim that instead of mere objects, we see meaningful equipment. We do not just see useful things soliciting us. We see useful things soliciting us *with attitudes*, not our attitudes but attitudes appropriate to the kind of useful thing they are. Money is seen as valuable, guns as threatening, and so forth. These attitudes are not imposed by us in any ordinary sense of imposition. We cannot make them go away by simply shifting our stance. We have to work hard to change them.

One does not want to reject subjective interpretation or ascription and say, instead, that the difference in our responses to the currencies must lie in their material-physical aspects. We do not want to say that any or all of the physical-material aspects in some particular set of configurations are what makes us see currency as valuable. For if our nation changed many of the material aspects and their configuration on the currency (for instance, its color, the monuments pictured, and so forth), after some experience, we would lose our sense that the old aspects looked valuable and see the new ones as valuable.

Charles Spinosa

Generalizing on the basis of this phenomenon, the valuable look of money, like the official look of a diploma, like the look of other socially constructed things comes neither from any particular physicalmaterial characteristics or configuration of characteristics nor from some particular interpretation or ascription we impart to it. Rather, the affective or attitudinal look (of being valuable, official, and so forth) derives from a category of being that is neither objective (in the thing) nor subjective (in psychological stances).

What is it? To hint at the answer briefly, notice that we respond to a look of the official, the look of the serious and valuable, and many other looks. Designers constantly develop these looks. They are the affective aspect of common meanings.[18] Common meanings are those meanings that are embodied in exemplars and dispose those who share them to act in accord with them. So, for instance, Marilyn Monroe was an exemplar of feminine beauty. Those who shared this meaning understood various looks and actions as Marilyn Monroe-like. They celebrated them and were thrilled by them. Like other common meanings, this one could be reduced neither to subjective preferences nor to objective features. We see subjects, objects, and situations in terms of these common meanings and the attunements they solicit because of the practices that make us what we are and make everyday objects what they are.

It is easy for us to believe that we see things through our moods. A bright day looks wonderful when we are in a happy mood and annoying when we are down. We all have felt infected by the exuberant mood of a party, even if we did not have the mood to begin with and even if nothing particular happened to us to put us in such a mood.[19] In the 1950s, Heidegger focused on the way things gather us to them, the way they draw us to regard them with a certain attunement. Think of wandering into a cathedral, for instance. It draws us to a certain reverential, awestruck attunement in dealing with it and the people inside, and we come to inhabit that attunement more and more as we get increasingly in tune with the cathedral. The more reverential we feel, the more we will see things as laid out in ways that confirm that mood.

In thinking about the Greeks, Heidegger came to notice that things draw our attention with looks that act as affective solicitation. We are drawn to feel reverential in the cathedral because it has an awesome look, with all the interplay of stone and light. Our practices for dealing with even everyday things include an affective solicitation beneath our notice. This solicitation determines the mood in which we will be disposed to act and the strength of our disposition to act. Heidegger sees the Greeks as allowing their sensitivity to these affective solicitations to move their culture in a different direction from ours. To understand better the presence of divinities, we need to see the differences between the Greeks and us more clearly.

III From What Gods Do (the Causal Power of Attuning) to What Gods Are

We are interested in causal powers, and so were the Greeks. We are particularly interested in causal powers in two registers of being. We are interested in the material causal powers of the natural kinds in the universe. That is what our science investigates. We are also interested in what individuals can do and ought to be held responsible for. Our social sciences and history, and sometimes our philosophy, investigate what individuals can do, and our law and jurisprudence, along with our ethical and moral thinking, investigate what people ought to be held responsible for. But the preclassical Greeks were comparatively weak in both of our familiar kinds of causal investigation. They investigated the causal powers of attunement much more than physical and intentional causality. Attunements do have such powers. Because our currency looks valuable, we handle it with care. Because other nations' currency looks like play money, we have to stop ourselves from using it unwisely. The mood of reverence enables us to see more of a cathedral than the mood of relaxed play lets us see. The power of shared affective attunements comes to life even more when we look at shifts in common meanings. Moving, for instance, from Marilyn Monroe to Madonna gives us a significantly different sense of what is erotically appealing. At the very least, we move from soft subservience to ironic assertiveness.

In order to see where gods come in, we begin by asking how we account for such changes in affectivity. Since, for the Greeks, the gods are the ones who give situations, people, and things their look, going from, say, Marilyn Monroe to Madonna would indicate that we passed from one goddess of femininity to another, and this change gave women their new look. How do we see this phenomenon today? We generally see our artists, particularly our popular artists, and our charismatic leaders as responsible for effecting such changes. But we do not see them as responsible in a legal sense or even, for the most part, as intentionally effecting the changes. Though the Beatles changed the way we saw many things, from lovers to political concerns, we do not believe that the change was something John Lennon or Paul McCartney or the commercial enterprise called "The Beatles" actively sought. The goal of the four musicians was to make their music popular. They matched their mannerisms and their dress to their music so they could present a coherent image to the public. But it is doubtful that they would have characterized their style in the terms in which it was affectively appreciated—and taken over— by the public. (Imagine how hard it is for us to predict how our styles will be taken over by our children.) The individual Beatles were probably as much changed by their music as we were. The artist is in the same position as the critic when it comes to saying what his or her work means to the culture. The eleventh- and twelfth-century troubadours who sang songs that wove elements of religious devotion into their descriptions of erotic love could hardly have said that they wanted to transform their common meaning called erotic love into something called romantic love. Yet they succeeded famously. For this reason, when we respond to art, we are not as interested in what the artist thought he or she was doing as in the changes the artwork made or makes in our attunements.

Nor can we convince ourselves that the changes the Beatles brought about were part of a general *Zeitgeist* or drift in our cultural practices. Surely, there was a drift in our practices toward certain kinds of irony and toward certain kinds of self-indulgences. The optimistic, smart, bravado of a John Kennedy who embodied young masculinity was replaced by the sweetly ironic, artistic spirituality of a John Lennon. We were transformed. But this transformation did not happen by cultural or practical drift. It was too much tied to the person of the artists. Thus, our accounts of changes in common meanings miss something that happens before our eyes. In this unremarked realm, the Greeks saw their gods. For Heidegger's Greeks, change in the look of things or in our attunement occurred when a god him- or herself looked at the thing—brought his or her energies to bear on it—or when a new god looked at it differently.

What is the nature of the agency that the gods brought to bear? When a god brings his or her energies to bear on something, it is not a matter of physical causation as it is studied in our sciences. A story about a god stopping the sun or living on Mt. Olympus does not tell us about an astronomical event or about a domestic address. The story about the sun's stopping changes the common meaning of the sun. The sun indicated orderliness and steadiness. That it could have been stopped tells us that wonder counts at least as much as order. Everything could be regestalted. To say the gods lived on Mt. Olympus is to say that that was how Mt. Olympus looked, just as our money looks valuable. When a god brings his or her energies to bear on something, the god changes the force or kind of its affective character. And the Greeks actually saw this change occurring; they saw the god acting. Heidegger follows the Greek formulation for identifying this power of common meanings by calling it the look of the look. By this he means the look of a god illuminating a situation in a certain way so that, for instance, everything is seen as erotic or as rationally disciplined.

We can get a feel for such power of illumination if we think of ourselves as designers and ask ourselves, what is the look of the look, say, of being valuable or official or (to attend more closely to Greek concerns) erotically appealing. Then, we may see why an account of this look must exceed the realm of simple objects. Why, that is, it could not be understood as an object in the world. Particular instances of the erotically appealing are shown to us on dozens of magazine covers monthly. But the look of this look, what this look is in general or as a whole is not something we imagine we encounter at all. When we are interested in the look of being official, we are not interested primarily in how academic regalia looks official or how judges' robes look official, but in the nature of the official look that pervades all of such items. We are interested in what, in our culture, something official looks like. If we imagine ourselves having to design an official-looking dress for a new adjudicating board, we would probably find ourselves leafing through magazines that showed various kinds of official dress in order to get a feel for what looks official. When we did that, what we would be getting a feel for is precisely the look of the look. A fashion designer who changes what we perceive as erotically powerful evening wear will succeed not just by selling many copies of a garment with a new look but by accentuating some grace that was missed before and that is now desired. Therefore, with this new cut, the general look of what we find desirable is changed. We need only leaf through magazines from past decades to see how much the erotically desirably look has changed in a short time.

Divine power is the look of things' looks when they are seen and felt most concretely. The divine beings have a power on a human or even animal order such that their looking at a situation can transform it. We have some small experience of this when someone with a very strong character comes into the periphery of a situation. We also can easily imagine how everything in a situation takes on a different look when we are told that a fierce bear is lurking about.[20] This power could be exercised by statues of gods. That is what made temples sacred. The statue or altar cross gives a situation in a temple or a cathedral its look and feel. Thus, for Heidegger the statue of the god "lets the god himself be present and thus *is* the god himself."[21] Now, we can say two things about the Greeks and their gods. First, because the Greeks were intensely sensitive to the affective power of the looks of things—that is, affective power of their common meanings—they could see and feel gods present in their statues and other artworks. Second, because they could see divine agents stirring affects, they had much greater sensitivity to common meanings in their world and to the ontological status of common meanings than we have. For common meanings are authoritative but neither subjective nor objective.

Art was not the only visual, bodily experience the Greeks had of gods. We can further understand what it meant for the Greeks to be looked on by a god from what we have just been saying. In situations such as graduations, weddings, and moments of inspiration when writing, things show up with a look different from the one they ordinarily have. People look more joyful at weddings than they do on most other occasions. At graduations everything seems touched by more dignity than we are generally accustomed to. At moments of inspiration, things appear with greater clarity than usual. For Greeks, these feelings, which we know are shared, would be enough to warrant a sense of being beheld by a divinity.

Though we might imagine ourselves seeing the look that a god casts over everything by way of a common meaning, it seems an excess of fantasy to imagine the god in full visibility somewhere on the scene irradiating everything with this look. However, if some person possessed by the spirit of a situation were really to speak, act, or think beyond him- or herself (as we know him or her), we would have little problem in saying that so-and-so was so inspired that he or she really expressed the meaning of joyfulness or dignity or clarity. When someone embodies the common meaning so thoroughly that their look entrances us—think of Marilyn Monroe—the Greeks would see the god as present in the form of the person. If the person is someone who has no previous memorable identity[22]—we might think of Mario Savio—then the god that pours his or her light into the situation is simply present on the scene. We should recall that Greek gods often impersonated mortals and often appeared as average people.

IV Seeing and Talking to a God

We can get a clearer picture of what the presence of a Greek divinity would be like if we examine the account of a typical fundamentalist Christian who encountered an angel.[23] This fundamentalist volunteered to purchase tickets for, and to put on a plane, four blind and wheelchair-bound children. Because of traffic, he arrived at the airport so late that there was no way he could both purchase the tickets and get the children to the gate. As he stood in consternation, a middle-aged man emerged from the crowd and asked if he could help. The fundamentalist felt strongly that the man was trustworthy, and with only a second to think he asked the man to lead the children to the gate and wait for him to arrive with the tickets. When he got to the gate with the tickets, he saw the man with the four children, waiting by the departure door. He thanked the man, who said that the reward was all his own. The fundamentalist turned and handed the tickets to the gate attendant whom he watched lead the children down the ramp. When he turned back, he could not find the middle-aged man. He searched the airport and had an announcement made. As he ran over the events in his mind, it made no sense that the man could disappear so instantly. Finally, he accepted what seemed to him to be the only sensible conclusion: the man had been an angel.

Of course, to skeptical, disenchanted ears, this conclusion does not follow at all. Each of us could give a perfectly sensible disenchanted account of what had happened. The middle-aged man had a blind, wheelchair-bound son, and his wife had called him just a few hours earlier to tell him that their child had died. Grief-stricken, he was rushing home when he saw the four children, who reminded him of his son. Sympathetic to the problems of caring for such children, he saw immediately what was wrong. He offered to help. Indeed, he was glad to help, because it relieved some of his pain. When it seemed as though an explanation would be required of him, he could not bring himself to tell his story. He just blurted out that he liked to help people. And with that, he ran off to catch his flight, which was about to leave, a few gates down. Could we, given this disenchanted description, describe the man's actions and demeanor as angelic? Most of us would allow such a usage, granting, of course, that we were comparing a regular living person to a fictional being. But now we come to the important questions. We have a fundamentalist who claims he has encountered an angel and our own claim that he has encountered an angelic person. What is the difference between the two accounts? And which does better justice to the phenomenon?

In answering these questions, we should not be thrown off the track by claiming that the difference between us lies in the fundamentalist's belief in a place called heaven where angels warble praises of God except when they are on holy missions. For such angelology plays no decisive role in the fundamentalist's experience. Similar angel stories can be found among those who have significantly dif-

ferent angelologies. Indeed, even people who are not fundamentalists report such encounters. We begin, then, by answering a simpler,
similar question that has the same ontological implications. What is
the difference between seeing our own currency as valuable and
seeing it as a piece of paper on which are printed many inscriptions
that can be analyzed to determine if it carries value?

When the fundamentalist sees the angel, what he sees is a perfect
embodiment of his subculture's common meaning of angelic action.
The angel made real for him (brought him into tune with) something that he had only understood before in the abstract. Indeed,
seeing the angel brought his beliefs into tune with his perceptions
and emotions. Such a sighting need be ontologically no different
from seeing a freshly printed $1,000 bill as a perfect embodiment of
our common meaning of valuable money.[24]

To see neither angels nor money as affectively valuable is ultimately to see nothing but wholly disenchanted things, things with no
affective meaning. Obviously, if we cultivated ourselves to see that
way, we would become a different form of life. It would surely be an
affectively diminished form of life with its sense of mattering wholly
absent. In place of mattering would lie practical considerations. On
this score, it seems obviously preferable to see valuable things as valuable. Why not see angelic actions as performed by angels? There is
only one reason. That could lead us back to all the metaphysical
notions of angelology. But there should be little problem if we could
keep clear that divinities are divinities only so far as they embody the
powers of affective common meanings.

So long as people can be seen either as agents of common meanings (culture figures, gods, or angels) or as objects, we should be able
to say that a world in which there are angels or gods makes sense. It
has all the advantages that seeing money as valuable has over simply
determining that money is valuable. But what about cases where a
god or angel appears out of thin air, when there is no other person
there whom we could say the god or angel is impersonating? How
can we assimilate actual divine presentations in terms of a common
meaning or an attitudinal look? In a famous scene in the *Iliad*, as
Achilles is about to pull his sword on Agamemnon, Athena grabs his
hair from behind, and when he turns, she tells him not to attack

because he will regret it. Suppose that the Greeks actually encountered gods this way. Nonbelievers would want to describe such an experience as hallucinatory and therefore as dangerous in a way that the angel in the airport is not. Let's look at such phenomena to begin with in an open yet skeptical way.

Let us start with a commonplace set of phenomena in the auditory sphere. When we are anxious to hear from a loved one, we may find ourselves thinking that we have heard our telephone ring. When we are in a situation where someone such as a parent regularly calls our name, we do sometimes hear our name called by that person even though he or she is not calling us. People who have grown familiar with spouses or parents will sometimes hear them say the expected thing even if they have said nothing at all. What is happening in such cases? We have not *simply* had an auditory hallucination. In these cases, we do not assume that there was no sound at all. We normally believe that the affect or the feel of the situation is so strong that it pulls sounds into the pattern that we hear. Indeed, such moments have been portrayed in literature and on film enough for us to say that they are paradigm embodiments of longing. If we had the sensitivities of the preclassical Greeks, we would be likely to say that the rings and spoken words were produced by the divine powers of longing. Indeed, the perceptual impressions here are just like the perceptual impressions of dignity at a graduation, joy at a wedding feast, and the valuableness of money, except that in the cases of the telephone ringing or the noise at the door, the common meaning misleads us by *disguising* the state of affairs rather than bringing the state of affairs to full expression.

We should not be distracted by divinities misleading us. Rather, we are interested in the power by which they can transform states of affairs, drawing from us immediately appropriate responses, as in the case of Achilles. In the real-life examples of our *current* responses to common meanings, we see and hear the affective aspect of common meanings taking over whatever perceptual material is available in order to express the power of the feeling of a particular situation. We do not infer that there is joy, we see intensely joyful weddings. We do not feel intense longing, we hear the phantom telephone rings. Likewise, we do not see a chthonic demon spooking us, but we hear noises at our door. Even with our modern ontology, our common meanings sometimes have enough affective power to produce perceptual effects as real as the god for the Homeric Greeks. But we call these events hallucinations.

The Homeric Greeks and other undisenchanted people would not have had to live with such a cramped interpretation. Indeed, just as we may hear a ringing telephone when none is ringing, the voice of a spouse when the spouse is absent, and someone breaking in when no such thing is happening, they would have experienced the voice of Aphrodite, the common meaning of desire; the voice of Hera, the common meaning of domesticity; or, let us suppose, the voice of Hermes, the common meaning of thievery. And the voice would say something fairly typical of that common meaning.[25] It would work on the undisenchanted Greek much the same way telling ourselves a story or more likely, watching a television movie works on us. It stiffens our resolve, intensifies our excitement, brings us more in tune with what we are feeling, gives us a keener awareness of the consequences of our actions, and so forth. That the voice of the divinity affects us in this literary register is what Heidegger means when he says that myth is the appropriate mode of relation to the divine.[26] Can we say that it makes sense to see a divinity in thin air?

So far, we have answered the simpler question: how does it make sense to hear the voice of a divinity saying particular things when in the world of objects there is no such voice? We hear voices when the power or feel of the situation is so strong that we construe random sounds as a voice. The pervasiveness of imperfectly distinguished noises in our environment together with the affective quality of common meanings ground these auditory phenomena. But visual phenomena tend to be different from auditory phenomena in that we see more transparently than we hear. While we work, we are aware of a din around us. But we tend to think that visual phenomena are far more determined, except in fogs, at dusk and dawn, in dense forests, in shadows, in conflagrations, in battles, storms at sea, and so forth. Making such a list makes us aware of how much our current forms of landscape and architecture enhance the determinateness of visual phenomena. Our lawns dotted with shade trees, our cleared fields, our straight highways, our wide streets and sidewalks, our street lights, our unflickering indoor lighting, our cleared park paths and trails, our towers all make vision regularly more determinate than it was in earlier times.

Sit around a campfire. Notice all that is to be seen indistinctly when we light our rooms with candles. Stare into the flames of the fire in the fireplace. If we focus on such times, when visual fields have much in them that is indistinct, we have reason to believe that we might well be drawn to see the common meaning affecting us. We can easily list cases where the common meaning of our situation determines what we see. When we are walking across a college campus, we are attuned to the academic life and world. On such occasions if a business acquaintance happens to be within our view, we will frequently not recognize her. In other situations, we can easily find ourselves seeing someone who looks just like another person we are expecting to meet. We may even begin speaking to the stranger before we realize our mistake. If we had less disciplinary forms of landscape and architecture, we would have more opportunity to become sensitive to visions which we now take as simple hallucinations or illusions.

But we have yet to reconcile the perceptual presence of divinities changing the attunement of situations with the skepticism that comes with our disenchanted ontology. For the disenchanted person, reports of divinities reveal various kinds of mistakes. In one case, the reports might be the sentimental misidentification of human actions for divine ones. In other cases, the reports would be stress-induced misidentifications of anditory or visual patterns as words or divinities. They could even be full-fledged hallucinations. For someone sensitive to the power of common meanings, the genuinely experienced god is the agency of the affective power of a common meaning bringing us into tune with our situation.

We experience such attuning when literary works or a television movie bring us into tune with changed situations. A figure like Marilyn Monroe or Humphrey Bogart brings us into attunement when she or he speaks and acts in such a way as to make us sensitive to the feel of things in our world and, thereby enables us to act more spontaneously and effectively. When this happens, such figures have been acting with a super-human power that we have called the divine. Since this power is neither subjective nor objective—it does not reside in either our subjective response to Marilyn Monroe or Humphrey Bogart or in them as people or even as actors—we should not be disturbed when the power comes free of subjects and objects. If a seeming subjective (sentimental) or objective (perceptual) "misidentification" brings us into tune with our world, then we are witnessing a divinity at work. Given these considerations, we should not say that, when we watch television, the Greeks and other undisenchanted peoples misidentify indistinct noises and sights unless we are prepared to say that, when we watch television, *we* misidentify images or people playing at being other people as attuning figures. For it is quite clear that our fully absorbed experience of dramas is not the experience of someone playing at being someone else. Yet we do not believe that, when we are in such an entranced state, we are misidentifying what we see.

Recall that so long as our ontology allows only for subjects and objects, we have no place for *seeing* money as valuable. Our experience of seeing money as valuable has to be accounted for as an act of ascribing or of interpreting. This limited ontology makes us unable to account for the effect that occurs when the figures in a movie bring us in tune with our lives. We cannot seriously say we see images and hear recorded sounds to which we ascribe or interpret certain feelings, motives, and so forth? We see and hear in a dimension that we may call mythic, attuning, extraordinary, or uncanny. (Heidegger uses all these terms.) With an ontology that accepts attuning and common meanings, we could experience the gods appearing out of thin air, "materializing" before us and yet not confusedly think that we are either hallucinating or seeing physical objects in unusual circumstances exhibiting their causal powers. Finally, we could see that phenomenon of materialization also taking place when an actor plays a character which becomes a culture figure or when an average person such as Mario Savio takes on a new luminescence in a movement. For someone is a culture figure at certain moments, in certain actions where he is bigger than himself. Those moments come and go, and no one can be fully in control of them. Either the god materializes as the culture figure or fails to.

When we are seeing or listening to voices and sights from this dimension whether it is like a movie or the value we see in the dollar,

Charles Spinosa

we are able to act more flexibly and decisively. Consequently, the movie figures and the value we see are attuning presences. Since our way of acknowledging this dimension is far less direct than the Greek way, we have a hard time saying that we see divinities. What we experience, therefore, has far less authority. We become attuned by indirect, furtive means. Our ontological neglect of both common meanings and attuning enables us to experience them only in a degraded form. Getting us to change our ontology to accept the experience we marginalize was, famously, Heidegger's project.[27]

12

Trusting

Robert C. Solomon

Until very recently, the philosophical literature was virtually silent on the topic of trust and trusting although trusting's importance was presumed at every level. One does not have to dig very deeply behind Kant's arguments in the *Groundwork* or Mill's utilitarianism or, especially, Aristotle's *Ethics* and *Politics* to find it loitering at every turn. Sissela Bok, in her popular book, *Lying*, repeatedly refers back to trust as the "atmosphere" or "climate" presupposed in every social interaction, "like the air we breathe." Religious faith can readily be viewed as a species of trust, and even epistemology might be viewed as an extensive concern about trust, trusting in other people's testimony (according to Tony Coady), trusting in one's own cognitive apparatus and good sense (according to Keith Lehrer).[1] But philosophers have been prodded to turn their analytic skills to trust only recently. (Annette Baier deserves credit as a philosopher who ignited the current interest in the topic.)

In sociology too, trust has emerged as a "hot topic." Bernard Barber wrote a study of trust back in 1976, the distinguished German sociologist Niklas Luhmann tackled the subject in his *Trust and Power* and more recently the dean of English sociologists, Anthony Giddens, has been pursuing the subject in a number of books and studies. And then there was Francis Fukuyama's well-known and rather controversial study in 1996.[2] The sociological literature has tended to substantivize trusting, turn it into a mysterious "thing" or medium, but as usual, there has been relatively little communication between the sociologists and the philosophers. Both have their obvious blind spots, and putting them together provides a much better opportunity for understanding the seemingly simple but in fact quite complex issue of trust. Fernando Flores and I have been working on such an investigation, and not too surprisingly we have found that a promising approach to the issue is by way of Bert Dreyfus's now seminal interpretations of Heidegger. On such an interpretation, trusting emerges neither as a Cartesian psychological state nor as a sociological "fact" but as a complex and dynamic social and transformative practice. In this chapter, in Bert's honor, I would like to summarize some of these ideas.

I   The Philosophy of Trusting

In a recent issue of *Ethics*, three philosophers—Karen Jones, Russell Hardin, Lawrence C. Becker[3]—take on the phenomenon of trust full-tilt and all make the point that trusting is no "thing" but an attitude or a stance. Accordingly, "trusting" is perhaps more appropriate than "trust," although the noun form is more common and I will use the two more or less interchangably (in part for grammatical reasons). In the *Ethics* symposium, the three philosophers raise the question, how "cognitive" is trust? How much does trusting consist of beliefs which in turn depend on evidence and calculation of probabilities? Hardin, who has written a good deal else on the topic, argues a sophisticated game-theoretical vision of trusting, pervaded as most such accounts tend to be with a certain presumption about human self-interestedness and (accordingly) more than a modicum of suspicion about people's trustworthiness. Consequently, in this article he focuses on "devices for commitment" which, he claims, make trustworthiness possible. Jones and Becker, by contrast, analyze trusting as an "affective attitude." Jones suggests "optimism" and Becker "non-cognitive security" as paradigms of trust, respectively. Ten years earlier, Annette Baier precociously introduced the topic, tracing her own interest back to her eighteenth-century ethical hero, David Hume.[4] She takes as her paradigm of trusting reliance on the other person's good will, though not, obviously, in the Kantian sense of that phrase.

The relatively new attentiveness to trusting betrays the damage that results from all of those years of neglect. I have my usual suspicions here, and this is what initially drew me to the topic. What caused the neglect of trusting (in part) was the avoidance of the "softer" aspects of ethics, of ethics as feeling or "sentiment," of ethics as an essential function of relationships. Too much of the current attention to trust still tends or tries to avoid these "soft" areas. Thus trust is reduced to beliefs about probability, to strategy and rational expectations, all familiar hard-headed terrain in modern philosophy.[5] Trusting is discussed as a risk to be justified instead of an existential stance in which such questions are transcended. But when the attention to trust turns to game theory and its rational decision-making kin, I think that it is seriously distorted and turned into something very different from trusting. (I am even tempted to claim that it is the very opposite of trusting, a kind of calculating distrusting.)

When trusting is treated as an individual's affective attitude, on the other hand, the danger is that either it is thereby reduced to a set of subjective probabilities (in which the rigorous demands of game theory and the like are suspended but the cognitive bias remains) or, worse, it is simply dismissed as noncognitive and thereby as nonrational and utterly impervious to evidence and argument. But whether cognitive or noncognitive, trusting is treated as a matter of individual psychology, a set of beliefs or attutudes one person has regarding another. It is not, except by vague suggestion, an essential ingredient in a relationship or a society. It is worth noting that most of the sociological literature takes exactly the opposite approach. There trust is treated as a kind of "medium" or "atmosphere" which is the precondition of virtually all of the activities of a social group. For example, Francis Fukuyama talks extensively about "high trust" and "low trust" societies, but then he hardly says a word about what it is for one person to trust another.[6]

My concern is that the phenomenon of trusting is often distorted as much as it is clarified when it is opened up to philosophical examination. As so often in philosophy, one topic is subsumed or embraced within the well-established methodology for dealing with other, often unrelated problems. Trusting in particular gets treated as one more philosophical abstraction requiring definition in terms of necessary and sufficient conditions. The accounts are accordingly "thin" as opposed to the rich, dynamic, and multi-dimensional phenomenon itself. Such thin and logical definitions lend themselves enticingly to paradox and counter-examples but not necessarily to understanding.[7] Trust thus treated is about as enticing and as practical as love treated as a philosophical abstraction, in Agathon's drunken *Symposium* speech, for example, or in many a male bachelor's crooning about this most celebrated passion. Such treatments may be edifying and ethically pure, perhaps, but they tend to be exceedingly limp on the messy dynamics and rather noncommital on the many complexities of erotic attachment.

What most of the philosophical views share, I think, is a failure to take trusting seriously as an element in dynamic relationships. They present "thin" as opposed to "thick" descriptions of a fascinatingly complex and variable phenomenon. And they treat trusting as an individual attitude or belief (or some such Cartesian psychological state) rather than as a phenomenon in social space. On most philosophical views, trusting smacks of solipsism. It represents the viewpoint of a threatened subject peering out suspiciously at a risky world. If trusting is discussed at all in terms of relationships between people the trusting itself is nevertheless discussed strictly from the first person point of view. Moreover, most of the examples tend to involve only two people (less often, a person and an institution).[8] Most of the examples are very specific, trusting someone to do something at or by a certain time, focusing on a single interaction or expectation rather than any more protracted relationship. But it is important to distinguish such single encounters (even if repeated) from ongoing trusting relationships and what sociologists call a trusting" atmosphere" or "climate." Thus Hardin sometimes treats trust as a reiterative prisoner's dilemma, far better than the one-shot paradigm that is sometimes employed, perhaps, but nevertheless minimizing or misunderstanding the role of relationships—including multi-party communal relationships, in trust. What the philosophers tend to neglect, in other words, is just what the sociologists tend to assume, the social nature of trusting.

In the "affective attitude" camp, Karen Jones and Larry Becker agree that trusting should not be construed as a matter of beliefs but rather, at least primarily, as a matter of "affect" or "emotion," and in particular emotions directed *at* other people. This is something less than social and still much too Cartesian, but it does capture something of the idea that trust "permeates" a society or a relationship and is not merely a set of expectations. Indeed, both Jones and Becker suggest that trust is actually compromised as it becomes more "rational." I think that this is an important insight that requires further explanation even if, as such, it is overstated. Baier, Jones, and Becker also agree that trust and trustworthiness cannot be "willed," a thesis which I want to question here. What underlies much of what I have to say, of course, is a claim I have been arging rather stubbornly for over twenty years now, that the distinction between "cognition" (in its various forms) and emotion is problematic and does serious damage in discussions about topics relating to emotion. The choice between trust as a set of beliefs and trust as a noncognitive "affective attitude," I want to suggest, is a bad choice indeed. It encourages us to conceive of trust either as calculating distrust or as dumb but warm feelings, neither of which deserves the important place trusting obviously occupies in virtually all of our social relationships.

In this chapter, I want to focus on several such matters. First, I would like to explore the notion that trusting is an aspect of dynamic human practices, interactions and relationships, not just a psychological state (belief or attitude). Second, I want to discuss the complex relationship between trust and distrust. Third and finally, I want to discuss the status of trusting as an emotion and suggest that we *resolve* to trust.[9]

II Trusting in Dynamic Relationships

From Heidegger and Dreyfus we get the claim that it is a mistake to try to understand human activity in terms of static properties, necessary and sufficient conditions, instead of in terms of shared practices. The claim is sometimes overstated by their fans and followers. I do not doubt that there are several sets of necessary and sufficient conditions which could be specified for trusting, depending on the general context (for example, in business partnerships, intimate relationships, civic and political associations). What gets left out of such characterizations, what gets lost in the Chisholming down of counter-examples and revised attempts at definition, is the rich picture of interaction and background practices that are involved in trust. The problem is not just another of those promiscuities of the English language, again as in "love," which serves as an all-purpose name for affection for one's lifelong soulmate, one's parents, one's children, one's dog, one's favorite book, and one's favorite vintage wine. Nor is it just to say (what is certainly true) that trusting is always contextual, that any general definition, even if correct, nevertheless leaves us uninformed about what is involved in any particular episode of building and maintaining trust. The problem is that leaves out what is most important and exciting about trust, the fact that trusting is an ongoing process, a reciprocal (and not one-way) relation in which both parties as well as the relationship (and the society) are transformed through trusting.

Several philosophers have argued, plausibly, that trusting should be distinguished from "confidence" or "dependability" or "reliance" or "predictability."[10] Talk about trust, they argue, is or should be limited to our dealings with other human beings, or, at least, with other agents. With this restriction, talk about trusting one's car to make it up the hill or to get through the winter should be understood as merely metaphorical. Machines cannot literally be "trusted." They can only be relied upon. Furthermore, this is not because one is more likely to fulfill our expectations than the other. A trustworthy person may or may not be more likely to fulfill his or her trust than a trusted machine. I once owned a vintage British sportscar (or did it own me?), and my proud owner's trust had far more to do with affection and hope than with scientific predictions and expectations. As the owner of a classic 1966 MGB, I necessarily had that "optimism" that Karen Jones describes. I nevertheless was prepared at every moment with screwdriver, pliars, and wiring, not to mention a monthly ticket for the city bus. What was missing was the fact that my "trusting" my car—in addition to being pervaded with distrust—did not and could not have had any effect or influence on the car itself, as trusting another person (and letting her know that you trust her) usually does.

The reason why trusting should be (strictly speaking) restricted to agents in relationships is not, as Baier famously puts it, because we rely on another's good will. It is rather because trusting is the product of participation and mutual communication in relationships. Trust is not a matter of reliance, and it is not just a matter of expectations (which presume a certain amount of risk, the dimension of trust much emphasized by sociologists such as Luhmann and Giddens[11]). A car "behaves" no differently whether it is trusted or not, despite the sometimes magical incantations and heartfelt confidences of affectionate owners. An employee behaves very differently depending on whether or not and to what extent he or she is trusted. Furthermore, the very fabric of trusting is built out of such exchanges as promises, commitments, offers, and requests and the response they receive. One might view the dependability of an object, say, an automobile or a suspension bridge, as a complex disposition, a structure which can be predicted to function or not function depending on certain variables. A car is dependable, for instance, on days when the temperature is over twenty degrees Fahrenheit. A bridge will bear a load of up to so many hundreds of metric tons. But when we consider whether or not someone is trustworthy, or (what is different) whether or not to trust him, we recognize that our behavior and our interaction and the background of the relationship is of critical importance, and not just by way of "depending on certain variables." It is kindergarten knowledge, that how you ask someone to do something (for example, by saying "please") has a lot to do with whether and how they will do it for you. But there is no simple formula that will capture the intricacies of such interactions and trusting relationships in general as there is, presumably, for Toyota cars or steel bridges with a span of so many meters. One must look at the dynamics of the relationship, not just the "structure" of one person's attitude and beliefs toward another. Trusting is a transformative practice, one that alters not only the trustor but the person trusted and, most important of all, the relationship between them.

The idea that trusting is an ongoing social practice rather than a specifiable state of mind suggests the rationale behind talking about trust as an "atmosphere" or "climate." When Fukuyama writes as if trust were a social medium, some pervasive foundational ingredient in which all other institutions and aspects of society are rooted, he is not simply talking about the sum total of all individual trustings.[12] But to say that trusting is an ongoing social practice is not to say that it is an unresponsive "atmosphere" or a "medium" but rather that it is the product (as well as the basis) of many particular human exchanges. Rather, following (early) Heidegger and Dreyfus rather closely here, we might say that what the sociologists recognize in their use of metaphors is that trust tends to recede into the "*background*" and become more or less invisible, taken for granted, in our everyday relationships.[13] So, too, we can better understand the plausibility of other "substance" and "stuff" metaphors such as "glue" (Kenneth Arrow), "lubricant" (John Whitney), "atmosphere" (Sissela Bok), "medium" (Fukuyama), and "stuff" (Barber) by taking them not literally but as a covert or confused reference to active but invisible background practices.

Trust is invisible (or "transparent") in many (or most) trusting relationships insofar as it tends to provide the background rather than the focus of our activities. But to take trusting for granted, to think that talking about trust is either redundant or ominous, is itself dangerous.[14] It ignores trust just when we need to be most concerned about it, when trust is flagging or betrayed, when trust is gone and needs to be recovered. We too quickly tend to assume that complex human practices are by their very nature "conscious" or "reflective," that is, that they are at the forefront—or at least the perceptible periphery—of consciousness, matters of attention or, at least dim awareness. But much of what we do, and most of what we believe and feel, is not so foregrounded or attended to at all.

We are brought up in a particular culture and a particular family setting, and within that culture and setting we learn all sorts of attitudes and ways of acting that may never be made the focus of teaching or learning or attention. Dreyfus tells the story, for example, of a Japanese baby versus an American baby, who is coddled and secured by its mother until it "learns to be a Japanese baby," opposed to the American baby, who is stimulated and teased by its mother until it becomes an American baby. So, too, Dreyfus points out, we learn the appropriate distance to stand and speak to someone, an appropriate "comfort zone." This need never be a focus of our attention. Indeed, most of us never notice it at all until we find ourselves talking to someone from a different culture and notice our discomfort at the violation of what we never thought before to be a "rule." Such subconsciously learned postures, stances, judgments, and attitudes obviously play a major role in our sense of trust,—whom to trust, when to trust, what to trust, how to trust. We simply "grow up" into certain patterns of trusting, finding certain people, certain situations, and certain routines familiar and comfortable. In such "simple trust," trusting need never emerge from the background at all. It remains there, unnoticed, not articulated, reflected or commented upon. Indeed, to bring it to our attention would be an annoyance, an inappropriate intrusion.

What does it mean for trust to be "in the background"? It is invisible only in one sense, the sense in which we are not paying attention to it and, perhaps, are so skillfully engaged in it that we could not describe what we are doing even if asked. One might pay close attention to one's position and efforts when first learning to ride a bike, but soon after one has learned one no longer pays any attention to any of this and might be hard-pressed to repeat the instructions that allowed one to make the first tentative moves. At the beginning of a love affair, one might pay careful attention to both what one says and what is said, to every move and, eventually, every caress. But once established, the conversation becomes much less self-conscious, the caresses become more automatic (without thereby becoming any less meaningful or caring). What was once a matter of keen attention and great concern now slips into the background, where it continues, in much the same way as before, but without the attention and explicit concern. But none of this goes away, needless to say, and any too inconsiderate comment or inappropriate caress might snap such matters back into the forefront of attention. As a generalization about human activity in general, we might follow Heidegger and say that it tends to be unreflective until it is shocked into reflection by some sort of breakdown. But this is not to say that it is any less human or any less activity. It simply appears to be the "medium" in which all sorts of other activities can then take place and occupy our attention.

The dynamics of trusting relationships depend on the specifics of the relationship as well as the dynamics of the particular relationship and, more generally, the culture and the social background. What counts as trusting in marriage is not the same as trusting in a business partnership, and neither much resembles the sort of trusting that is appropriate between citizens and their leaders or the trust of an infant for its parents or caretakers. Trusting in the context of a business deal largely depends upon the contractual, institutional, and market constraints on the relationship. But trusting should not be confused, as it often is in business, with a contractual relationship. It is often said the contracts establish trust, but I think a good argument can be made that contracts often indicate lack of trust. Particularly when there are enforcement provisions and sanctions, it would seem that a contract is both more and less than merely a trusting agreement. It is protection based on distrust. It is also said that trust is required as the basis of any contract which does not have decisive sanctions. This is true, but incomplete. Trust not only precedes but can trump the contracts that are based on it. A Japanese bank, because of severe financial duress, recently reneged on a contract with its American counterpart. The Americans were furious and threatened suit. The Japanese replied that they considered the ongoing working relationship as primary, the contract secondary and unimportant. (What the Americans did, of course, was have their lawyers redraft the contract, thus misunderstanding the nature of the dispute.)

Every trusting relationship, no matter how "easy," proceeds by way of its individual dynamics. Here is a familiar example: one person is punctual and expects the same of the other, who is habitually late. The reason may be overscheduling, or a casual indifference to time, or the false belief that one ought to be a fraction late for all non-work-related appointments. The explanation does not matter. (Indeed, if or when the tardy person begins to explain his or her lateness, that is in itself a new development in the relationship, and not necessarily a positive one.) The punctual person, on the other hand, silently simmers, sooner or later coming to expect the other to be late. Coming to expect the other person to be late ends the period of dashed expectations (now the punctual person makes it a point to have a good book while waiting), but that period of anger and frustration is replaced by another, potentially more damaging.

The late arrivals, now expected, are seen no longer as irresponsibility but as disrespect, or even as contempt. Trust, accordingly, is eroded. The lateness begins to poison the relationship. For some time, the perpetually tardy person does not realize that his or her behavior is not only discourteous but trust-destroying. Depending on the relationship, the outspokenness of the punctual person, and the sensitivity of the tardy person, this period may be protracted. But once the conflict is aired (which might be provoked by excuses on the part of the tardy person), the dynamic changes. It becomes mutual, a problem to be solved, in place of two independent behavior patterns that have resulted in unintended conflict. A conversation leads to a concrete program, a new resolve, on the part of the tardy person, to be on time. It may or may not lead to a promise, an explicit commitment, but it is clear that the conversation as such amounts to a commitment of sorts. Future tardiness will now be viewed as betrayal, a serious and direct expression of contempt. On the other hand, future punctuality may well be rewarded, if only by a word of praise or an extra gesture of affection. The resulting collaboration converts the former source of distrust into a strong source of trust, as the tardy person's effort to overcome old habits in sole consideration of the feelings of the punctual person is appreciated.

This example may seem trivial and insignificant, but trust in relationships is built out of such "trivia," such routine everyday making and keeping of promises and commitments. I want to suggest that trust in any relationship is built out of (and destroyed in) such routine frustrations, promises, and commitments. Indeed, one way of understanding relationships is by understanding the importance and the intensity of these everyday and ongoing encounters. Recent philosophy sometimes talks in grandiose terms of "teleology" and "shared values," but paying attention to our own relationships seems to show that such concepts are often irrelevant or secondary. Couples function harmoniously despite considerable differences in political ideology or religion. The surprising but successful marriage between Mary Matalin, chief campaign strategist for the Bush presidential

1992 campaign, and James Carville, chief Clinton strategist in the same election, is but one of many examples. They had not only opposed but urgently competitive jobs. They needed to keep secrets from one another and played serious tricks on the other side. But the marriage depended not on this so much as on the routine promises and commitments that every couple makes and lives with. It is in being conscientious to "trivia" that trust is generated.

Of course, conscientious habits regarding trivia readily become conscientious habits regarding the most major matters. In the military, it is not anal compulsiveness that leads sargeants to insist on mirror-shine spit polish on the boots of their recruits. It is the secure knowledge that soldiers who are conscientious about the details of their appearance because of the demands of their superiors will become equally conscientious in their dealings with military authority in matters much weightier, when lives are on the line. Couples who are attentive to their most trivial promises and the expectations of their partners are also couples who will weather the deep divides that tragedy introduces unwelcome into every relationship. Business relationships show much the same logic of "trivial" promises and commitments. At a major Manhattan bank, for example, bank officers who are caught in even the smallest infraction are fired, not because of the seriousness of the infraction itself, but because such behavior is corrosive of trust. Executives who worry how they can improve trust in the corporation and limit their attention to grand compensation schemes, profit-sharing programs, for example, are missing the obvious. It is well-documented that employees are not so much upset by the astounding differential between executive salaries and their own as they are by seemingly minor disappointments of reasonable expectations. A bonus program is announced in January; in November, its terms are altered. A disruptive and unproductive assistant manager is promoted only because he is a friend of the vice president. The company Christmas party is cancelled to save money. For all of the proper commotion about "down-sizing," distrust in corporate America is arguably as provoked by "trivia" as by the disruptions that make the headlines.

III Trusting and Distrusting: A Virtue and Its Shadow

Distrust is not the failure of trust nor is it a preliminary to trust ("we will wait and see if we can trust you"); distrust is an essential aspect of trust itself. The dialectic of trust and distrust is the most exciting part of the story of trust, and philosophers who just treat them as "opposites," without further analysis, are thereby missing the very nature of the dynamic of trust. Karen Jones makes the good but overly neat logical point that trust and distrust are *contraries* rather than *contradictories*, that is, one need not either trust or distrust; one may remain merely indifferent. I may not trust Sally because I have no dealings with her. But I do not therefore distrust Sally either. But what gets left out of this neat logical picture is the convoluted "logic" of coming to trust while grappling with distrust, and vice versa, not to mention the logical nightmare of "mixed feelings," that is, trusting and distrusting the same person at the same time (and even in the same respects). This is what I want to call "authentic" trust, trust that has all of the considerations for distrust already built into it, trust that is neither simple nor "blind."

I want to make a number of distinctions here, not between "kinds" of trusting so much as between two primitive analogs of trusting and authentic trust. I distinguish between *simple trust*, naive trust, trusting as yet unchallenged, unquestioned (the faith of a well-brought-up child), *blind trust*, which is not actually naive but stubborn, obstinate, possibly even self-deluding, and *authentic trust*. In many of the current articles on trust—and in most of the popular literature on the subject—simple trust is taken to be genuine trust (Becker's emphasis on the "non-cognitive" seems to entail simple trust.) In manipulative and fanatical groups, blind trust is often taken to be the paradigm. ("You don't really trust someone unless you trust them *all the way*,"—echoes of the late Frank Sinatra.) One might also talk here about what Erik Erikson called *basic trust*, which consists in the sense of physical and emotional security which most of us happily take for granted, which is violated in war and in acts of random violence and whose loss causes anxiety or *angst*, but this would take us too far afield.

Blind and simple trust may share some features with authentic trust, for instance, a degree of confidence or what Jones calls "optimism" (to be distinguished, she says, from "looking on the bright side of things"—reminiscent of a favorite Monty Python song). They also include vulnerability and risk. But, nevertheless, they are very different, particularly in their relation to distrust. Simple trust is devoid of distrust. Blind trust denies the very possibility of distrust. Authentic trust, however, trust articulated and "spelled out," necessarily recognizes the alternative of distrust and has taken into account the arguments for distrust, but has nevertheless resolved itself on the side of trust. One might distinguish other possibilities too: prudential trust, which takes up trust as a matter of strategy, fully aware of the likelihood of betrayal, operational trust, trust carefully limited to this or that task in this or that cooperative context. But what I want to emphasize is the importance of that form of authentic trust which survives and transcends distrust and at the same time makes sense as a cultivated, intelligent, emotional attitude.

Authentic trust is constituted as much by doubts and uncertainty as by confidence and optimism. (One might compare Augustine's and Dostoyevsky's accounts of religious faith.) Simple trust may be a kind of paradigm (for instance, for Baier's infants and for Becker's innocents), but simple trust can easily be naive, uninformed, taken in. Blind trust can be downright foolish, even tragic, for example, in the much-discussed case of Othello.[15] But authentic trust embraces distrust and involves the willful overcoming of it. Authentic trust differs from blind trust in its acceptance of the evidence for distrust, although it is similar in that it ultimately insists on trust nevertheless.[16] Trust, that is trusting, is a decision, not a probabilistic or strategic conclusion.

Authentic trust is most evident in politics. What Fukuyama calls a "high trust" society may itself not be particularly trustworthy and in any case an argument can be made that one ought to embrace distrust. A "high trust" society may become victim to grotesque abuses of power (the fact that Germany and Japan are two of his three primary examples is suggestive). Distrust, on the other hand, can be a political virtue. Distrust of government—and the more power, the more distrust—is often appropriate, sometimes even wisdom. The ancient philosopher Chuang-Tzu is eloquent on the subject, as is our own Thomas Jefferson. And yet, cynicism toward government has become a serious problem in many countries, threatening ungovernability. And so author after author tells us that trust and not distrust is essential to cooperation and prosperity in politics, business, love, and other personal relationships, but the truth seems to be that both are necessary, in healthy proportion. What gets left out of most accounts of trust is an account of the ways in which trust fails, the ways in which trust can go wrong, the ways in which trust is constantly tested, or taken for granted, which leads (not inevitably) to its disintegration. Trust alone (like love) is not "the answer." But to leap from the observation that trusting is sometimes foolish or disastrous to the conclusion that trust is, after all, a question of justification, evidence and warrant is itself unwarranted. To point out that trusting (or any interpersonal attitude, love or even hate) can break down is not necessarily to indicate the need for what Jones calls evidentialism. Love also goes wrong, but it would be a mark of perversity or cynicism to insist that love must therefore be prepared to defend itself with reasons.[17]

What leavens distrust and makes it possible to overcome it is a modicum of trust. Pure distrust, as Kant and almost everyone else has speculated, is no basis for a coherent society (the celebrated Ik notwithstanding). At the bottom of the spiral is *paranoia*, which deserves its own protracted philosophical treatment. Paranoia is a much-explored realm in psychiatry, of course, but the phenomenology and logic of paranoia is surely worthy of extended exploration as well.[18] Here is one suggestion: paranoia is often described in terms of delusion, seeing and suspecting what is not true or plausible, or, only slightly epistemically more respectable, forcing implausible interpretations on what may or may not be confirmable facts. But these dismissive views of paranoia miss the insight of that familiar joke, "sometimes they really are out to get you." Paranoia need be neither a falsification or the imposition of an implausible interpretative scheme. What it is often is a perfectly plausible but ultimately self-destructive perspective on the way things really are. It is being locked into a vision which, even if true, makes life and human relationships impossible. (It is well confirmed in the social science

Robert C. Solomon

literature that people who have a more accurate estimate of the likelihood of failure and betrayal do far less well than people who are "overly optimistic."[19]) But this is an essay on trust, not on distrust and its extremes. The point is that distrust—though certainly not paranoia or its pathological kin—is not so much antithetical to trust as it is an essential part of authentic trust.

IV Conclusion

Why are we concerned with trust? The reason for talking about trust is not just that trust needs to be analyzed as a philosophical concept but also that trust as a practice can thereby be implemented and restored. Not talking about trust, on the other hand, can result in taking trust for granted and distrust as a phenomenon beyond our control, resulting in disintegrating trust and continuing distrust. Trusting, whether it involves social or institutional constraints and sanctions or not, is more than a matter of individual psychology or personal "character." It presents us with an *existential* dilemma, one captured well by Fichte, who insisted that "the sort of philosophy one adopts depends on the kind of [person] one is." We should by now be tired of the once-bold cynicism borrowed from Hobbes *et al* that tries to appeal to irresponsibilty and human weakness and inescapable circumstances. What we believe philosophically makes a difference. Believing in the viability and necessity of human commitments is the necessary first step in making ourselves trustworthy, and it is the presupposition of trusting as well. Thinking of trusting as a shared social practice in which we willfully participate transforms both trustor and trustee. Trusting is not a matter of prediction and probabilities, not a matter of belief, not to be compared with machinelike dependability nor confused with reliance.

And that, by the way, is why trusting is yet another thing that computers cannot do.[20]

13

Emotion Theory Reconsidered

George Downing

The debts owed by the philosophic community to Hubert Dreyfus are many. One major theme Dreyfus has consistently highlighted is the role of skillful bodily practices in making our world intelligible. I here extend a similar line of thinking to the topic of affect and emotion.

Once it could be said that philosophers ignored emotion. No more. The last thirty years have seen the remarkable rise of what has come to be called "emotion theory." A substantial philosophic literature already exists in this new field—more than a dozen books, many articles. Nor is emotion theory limited to philosophy. A parallel growth of interest has taken place in experimental psychology, where emotion, long left aside, has almost overnight become a favorite research topic. Interestingly, a certain reciprocal influence between the two currents has taken place as well. The philosophical literature has at times helped shape the questions researchers choose to ask.[1] And certain research findings have had no small impact upon philosophic accounts. Discussions of emotion theory by anthropologists, sociologists and psychotherapists have added to this interdisciplinary atmosphere.[2] Impressive amounts of new laboratory data concerning the biological and chemical underpinnings of emotion have also been assembled by neurophysiologists.[3]

Descartes, Hume, Spinoza, and others in the history of philosophy have had insightful things to say about emotion.[4] But contemporary emotion theory, both in its sophistication and in its glimpses of wisdom, has taken the subject much further. For the reader unacquainted with this field as it stands today one can make several recommendations where to begin. William Lyons's *Emotion*, tightly argued and eminently readable, provides an excellent panorama of many of the dominant issues.[5] The first chapter of Justin Oakley's *Morality and the Emotions* nicely summarizes much recent philosophic literature.[6] (Oakley's account of the relation between emotion theory and moral issues is also of interest.) Robert Solomon's *The Passions* remains, to my mind, one of the richest philosophic treatments we possess (even if I disagree with Solomon about several important matters).[7] Nico Frijda's *The Emotions*,[8] Richard Lazarus's *Emotion and Adaptation*,[9] and Ekman and Davidson, editors, *The Nature of Emotion: Fundamental Questions*[10] are good places to start for more acquaintance with the experimental psychology research.

My concern here is with the philosophic literature. So much has been discussed, and so much brought into focus by the new philosophic literature, that it seems almost impossible a major theme could have been omitted. Yet one has been. Or so I will here argue. The role of the body in our experiences of emotion has been almost entirely overlooked. And in the few instances where not overlooked, it has been poorly understood. A more dramatic oversight is hard to imagine.[11]

I

However did it happen, this forgetting of the body in emotion theory?

One could speculate on many levels. I will mention just one important reason, however. Most of the progress in the new philosophy of emotion has been unleashed by a single key move. Let us look at emotion, proposed Kenny, Solomon, Lyons, and a host of others since, as a special form of cognition.[12] What drives an emotional experience must be a series of evaluations, appraisals, judgements, construals. Do I feel afraid? Then I have judged an object or situation as dangerous, and as threatening myself. Do I feel angry? Then I have appraised someone as having wronged me. Even when angrily kicking the flat tire of my car I have construed it, comically enough, as a being with agency, and which has acted unjustly, and which now is deserving of my wrath.

What makes these "special" cognitions different from emotion-free cognitions? How are they woven together with other cognitions and beliefs? How might we, by teasing out their cognitions, better define the distinctive nature of separate individual emotions? What is the relation of these cognitions to desire? To action? To reasons for action? To causes of action? These and a good many related questions have been extensively treated in the philosophy of emotion. About some there is now a rough consensus concerning their answers; about others, total disagreement. But almost everyone writing on these issues would assent to one point: it has been this focus on cognitive evaluation which has opened up the overall discussion in the first place.

I will not dispute that point either, as I thoroughly agree. Nor will I here say more about the controversies, themselves frequently fascinating, which have grown up around these various subsidiary themes. Instead, let me turn directly to the problem at hand.

Starting with what the recent literature has said about the body, I will argue that the typical claims to be found there lead inevitably to contradictions. I then will propose an alternative view, one giving a larger place to the role of the body in emotion. I will try to show how this perspective not only overcomes the former contradictions, but also allows us to make much more sense of many of the significant details of an emotional experience.

II

First, a more exact statement of what I mean by claiming the body has been left out.

I am talking not about the biochemical substratum of emotion, but about subjective body experience; about what we feel going on in our bodies, and what we do with them. Merleau-Ponty liked to speak about "the lived body."[13] It is the body as we live it, during emotion, which I am proposing deserves theoretical attention.[14]

What has been said up to now, in the emotion theory literature, about bodily experience? The few discussions which do exist might be grouped into three positions.

Position 1. The best step, for an understanding of the nature of emotion, is straightforwardly to put bodily experience to one side. Dismiss it, philosopher; it will only confuse and mislead you. Such, for example, is the clear message of Solomon (whose writings, let me repeat, are nevertheless among those I most admire, albeit for other reasons).[15] This is a position which has been inherited from Sartre.[16] A part of its intent is to maintain as much distance as possible from the old James-Lange theory of emotion. (James and Lange identified emotion simply and squarely with conscious body sensation, nothing more. A view which almost no one today, myself included, would want to defend.)[17]

Position 2. Our bodily experience of emotion, while not unimportant, is just a qualia, *a twinge-like something, about which nothing more can be said.* Of the three, this is the most prevalent position. Typical is Gordon.[18] Proposing (e.g., pp. 92f.) that what we sense going on in the body deserves mention, he then quickly decides there is nothing further to say about it. Nor is this a problem, thinks Gordon, since one can analyze the core of emotion, that is, its cognitions, quite independently of reference to the body.[19]

Position 3. Our bodily experience of emotion serves the limited purpose of assuring us that some form of emotion is indeed going on. This is the position of Lyons, who takes the rare step of actually discussing bodily experience in a more than cursory fashion.[20] Observing that the relation between emotion and the body is "a particularly neglected area in the philosophy of the emotions," Lyons spells out persuasive reasons for why this neglect should end.[21]

Beyond that admirable admonition, however, he manages to draw few other conclusions. The single more specific claim he makes is the one just stated, that the bodily dimension of an emotion is an indicator (both to oneself and to outside observers) that one's present state is in fact an emotional state.

Now certainly this is right, I think. Of these three positions it is Lyons's alone which accords well with the point of view I will propose below. Lyons genuinely broke new ground. Nevertheless, there is considerably more about the body and emotion which merits our attention.

III

Before moving to the view I advocate, I want first to show more clearly how strong our need is for some such alternative. Therefore a preliminary claim. It is that attempts to specify the nature of emotion without any reference to subjective bodily experience lead to inevitable contradictions. Here are three arguments in support.

1. *The intensity argument.* Surely the factor of degrees of intensity is a key aspect of what we mean by "emotion". I felt only a trace of sadness. I was overcome by a paralyzing fear. Although light at the start, the more she talked the stronger her anger became. An implicit scaling of the strength of emotion is built into our very notion of it.

Now, however to make sense of this factor of subjective intensity without referring to one's immediate bodily experience? Just try. One ends up almost at once speaking about the pounding of the heart, the catching or shrinking or expanding of the breath, the buildup or slackening of tonus in certain muscle groups (my hand starting to shape itself into a fist, etc.). Nor is this true only of the upper reaches of the scale of intensity. A subtle shift in breathing, a moment of softening or warmth around the eyes, barely perceptible: so for a split second my sadness occurs, like the touch of a feather.

This in no way implies that, for example, a softening of the eyes is all there is to a passing emotion. First of all, cognitive appraisals will also be an essential component. My sadness will be "about" something, and to unpack that "aboutness" is to refer to appraisals and beliefs. Second, a wish, a desire, a motivation toward some action (even if I cannot define at once what that action might be) will be another component. I am not trying to return to James-Lange. I am saying just that to talk about appraisals and beliefs, plus consequent desires and motivation as well, is not enough. Either one must deny that the scaled intensity is a part of what we mean by "emotion"— and who would want to deny that? Or else felt bodily experience is going to have to be brought into the story.

George Downing

It is instructive to see Armon-Jones, in her generally excellent *Varieties of Affect*, valiantly try to circumvent the issue of intensity.[22] She does at least recognize the problem. Incredibly, however, she proposes that when an emotion is intense, it is because, phenomenologically speaking, the *cognitions*, the thoughts, are intense! But what, other than accompanying bodily experience, could ever render a thought "intense"? The clarity of the thought? But thoughts can be clear without an occurrent emotion being present. A repetitive or persistent recurrence of the thought? But, first, a thought can naggingly keep recurring with a nevertheless low emotional aura to it. Second, a strong emotion can (this certainly happens at times) come and go quickly; in which case a repetitiveness of its cognitions could not be the defining aspect of its intensity.

I do not mean, by the way, that there cannot be another sense of "emotion" which does not require reference to any immediate experience whatsoever. We say Jack took action *X* because of his love for Helen, even though perhaps at the moment of doing *X* Jack felt, in his occurrent awareness, nothing particular on an affective level. In this case we are using a dispositional sense of "emotion." As others have cogently argued, this dispositional sense is derivative. It depends upon our understanding of emotion as episodes of felt experience.[23]

2. *The location argument.* Consider a test anyone can try. Next time a friend tells you about an emotion he is feeling at the time, ask, if circumstances permit, where in his body he is experiencing it (a familiar mode of exchange in psychotherapy.)[24] What I call "experiential interventions" are questions such as "What are you feeling?" "What is going on in you right now?" and the like. An important subtype is "experiential interventions focused on the body", for example, "Where in your body do you feel that?" "What is it like there, describe it more," etc. Or put the question to yourself at a moment you are feeling an emotion.

Almost always an answer can be given. The sadness makes itself felt in the throat, or in the chest, or around the eyes, or deep in the belly. Or in two or more places at once. Or globally, a diffuse spread-through-the-body wave. And it is the same for other emotions; there is a bodily location to notice.

How could such a question so easily make sense (let alone be productive in a therapy setting) if the dimension of bodily felt experience were not an inherent part of what we mean by "emotion"?[25]

3. *The "no object" argument.* A claim made in much emotion theory is that emotion always has intentionality: an emotion is always "about" something. I fear the snake, I am happy that Susan is coming to see me, I am anxious about life in general. No intentional object, no emotion.

Unfortunately this popular tenet, so stated, simply does not hold up. Consider another example from psychotherapy. Nothing is more common than for a patient to remark, in the middle of a session, "Right now I am feeling sad (or angry, joyful, etc.), but I don't know what about." As for an intentional object, she or he is aware of nothing whatsoever.

In the theory of emotion one familiar move designed to deal with such counterexamples is to distinguish between "emotion" and "mood." A mood is said to be more global, more diffuse, more lasting, and—devoid of an intentional object. Or, if not devoid, then (according to some authors who on this point follow Heidegger), having only the world in general as its object.

But that will not do. The psychotherapy patient who suddenly feels a sadness with no defined "aboutness" is not in a mood. The sadness is (often enough) not lasting, not diffuse. It may be quite sharp and defined in its quality; and, moreover, present for only a minute or minutes. In short, its experiential tonality may be thoroughly like any other sadness; the subject is just not aware of an object. Of course one could call it a mood anyway simply by definition, but only at the price of circularity.

Nor can we resolve the issue by pointing out that the subject may well, five minutes later, "get in touch" with an intentional object. For five minutes she feels sad; then an image of her grandmother swims into view, memories unroll, and the "aboutness," now brought into focus, becomes a theme for therapeutic discussion. First, for the initial minutes, before the image, the emotion was nevertheless without a *conscious* object; and a conscious object is what is required if our very concept of an emotion is to imply that it has specific aboutness. Second, plenty of times a patient will become sad, will search for what it might be about, and will "get in touch" with nothing whatsoever. Naturally a good working hypothesis for psychotherapy is that there was nevertheless an unconscious "aboutness" which failed to become conscious. But this is only an empirical claim, and a very rough one. Whereas the tie between emotion and object asserted by most emotion theory is held to be a logical tie.

What then is implied if I can feel angry, joyful, etc., yet not have conscious intentional objects for these emotions? Obviously, that my everyday sense of what counts, in general, as an emotion is what I find in my direct bodily experience. Granted, there exist some emotions which must, intrinsically, have intentional objects in order to count as that emotion: to experience envy arguably there must be a specific object of my envy about which I have formed some cognitive judgements. Nevertheless this is not true of many emotions; and hence not true of what counts for us as an emotion in the first place. We see once again that to deny the centrality of subjective bodily experience is to land ourselves in major inconsistencies. Whereas once we restore bodily experience to its rightful place—that is, to a theoretical position as central as that of cognitions—these artificially created perplexities fall away.

Two asides before continuing. First, I do think there is a way to salvage the claim that emotion essentially has intentionality. I will not develop the argument here, but only hint at it. When we feel sad, but do not know what about, we seem all the same to have a tugging sense of *a missing object*. Rather as when, speaking, one begins a sentence and then forgets how he meant it to end. In an analogous sense one might think of emotion as still displaying the basic structure of intentionality even in those instances where a blank occupies the place of the missing object. Indeed, that would explain why we are so aware of the blank as blank. This line of analysis, however, though it might well rescue intentionality, still cannot rescue a conceptual picture of emotion which leaves out bodily experience. (A point easily supported. Those instances of emotion where the blank alone is present will require a reference to something other than the blank itself in order to count the emotion as emotion.)

Second, let me be clear about what I am not saying. I am not proposing that what we mean by emotion words is *primarily* what is felt in the body. Nor am I implying we first learn the meaning of emotion words through something like introspection. (In both cases, I in fact believe the opposite.) My claim is merely that if we look at the conceptual role played by emotion words, then (a) we find a clear niche there for attributions of subjective body experience, and (b) the full role of emotion words cannot be made coherent without a recognition of this niche.

IV

Suppose then, we grant that what we feel going on in our bodies is a central component of emotion. Not the whole story, as William James thought, but a key part of the story. What else can be said?

Substantially more. But before considering the function of bodily experience we need to look closer at what is involved. One difficulty is that the sheer complexity of our bodily experience has been too little recognized. To be all too brief,[26] three distinct aspects must be pointed out.

1. *Autonomic nervous system activity.* I am speaking of course not about the physiological processes in themselves but about how they are subjectively felt. When an emotion is experienced our respiration alters, our heart beat speeds up or slows, etc.; and we feel some of these bodily changes, whether marginally or in a focused mode. Generally speaking, the stronger the emotion, the more such subjective correlates will be present. In intense fear we feel our hands sweat, our limbs tremble.

From Aristotle onward whenever philosophers have mentioned the bodily dimension of emotional experience they have almost exclusively described these felt autonomic phenomena. The same is true of the new philosophic literature. Physiological agitation caught by conscious perception—here is where the body is acknowledged when it is acknowledged at all.

Naturally an open question is to what degree, and in exactly what manners, these autonomic processes impinge upon our awareness.

Take, for example, electrodermal responses (changes in electrical conductance in the skin, measurably present during some emotions).[27] Do we have, at times, some marginal awareness of skin conductance? Or even, at times, a focused awareness? When subjects speak (as they do) about their skin burning, or crawling, or having "currents" shoot along it, are they referring to a perception—vague, but still a perception—of electrodermal changes?[28]

I am here not taking a stand on this particular question. My assumption is more limited. It is (a) that to some extent, autonomic activity is entering into our perception, however marginally; and (b) that this perception is a part (but only a part) of what we commonly mean by felt emotion.

2. *Motor preparations.* Our muscles are differently activated whenever we feel an emotion; and probably always so. This interesting side of affective experience, almost totally ignored in the philosophic literature, has been pinpointed and researched by some experimental psychologists.[29]

As we feel anger, for example, our posture and facial expression shift. Perhaps the shift is large, perhaps minute. When we choose to mask it sometimes it is almost imperceptible. But it is present; likely it is inevitably present.[30] Bodily we find ourselves preparing to attack. This may manifest itself as a muscular mobilization (again, perhaps almost imperceptible) of the jaw, as if we were preparing to bite; or a setting (perhaps almost imperceptible) of the shoulders, as if we were preparing to hit; or in similar ways. Most often muscles tighten. On occasion they slacken: with shame, for example, the neck loses tonus, "preparing" for what, if allowed to develop further, would become a slumping of the head.

Demonstrated rather conclusively in research settings is that anytime a subject reports herself feeling an emotion, some muscular activity is taking place in the face. Less research has been carried out with respect to the rest of the body. But what has been carried out, indicates that equivalent postural and muscular prepartions are also occurring.[31]

How present are these subtle mobilizations in our awareness? Quite a bit, I suspect, at least in a tacit mode. Certainly it is no accident, for example, that patients in psychotherapy, when asked to attend carefully to what they are experiencing when they sense an emotion, refer often to such muscular phenomena along with autonomic reactions.

3. *Body defenses.* Amazingly, this aspect has not been researched in experimental psychology. But it is so important I will mention it too, even though it is not necessary to my argument. It is familiar ground to many psychotherapists.[32]

When an emotion first emerges, we tend almost always to defend against it, bodily, to some degree. We use the body to reduce it, to keep its intensity down. Suppose that my anger subtly mobilizes my jaw, as if "preparing" it to bite; in that case certain other muscle groups are likely to tighten in opposition. These are unconscious habits of course. Probably they are learned in early childhood. Anytime an emotion makes itself felt they tend also to be in play.

"Anytime" is an informal guess, naturally. Exactly how often these body defenses manifest themselves—and with what degree of tightening and/or slackening correlated with what circumstances—are open empirical questions, ones which beg for serious research. Likely there are many forms of such body defense. They appear also to be intricately orchestrated. They can swing into play even when an experienced emotion is mild and passing. In fact they may function (this can be observed from the outside) even in situations where (a) one would expect a subject to feel emotion but (b) she does not. Which invites the hypothesis that the subject has prevented, that she has suppressed the experience, precisely by, in part, an unconscious use of these body defenses.

Clearly such body defenses are not a part of the emotion itself. They happen alongside of it, so to speak. They are worth mentioning, however, for reasons which will soon become apparent.

To summarize, whenever we have an emotion our bodily experience instantly becomes more complex. Not only is a lot going on, physiologically speaking; many elements of this physiological buildup impinge upon our subjective awareness. What then is the significance of this rich, intricate activity?

V

Almost every theory of emotion at a certain point turns down a speculative road. And ought to. Because a compelling question arises: that of function, purpose, *telos*. Why do we have emotions in the first place? What purposes do they serve? I want to sketch an answer which hopefully will do justice to the diversity and complexity of emotion.

Let me turn first to some creative suggestions advanced in recent years by certain experimental psychologists.

An emotion, argues George Mandler, tends to "interrupt."[33] It intrudes, it breaks in. This is one of its most striking qualities. Either it distracts me from the activity I am engaged in (I was reading a book, a sadness about a recent loss swims through me) or, if an emotion about that activity itself (as I talk to Kate I feel happy we are talking), it highlights certain qualities of the activity (or object) and obscures others. An emotion unsettles the phenomenological field. Our immediate relation to the world has been problematized. The stronger the emotion, the more disruptive this unsettling.

Consider next the helpful metaphor of Keith Oately, another leading experimental psychologist: an emotion brings us "news."[34] Like a red warning light it wants to inform us, to tell us something. This information is about a change, about something new we must take into account, concerning our plans and intentions. It is like a status report. Some significant situation has been altered in some way; one or more of our plans must be reworked. A dangerous animal appears from behind a tree: my fear tells me that my general intention of staying alive is now in jeopardy, it has an altered status. My friend has died: the grief sweeping through me announces, tacitly, that a host of projects concerning our relation has just crumbled.

Now add a third idea: an emotion creates in us a condition of "action readiness." This concept has been developed especially by Nico Frijda. The autonomic nervous system arousal, together with the muscular prepartions, key us up; we are poised to act. Perhaps better said, the emotion brings a shift in our action orientation. Anger throws us into an aggressive, high-arousal stance toward the world, for example. Whereas sadness more tends to disengage us slightly. We yield and soften, and ready ourselves as well, on a primitive body level, for the possibility of someone else consoling or taking care of us. (Of course one's habit may be never to let anyone take care of himself. All the same in sadness the body prepares for that.)

So, an emotion "interrupts," it announces "news," and it shifts my mode of "action readiness." How do these elements work together?

How they work together is the heart of the matter. With my attention caught, and my body in a changed state, I now enter into a process of what might be called *interrogation*. Bringing news, the emotion warns that something in my life—something, however small—is now different. But what is different? How is it different? And with what implications? Which sector of my belief-desire network requires revision? And at what level of generality?[35]

The key point is that I carry out this interrogation *with my body*; with, more exactly, a special form of embodied attending. The emotion has "cooked up" in my body. Maintaining this body state, letting it continue, I see how the object-situation (what the emotion is about) newly arranges itself in my perception. I read the situation, allowing one new aspect after another to emerge; and I do so using my body as a kind of instrument. Rather, as with visual perception, I must position my head so that my eyes can see, so, analogously, I utilize my body in its affective state to bring out what the new situation fully means to me. Often language is involved too; I look for words for the new situation. But even the search for words is supported and guided by this concrete deployment of my body.

Obviously this implies a complex set of bodily practices, of bodily skills. The emotional state must be not only maintained; it must be put to use. Felt bodily nuances must be welcomed, tracked, and allowed to develop; while at the same time the situation is allowed correspondingly to unfold itself in new guises.

There is a complex intentionality at play here. The body is playing several roles at once. Partly it operates outside of consciousness, as always; it sustains the intentional arc, in Merleau-Ponty's (1962) sense. But it is also, however marginally, present to perception. We might say that during moments of affective resonance it becomes more present, in an instrumental mode. It gives me both access to the world (prior to consciousness) and helps me (consciously) read the world.[36]

VI

It might be objected that an emotion sometimes comes and goes so quickly that no such interrogation takes place. But these are limit cases. For example, perhaps the interrogation process is condensed, it unfolds instantaneously. I was crossing the street—and suddenly I find myself crouched on the curb, sweating and shaking. A speeding car has just whizzed by, nearly taking my life with it. The emotion is fear, the cognitions are something like "danger, urgent, highest priority, move fast." But these are unconscious cognitions, a burst of high-speed automatic processing. Mobilization led directly to movement before any conscious choice could even be considered.

This foreshortening of the normal exploratory process is exceptional, however. It is more reasonable to call it a variant rather than a prototypical example of what we mean by emotion. Notice too, by the way, that even in this example the process of interrogation does not really disappear. It is merely displaced, as it were. Standing there on the sidewalk in my state of terrified arousal I will replay the incident, unfold its nuances, find language for it, and the rest. Using the double intentionality of my body state I will likely "work over" my perception of the event at some length.

Another limit case concerns emotions which come and go so fleetingly, nothing whatsoever happens beyond the felt bodily trace itself. Perhaps a twinge of anger goes through me but I distract myself as fast as I can. Here the interrogation process is truncated, rather than foreshortened or displaced. This is analogous to when a conscious visual perception, initially only a blur, is neglected and passed over rather than brought into focus. Were we to take such a moment as prototypical for visual perception in general, obviously we would understand little. The same for fleeting, undeveloped emotions. In their case the "news" is never delivered. There is a call to unfold meaning but the call is ignored.

Yet another limit case has to do with emotions artificially produced by biochemical means. A drug, or stimulation of the brain, may create a conscious affective state as intense as any. Here the announcement of "news" is in a certain sense a false announcement. What happens, subsequently, is of theoretical interest all the same: typically the interrogation process takes place anyway. It may be a derailed, comical interrogation; it may lead to evaluations and appraisals in their way as erroneous as when brain researchers artificially stimulate a subject's visual images. Nevertheless we see in this example too a version of the normal process which has simply gone awry.

In sum, a paradigm unit of emotion is an extended, complex act. It is simultaneously a bodily sensing; an aligning of this sensing with the relevant situation; and a forming of cognitions. This act has a certain brief duration in time.[37] It unfolds. It can last a second, several seconds, minutes even.[38] How long? An open question. I am making a claim here only about the minimum duration of prototypical cases of emotion. I am saying that an emotion in this sense lasts at least long enough (e.g., a second or several seconds) that a certain evolution of the feeling, however limited, can be consciously noticed.

We can also find examples which are reduced versions: no cognition results, or the body-sensing is almost eliminated by instantaneous action, for example. These partial versions can be easily understand as variants of the fuller version, however. Regarded only by themselves, on the other hand, the partial versions would never let us adequately grasp the workings of the fuller version.

VII

An implication of this analysis is that we must talk about practices and we must talk about choice. First, practices. If I am right that one uses her body to let the emotional qualities of a situation more fully emerge, then it makes sense to speak about doing this well or badly. We are talking about a group of skills which may be more or less well developed.

I will call these *body micropractices*. They include, for example: (a) the capacity to sense a buildup of emotional feeling in the body; (b) the capacity to allow a bodily state to be there, present and conscious, without cutting it off; (c) the capacity to use this state, like a lens, to explore the relevant situation; and (d) the capacity to follow the continuing nuances and modulations of the bodily state. Additional body micropractices overlap with linguistic practices: for example, (e) the capacity to combine affective sensing with a search for language for the newly emerging aspects of the situation; and (f) the capacity to confront one's intention hierarchy, locating the level of the hierarchy which best "fits" the intensity and import of the emotion (more shortly about the lattermost).

This is, of course, to describe body micropractices at a very general level. Their richness and complexity become more apparent when we enter into detail concerning distinct affective states. Then one can talk about the distribution of bodily attention, the functioning of breathing and movement, the contracting of specific muscle groups, and the like.[39]

A helpful idea has been proposed by Theodore Schatzki. In his *Social Practices: A Wittgensteinian Approach to Human Activity and the Social,* he distinguishes between what he calls *dispersed practices*—such as describing, ordering, explaining, questioning—and *integrative practices*—such as cooking practices, farming practices, recreational practices, etc.[40] Though both forms are cultural, dispersed practices are more basic and more widespread. They are also presupposed by almost all integrative practices, and enter into the latter as constitutive components.

The body micropractices I am describing seem to me clearly also to belong to the category of dispersed practices. Schatzki's list, which consists mainly of types of speech act, should be expanded to include them.[41] Body micropractices have a like pervasiveness in our lives, and a like basic quality. They also enter into many of our integrative practices in a similar fashion, that is, as constitutive components.[42]

One might object that, unlike speech acts, affective body micropractices have a strong biological "instinctual" element to them. But this objection is easily answered. Whatever the biological thrust to what we do with our bodies during emotional states, a substantial part of what we do is culturally shaped. In order to categorize body micropractices with other basic practices, all that is required is that a part (of the former) be culturally shaped.[43]

VIII

More about the cultural dimension of body micropractices.

From one person to another there can be tremendous variations with respect to these affective skills. Even for a single individual, his or her degree and mode of development may be noticeably different depending upon area of emotion (sadness, anger, etc.), level of intensity, interpersonal context (sending and receiving skills, etc.), and the like.[44] On top of this, there are the variations from culture to culture, social group to social group,[45] and family to family. How and when are such variations learned?

We are beginning to know something about this. Thanks to extraordinary progress in recent years in the experimental research of infant development, a solid hypothesis can be advanced.[46] Body micropractices are, for the most part, formed quite early. They are shaped by the minute specifics of repeated interactional exchanges during the first two years of life. Naturally genetic and constitutional factors have an effect too. As do, so far as can be determined, influences from later childhood, for example, imitation of peers, instruction in practices such as sport, and even trauma (which may leave a residue of new body defenses). But the impact of the preverbal years appears to be immense.

I have elsewhere discussed this research at length.[47] Much of it is based upon the analysis of videotapes of parent-infant nonverbal interaction. (There are quantitative means of doing so.) Let me here mention just an example. Daniel Stern has shown, with great precision, one series of typical formative patterns. Some parents, when the infant begins displaying a particular emotion (sadness, anger, joy, etc.), with their own adult bodies first join or mirror the rhythmic movements of the infant. Then, systematically, they subdue their rhythms, leading the infant in a like manner to dampen his (i.e., the infant's) expression. Others join, then systematically increase their movements, taking the infant with them into an expression patently more intense than the infant intended. Others join; and then, neither undermatching nor overmatching, permit the infant to feel out and explore her own evolving rhythm (the best outcome, needless to say). Others fail to join in the first place—no reciprocal rhythm, no matching. This leaves the infant isolated, so to speak, in his emotion (the worst outcome).

At Salpêtrière hospital, where we use videotape analysis of parent-infant interaction for both research and treatment purposes, we are confronted daily by these realities. What is remarkable is how these formative actions are mainly unconscious on the part of the parent. Yet they are systematic (the adult does them consistently over the months). And many of their effects are lasting (so far as, to date, it has been able to be determined).[48]

What such research demonstrates is a fascinating paradox concerning emotion. All of us tend to think of emotion as the most "natural" thing there is in us—the quintessence, for better or worse, of the instinctual, the precultural. And partly this is right; there exists a core of expressive movement tendencies which, as some excellent studies show, is clearly wired in, universal, operative equally in China and Mexico, operative equally in infancy and adulthood.[49] But mostly this image is wrong. The larger part of how we conduct our bodily practices during emotional states is the result of our having been exquisitely trained to do so.[50]

The implications I myself draw are somewhat different. Even though he often invokes "the body" it turns out that what Gendlin means is simply whatever a person might sense around the middle of her or his torso. This seems a surprisingly limited vision of embodiment. My preference is to emphasize, in therapy, a wider range of forms of contact with the body, as well as a more systematic reorganization of what I call affectmotor schemas (Downing, 1996). How this should be intergrated with the rest of the therapy is also more specific to the patient, the institutional or work setting, the therapeutic goals, and the like. Granted, one's "trainers" (fathers, mothers, grandparents, siblings, etc.[51]) were little conscious of this influence, this transmission, just as we in turn are little conscious when, as parents, we take over the role of initiator. That unawareness is no barrier, however. If anything, as Foucault well understood, it would seem to strengthen the sheer power of bodily cultural shaping.[52]

IX

There is a further fundamental point which at this time I can only mention. The discussion it deserves would require considerably more space.

So far I have talked about emotion episodes as if they basically implicate one person alone. But emotion also has a strong interactional component. This means not just that our early affective micropractices are built up in an interpersonal context. It also comprises the reality that our emotional states are often interwoven with those of one or more persons immediately present. When that is the case, the links are many and subtle.

Concerning an adult, we need to think about two sets of micropractices. One is those he mobilizes when alone; the other, those which come into play in contact with someone else. (Naturally the two sets overlap.) The interactional set includes, for example, (a) embodied skills for the "sending" of emotion to another person; (b) skills for the "receiving" of emotion from the other; (c) skills for "negotiating" such exchanges[53]; and (d) skills for using shared affective states jointly to disclose aspects of the world. I see this interactional dimension as having functions just as critical as those which operate on an individual basis.

This is a complex claim, however, and I must pursue its implications elsewhere.[54] In what follows I continue to focus upon the individual functions of affect only. The reader should keep in mind that half the story thereby remains untold.

X

We can now pass to a question which has generated considerable confusion in discussions of emotion: the question of choice. Some historical background is first necessary.

Traditionally, throughout the centuries, emotion was seen as "passion": it simply happens, the subject is "passive" before its onslaught. Choice was viewed as belonging only to subsequent actions: in anger one does or does not physically strike out, etc.

George Downing

An important countercurrent began with Sartre. In his *Sketch for a Theory of the Emotions* he took the position that we choose our emotions; and that we do so for strategic ends, whose exact nature we often camouflage from ourselves. Far from "suffering" an emotion, we implement it. A quite elaborate philosophic account of the nature of self-deceit accompanied this explanation. (Much of Sartre's later, best-known work, *Being and Nothingness*, in fact represents a continuation of these reflections upon self-deceit.[55]) In contemporary emotion theory a modified version of the same point of view has been advanced by Solomon in *The Passions*. While removing much of Sartre's accent upon manipulativeness, Solomon affirms the same basic claim that at bottom we choose our emotions.

Interestingly, this countercurrent has also surfaced in the field of psychotherapy. The same year Solomon published *The Passions*, Roy Shafer brought out *A New Language for Psychoanalysis*, a book which was enormously influential in psychoanalytic circles.[56] Shafer too, held that emotions do not happen to us. They are actually "willed actions"; we construct them, he thought. Why then does ordinary language describe emotions as simply occurring like the weather? Because, proposed Schafer, ordinary language bears the imprint of our avoidance. When we talk this way we collude in a flight from autonomy and responsibility.[57] A few years later a similar constellation of ideas gained currency among a number of "humanistic" therapists (principally in certain sectors of Gestalt therapy and Transactional Analysis). And it remains a point of view one hears often invoked.[58]

So which view is right? The traditional, that emotions happen to us? Or the new, that we cause them ourselves?

As I see it the question has been wrongly posed. Up to now the terms of this debate have been: do we have choice *of* an emotion or only *after* an emotion? But the analysis of emotion which has been developed here makes clear there is a third alternative: that of choice *during* an emotion.

A great insight, I would suggest, lies buried in the Sartre-Solomon view: that in our experiences of emotion there exists far more potential for the exercise of agency than we normally think. What is mistaken, however, is the Sartre-Solomon portrayal of what this agency can do.

Lengthy, persuasive criticisms of the countercurrent position have already been made.[59] Rather than repeat them here I will just state my agreement. In normal instances (i.e., apart from special cases involving manipulation) it makes no sense to say we choose to have an emotion. Emotions do *happen to us.* We react; and that reaction—including both a first cognitive appraisal and some first physiological stirrings—is underway, is well in movement, before we really know what is happening.[60] Up to this point the traditional view is quite right. We discover ourselves in the middle of our emotion as if we have been dropped into the sea.

But does that imply no dimension of choice is involved? Not in the least. Once the first wave of these parallel events (the initial appraisal, the autonomic reactions, the muscular activations) has crossed the threshold of consciousness, *then* we can talk, and should, about parameters of agency. We can talk about the various ways a person might steer his emotion; or accentuate or attenuate or interrupt it; or interrogate it; or refuse to acknowledge it; etc. We can talk about the perception, or the lack of it, of a steady stream of minute potential decision points. All of this comes after the emotion's onset, yet during its duration.

Once this essential distinction is understood a more precise critique of the countercurrent view can then be formulated. This critique applies equally to the versions advanced by Sartre, Solomon, Shafer, and those humanistic therapists advocating a similar perspective.

1. The idea that we are the authors of our emotions represents a basic misunderstanding of their function. Consider how things would be otherwise! Of what benefit would our emotions be if they did not literally force us to re-evaluate the world around us? What usefulness would these delicate instruments have if they were registering only the whims of our own choosing? That would be a curious way to live indeed. It would amount to a kind of autistic short-circuiting, a closing off of key channels of information. At bottom, survival itself would be rendered problematic—let alone the richness of a full emotional life.

2. A strength of the new view is that it tries to explain why it should be, in emotional experience, that we so often fail to perceive the potential for the exercise of agency. A weakness is that the new view

here gives too simplistic an answer. It pins the entire blame on self-deception: we hide our options from ourselves in order to evade responsibility. But clearly that is only one factor in play. A factor likely carrying far more weight is the degree of lack, for any given person, of the necessary bodily skills and habits.

I do not mean that the avoidance of responsibility counts for nothing. I too am convinced that self-deception can at times play a role. But it is an error here to see only the patterns of avoidance and to miss the deficit.[61] If I am right that not one but a series of skills are involved; and, as well, that they are complex, subtle skills; then no amount of "taking responsibility" can substitute for the gradual, step-by-step process of acquiring and/or refining those skills.[62]

3. The countercurrent view also ignores the fact that the physiological buildup has its own momentum, its own forward flow. Remember again how much is happening concurrently: (a) the autonomic phenomena (heart rate, breathing, sweating, etc.), and (b) the muscular mobilizations (e.g., jaw muscles subtly altered in preparation to bite, etc.), together with (c) the prechoice mobilization of the body defenses. One can no more "will" this collective pressure instantly to disappear than one could stop a heavy moving object in its tracks.

This is not to say that such physiological processes lie in one realm and choice in another. On the contrary. To the extent these processes are subjectively perceived they can be guided and modulated. For example, I can clearly affect, if in limited ways, the emerging muscular phenomena (both the muscular preparations and the counteraction of body defenses). Along with this I easily affect the emerging patterns of breathing (a leverage point of great psychological importance, incidentally). Likely too, I can affect a part of the additional autonomic nervous system phenomena (e.g., heart rate). (Research strongly suggests our autonomic responses are far more subject to voluntary control than one would intuitively think.) I can affect these body phenomena in themselves, and I can affect extensively how they are used to interrogate a related external situation. Nevertheless I cannot simply "will" that those processes not be there. Nor can I "will" that they have no forward drive, no ongoing momentum.

Only by taking account of these several restrictions is it possible to delineate the true locus of choice. We then give choice its due, acknowledging its pervasive presence in emotional experience. Yet we no longer envisage choice as total. One could say that the Sartre-Solomon view rightly confronted one area of human denial, that of responsibility and autonomy, only to collude with another area of denial, that of the reality of our embodiment.

XI

More about choice. An emotion brings "news," as already said. The news concerns a need to revise my belief-desire network. But right when I first grasp what the news seems to be about (i.e., when an initial version of an intentional object comes into awareness) there sometimes emerges a complication. My intentions and their supporting beliefs rarely exist in isolated forms: usually project A is a subproject of project B which in turn is a subproject of project C, etc. So just where in this nexus should I focus my attention? This is not always evident. Two or more contexts may appear equally relevant. I may find myself facing an inherent ambiguity, and forced simply to choose.

Consider an example. I hang up the phone. My cousin Robert has just informed me that something I said yesterday quite strongly hurt his feelings. (We had been trying yesterday to resolve a difficulty about a planned joint vacation.) In response I feel surprised, as I had not anticipated he would react this way, and disappointed, and angry at myself, and remorseful. Reeling somewhat, I grope for what it is in this situation which, using my activated body state, I want and need to scrutinize. As during any affective unfolding, partly I must feel out: *how much does it matter to me?* But in this case I must determine something else as well: *what exactly here is the "it" which matters?*

Is it my intention, now in doubt, of organizing the planned vacation? Or is it my larger project, in this (let us say) often strained relationship, of trying to bring about a better rapport? Or is it a still larger intention (adopted in recent years, let us say) of wanting more satisfying connections with my family as a whole? Or perhaps a wider intention still, of giving more attention in general to what happens between myself and others? Boxes nested within boxes nested within boxes. Which box now deserves my attention? At which level of description shall I focus my embodied attending?

The point is that occasionally one finds no fact of the matter here.[63] The emotion simply points, we might say, in an ostensive mode. "Pay attention now to *this*." So in one sense the givens of the revealed situation are crystal clear. Yet nothing is fixed with regard to which frame—a narrow one? broader? very broad?—to select for the unfolding of the interrogation. I have to leap, and in the instant.

It is this ambiguity of context in affective interrogation which, I would suggest, underlies some seemingly puzzling remarks about emotion made by Heidegger in *Being and Time*.[64] Discussing anxiety, for example, he first insists that it is different from fear. Now this is a common enough distinction. But Heidegger goes on to say that the true object of anxiety is not any concrete situation but rather the world as a whole. And shortly after that, the object of anxiety, instead of being "the world," is said to be my lifetime taken as a whole, my "being-towards-death" (i.e., my anxiety is about the fact that I might die without having realized enough of what is significant to me[65]).

At first glance what should appear a problem here is that anxiety, taken in an ordinary sense, is a common emotion. We all feel it often. Whereas Heidegger ends up forced to claim it is "rare," or that "true anxiety" is rare (1962, 234). He contrasts anxiety with fear in this respect, claiming the latter alone can be a mundane experience. Anxiety as a hidden potential is said to "underlie" fear, making it possible (1962, 234). But it is only fear that, according to Heidegger, we ordinarily sense. (He even manages to sketch a number of descriptions of types of ordinary felt fear [e.g., 1962, 181f., 391f.].)

Now one way to take all this would be simply to grant Heidegger his own semantic convention, and then assume that he has—astoundingly—nothing worth saying about anxiety as it is commonly referred to. I think there is a more interesting way to approach his comments, however.

When we consider the context-ambiguity often present in the intentional object of emotion, however, these comments no longer look contradictory. A strong emotional experience contains within it the possibility, should I so choose, of radically confronting my hier-archy of intentions at even its highest levels. My fear/anxiety can remain focused within a narrow context; or I can choose a more inclusive context; or I can even jump, should I so decide, to the broadest contexts possible. At the limit this can develop into a self-confrontation concerning, for example, my time on this earth as a whole. Deep inconsistencies may emerge in what I have held to be true. My strongest values may be brought into question, as well as central beliefs about self and others.

I prefer this reading as I find Heidegger's discussion in general a profound one. Many of Kierkegaard's finest reflections are also about precisely such affective escalations.[66] Kierkegaard speaks not only about our need for these experiences, but also about how they can be undergone wrongly or rightly—how they can become either traps of self-torment or pathways toward productive change.[67] He develops this point not only about fear,[68] but also about sadness.[69] I would suggest there is a like analysis to be made, though I will not take it up now, about both anger and happiness; perhaps certain other emo-tions as well.

Need I add that here too we are talking not only about choice, but also about a set of background skills which underlie the capacity for choice? Certainly that is one reason Kierkegaard says so much about repetition. In Kierkegaardian repetition, if one looks carefully at the texts, it is not only a matter of picking up the slipping-away threads of some recent emotion-based reworking of projects and beliefs. It is also a matter of learning how to do it. This can only be achieved, Kierkegaard sensibly holds, by over and over engaging in the process itself.[70]

XII

Some last remarks. Cognitive theories of emotion are fond of accent-ing its affinities with rationality. Typically they support such an idea in one or both of two ways.

First, as summarized above, each emotion type is said to have a cognitive kernel consisting of several judgments expressible in propositional form. An emotion thus has a kind of internal

George Downing

propositional structure. And where we have propositions, we already have at least the building blocks of rationality.

Second, cognitive theories often point out how pervasively we tend to think of occurent emotion episodes as being appropriate or inaproriate to their objects. When we say of a fear it is exaggerated, or on the contrary that it suits its object, we invoke normative constraints, a mind-world fit.

Both claims seem to me justified. I think there is more to be said on the subject, however. If anything like the analysis I have given here is right, then there exists a deeper sense in which our emotions are interwoven with rationality. Emotions have the function, I have argued, of bringing us face to face with discrepencies in our belief-desire network. They do not merely deliver information; they pressure us to revise some specific grouping of inconsistent beliefs and intentions.

To say this is not in the least to portray human life as excessively rational. By "rationality" here I mean simply the norms of noncontradiction together with simple induction.[71] It is only against this backdrop of norms that any lack of coherence can be seen as such.

In point of fact I see our lives as fraught with inconsistencies major and minor. Precisely what is so fascinating about emotion is how it ferrets out irrationality in this technical sense. No less fascinating is how such acts of revision depend upon the exercise of embodied skills.

14

Heideggerian Thinking and the Transformation of Business Practice

Fernando Flores

Hubert Dreyfus's interpretation of Heidegger has led to changes in theoretical work and in practice in fields usually thought of as quite distinct from philosophy. His work is, for instance, ever more widely disseminated in the information technology community.[1] I believe that Dreyfus's Heidegger opens up even more profound possibilities for change in business management. With Dreyfus's Heidegger as a cornerstone of our thinking, I and my colleagues at Business Design Associates (BDA) have been developing, and applying with our clients, an alternative description of business that both challenges the interpretations held by most business consultants and people trained in U.S. business schools and leads to significant increases in competitiveness. I will show how certain claims derived from Dreyfus's Heidegger drive our work.[2] But since our work is moving business in an unusual direction, I will begin by reviewing the standard interpretation of what business is about. I will then turn to our reinterpretation of business, and elaborate the consequences in five prominent areas of business activity: (1) understanding the customer, (2) designing business processes, (3) finance, (4) implementing of strategic change, and (5) entrepreneurship. (This understanding of business also has important consequences for understanding power, strategy formation, and marketing, but space limitations prevent me from entering into these discussions.) My general thesis is that business thinking and practice should be understood as a branch of the humanities. When they are not, all of us lose, whether we are directly engaged in traditionally commercial activities or not. There is a second thesis that I will not argue, but merely state as a belief: it is the duty of practitioners of the humanities to give business studies their appropriate place in educational curricula.

I   Business Practice as Commonly Understood

Most management consultants and managers who adhere to their Master of Business Administration (MBA) training believe that human beings are best understood as rational beings with desires. Such beings use their reason (sometimes with and sometimes without active deliberation) to analyze their feelings into desires. They then use their rationality to invent ways to satisfy these desires. So far, in this account, there is no business. Business comes on the scene as the primary means we invent for allocating goods that satisfy desires. All who engage in business—that is, virtually everyone—allocate satisfaction by exchanging valuable goods and services. Consequently, theories of business have focused on exchange, and modern business has developed from the attempt to produce the greatest aggregate exchange value at the least cost. Consultants and managers advocate a variety of measurements for this kind of exchange value production. Raw profit, operating margins, cash flow, and market share are the standards, but one has only to pick up a *Sloan Management Review* or *Harvard Business Review* to find business thinkers proposing more and more elaborate measures such as the cost of capital and return on investment.

Because the exchange-centered account ignores what makes business activity fully worthwhile for us as human beings, it leads to an enormous amount of wasteful business behavior. Worse, it turns those business practitioners who try to follow it into optimizers who act as if their lives would not be worth living if the price of their companies' stock were to decline. Such a life is one of frenzy or resignation, each of which disables innovation and commitment.

What alternative description of business should we construct? First, we should replace the Enlightenment view of human beings that undergirds so much business thinking. Here Dreyfus's account of Heidegger becomes relevant. Human beings are not desiring subjects, though they have fashioned themselves that way since Descartes. They are beings who cope skillfully with their environment and each other in a coordinated way. As such, they acquire shared skills (which we, following Wittgenstein and Dreyfus, call practices), and establish equipment and roles. Together, practices, equipment, and roles help determine how things and people are encountered. For example, given one set of practices, equipment, and roles, people will be dealt with as saints and sinners; given another set, they will be dealt with as independent, choosing beings. We are capable of encountering desks, chairs, and professors not because they have some *essence* that we apprehend, but because we have a context of objects like desks, tables, lecture halls, universities, degrees, books, and so forth. Of course, these interrelated pieces of equipment, people, and institutions are not enough to make chairs, desks, and so forth, intelligible. We must also have shared practices for using chairs, for writing or reading at a table, for listening to lectures, or entering into discussions with a professor. It is in this equipmental, institutional, and practical context that we can identify a chair or a classroom. But we need more than equipment, institutions, and practices to identify human roles such as a professor or a student. Certain related practices have to be collected together so that they reveal *a way* of dealing with equipment and other people, and that way has to be taken as worthwhile. When a way of dealing with equipment receives general recognition we see it as a role, for instance, professor or student. Of course, it does not follow that things and practices from other cultural contexts are invisible to us. They appear as strange rites and artifacts.

Human beings, then, disclose or open up shared contexts in which things and people can appear as the particular things and people they are. That we are disclosers is one of the critical notions that we at BDA have appropriated from Dreyfus's teaching of Heidegger. We also appropriate an observation that for Heidegger follows from the last. We are at our best when we are acting in a way that reveals us to ourselves as disclosers.[3] Acting as though we are desiring subjects, which we now tend to do unreflectively, opens up a world of equipment and roles but does not open up a sensitivity to ourselves as those who create and preserve the world in which things and people show up in a particular way. If we look for evidence that we assess ourselves to be experiencing life at its best when we are disclosing, we can find it in many simple cases. We might consider how we have felt when, with others, we were setting up institutions in which things were going to appear in a distinctive way. Other examples are entering into marriage and other forms of partnership. Most of us can remember the flurry of engaging activity at such creations. We can even remember the wonder we experienced as we formed new practices such as joint financial accounts that enabled us to see and experience new things such as financial responsibility. "Life at its best" is the term we use at BDA to indicate the phenomenon Heidegger calls authenticity.[4]

II Understanding Needs and the Customer

The light that this way of thinking about human beings shines on business activity is rather surprising. If we begin to think of ourselves as disclosers, our descriptions of most businesses that we care about will change. We will no longer see them as doing a good job at supplying a widget. Rather, we will see that the business is valuable because it enables us to have a new need for the first time, and in so doing, it encourages us to develop new practices that inflect or reconstitute our world in some small way. Such a business is sensitive to the tensions in the lives of its customers—tensions that the customers may assume are unavoidable—and produces a product to relieve them. For example, no one needed the first disposable razor. No one needed the first speed bumps. No one needed the first frequent flier mile. No one needed the first computer mouse. But once created, the need seems to live on its own. Indeed, businesses act as though the need had been discovered and try to prevent other businesses from producing a competing good to satisfy that same need. However, in focusing exclusively on the need, average businesses overlook the relationship with the customer that led to the production of the new thing in the first place. Because they do not see this relationship as one where people are collaborating on a new way of constituting reality, they tend to merely offer a product that will satisfy a preexisting desire. When they have succeeded, they then look for another unmet desire. Many businesses, then, do not see how they can play a continuing role in developing the new world opened by the new product. The computer industry's sponsorship of users' groups provides one example of how this can be done.

What is the lesson to be drawn from this? Business is not primarily about exchange, but rather about establishing relationships with customers that "articulate" the customers' concerns and needs. Effective business sensitizes all engaged with it to our nature not as desiring beings but as disclosive beings. The basic relation to the customer, as exhibited in the businesses we most appreciate, is world building, not exchange.

Most MBA graduates would summarize this by saying that effective businesses listen to the customer and innovate, and that these activities must be added to the core activities of producing quality goods for exchange at low cost. But as businesses are currently constituted, the drive for cost cutting and quality usually hinders the establishment of innovative relations with customers and produces goods only slightly different from those of competitors. The reason is that executives who focus on cutting costs frequently eliminate all that is experimental, and their efforts also dampen the motivation to listen attentively to customers' tensions or concerns that do not directly address the existing product.

As understood within the dynamics of exchange, quality means getting a product to the customer quickly, making accurate assessments of the customer's need, telling the truth, treating customer complaints fairly, and so forth. One week, I interviewed a major automaker and a leading medical supplies producer. Executives from both companies were proud to show me their lists of corporate values. They were identical. Each company was trying to establish the same relationship with its customers. They cared about on-time delivery, low product breakdowns, and so forth. The car company did not include among its values the love of driving, cool cars, or of comfortably driving the family on vacation. The medical supply company did not extol the love of an active life, freedom from disability, responsiveness to the stresses of physicians, or anything of the sort. Both companies will make incremental improvements in the convenience and prices they offer their customers, but it would be unwise to expect them to show their customers that something previously thought impossible is in fact possible. Consequently, it is unlikely that most customers will come to care deeply about these companies or love their products. Yet, these companies both understood themselves as beings sensitive to the customer and innovative. And according to the current standards of business thinking, which do not acknowledge the constituting of worlds, they are.

III Designing Business Processes

If the basic activity of a business is forming relationships that articulate its customers' concerns so as to disclose new worlds, how is such a business to be designed? We find that we can bring out the disclosive nature of people by focusing on a business's most important commitments, which are overlooked in most everyday transactions. By attending to the structure of commitments, we also show how the roles of the parties can be reconstituted through the formation of new commitments. For instance, if salespeople can only make requests to delivery people, then salespeople become order-takers. When they can make requests to R&D, they become, in part, innovators. By changing the structure of commitments, we can redesign a company to begin making flexible offers. Seeing our actions as guided by explicit commitments is one of the marks of modern, contractual culture. The customs and duties of traditional cultures and some companies run by tradition are relatively hard to change. But if one sees obligations in terms of commitments, one can make commitments that go beyond what is customarily done. Thus, recognizing commitments makes for greater flexibility. Today's flexible, disclosive organization is best understood, then, as a network of commitments. Once we see this, we can both diagnose and design an enterprise according to the kinds and structure of commitments it seeks to perpetuate.

How does an enterprise look when it organizes its business practices around its commitments? Let's start with the basic elements of commitments: (1) requests and offers, (2) promises, (3) execution of promises on the basis of interpretations of these promises, and (4) assessment of the relationships constituted by the promises.[5]

Businesses are frequently organized around those issuing requests and those executing them: bosses and employees. A business is considered efficient if many of the requests are standing requests—like teaching so many courses each semester—that do not require an explicit statement of the request or any interpretation in the execution. This kind of arrangement makes sense when the business is organized around processes for dealing with things. But innovative and customer-sensitive organizations are designed to replace the standardized request and execution relationship with requests, offers, promises, and interpretive execution.

To get a feel for the significance of adding promises, think of the difference between Federal Express and the U.S. Post Office. Federal Express *promises* to have your package arrive at a certain time—and there are many stories about Federal Express employees who have gone beyond standard procedures to fulfill that promise. The U.S. Post Office, by contrast, *predicts* when your package will arrive. To bring this difference home, compare a 911 service that promises the police will arrive within three minutes with one that predicts they will arrive within three minutes. And to see the difference between execution and interpretive execution, contrast the babysitter who says at the end of your evening, "Your son ate at seven, went to sleep at eight and is fine now," with the one who tells you about the conversation she engaged your son in while he was eating, who delights in the inventive game they came up with together, who encouraged him to brush his teeth by telling him a tale about crocodiles, and who then read him a story that teaches a lesson she loves. The first has executed her instructions. The other has actively interpreted them and is checking the interpretive execution with the customer.

The distinction between normal business and commitment-based business comes out clearly when we look at simple institution-building. Compare the proposal of partnership that is met with a promise and the one that is met with a prediction, as is frequently the case today when people respond with predictions about when they can think about this or that proposal. Compare the marriage in which each partner says, "I do it this way," with the marriage in which partners say to each other, "How shall we agree to do X?"

At BDA, we organize a business's practices around the commitments that people in the business make to each other and to customers. Managers observe and manage certain kinds of commitments. Assessment of the relationships that are established occurs regularly so that they can be adjusted. Employees make offers and promises, and perform interpretive executions. Finally, commitments are organized so that the customer's concerns are always kept under consideration by an internal customer who represents the interests of the external one. Such organization enables a business to have a relationship with its customer that can regularly bring delight to each. It is like the innovative marriage mentioned above, rather than the routine one.

IV Finance

To understand the world of finance as it is currently constituted, one has to imagine commerce starting with desiring, rational agents in a state of scarcity and need. One sees them squaring off against each other, taking each other's measure, and concluding that it would be better to make a compromise involving an exchange than it would be to battle for everything. Hence, in finance, commitments are not basic; bitter, oppositional need is.

Of course, few economists or finance directors will say they literally believe that this is how commercial activity began. But they will say that thinking this way provides the best model. In our view, this model has at its core certain key elements that lead to wastefully antagonistic relationships among a company, its customers, and its suppliers. First, the products exchanged are taken to pre-exist and have fixed values independent of the exchange relationships.[6] Second, the negotiations involved in the exchange are seen strictly as short-term, zero-sum transactions in which one party profits in the deal and the other loses. This model does not predict behavior so much as lead to pointless waste and antagonism. The wastefulness comes out most clearly in the way working capital is handled.

Working capital management is a matter of predicting the flow of money into and out of accounts and timing billing and payments so as to maximize cash on hand. For simplicity's sake, we will say that the management of working capital, which falls on finance departments, amounts to an effort to squeeze as much as possible from those indebted to the company and to pay as little as possible to the company's creditors. This gets complicated as finance managers develop strategies for acting on the basis of predicted flows of capital. For instance, if inventory expenses are mounting, a finance manager might order salespeople to discount the price of the product. But such discounting could significantly reduce the funds available to pay vendors before they initiate litigation. Timing counts. Even then, if that reduction exceeds the savings in warehousing costs, the sale failed. If not, it then succeeded.

Working capital management gives us a glimpse of the original state of human beings as understood by economists and MBAs. Though contractual commitments and custom govern much of what we do, whatever they do not govern is open to the wits and tactics of finance departments, whose job is simply to take as much as they can get away with. In this context, customers and suppliers are treated like enemies.

What is BDA's response, philosophically and practically? Philosophically, we follow Dreyfus's Heidegger. Heidegger believes we will never understand the meaning of our activity if we try to find a starting point before there were human beings dealing with each other. Similarly, we believe that for understanding commercial activity, we must begin with the earliest relationships that articulated concerns as needs. In both cases, the basic claim is that any activity can only be explained by taking into account what worthwhile way of living the activity came from.[7] It cannot be made intelligible by examining an earlier way of living or a bunch of motivations, actions, and so forth that are not already linked to one another by considerations of worthiness. Before relationships that articulate concerns as needs, there is neither business nor incipient business.

If forming commitments is a basic part of the business activity of articulating concerns, then any area in which there are concerns to be articulated but no commercial commitments obviously presents a commercial opportunity. That is the situation in the maneuvering that goes on over working capital. Therefore, at BDA, we help our clients see that even the company that is winning the working capital war is in a losing commercial position overall. We have found that it is almost always possible with modern communications networks for two companies to develop and manage working-capital commitments collaboratively and thereby handle collections and payments to the advantage of both. Game theorists maintain that informal agreements of this sort should always fail because there is invariably one business that will grab the opportunity to take advantage of another even if it reduces overall revenues to both. But we know that friends tend to avoid injuring each other merely so that one can have an advantage over the other at the cost of both. Likewise, we find that those businesses that are constantly in communication and jointly striving to keep the working capital of each at zero tend to keep such agreements and avoid the game theorist's zero-sum game.

In general, we teach finance departments to understand their accounts in terms of the underlying commitments that they measure. Accounts payable is the name of the journal in which we keep track of the promises we have made to suppliers in exchange for promises they have made to us. Accounts receivable is the equivalent journal for our relationships with our customers. Payroll is the journal in which we watch the fulfillment of promises made to employees in exchange for employees' promises to the company. Inventory is the result of procurement and production in absence of, or out of timing with, requests of customers.

By helping our clients see these accounts as measures of promises and synchronization of promises with delivery, we spur the realization that careful attention to all the elements of a commitment builds relationships in which parties are disposed to treat each other with respect and not as enemies. Once members of finance departments see their accounts as measuring promises kept in a timely way *inside relationships*, problems can be understood in terms of relationships. Thus, for example, the question of timeliness of payments may generate the following sorts of questions: *On what payments are we late? Have we overcommitted? Are we in condition to fulfill our promises? Are our suppliers fulfilling their commitments to us?* Such questions represent a huge transformation over the standard attempts to pay as late as possible, make as many commitments (sales) as possible, and try to pay less to suppliers.

Asking our questions leads to the building of innovative relationships in which concerns are articulated so that they can be turned into needs for which mutually beneficial exchanges can take place. Bringing this relationship-based perspective to our clients' businesses has often allowed them to cut more than 30 percent of the current costs of operations. That should show even the most hardened finance director that the standard model governing his behavior fails to capture the nature of commercial enterprise adequately.

V Implementing Strategic Change

1 The Common Understanding of Implementation of Strategies

For the most part, strategy implementation supposes that both desire and rationality are clear and controllable. Rationality operates over various domains of facts that are clear to all. People are understood as being good at calculating within these domains. Desires are changed by changing reward structures. The activity of strategy implementation then depends on leaders who have wills strong enough to overcome ingrained habits, both in themselves and in others. It should come as no surprise that strategy implementation is one of the most vexing parts of standard business activity. Let's examine the four basic elements of traditional strategic implementation.

First, rationality is assumed to work on clear facts and therefore produce results clear to all. The common understanding is that before proceeding to implement action, a strategic objective must be set and well understood by everyone. For the most part, the objectives are determined by a small group of people or a single high-level executive.

Second, people are understood in terms of their calculative ability, not their ability to manage commitments and trust. The team designated to implement a strategy will then be the team with the appropriate calculative skills. In addition, the structure of implementation teams are set up so that being selected to implement the new strategy is seen as desirable. Consequently, the power structure of the organization changes with the constitution of the team. Those that are on the team are now seen as having power to make changes, whereas before, power lay elsewhere in the organization.

Third, we see that although simple behaviorism is dead in the academic world, it lives a hardy life in the corporate human resources environment. There, it is assumed that implementation is best achieved when incentive structures are aligned with the strategic objectives of the organization. People must be rewarded for acting in accord with new goals of the organization and punished if they act otherwise. Often this takes the form of basing a percentage of employees' compensation on altered behaviors favoring the new corporate values. For example, if the strategic change is to establish a customer focus along with empowerment of employees to address customers' concerns, employees who respond to customer complaints by making a decision on the spot will be rewarded for these actions with increased compensation.

Fourth, we are also habitual beings. The role of leaders in implementation is that of establishing and maintaining the new standards that provide the means for achieving the corporate objectives and supporting the overcoming of old habits. The view of human beings as rational, desiring agents is clear: give employees the appropriate procedures, and if there are financial incentives to apply them, they will do so. The leader must constantly and willfully maintain the standard and make sure people do not fall back to the old way of behaving.

2   Our Response: Style

Understanding human beings as desiring, rational animals causes business theorists to miss precisely what is most important and difficult about making a strategic change. Changing compensation structures in order to change desires and isolating clear goals to appeal to rationality reveal enormous blindness to the organization's way of being, something Heideggerians care about. This is not to say that a business enterprise as a social type has a way of being that is different from that of a church or a university, (although this is true) but that each business enterprise has its own way of being, which we call a "style," focused in exemplary acts that are most admired by people in the organization.

At Apple, for example, the exemplary act could well be the work of the "hot group" led by Steve Jobs that spawned the Macintosh. If it is, we would expect that people at Apple would feel at their best if they are working in hot groups. Development of anything would appear as the occasion for a hot group. A career would be understood in terms of a series of hot groups. Power would be measured according to one's ability to constitute hot groups, and so forth. Based on the Macintosh hot group, Apple would have a rebellious, hyperflexible style. High-tech companies in the genetic engineering field tend to have academic nurturing styles. Companies founded by engineers cultivate managers who try to bring employees, suppliers, distributors, production schedules, and everything else under control as though they were all forms of equipment. Thus each type of company, as well as each enterprise, manifests a different style or way of being, focused in a different type of exemplar.[8]

Even those business theorists who recognize that companies have different styles—bureaucratic, lean, competitive, monopolistic, marketing oriented, or production oriented—miss the effects of those styles. The style of a company determines what possibilities are noticed and what is considered important in the company. People in a flexible, hot group company will look for opportunities to be in a hot group that goes against the norm. They will seek opportunities for discontinuous innovation. As a result, they will miss many opportunities for continuous improvement. People in a company with a nurturing style will work on their own projects without much concern for the customer, whether their work is central to the company, or whether it runs against the corporate grain. They will seek opportunities for independence.

Since corporate style determines how people in a company assess what is important and what it makes sense to do, any change in strategy, which redirects the focus and energies of the company, will require the implementation of a new corporate style. Currently, when corporate leaders come to see that they need a culture change, they tend to think they must fire a lot of people who have the old temperament and hire others who have the new one—fire lots of introverted engineers and hire legions of extroverted marketing types. Such an act almost always lowers esteem for the new strategy and raises levels of distrust to enormous and quite costly heights.

Strategic implementation, we believe, requires recognition of style change, and style change involves three basic components: (1) the development of a new admired exemplar, (2) the institution of new commitment structures that give people worthwhile roles conforming with the new style and revealing internal and external customers to them in a new way, and (3) the cultivation of trust.

3 Exemplars

Conventional strategy consultants will advocate the strategic direction that promises the greatest sustainable competitive advantage. They will then attempt to form a strategy appropriate to the company's resources, but the emphasis will be on finding a niche in which the cost of competing with the company is prohibitive. Then, given such a strategic goal, companies try to implement it by finding people with the right functional capacities, changing the compensation program, and then moving at once. But since a style change is required for such a change in strategy to stick and for people to care about it, this approach produces at best incremental changes, even when incredible forces of will are exerted by the executive team. The reason is simple. People know only the goal they are shooting for, not how their concerns, ways of working together, sense of possibility, and sense of the customer's concerns must be changed to make the plan work. In short, they do not have a good example of what their company should look like with the new strategy, or a sense of the new style they will need to embody.

Goals such as product development and increases in market share can be pursued with different styles. Questions proliferate. Should costs be cut by trying to get better control of everyone's time? Or should highly coordinated just-in-time strategies that require careful use of communications systems be implemented? In the one case, the company develops a highly supervisorial, controlling style. In the second case, the company develops a collaborative, team-playing style. But if managers institute the strategy using different styles from one division to another, they will produce all sorts of breakdowns in coordination, communication, and trust across divisions.

A small-scale project that institutes the new strategy in the division where it would be most congenial makes for a much better beginning. To make the strategic change, that division may draw on practices that are relatively marginal in the company. One of our favorite examples is a cement company we worked with. This company was famous for keeping costs low and margins high. It saw the world through the controlling eyes of engineers. But customer satisfaction with its quick-drying ready-mix product was low. The company claimed to deliver the product at the time the customer requested it. If it arrived late or early, that was because the customer's organization (usually the customer was a large contractor) was a mess, according to the company. Customers, in contrast, told the cement company that it was rigid, inflexible, and did not understand that in the contracting business many changes had to be made over the course of the day. Customers wanted to call the cement company and reschedule as late as the morning of the delivery. This seemed impossible. We asked the cement company how it could take its customers seriously. We looked at emergency rooms, 911 operations, fire departments; the joint BDA-cement company team emerged with the overall sense that the cement company was really supplying crisis managers, not orderly builders. They then examined their own practices for handling internal crises and worked to develop these practices for application to the customer. The results made the ready-mix business so able to dominate the market that the company had to worry about antitrust pressures. This new style of working with contractors is now beginning to pervade the company. An exemplar like ready-mix operations gives managers in other areas a stimulus to form their own interpretation of the ready-mix success. Since the change is being made division by division on the basis of an exemplar rather than through a changed set of procedures, each division gets to determine how it makes sense of the success of the exemplar and thereby feels ownership for what is done on the basis of that interpretation.

4   Redesigning the Structure of Commitments

While the exemplar sensitizes managers to a change in style, the managers actually bring the new style into their own areas by redesigning their business practices. Business practices are essentially the practices that articulate a concern in such a way that the concern may be addressed by satisfying a need. Such articulation happens inside commitments. Hence, in changing the style of his or her area in order to implement a new strategy, a manager establishes a new structure of recurrent commitments. He or she also determines the competencies of people who will fulfill the commitments and of those who will evaluate how the commitments have been fulfilled. Furthermore, the manager establishes the new understanding of the customer. Is the customer extremely cost conscious? Does the customer want to be delighted by new products? Does the customer want to be served in a particular way? The manager answers these sorts of questions in terms of the new exemplar he has been given. In the case of the cement company, the customer wanted to be saved from a crisis. The commitment structure that was developed did not call for long-range plans but for flexibility. It involved offering emergency rerouting of quick-drying cement at special prices.

In restructuring the commitments of their areas in this way, managers establish an environment in which their employees articulate the style and the strategy according to their best lights. The new style is reflected in who makes promises to whom. If the company wants lots of product development, then someone from product development must be involved in making commitments to customers. Product development is in the loop that considers customer complaints and so forth. If cost cutting is the issue, then people representing finance are involved in important commitments. When the structure of commitments is carefully adjusted, employees actively—rather than reflectively—buy into and promote the change each time they make a commitment.

However, getting employees to take commitments seriously is quite difficult. Even senior managers tend to fall back into standard ways of acting. For this reason, commitment coaching is an essential part of any implementation scheme. Hopes, complaints, statements of procedure, wishes, guesses, and so forth all have to be turned into requests. Perceptions that others are confused, and know-it-all claims about what will happen, have to be turned into offers. Predictions have to be turned into promises. Without such coaching within the new commitment structure, the new strategy will be implemented only at great cost. Coaching also produces a change in background dispositions to act and speak that enables people to deal with themselves as disclosers of situations rather than as rational, desiring beings. How this works will become clearer in the context of the cultivation of trust.

5   The Cultivation of Trust

Few corporate actions produce distrust, resistance, and resentment as much as changes in and implementations of new corporate strategies. Most of us see this as an empirical truth with obvious causes. Changes in strategy threaten jobs and ways of working to which people have become accustomed. A company that threatens the welfare of its employees and its suppliers undermines their trust. However, the trust that is weakened here is not the best form of trust and would be better termed a sense of security. This security depends on an underlying feeling that our identities are fixed, fragile, and constantly under threat of attack. Heidegger, according to Dreyfus, saw that this view of the self is strongly enhanced by certain prevalent structures of modern organizations that involve trying to look good, fitting in, gossiping, and so forth.[9] In such an environment, things are normally spoken behind people's backs. Credibility is built and harmed anonymously. Distrust flourishes on most occasions. Add to the fearful swirl of gossip a directive to change, and what little stability that does exist, is lost. For this reason, any institution of a new corporate style and strategy has to be implemented with trust-building practices.

Building trust requires change in many areas of organizational design, commitment formation, and role formation.[10] Initially, it means learning to make assessments of others' sincerity, competence, and his or her care for one's own identity. (Care for one's identity means most importantly helping one form and fulfill commitments and helping one maintain high credibility as someone who makes and fulfills important offers.) For this reason, one of the main trust-building practices must be *regular* and honest assessments of managers and employees, mostly made openly among team members. I emphasize regularity because at first people will game assessments using them to enhance their own power and diminish that of others. But if assessments are made regularly and publicly, power games become obvious after a while and the styles of speech that breed distrust become far less influential. Even more important, people come to see that their own speaking, as opposed to the general swirl to which they contribute, can change others and themselves. They thus learn what it means to disclose a new way of being, and discover that they do not have fragile, fixed identities. The activity of articulating concerns and developing a new style becomes more powerful when participants have transformed themselves into trusting colleagues.

VI Entrepreneurship

As should be evident from this discussion of businesses creating new relationships with customers, our view of business is quite entrepreneurial. Indeed, we take the innovative entrepreneur to be the paradigmatic business figure. Moreover, we believe that Dreyfus's interpretation of Heidegger's ontological account of thinkers and artists illuminates the work of entrepreneurs.[11]

Current business thinking sees innovative entrepreneurs as gifted arbitragers who find certain things that are not highly valued in their home contexts and could be sold at great profit in some other context. So, according to the standard view, King Gillette saw that the abilities required to make a disposable razor blade and the materials to make it would not be valued highly in most economic contexts but if put together in the production of disposable razor blades would be extremely valuable. Such an account captures a small and nonessential part of what entrepreneurs do. The critical contribution of King Gillette was to see the *possibility* of the disposable razor blade. The skills to make such a product did not yet exist, though, there were, of course, skills to deal with metal and to grind sharp edges. Furthermore, it is quite clear that many innovative entrepreneurs have been only mediocre at bringing together the skills and materials to make their products in a cost-efficient way. Such entrepreneurs do not become wealthy, but this does not make them any the less entrepreneurial. The crucial abilities of an entrepreneur are seeing new possibilities for products and services and gathering people together into an organization to produce and market a product that realizes these possibilities.

How, then, do innovative entrepreneurs happen upon new possibilities? Like artists, political leaders, and other cultural innovators, entrepreneurs are sensitive to marginal practices that have the potential to give our way of life a whole new style. Heidegger believed that Nietzsche was sensitive to the marginal flexible technological practices of his day and wrote to get people in tune with them.[12] Likewise, King Gillette noticed the peculiar invention of disposable bottle caps and was captivated by the exceedingly marginal practice of disposability. He wanted to extend that practice, and spent years looking for the right way to do so. Finally, he hit on the razor, an instrument associated with masculine duty and impeccability. With the disposable razor blade, he helped to bring about a change not only in shaving but in our understanding of ourselves, things, and other people—in short, in our understanding of being. He helped change the style of our everyday practices to such an extent that we take disposability for granted and just read it back into previous human history. I can even remember interpreting the Genesis story this way. In my youth, I thought that the point of God's giving man dominion over nature was that man could use natural things and throw them away as he pleased. Scholarship has since taught me that dominion as disposability is a modern phenomenon, but we still live in Gillette's age, which is also to say that we live in a particular version of Nietzsche's technological age. Reconfiguration is the term we at BDA use to designate the entrepreneurial process of bringing marginal practices like disposability to the center of a culture.

Gillette did not reconfigure by coming up with the idea of the disposable razor blade. He had to gather people together to see its possibility, to work for its production, and to market it to others. In short, he had to establish an organization whose product people cared about. Entrepreneurs attract people to work in their organizations by showing how their product and vision will make a difference in a particular context of people's lives. In constituting their organizations, entrepreneurs bring practices into their employees and allies' lives that these associates find valuable but which they could not have produced themselves. Also, once the entrepreneur's organization is constituted, the entrepreneur must regularly put employees in touch with their innovative roots by bringing back to their attention and updating practices that have fallen into disuse. All of these actions help to make people aware that they are sharing in the disclosure of a particular cultural world.

Because entrepreneurs change our culture's stand on what things mean and how they matter, we say that they are history makers. They allow themselves to be captivated by practices that are now anomalous but that, if embodied in the right way, will shift the culture's style of dealing with everyday things. What is important from this perspective is not whether, for example, flexibility or treating ourselves as disposable is an improvement but the fact that the ability to change our understanding of being is what makes us most human.

When we first started using this Heideggerian interpretation of entrepreneurs, we ran into many MBA types who thought it was nonsense. Entrepreneurs were just self-interested arbitragers, they said. At first we replied that we were simply describing the practice of entrepreneurship, not the psychological motivations of entrepreneurs. But as we have spoken with more and more entrepreneurs, we have found that they have an account of history and understand themselves as engaged in changing it. In short, they are not out of touch with the disclosive nature of their activity. They see themselves as giving their customers something new to love that will change their lives or blow their minds. Entrepreneurs and those who seek entrepreneurial businesses see that, when structuring a business, there must be room for exploring the anomalous and the marginal.

In the worlds of the academy, politics, and culture, commerce has usually and wrongfully held a secondary status. It has been depreciated because it is the rationalization of need and not of freedom.[13] Not only have the critics of commerce made this claim; many in business have accepted its truth themselves and thereby conspired in their own cultural devaluation. Moreover, some have taken advantage of this status to justify lower ethical standards in business transactions. The caveat emptor of the old open markets is perhaps the most notorious example. Today's unscrupulous behavior would be more on the order of promising that one's own software program will come out soon (although it is still early in development) just to keep one's customers from turning to a competitor's product and thereby bankrupting the competitor.

I do not want to debate whether such a policy is ultimately justified. Rather, I want to revert to my basic contention that business as much as any other highly prized activity enables us to disclose new worlds and to disclose ourselves as disclosers of new worlds. On my interpretation, disclosing is our highest ethical good, and a business promotes this good when it listens to customers to articulate their needs, when it designs itself around commitments, when it turns suppliers and customers into collaborators, when it cultivates new company styles, and when it enables entrepreneurs to open new worlds. The ethical standards to which commerce should be held, then, are those of our most disclosive activities. We are having success in enabling those engaged in business to see this, but we only came to understand it in a world opened up for us by Hubert Dreyfus's interpretation of Heidegger.[14]

The Quest for Control and the Possibilities of Care

Patricia Benner

By working out the phenomenon of care, we have given ourselves an insight into the concrete constitution of existence.
—*Martin Heidegger*[1]

In this chapter, I will describe how Heidegger's recovery of ontology and his insights on thinking, language, openness, and engagement have shaped studies of clinical and ethical expertise in nursing practice. As an experienced nurse I found that Heidegger's understanding of practice and his ontological project of working out the phenomenon of care, the basic stance of being connected regardless of the quality or content of connection, gave insights and language needed to articulate the intents and meanings of the everyday caring practices of nursing.[2] Heidegger defines solicitude as the "authentic care" that allows for the existence of the Other to be seen and responded to:

This kind of solicitude pertains essentially to authentic care—that is, to the existence of the Other, not to a "what" with which he is concerned; it helps the Other to become transparent to himself *in* his care and to become *free* for it.[3]

Heidegger's notion that we are finite beings "thrown" into a world constituted by others discloses the limits of the possibilities available in everyday caregiving relationships. As a finite being one does not fully and freely choose to care, nor does one control how a caregiving relationship will unfold. One's capacity for understanding and responding to those in the caring relationship is dependent on one's openness. Though the expert caregiver must develop expert attunement to the other, no "technique," personal attribute, or skill can guarantee that the other will respond. On the other hand, the effect of the response may be far greater than what the caregiver would predict based upon what he or she offers. Because solicitude itself is shaped by finitude and thrownness, being *in* a particular human relationship precludes clairvoyantly choosing what to offer or what the offering will mean to the other. Such a dynamic and co-constituting relationship is better understood in practice and narrative than in formal theories and laws.

Heidegger's early writings on care, solicitude, finitude, thrownness, and the priority of practice over theory, have influenced my work.[4] These insights are enhanced and clarified by late Heidegger's critique of technology as having the potential of turning human beings into resources. Late Heidegger warns that the kind of ordering characteristic of technology, which he calls enframing, causes us to experience everything as resources in a system that is to be enhanced and controlled. Such enframing may prevent us from seeing and relating to the concrete other and are the relational dangers that nurses face daily in their efforts to care. The possibility that receptivity, responsiveness, and attunement can counter the dangers of enframing are drawn from both early and late Heidegger and are amply demonstrated in excellent caring relationships.

The aspects of Heidegger's project just described did not serve as a "theoretical" framework for my studies. I doubt that these thought projects would have been accessible to me (or in Heidegger's terms, would have created a clearing for me) if I not been a nurse with a practical, experiential understanding of the everyday caregiving of nurses, and had not already been frustrated in my attempts to translate experiences of attuned and authentic care into scientific and technical language. Also, Hubert L. Dreyfus's[5] practical projects of examining artificial intelligence through Heidegger's insights and his collaborative work with his brother, Stuart Dreyfus,[6] on skill acquisition, gave concrete models for applying Heidegger's thinking to the study of everyday social practices and skillful ethical comportment. However, no amount of theory or modeling would have created the vision and possibilities extant in nurses' stories and in what was evident in observing their everyday practice. My interpretive efforts and explanations do not go beyond the nurses' stories and actual practice. Furthermore, the positive reception of my work would not have been possible had not others understood the nurses' stories that my collaborators and I collected.

The thinking of Heidegger, Dreyfus and Dreyfus, Charles Taylor,[7] and Jane Rubin[8] have strongly influenced four interrelated areas of study in nursing: (1) the study of nursing practice and the ethics of that practice[9]; (2) the study of skill acquisition and the nature of human expertise[10]; (3) the study of stress and coping in health and illness[11]; and (4) the development of a hermeneutical phenomenology for the study of human practices and concerns.[12] Drawing on Heidegger's ontology, this chapter will study nursing practice as a way of knowing.

By "knowing," I do not mean disembodied cognition. Instead, following Heidegger's hermeneutic phenomenology, I define knowing primarily in terms of "knowing how" to take action in particular situations, in and defined by human social relationships. The type of knowing involved in abstract scientific and social theory, as well as in applied technology, obviously helps to inform nursing practice, but such knowing cannot be the only or ultimate basis for such practice. According to Heidegger, humans are not worldless intellects, but instead are always already concerned about the things that they encounter in everyday life, and solicitous toward the other people with whom they customarily interact. "Care" constitutes the human mode of being. Technical and theoretical knowing, as well as practical know-how, are all undertaken because human existence cares about itself, other people, and things. The everyday practices that embody our capacity for knowing how to do things take place within what Heidegger calls the "world," the taken-for-granted set of complex and coherent social relationships, possibilities, and avenues for activity. The "Worldhood" of the world refers to the ultimate significance or meaning of all those complex, interrelated activities. Such activities are undertaken for the sake of human existence itself. The world of practices that humans create for themselves, including the skills necessary to use technical equipment, is disclosed because human beings care about self, other, and things. Heidegger's account of world, significance, and care have allowed me to interpret and understand narrative accounts of nursing practice in ways that keep intact the context and relations which are internal to that concernful, worldly activity.

The traditional academic strategy for developing nursing "knowledge" involved establishing explicit, context-free, formal theories and principles of practice that nurses should then "learn." Indeed, anything less than such decontextualized, formal theories and practices was considered ignorance rather than knowledge. Upon entering academia, nurse educators were pressed to give scientific and technical language to all of nursing knowledge and the practices of nurses, in order to structure nursing curricula according to the natural sciences and to formal theories about human growth and development and social life and thereby to legitimize nursing knowledge. While enhancing nursing's scientific and technical knowledge clears up many false beliefs, unwarranted practices and superstitions, this "knowledge production" falls short of capturing, and even obscures, much of the knowledge embedded in caregiving relationships with particular patients, families, and communities.

While falling short of capturing the intent and content of nursing practice, this enterprise of knowledge production also confronts the limits of formalizing (decontextualizing and making explicit) any social practice.[13] Nursing educators created endless lists of behaviors, tasks, diagnoses, and interventions, all of which could spawn new lists. Even more troubling, once nursing practice was defined as isolated units of behavior, diagnoses, and interventions without the significance of those actions (the in-order-to's, and for-the-sake-of's, for-that-purpose, to-that-end), there is no way to get back to everyday integrative clinical knowledge that always entails engaged reasoning in particular clinical situations. Thus, articulating nursing knowledge into the available economic and scientific language creates conflict and incongruities with the knowledge and ethos embedded in the actual caring practices of nurses.[14]

Significance, relationship, context, and the import of timing are left out of context-free lists of processes, structures, procedures, and diagnoses used to structure academic nursing curricula and account for nursing action in health care institutions. Nursing had fallen into what Heidegger calls the "enframing" or technological way of ordering its knowledge and this mode alienated nurses from their understandings and practice. Heidegger strikes close to home with his remark:

If man is challenged, ordered . . . then does not man himself belong even more originally than nature within the standing reserve? The current talk about human resources, about the supply of patients for a clinic, gives evidence of this.[15]

This statement about ordering and moving supplies around to have them available describes today's commodified health care system that focuses on technical procedures and economics. Nursing is a complex, invisible, and devalued caring practice. Like medicine in general, nursing is threatened by the trend to view health and wholeness technically. That is, to regard the body as a machine; to make the individual the unit of analysis; and to portray the health care system as a techno-cure commodity to be sold to economically free agents—medical consumers.

The technology of organ transplants, for example, creates the ethical dilemma of seeing the dying person as viable tissue transplantation to be bought and sold, while overlooking what currently sustains organ transplantation as a practice, that is, the vision of rescuing life from tragedy through the opportunity to give heroically in the midst of death. The "business" of organ transplantation driven only by economics brings the medical world chillingly close to enframing human beings as resources or standing reserve.[16]

In a technological understanding of health care, patients too easily become pawns in a supply and demand economic system, and behavior and energy become resources to be managed and controlled. Hospitals openly began introducing techno-cures as commodities and diseases as "product lines" only in the last twenty years.[17]

The objectification of people in the commercial medical contract mirrors the objectification of human beings in science. Medicine has adopted the model of knowledge developed by modern physics. Heidegger asserts that:

Modern science's way of representing pursues and entraps nature as a calculable coherence of forces. . . . [p]hysics . . . sets nature up to exhibit itself as a coherence of forces calculable in advance, it orders its experiments precisely for the purpose of asking whether and how nature reports itself when set up in this way.[18]

Heidegger's insight that method and language set up what can be revealed, along with his view of thinking as integrated with skill and action, provide an alternative way of exploring and articulating the knowledge embedded within nursing practice. In studying the everyday practices of nurses, I sought to recover nonmanagerial, nonenframing ways of being with patients in order to reveal what was being lost by the informatics approach to medical planning and decision making.

Adopting the Cartesian Medical Model of knowing has been a persistent, if uncomfortable, temptation for nursing since its beginnings. Heidegger's critique of Cartesianism and technological enframing and his vision of thinking offer a strong alternative to technical knowing, one that more closely matches what and how nurses know in their practice about being with and caring for others. Heidegger's work gives permission to reconsider thinking as engaged action:

Thinking does not become action only because some effect issues from it or because it is applied. Thinking acts insofar as it thinks. Such action is presumably the simplest and at the same time the highest, because it concerns the relation of Being to man.[19]

The understanding that thinking "acts insofar as it thinks" gives a practice such as nursing, with a long tradition of acting and thinking, a place to stand that is grounded in experiential wisdom and everyday situated actions. Though I am making this case for the clinical practice of nursing, I believe that a similar case could be made for other clinical practices. Heidegger's understanding of thinking and language invites the thinker to generate a language appropriate to actions and concerns. The nurse clinician is called to think, that is, to act knowingly. It is essential that nurses know the particular patient/family as other and not a mere projection, and that they recognize the situation for what it is rather than overgeneralize it.[20] They must engage in developing a historical understanding of the situation as it unfolds.

To better understand and articulate the caring practices of nurses I have interviewed nurses in small groups, having them tell stories of clinical situations that stand out in their memory for having taught them something new or being an example of the best or worst of their nursing care. The small group interviews set up a communicative context where dialogue, comparisons, and questioning could elucidate the meanings of the story from the storytellers and listeners. Also, participants were instructed to talk to one another in the most natural ways of telling their stories from practice. This was to facilitate the natural everyday language of nursing practice and to avoid having the participants talk up or down to the researchers. These narrative accounts of practice were tape-recorded and transcribed so that the group could be asked in subsequent interviews to clarify any puzzles and so that the text could be studied using Interpretive Phenomenology, as described by Heidegger.[21] In addition to the group interviews, we made observations and taped-recorded interviews of nurses at work. The observations were considered necessary to augment the narrative accounts in order to see the thinking embedded in the skilled actions and responses of nurses. Heidegger again describes an analogous phenomenon:

But the craft of the hand is richer than we commonly imagine. The hand does not only grasp and catch, or push and pull. The hand reaches and extends, receives and welcomes—and not just things: the hand extends itself, and receives its own welcome in the hands of others. The hand holds. The hand carries. The hand designs and signs, presumably because man is a sign. . . . Every motion of the hand in every one of its works carries itself through the element of thinking, every bearing of the hand bears itself in that element.[22]

Observations of actual skilled actions were required to capture the response-based knowledge of the expert practitioner. For example, the titration of pain medication and vasoactive drugs were based not on physiological parameters alone but on knowledge of the particular patient's responses.[23]

Narrative accounts of actual practice told to colleagues were chosen to give access to natural language and the sayings of nurses, and these sayings typically created a profound response of recognition and membership of the participating nurses. Again, Heidegger helps describe this approach.

[I]n speech the speakers have their presencing. Where to? Presencing to the wherewithal of their speech, to that by which they linger, that which in any given situation already matters to them. Which is to say, their fellow human beings and the things, each in its own way; everything that makes a thing a thing and everything that sets the tone for our relations with our fellows. All this is referred to, always and everywhere, sometimes in one way, at other times in another. As what is referred to, it is all talked over and thoroughly discussed; it is spoken of in such a way that the speakers speak to and with one another, and also to themselves.[24]

While the purpose of the "storytelling" interviews was research, they served as an unexpected point of reengagement with nursing practice for the participants. They frequently stated that the stories had reconnected them to what was important to them, recovering meanings that sustained them in their practice. Nurses, in general, responded to this initial work with reviews and statements that the stories or exemplars of other nurses had captured what they knew in their practice but had not been able to say or read in academia.[25]

When studying nursing practices that have deteriorated into mere technique and consumer contracts, I find a language of control, coping mechanisms, deficiencies, problems, diagnoses, and the covering over of significance issues and human concerns. However, the best of nursing practice is infused with an understanding of caring as actions that nurture, foster growth, recovery, health, and protection for the vulnerable. In the moments that nurses hold out to themselves and to others as their finest, the nurse stands alongside the particular patient and family and responds to their concerns.

Terri Holden, a nurse in a coronary care unit, provides a narrative account of lifesaving caring practices in that highly technical environment. Her narrative is presented to illustrate the nurses' ways of thinking and being with the other in authentically caring ways. In the following example, the cure is dramatic, but the possibility for cure is based on artful and skillful caring practices of nurses and physicians:

Joan, a 52-year-old woman, was admitted to the coronary care unit because of her congestive heart failure which she had developed at the age of 36 due to rheumatic fever she had contracted at the age of 8. She had refused follow-up care for a number of years due to the financial burden she felt it placed on her family. She had been non-compliant with her medications, and she had quit smoking only three weeks prior to her admission. . . .

We began our assessment by connecting her to the cardiac monitor (which showed atrial fibrillation), starting I.V.'s and preparing for insertion of the pulmonary artery catheter. Joan's eyes kept darting back and forth from the staff to the ICU equipment. Her frightened look told me that she would require a great deal of emotional support and patience, as well as continual orientation. . . . It took six weeks before Joan was stable enough to undergo cardiac catheterization which concluded that she had normal coronary arteries, the one thing in Joan's favor!!

I find it remarkable that Joan was cared for fully for a month while she was disoriented and combative, and yet cost/benefit language is missing from the narrative. She required constant skillful, attentive care. Her mother was closely involved. It is remarkable that the nurses were able to keep Joan's blood pressure and heart rates within safe ranges with careful titration of medications and keep her invasive lines from causing overwhelming sepsis for two months. By skillful care they were also able to keep her skin intact despite total bed rest.

Unfortunately in the third week of admission Joan developed respiratory distress and required elective intubation. She was placed on a respirator. This hindered our communication efforts even further.

Now Joan was unable to talk, added to the fact that we had to continue to restrain her to protect her from pulling out the endotracheal tube which connected her to the respirator.

It was a matter of experimenting creatively and with a lot of PATIENCE to find a solution that worked for both Joan and us. . . . We were able to get her to write simple phrases, although at times it usually proved too tiring due to Joan's physical condition and too cumbersome due to her invasive lines.

We needed to find other alternatives to communicate with Joan. We could not be entirely dependent on written communication.

An oriental fan came to the rescue and became our alternative to written communication! Joan's husband brought her this fan from home. Joan was always warm and used the fan most of the day. She would gesture often with the fan as if she was directing an orchestra. This fan became Joan's sign language with which she communicated some of her basic needs. The staff and Joan worked out the following signals: For instance fanning the left side of her face meant that she needed a blanket for her feet (which were always cold due to her poor perfusion); fanning the right side of face meant that she wanted the covers removed; pointing it to her throat, of course, meant that she needed to be suctioned. If the fan was folded and placed by her side and Joan closed her eyes . . . it meant "I need some rest!" And if the fan was pointed at one of us it was Joan's simple "thank you". This sign language was incorporated into our care plan. Actually it proved quite effective in meeting some of Joan's basic needs. . . .

All the staff became personally involved with caring for Joan's emotional and physical needs . . . our goal was to get her to surgery. We came to know Joan so well over the two months she spent in our unit that we instinctively knew when a change was to occur in her condition and if it required us to call the resident. Joan exhibited periodic anxiety attacks manifested by holding her breath which subsequently caused her heart rate to fall into the low forties and thirties. We could usually anticipate these anxiety attacks when her eyes looked frightened and wide, and her cheeks began to puff out. We would calmly talk to her using relaxation breathing techniques, but this was not always effective. Several times she required medication (atropine) to bring her heart back to normal limits.

In conversation with Joan's mother, we discovered a pleasant memory we felt could possibly help Joan work through her anxiety. It was worth a try since her emotional response caused her heart rate to slow. As a child, Joan loved to visit her grandmother on her farm in Tennessee. She had fond memories of listening to the rain and watching the thunderstorms from the security of a porch swing in the company of her grandmother. We called on our resources in Occupational Therapy for assistance. They had a collection of environmental tapes which include some great thunderstorms and sounds of the rain falling. I can't describe the look on Joan's face when the earphones were turned on!! We had no further episodes of bradycardia that could not be resolved with thunderstorms!! . . .

A week before Joan's scheduled surgery we took the opportunity to orient her to the outside world instead of her daily view of the wall across from her bed. Our other purpose was to begin to prepare her for leaving the unit. We asked the resident (or rather directed him) to write a nursing order. The new wing of the hospital had just opened and the access to the wing was across a catwalk which had a magnificent view of the Chicago skyline. We gathered our resources—respiratory therapy to ventilate, residents to push the bed, and our staff as the tour guides. At first Joan was hesitant to leave the unit, but with a little bit of coaching and cheerleading from the staff, she conceded and it turned out to be great therapy. . . . On March 1st, she was taken to the operating room where she underwent triple valve replacement. Her postoperative course was relatively uncomplicated and she was discharged home on March 23rd.

She cares for her own home, sings in the church choir, and plays bingo several times a week. She is totally oriented and has a wonderful personality. She sleeps with one pillow and is compliant with her medications. Joan has come back to the unit to visit several times and reports how much she is enjoying life![26]

In this narrative of care, the dialogue is local and specific, filled with details. The boundaries between the human and the medical, the illness and the disease are easily transcended and the use of the technology is guided by the concern for Joan as particular member and participant complete with concrete experiences and history but also as other. This detailed narrative gives life to Heidegger's much more abstract account of the same phenomena:

Everyday Being-with-one-another maintains itself between the two extremes of positive solicitude—that which leaps in and dominates, and that which leaps forth and liberates. It brings numerous mixed forms to maturity. . . . Solicitous concern is understood in terms of what we are concerned with, and along with our understanding of it. Thus in concernful solicitude the Other is proximally disclosed.[27]

Joan's world had shrunk to a narrow safety zone in the center of her bed. The festive gesture of taking Joan outside the unit to the skywalk to see the lights of Chicago is an example of what Heidegger describes as solicitude that "leaps forth and liberates." Initially, Joan resisted this gesture, but the successful excursion demonstrated to her that she could leave the unit and return safely, a realistic rehearsal for leaving and returning from surgery. Being with Joan dictates the ethics, craft, and tact of caregiving. The early recognition of anxiety attacks, the creative use of the thunderstorm tapes to interrupt them, and the use of the fan to communicate were all forms of solicitude that allowed Joan to be a participant and member in a human world despite her debilitated state. The nurses' care leaped ahead in order to liberate rather than dominate her spirit. It is a remarkable achievement of human care to allow concrete others to experience care even though they cannot assert their rights or "fight" for what they need. The nurses see Joan as a person even during her combative and disoriented states. That every nurse learned the "fan system of communication" was a powerful symbolic message of attentiveness and care.

The narrative about Joan is also remarkable because Joan could easily have been dismissed under the rubric of cost-benefit analysis, rational calculations about the "quality of life," and distributive justice. Distributive justice is an issue both on the personal and societal level. Joan's health had deteriorated to a life-threatening extreme due both to insufficient funds (which prevented her access to earlier treatment), and to her inability to give up smoking. In the current moralistic climate of exclusionary insurance entitlements, Joan was in danger of being "unentitled" to treatment because she failed to take adequate "personal responsibility" for her health.[28] However, this is not a narrative of equity and contractual agreements about rights between autonomous agents. It is a narrative of liberating concern and generosity where the nurses' care attempts to make up for past injustices.

The replacement of three heart valves is a heroic achievement, a technical triumph that cannot be overlooked, but it must not dwarf the story of compassionate care that created the possibility for surgery. The nursing staff became Joan's community and that community became healing. The enframing discourse did not triumph. We must clarify and make visible these triumphs of caring in order to guide our understanding of the possibilities and limitations of high-tech cures. This exemplar calls us to think about the tragedy of providing only highly technical medicine in the absence of accessible preventive low-tech care. It also calls us to question the problems of the moralism inherent in the view of the person as a self-of-possession who can take clairvoyant control of health regardless of social circumstances and structures for health promotion.[29]

Intensive care nurses debate about what is authenic care and what are reasonable interventions versus neglect, or unrealistic futile treatments. To come to terms with these essential qualitative distinctions in highly technical health care, we will need to study the best of our specific helping relationships from the perspectives of all those involved.[30] Health care ethics must be lodged in being-with-the-other in order to allow the other to be seen, understood, and to be.[31] Studies of health care ethics and practice must be more than the current principle-based quandary ethics that explore breakdown and puzzle cases. They must consider everyday skillful ethical comportment.[32] Clearly, highly technical health care gets carried away by unrealistic heroics at times, but identifying general rules of inclusion and exclusion for technical interventions must not replace the concernful, respectful, ethical, and clinical practical reasoning about particular patients. The danger is that we will want large population statistics and rules that will prevent us from having to exercise engaged, practical, moral, and clinical reasoning in particular cases. Our Enlightenment quest to be fair through abstraction and disengagement may lead us to be unwise in our practice, or lose our ability to be merciful and just in particular relationships to others.

Clinical and ethical judgments are inseparable and must be guided by being with and understanding the human concerns and possibilities in concrete situations. One way of clarifying the problems and solutions is by studying practical situations that give us clearer visions of the best of our caring relationships.[33] Theoretical or economic formulae cannot replace a first-hand knowledge of the patient, family, and community. The full press of enframing in health care sets up the possibility of seeing the practices that we are endangering by this calculative view. Heidegger says:

Thus where enframing reigns, there is *danger* in the highest sense. [citing Hölderlin's poem]

But where danger is, grows

The saving power also.[34]

The caring practices evident in Joan's narrative have been rendered invisible and marginalized by the current accounting practices in health care where only the high-tech procedures are visible and payable in the system. Indeed care is interpreted as a "cost center" to the insurance company, and procedures and treatments are "sources of revenue." This "accounting" view dictates cutting back care while increasing billable procedures, even though the care is more humane and may cut costs to insurers and patients in the long run (for example, patient attentive care to foot ulcers that prevent intrusive surgeries). In the midst of the highest techno-cure we are reminded of our commonly held human condition—our embodiment, finitude, our need for care, and the unsustainability of many of our technical interventions. Health and recovery require that a person's embodied capacities fully return or that our technological dependency be humanly acceptable.

The recognition practices evident in the careful attention to Joan's embodied spirit and personhood rescue techno-cure from the realm of torture and call us to offer care earlier so that heroic techno-cures are used less often as a substitute for care. These nurses provide an example of what Heidegger calls a free relationship to technology, and an example of a marginalized saving practice that, if recovered, could alter the crisis in the challenging forth of techno-cure. A recovery of the understanding of the person as a member-participant and the ethical comportment of health care practitioners as a process of being-with and letting-be could alter the dangerous atomistic view of the self as a mind that is responsible for controlling an object-body.[35] This human possibility could save us from adversarial and distrusting entitlement arguments that are based upon the fear that our health care is *only* an economic issue and that we ourselves are the raw material for a profit-oriented commercialized health care system.

My observations of nursing practice have occurred at a time when the notion of atomism and a contract society have reached a new high point. When health care is viewed as a commercial contract between completely autonomous free agents, health is viewed as primarily an individual responsibility. Health care is oriented toward cures and technical fixes, and illness prevention is aimed at the individual's control of the body, emotions, and health. Much of popular psychology and pharmaceutical approaches to managing our emotions may be interpreted as understanding even our feelings as one more resource to be managed. If Heidegger is right about our emotions giving us access to our being, then this approach deprives us of our human ability to open ourselves to things and people as mattering.

Care is an embarrassment to a technical control paradigm of health. If we can give up the grandiose technical vision of disemburdenment from care, we can improve our health through everyday caring practices that focus on building our communities and environment for health.[36] The Enlightenment promise that we should eventually be able to overcome the burdens of care because scientific progress should dis-burden us from the vulnerability of embodiment and disruptive emotionality that require care, is an expensive and disappointing illusion. With our quest for control, we cover over the fact that we do not spring from the womb as autonomous and educated, nor do we go to our graves without requiring care, support, and sustenance. We deny what Heidegger calls our thrownness. The quest for an insular self who must be protected from the contaminating "unhealthy" influence of the community is both mystifying and radically unhealthy.[37]

The study of expert nursing practice contrasts expert caring, which focuses on enhancing and elaborating strengths and capacities, with its competitor within the profession, social engineering and its expert knowledge which objectively assess the individual and community from an outsider's stance and prescribes solutions to problems based upon a diagnosis of defects and deficiencies. These two ways of helping need not be completely oppositional. Each can serve the other since an understanding of what is missing propels change and growth. However, the pathological approach—that is, identifying defects and measuring how far short of the norm someone falls—can take over the discourse setting up power relations that blind the clinician to the actual possibilities in the situation. The study of clinical and ethical excellence in nursing has relevance and implications for the gaining of expertise in any complex human skilled performance that requires relationship with a particular situation or person, embodied intelligence, pattern recognition, commonsense understanding, skilled know-how, the development of socially embedded practical knowledge, a sense of salience, and a historical understanding of the situation. Heidegger has his own example:

A cabinetmaker's . . . learning is not mere practice, to gain facility in the use of tools. Nor does he merely gather knowledge about the customary forms of the things he is to build. If he is to become a true cabinetmaker, he makes himself answer and respond above all to the different kinds of wood and to the shapes slumbering within the wood—to wood as it enters into man's dwelling with all the hidden riches of its essence. In fact, this relatedness to wood is what maintains the whole craft. Without that relatedness, the craft will never be anything but empty busywork, any occupation with it will be determined exclusively by business concerns. Every handicraft, all human dealings, are constantly in that danger.[38]

In the above passage Heidegger points to the kind of thinking and skill involved in attunement and response-based action that is common in human expertise and which shapes notions of excellence within a practice.[39] Thus the expert clinician's concern is not limited to well defined, prespecified problems. The expert can identify or find problems because of a deep background of perspectives that are available from past clinical situations. Heidegger tells us:

From the earliest times until Plato the word *techne* is linked with the word *episteme*. Both words are terms for knowing in the widest sense. They mean to be entirely at home in something, to understand and be expert in it. Such knowing provides an opening up. As an opening up it is a revealing.[40]

Consequently, expert clinicians do not just engage in knowledge utilization; they develop clinical knowledge. A practice in this view is not a mere carrying out of an interiorized theory; it is a dynamic dialogue in which understanding is refined, refuted, altered, enhanced, and at the very least filled with nuances and qualitative distinctions that are not captured very well in theoretical terms.

Nursing practice is a socially embedded way of knowing and revealing. I find Heidegger's phenomenology helpful in trying to re-open questions of the relationships between theory and practice and to see that explanation without understanding is empty. Understanding requires expert practitioners who must always learn how the explanation works, when it applies, when it is irrelevant, and when it may unwittingly do violence to competing goods. We can better recognize the tyrannies of both theories and practices if we question the assumptions that theory *always* liberates and practice *always* enslaves.[41] Innovative caring practices can help us to overcome our fear of involvement and care in an age of "theoretical" human relationships between atomistic individuals. The best of our caring practices, as exemplified in the story of Joan, can help us return recovery, alleviation of suffering and healing to our commodified techno-cures. In stories of actual caring relationships, we can rediscover the possibility of community, habits of attentiveness and human caring so that our vision of connection is not limited to applying techniques to increase predictability and social control.

Heidegger's explication of a technological self-understanding clarifies why our quest for holism keeps getting derailed into the totalism of the control paradigm.[42] Totalism replaces holism when we opt for increasing control of our bodies as resources through medicalizing more and more arenas of our lives.[43] When love and leisure become one more form of cure, and our stress reduction strategies unwittingly call us to increase personal control to the exclusion of being with others, we might conclude that our whole life has been taken up in the service of engineering our health in the same technical ways that we approach curing our illnesses. It is here that Heidegger's insights on our current technological self-understanding are helpful. Are we called to care or to control? Is health care a commodity, or good in itself, a basic right or a practice of commitment? It is impossible and undesirable to turn our backs on technology, but we can allow the best of our caring relationships to guide our technology and help us resist a technological self-understanding.

The question is whether we can as a society see the web of care that constitutes socially embedded practical knowledge, the knowledge associated with preserving human worlds, and come to value this skillful, courageous comportment. All of the caring practices such as nursing, mothering, fathering, education, child care, care of the aged, social welfare, care of the earth may be potential saving practices even as they are threatened and marginalized by a society that creates myths about ever expanding possibilities to manage and control all aspects of life. Explanation and detached, theoretical ways of knowing cannot replace the situated action and possibility created by being with particular concrete others.[44] Without the faithful, skillful care required for rearing children, educating young and old, caring for the sick, and caring for our earth, our technological breakthroughs are meaningless. Indeed we will not have the necessary safety net for the breakthroughs since each breakthrough brings with it a potential fallout requiring new networks of care.

IV

Responses

Responses

Hubert L. Dreyfus

Half the contributors to this volume deal with issues that grow directly out of my work. For the most part they are critical of one or another of my central theses. I have, therefore, tried to answer these critics as fully as possible, but, in so doing, I have used up all my allotted space. Each of the other contributors has developed ideas I find fascinating and well worth discussing. I am as grateful for these contributions as I am for the critical ones, but the conversations they open up will have to be put off to another occasion. For the time being, I want to thank all my friends and former students whose work is represented here for giving me an exhilarating sense of the breadth and relevance of the issues with which we are all concerned.

Reply to Joe Rouse

Papers like Joe Rouse's make being the subject of a Festschrift worthwhile. Joe not only gives the clearest account I have yet seen of my understanding of coping skills; he does so while leaving out my understanding of how the various kinds of coping practices are related to each other. He thus suggests, from the start, that I could and should stick to my phenomenology of skilled activity while dropping all my distinctions between kinds of skills and their dependence on each other. Joe thereby challenges me to defend the distinctions of levels of skill that marks off my Heideggerian/Merleau-Pontyian view from his account of all skilled activity as simply linguistically permeated coping. I grant Joe's claim that, once we have language, all coping is permeated by it, but I do not think this undermines the distinctions that Heidegger and Merleau-Ponty think must be preserved if we are to understand the essential structure of human being-in-the-world.

Rouse defends an all-embracing pragmatist holism that levels all my distinctions. Specifically, he wants to deny two distinctions I find basic: (1) the distinction between transparent coping[1] and explicit articulation and (2) the distinction between explicit articulation and theory. He also wants to level my distinction between coping skills, on the one hand, and norms of good/bad and of right/wrong, on the other. He even wants to level my distinction between these two kinds of norms. Every distinction I care about melts away in the all-embracing soup of linguistically permeated coping. In response, I will use what I am beginning to see as my philosophical method (I did not know I had one): look to Heidegger's and Merleau-Ponty's distinctions for a clue to the phenomena in question and then to those phenomena to test and further develop Heidegger's and Merleau-Ponty's distinctions.

As Rouse well knows, Heidegger distinguishes three modes of being which he names availableness, unavailableness, and occurrentness, and correlates each with corresponding ways Dasein deals with things: circumspection (*umsicht*), explication (*auslegung*),[2] and knowing (*Erkennen*). He then adds a second way of dealing with the occurrent, theoretical discovery. Merleau-Ponty, given his interest in perception and the embodied skills we share with animals, finds a level beneath all these ways Dasein deals with things. We will need to be clear about all five of these kinds of activity to respond to the fundamental problems Rouse raises.

At the simplest level we find the skillful things that we and animals do, like walk, climb trees, get around obstacles, hide, eat, get the right distance from things so as to see them clearly, and so forth. These are all cases of what I call transparent coping. Merleau-Ponty points out that in such activity we are solicited by the situation as by a gestalt tension to respond in such a way as to reduce that tension and arrive at a sense of equilibrium. Perhaps it would be better to speak of being solicited by the context rather than the situation since, strictly speaking, only human beings, who can envisage being in other situations than the one they are in, are capable of being in a situation.

Heidegger's account of circumspection is similar to Merleau-Ponty's account of skillful coping in that Dasein simply does what the situation calls for without reflection, deliberation, or mental states with propositional contents. Rouse gives an excellent account of this kind of coping which, as he puts it, responds directly to the presence of affordances. Heidegger only differs from Merleau-Ponty in that he stresses that for Dasein such coping takes place in a world of roles and equipment where things have significance and are, from the start, experienced as shared with others. Heidegger would not want to draw on experiments with neonates to back up his claim that Dasein is always in a shared meaningful world, but I think he would be happy to learn that the work of Daniel Stern[3] and others suggests that infants from birth respond selectively to their mother, to language, to faces, and so in a minimal way to a shared social world. There is evidence that babies also pick up the style of their culture—nurturing, aggressive, authoritarian, or whatever—from birth, so that they always already share their culture's understanding of what it means to be.[4]

Noting the relation between the phenomena Merleau-Ponty describes and those described by Heidegger lets me correct a mistake of mine that Rouse has helpfully noted. I should never have said that for Dasein the animal way of coping is more basic than the social way, and I should certainly not have "assimilate[d] the contrast between bodily coping and social normativity to the more basic contrast between practical coping and the *explicit* articulation of propositional content."[5] As the Japanese baby example suggests, rudimentary social norms are already in force at the level of transparent coping.[6] I now think that asking which is more basic, Merleau-Pontyian gestalt-governed coping or Heideggerian socialization into the style (and language) of the culture, is the wrong question to ask. Clearly, the human baby could not acquire coping skills, animal or cultural, without the ability to respond to the gestalt solicitation of the situation, and clearly a neonate would not be Dasein if the coping skills it acquired were not always already colored by its culture. So the Merleau-Pontyian animal level of skillful coping is always present in Dasein's always already socialized activity and vice versa.

If there is some disturbance, and ongoing transparent coping is interrupted, we normally stay involved but pay attention to what is going on in the situation. This is the level of explicitation. Here it makes sense to speak of beliefs, desires, goals, and, in general, of propositional content. This is the level of intentionality explored in different ways by Husserl, Searle, Davidson, and Brandom. Heidegger and Merleau-Ponty both acknowledge the importance of what they call representational thinking but both would say that all thinkers who begin their analysis on this propositional level begin one level too late. Rouse goes further and denies that there is even a distinction between transparent coping and content-mediated deliberate action.

We can also become detached and just stare at things independent of any specific practical situation. Then we encounter them as occurrent substances, and we can come to know their properties. Finally, we can explore things without regard to the human world and propose and test theories about them. This is the level of scientific discovery. Rouse thinks these distinctions too lose their significance once we understand that transparent coping and the world it deals with is "wordy" through and through.

Before defending all these distinctions as important and not to be levelled, I want to make sure we have the relevant phenomena in view. Heidegger uses the activity of hammering to distinguish the above four levels of Dasein's coping. One can use the hammer transparently in circumspection. Then it withdraws, Heidegger says. One can find that the hammer is too heavy for the job one is doing and so unavailable. Encountering the hammer as too heavy is a case of explicitation. Or one can come to know that the object one has been using as a hammer is a substance with the property heaviness. Note that there is a clear distinction between what we might call a *situational aspect* of the hammer (it is too heavy for me to do this job) and a *desituated property* (it has heaviness in any situation). Heidegger never adequately thematizes the level of the unavailable and the related distinction between aspects and properties but it, nonetheless, plays an important role in *Being and Time*.[7]

Finally, Heidegger goes beyond Aristotle and introduces a modern sort of dealing with things which he calls theoretical discovery. Theoretical discovery occurs when one brackets not just the situation but the shared meaningful world. If one "de-worlds" the hammer and reintegrates it into a theory, one can then discover the hammer-thing, not just as an occurrent object with the property heaviness, but as an entity that has a certain mass.

With these distinctions in mind we can turn to Rouse's attempt to level them.

Objection 1. There is no philosophically interesting distinction between transparent coping and deliberate or explicit coping because they are both cases of practical linguistic skill. As Rouse says, "Why shouldn't explicit articulation in words . . . be regarded as exemplifying, rather than contrasting to, practical coping as a mode of intentionality?"[8] My answer is that there are two important distinctions being levelled here. First, sometimes words are, indeed, used as equipment in the local situation and language functions transparently in a nonpropositional way. In my *Commentary* I use the example of a doctor, intent on an operation in progress, saying "scalpel" to her nurse and soon finding one in her hand. But often language is used propositionally as when there is some disturbance and the carpenter says that his hammer is too heavy and asks a coworker to hand him the lighter one.

This leads to the second distinction. Once the elements of the situation have been made explicit, one kind of linguistic coping—like asking for the lighter hammer—takes advantage of lexicality and all sorts of specific aspects of the situation. But an equally important use of language, the one Heidegger stresses, uses language for passing the word along outside the local situation. Most of the time we use language to make assertions about objects and events that have no immediate relation to our local situation at all. Then, I grant Rouse, we are still using a practical skill, but it is a very different skill from speaking about something in our shared local *situation*; our desituating skill enables us to speak of anything anywhere in the *world*. In both cases, as Rouse points out, the speaker dwells in his or her language as "a richly configured field of articulative possibilities" (19). But it is misleading to characterize this dwelling in the field of linguistic possibilities as dwelling in "the situation at hand" (20). If one conflates how we dwell in language with how we dwell in our specific practical situation, one levels the distinction between the way assertions are constrained by the shared local situation and the way they are constrained by the shared understanding of what Heidegger calls the average intelligibility of the public world. Then one gets the pragmatic platitude that "Making things explicit . . . turn[s] out to be the skillful use of words and sentences as equipment for coping with one's surroundings" (20).

It is always important to keep in mind the phenomenon. Heidegger wants to distinguish the way the carpenter can make the fact that the hammer is *too heavy* explicit by laying it aside "without wasting words,"[9] from the way he must use language to make its *heaviness* explicit. But then language must be a very special kind of practical coping skill. As Rouse is well aware, situational coping skills "fall apart in the absence of their intended setting" (20). Thus nonpropositional practical skills refer only when they are in a specific situation, while propositional language can refer to objects in other situations and even nonexistent objects. Rouse next tries to level this fundamental distinction.

Objection 2. There is no philosophically interesting distinction between linguistic coping with things that are present and with things that are absent or non-existent. Rouse correctly points out that I follow Heidegger in rejecting the Frege/Husserl appeal to mental contents to solve the problem of reference. I follow Heidegger too, I think, in claiming that there is crucial difference between the way language refers lexically in a local situation and the way it refers to things and events in the rest of the world. This special de-situating capacity of language is made possible, Heidegger claims, by the fact that the referential totality of equipment allows us to single out significances—nodes in the equipmental network—on the background of the shared average intelligibility of the one (*das Man*). Once we attach words to these significances we can, without our linguistic skill breaking down, refer to them outside any local situation and we can even purport to refer to them when they are not there.

Rouse finds this account "opaque" and I agree it is simply a description of the phenomenon, not a theory of reference. I think Heidegger believes that any general theory such as Frege's would, by the nature of theory, have to abstract from our embeddedness in the background intelligibility and referential whole that makes reference possible. Rouse would agree, but he, nonetheless, offers a pragmatist explanation. He proceeds by levelling the distinction between the situation and the world and then generalizing—illegitimately, I think—from the way reference works in the local situation to the way reference works in the world. He says, "[L]anguage use is . . . directed toward its surroundings, and *like any other form of practical comportment,* its coherence depends upon sustaining a practical hold upon *actual* circumstances" (21). The fast move, it seems to me, is to expand "actual circumstance" from present situational circumstances, which are literally *circum*-stances, to states of affairs anywhere in the universe. To hold that the Davidsonian principle of charity that says we all must share a *common world* or background intelligibility can give one a practical hold on *actual circumstances* seems to me to explain the opaque by the more opaque. Granted, that "[L]ike other practical coping activities, the sense of asserting falls apart unless it sustains a substantially 'correct' hold on its actual circumstance" (22), I do not understand how this is supposed to explain how one can refer to things outside their current local circumstances and to things that do not even exist.

Furthermore, it seems a mistake to hold that "assertions refer . . . to the whole setting in which . . . an assertion would be significant" (22). Assertions can both refer *in* and to a situation, but they do not refer *to* the very situation they refer *in.* This is not to deny that "assertions . . . function through a practical grasp of their whole 'context'" (23), but context is ambiguous here; assertions function differently where the practical grasp in question is of the situation or of the world. It is fascinating that Rouse thinks that the appropriate way to think about reference outside the local situation where one can actually point is to see it as the use of equipment to act at a distance. The kind of reference and knowledge that is possible at a distance has given rise to a new field called "telepistemology," the study of the problems raised by reference to something not present. To use Haugeland's terms, when one engages in telerobotics one changes from a broad-band relationship to what one is dealing with, of the sort Heidegger and Merleau-Ponty describe, to a narrow-band relationship of the sort Descartes proposed, and that change raises a host of special epistemological and ontological difficulties, including the problem of reference at a distance, so to speak.[10]

I must be missing the point, but it seems to me that, rather than showing that it is an "illusion" that "assertions are a 'special' kind of equipment," (22) Rouse has simply ignored the distinction between the local situation (actual circumstances) and the world (our public shared average intelligibility) so that he can dogmatically assert that language functions the same way in each.

Objection 3. There is no philosophically interesting distinction between explicit articulation and theoretical explanation. Here Rouse, having attempted to level the distinction between situation and world, now tries to level the distinction between the world and the universe. Again everything turns on the role of coping practices. Rouse explains in convincing detail the role of coping practices in doing science and in referring to the entities science studies. I want to argue that all of his detailed descriptions are accurate and illuminating, but that the way he uses the phenomenology and sociology of the work of scientists levels the distinction between *constitutive* practices and *access* practices. If the universe has a structure and is divided up into natural kinds, a big claim that I defend elsewhere,[11] then one could view the practices for getting at these natural kinds as contingent rather than constitutive. They would then involve a form of rigid designation which would, indeed, be a radically different kind of intentionality than everyday coping. I have gone into this question in detail in the paper, so I will not try to defend the distinction here. But one thing is sure. This is no merely academic debate. The status of natural science—its authority, its funding, how it should be taught, and so forth—depends on getting this distinction right.

Objection 4. There is no philosophically interesting distinction between transparent coping and social norms. Rouse contends that "skills are irreducibly 'social' " (26). This claim seem to me just plainly false. Unless one wants to deny that the higher mammals have skills, it is apparent that many kinds of animals have nonsocial skills.[12] And, in spite of the pervasiveness of language, people still have nonsocial skills. They can, for example, localize sounds, hide from predators, and climb trees.

Within the domain of social skills, there is another important distinction that Rouse would like to gloss over. I grant that social skills are a form of normative transparent coping different from mere success and failure—as when I trip and fall—which need not be social at all.[13] It does not follow from the fact that social skills can be evaluated normatively, however, that all social skillful acts are fully normative in that they presuppose membership of an individual in a community in which one can assess members' acts as right or wrong and assign responsibility for them. My favorite example has always been distance-standing practices. We are socialized into these norms at a very early age—before we are individuals—and they are reinforced by unconscious social pressure. John Haugeland has a good account of how this works.[14] Merleau-Ponty would presumably add that, when we are not conforming as we have been trained to do, we have an uneasy sense of deviation from some comfortable equilibrium. These nonpropositional, but nonetheless normative, social skills are talked about, when they are noticed at all, in terms of the difference between good and bad, as in good and bad posture, or good and bad pronunciation, and experienced, when they are experienced at all, as being in sync or out of sync with the situation. They underlie and make possible the "interaction with other agents" whom we "*recognize* in practice as intentionally directed toward a shared *world*" (27). Babies do not need to recognize anything nor to have an I-thou relationship in order to be socialized. Approval or disapproval is essential, but accountability to others comes in much later. Again it seems that Rouse and, on his account, the Brandom-type pragmatists start one level too late. This is not merely an academic distinction. Pierre Bourdieu is dedicated to pointing out that social power rests on the level of the embodied and transparent *habitus*.

At the next level we do, indeed, find practices that can be right and wrong, correct and incorrect, as in making grammatical mistakes, or driving on the wrong side of the road, taking property that does not belong to one, and so forth, and we experience ourselves as agents. Here we hold people accountable in a way that they are not accountable for their pronunciation. These explicit norms can, in turn, be codified and stated as principles, laws, and rules.

Hubert L. Dreyfus

Whether or not my attempt to distinguish context, situation, world, and universe, as very different loci of practical coping, ultimately holds up, I am immensely grateful to Joe for having challenged me to defend these distinctions. In trying to do so, I have learned to distinguish Heidegger's and Merleau-Ponty's phenomenologies from Joe's form of pragmatism.[15] So now a whole new issue for discussion is opened up for us. What is to be gained by saying (truly) that everything people think and do involves language-permeated skills? Just why is Joe so eager to deny the significance of the distinctions honed by existential phenomenologists? And, conversely, just what is the philosophical and existential importance of these distinctions that makes me so determined to defend them?

Reply to Ted Schatzki

I am grateful to Ted for a very careful reading and critique of my phenomenology of skillful coping. I appreciate and generally agree with his extension of my account to people coping with one another. I also agree with, and henceforth will use, Ted's formulation of the way people's mental states can be understood to affect their actions by determining what it makes sense to do. Therefore, in the little space I have, I will take up and try to answer Ted's objections to certain of my views concerning coping. These objections are important to me because they force me to make clear why I am so committed to *transparent*, that is, nonthematic coping.

I will sum up my reservations concerning Schatzki's defense of the importance of thematic coping in four theses:

1. Schatzki agrees that in active coping I need not be thematically aware of my current activity and I just want to add that, if I am, it will almost surely mess me up.

2. When I am coping transparently, I may well be thinking of something else and usually am, but that is not necessary for successful coping.

3. I may need to be explicitly aware of the environment as in Schatzki's examples of skiing and of needing to inspect instruments

to carry out some skills, but for most skills I can simply respond to the overall gestalt or affordance and not be aware of it at all, as in my examples of distance-standing and of gear-shifting. Likewise, one can be anxious, or in all sorts of moods, without being thematically aware of them.

These first three phenomena support my claim that, to act skillfully, it is not necessary to be *explicitly aware* of anything, although one must be sensing whether one is in sync with or is deviating from a sense of equilibrium.

4. I disagree with Ted's claim that "an agent is *always* . . . aware of something" (38, my emphasis). It seems that, for some highly skilled activities, one must necessarily not be aware of anything. Larry Bird says that sometimes he is not aware until after he has passed the ball of what he has just been doing on the court, and an Israeli pilot once told me that to fire all of his various sorts of missiles and fly his fighter plane during a dogfight, it seemed he had to black out and could not remember afterwards what he had done. Maybe in an extreme crisis the brain has to dedicate all its blood to its skill module and has none left for its consciousness module. In such extreme cases, it may be that even nonthematic consciousness only gets in the way. Nietzsche and Dewey would have loved the idea.

So my strongest thesis is that neither thematic awareness *nor even nonthematic awareness* is necessary for highly skilled activity. The point of this, I now realize thanks to Ted's pressing me, is that background coping is necessarily nonthematic and largely unconscious. The phenomenon has been most fully explored in Pierre Bourdieu's account of how *habitus* works through posture, mood, and so forth. This phenomenon is what allows Heidegger to claim that such coping is not a kind of intentionality at all and can, therefore, be a candidate for the condition of the possibility of all intentionality.[16]

Reply to John Searle

Since I have always taken John Searle's account of Intentionality and the Background to be the most important and well-worked-out contemporary account of these subjects, a great deal of my reading of Heidegger has developed in response to them. It is, therefore, very important to me to get Searle's arguments right so that my Heidegger is not arguing against a straw man. Although it would be illuminating for the history of phenomenology if, in addition, Searle's views turned out to be like Husserl's, that is not nearly so important to me as whether his views are the best version yet articulated of the position Heidegger opposes, so I can marshal the best Heideggerian objections to them and then see if Searle can successfully defend them. This current exchange is the latest stage in this ongoing debate.

But before I can get to the deep issues that divide us, I have to clear up four terminological points.

1. It has never been important to my argument against Searle's account of intentionality to state his views in subject/object or inner/outer terms. For my purposes his mind/world dichotomy would do as well. What is important for me is that, for Searle, all Intentional content and even the Background that makes conditions of satisfaction possible, are in the mind/brain and so could, in principle, be completely preserved in a dream or in a vat whether the world existed or not. If it makes Searle unhappy to call what remains in the vat a self-sufficient subject, I can drop the term, but the fact remains that his view sounds very much like Husserl's Cartesianism and Searle himself says: "I am in agreement with various philosophers who are trying to get at Intentionality with such notions as 'methodological solipsism,' 'the transcendental reduction,' or simply the fantasy of 'the brain in the vat.' "[17]

2. Likewise, my problems with Searle's account of the Background do not hinge on the terminology each of us uses. He and I began discussing intentionality shortly after I arrived in Berkeley, and I soon found his view that the Background provides the nonintentional conditions that make intentionality possible very close to what Heidegger means by "the background of a primary familiarity which is not ... intended but is rather present in [an] unprominent way."[18] In 1980 and again in 1992 we gave a joint seminar on the Background which I found very illuminating, but the more I have

read since of what Searle says about the Background, the less I understand his view.

The Background, Searle says, is made up of skills and capacities as well as a certain readiness for what might normally happen in a situation. I would have thought that at least some of the capacities, skills, and readiness to respond, which make up the Background are bodily rather than mental, and, indeed, Searle says in discussing skill acquisition that "repeated practice enables the body to take over and the rules to recede into the Background."[19] But Searle also wants to say that the Background is mental, where "mental" means that "all my Background abilities are 'in my head'."[20] But since the head and the brain are parts of the body, I am confused as to where the Background resides. Is it a first-person experience in the mind or a third-person mechanism in the body? I can well understand that Searle is "unsatisfied . . . with the traditional vocabulary of the 'mental' and the 'physical,' "[21] but what other ontological vocabulary does he have? Merleau-Ponty says that the lived body is neither mental nor physical but "a third kind of being"—"motor intentionality,"[22] or "intentional tissue" as he sometimes calls it. Does Searle want to say the same about the Background? I doubt it, although I would be delighted if he did.

3. Searle and I agree that, when one follows rules in acquiring a new skill "repeated practice enables the body to take over" (*Intentionality*, 150). But I cannot accept Searle's view that, when one becomes skilled, the rules recede into the Background rather than being left behind like training wheels. Take his example of driving on the right. I agree that if I learned to drive by following the rule "drive on the right," then, when I was learning, that rule played a direct causal role in my behavior. I also agree that, for this reason, we can say that that rule is now indirectly playing a causal role in my behavior since I would not now be driving on the right if I had not once followed it. But it seems to me obvious that, while my skilled behavior still *conforms to* the rule, I am no longer *following the rule as a procedure* in the way I was when I was a beginner. The rule once guided my behavior step by step. In so doing it produced a structure in my brain. Now it is that structure, no longer the rule itself, that is governing my behavior. To say that I am now "unconsciously

following the rule" (87) covers up this important change. For the same reason, it seems misleading to say "my behavior is 'sensitive to the rule'" (87) if this means my *current* behavior.

So I agree, with the *scientific* claim that my current behavior is *indirectly caused* by the rule, and with the *logical* claim that to understand my behavior one has to *allude to* the rule. (This explains why, when asked to explain what I am doing, I invoke the rule.) But the ostensibly *phenomenological* claim that in my current driving I "follow the rule unconsciously," or that I am now "sensitive" to the rule, seems to me either a very misleading way to make the above true claims, or just plain false. I can't understand why Searle both insists he is not doing phenomenology and then persists in using this obfuscating phenomenological terminology.

4. I do, indeed, say that Searle holds that we are "interpreting" brute data when we see a house or hear meaningful words. I grant that this is a misleading way to describe his view and I agree with him that we should use "interpretation" in the normal everyday way in which "literal cases of acts of interpretation are rather rare" (73). What worries me, however, is not whether we need to *interpret* the data, but that Searle holds that to see a functional object like house we have to *assign a function* to some physical stuff of the universe. As he puts it:

The important thing to see [is] that functions are never intrinsic to the physics of any phenomenon but are *assigned* from *outside* by *conscious* observers and users.[23]

Literal acts of assigning and imposing are rather rare too, and Searle cannot be using these terms in an everyday way. So, for example, Searle holds that to hear meaningful language we have to impose intentionality on the acoustic blasts coming out of people's mouths. Several different possible questions need to be distinguished here. It is certainly a legitimate project for neuroscience to explain how acoustic waves get processed in the brain so that they are responded to with certain movements. One can also ask, as Searle does, what are the logical requirements for a stream of sound's being a speech act. However, to ask how the *experience* we have of the meaningless noises coming out of people's mouths can become the *experience of speech acts* seems to me wrong-headed; that question is based on the idea that we normally experience meaningless noises coming out of people's mouths, but we do not. When Searle says "the child . . . learns to treat the sounds that come out of her own and others' mouths as standing for, or meaning something,"[24] this is at best highly misleading since, although the child's *brain* is gradually organized to process the acoustic blasts coming out of people's mouths so that the child hears meaningful sounds, the *child* does not *learn* to *treat* these noises as meaningful sounds at all, because, from the child's point of view, the job has always already been done.

When I hear terms such as "assigning" or "imposing," terms that normally describe mental activity, used to explain how brute stuff acquires intentionality, I cannot help thinking Searle is doing neither brain science nor logical analysis, but is engaging in bad phenomenology. But in his book on social reality Searle defends his method. He says he is only asking and answering the logical question, definitely not doing phenomenology, and adds, "I will use a first-person intentionalistic vocabulary to try to lay bare certain elementary features of social reality."[25] What I do not understand is why, if he is not doing phenomenology, he uses first-person vocabulary? It is precisely this vocabulary that misleads someone like me into supposing that, since this activity of imposing is not conscious, it must be unconscious. Husserl calls such postulated mental activity, that is neither conscious nor unconscious, "transcendental," and speaks of transcendental consciousness "taking" the brute data as meaningful, but I could never understand what that meant. It seems like slight-of-hand to describe the assignment of significance as a first-person mental activity but then take away the psychology.

Now, at last, we come to the serious issues. Searle and I differ on three basic questions. (1) What is an intentional state? (2) What sort of intentional state—propositional or nonpropositional—causes movements and constitutes them as actions? and (3) Is Searle doing logical analysis or phenomenology?

Hubert L. Dreyfus

1. What Is an Intentional State?

When I first began writing about intentionality, I claimed that Heidegger and Merleau-Ponty had an account of everyday ongoing coping as a response to the solicitations of the situation that did not require consciousness nor intentionality.[26] Searle pointed out to me that even skillful coping can succeed or fail and therefore has conditions of satisfaction, so it must be a kind of intentionality. I missed this point in my earlier papers although I should have known better since both Heidegger and Merleau-Ponty affirm that they are studying a more basic kind of intentionality, but a kind of intentionality nonetheless. I thank Searle for calling my attention to this mistake.[27]

I do not dispute Searle's minimal logical condition that all intentional states must have conditions of satisfaction, but it turns out that Searle also defends the strong substantive claim that these conditions of satisfaction must be "mental representations." It is not the terms "mental" or "representation" that matter, but Searle's controversial claim that the contents of the conditions of satisfaction must be propositional. As Searle puts it, his use of "representation" can be dispensed with in favor of all the notions that are used to explain it such as the logical requirement that the action have conditions of satisfaction and (what I would call the phenomenological requirement) that those conditions have "propositional content."[28] Following Heidegger on action and Merleau-Ponty on perception, I contend that the conditions of satisfaction involved in perception and action need not be propositional in the usual sense.[29]

2. What Sort of Intentional States—Propositional or Nonpropositional—Account for Actions?

Searle and I agree on the logical requirement that, for a bodily movement to be an action, it must be caused by its conditions of satisfaction, where this might mean just being sensitive to them as constraints on the success of the motion. However, Searle seems to me to be doing phenomenology when he adds that, for an intentional state to account for an action, the propositional contents that represent the action's conditions of satisfaction must accompany and guide the appropriate bodily movements. What looks like logical analysis to Searle looks like phenomenology to me because there is another way the movements can be caused. Merleau-Ponty claims that in ongoing skillful coping one is guided by sensing the tension of deviating from a satisfactory gestalt, and that therefore one only senses in retrospect, after one has settled into a satisfactory gestalt, what one has succeeded in doing. This final gestalt cannot be represented in propositional form in advance or even after one is in it.[30] The weak logical condition is not in dispute between Searle and existential phenomenologists such as Heidegger and Merleau-Ponty; but existential phenomenologists do dispute Searle's strong phenomenological requirement.

We existential phenomenologists do not claim Searle's account is bad phenomenology but rather that it is the phenomenology only of effortful, deliberate, thoughtful action, like lecturing on or writing about philosophy, and so leaves out the sort of skillful coping one experiences in the flow of sports or in simply finding one's way about in the world. I thus agree with Searle that doing philosophy is a "paradigm case of intentional mental behavior." But that does not show at all that my view that much of the time we are not engaged in what Searle calls mental behavior is "self refuting." In fact, I think that Searle's phenomenology is support for my view. My claim is that, although we often engage in what I call deliberate activities, such thoughtful activity is not the only, nor the most basic, way we relate to the world.

This issue comes to a head, as Searle makes clear, in sports. In his description of a tired competitive tennis player who is falling behind and trying not to lose his concentration, Searle gives a convincing description of what it is like to be driven to win. I grant such a person is fighting hard to achieve certain specific goals. I take Searle's word for it that in a certain sort of "serious competitive activity" trying hard is the name of the game. But not all athletic activity need be so stressful and not all tournament tennis need be either. If Tim Gallwey, from whom I once had a tennis lesson, had been the coach, he would have recommended that Searle's pressured player let go and just respond to the situation as a Zen master would.[31]

Searle is so convinced that the agent is always trying that he takes my example of Larry Bird's reporting that he often does not know what he is doing on the court until he has done it as a case where "we are unable to get at the actual conditions of satisfaction; we are unable to get at what the agent is trying (sic) to do."[32] Searle therefore thinks my descriptions of Zen-like flow are irrelevant precisely because he hears them as claims that the trying is unconscious. But my claim is that in such cases the agent is not *trying* at all. Moreover, it is not a question of what percent of his time an athlete spends in effortless coping and what percent in deliberate trying. The important thing is that there is a kind of prelinguistic, nonpropositional coping, that goes on in the best moments in sports. In such cases the agent is not consciously trying to do anything and there is no reason to think he is unconsciously trying either.

Heidegger and I also want to claim that this responsive, nonpropositional ongoing coping makes possible the deliberate, propositional, trying Searle describes so well. But Searle resists this move. He holds that, even if there were the kind of responsive coping I describe, trying is more basic because it plays a causal role in governing all skillful activity which is "intentional behavior right down to the ground" (81). One cannot just be responding to a gestalt; one must be responding to it in the service of something one is *trying to do*. This makes sense in the case of many kinds of action. I normally do not just skillfully move my tongue, but I move it in the service of pronouncing words to get you to understand what I am saying, and I normally move my arm in the service of hitting a tennis ball in order to win, or play well, or get exercise or whatever. In such cases intentionality, as Searle claims, always rises to the level of skill.

But, as I have pointed out, there are other activities, such as the way we stand the appropriate distance from people without noticing we are doing so as well as the ways we unconsciously orient ourselves and find our way about in the world, which do not serve specific goals like winning a game or winning a point. In these cases there is no representational intentionality, rather, we could say that there is Background skill all the way up. Searle would no doubt respond that, even if I am unconsciously sensing a tension drawing me closer when I am standing too far from my interlocutor, this could only be happening because I was trying to carry on a conversation or realize some other goal. I would answer that I normally stand the appropriate distance from people, face them, etc. even when I am not trying to do anything with them at all. More generally, Searle could always say that all my activity as I find my way about in the word—all my orienting and coping practices as I walk, wear my clothes, sit in chairs, get on and off the buses, etc.—is caused precisely by my trying to get around in the world. But I do not see what is gained by this empty claim. It seems to me at least as accurate to say that I could not carry out any of my conscious deliberate actions if I were not engaging in the kind of prelinguistic, nonpropositional coping that Merleau-Ponty, Heidegger, and others like Dewey describe. Heidegger's background, I would contend, is not just an ability, capacity, or skill; it is a kind of *activity* whose conditions of satisfaction are just doing what feels appropriate without any propositional content that specifies what goal one is trying to reach.

To sum up, Searle sets forth both a *logical* and a *phenomenological* condition for a movement's being an action. The weak logical condition is that the movement be caused by the action's conditions of satisfaction. The strong phenomenological claim is that the movement must be caused by a propositional representation of those conditions. If put in a sufficiently minimal way, the logical conditions for intentional comportment are not in dispute between Searle and me. Even though the tennis player in my example does not know what the optimal gestalt is, he senses when he is moving toward or away from it, so conditions of satisfaction do play a causal role in directing his behavior. If that were all that the causal role of intentional content meant, who could deny this requirement? But I *do* want to deny Searle's strong phenomenological requirement that the intentional content (i.e., the representation of the conditions of satisfaction) that governs an action must be mental, that is, propositional. I am claiming that, in ongoing coping, the tennis player cannot represent propositionally the optimal gestalt that, nonetheless, directs the movement of his body. As Merleau-Ponty, to whom I owe this description, puts it: "Whether a system of motor or perceptual powers, our body is not an object for an 'I think', it is a grouping of lived-through meanings which moves towards its equilibrium."[33]

I do not see why Searle opposes this phenomenological claim with his phenomenological counter-claim, especially if he is concerned only with the logical conditions for a movement's being an action. I suspect there are two reasons he feels he must deny that there is a gestalt-governed way of acting and that it is more basic then the kind of willful propositionally governed action he so well describes. (1) He wants, I think illegitimately, to include in his logical analysis of action the claim that the movements making up *any* action must be caused by a propositional representation of its conditions of satisfaction. (2) There is no place for body-intentionality in Searle's subject/object ontology.

3. Is Searle Doing Logical Analysis or Phenomenology?

As we have seen, although Searle expends a lot of effort contesting my Merleau-Pontyian phenomenology in the name of his own strong phenomenological stand, his fall-back position is that he is only doing logical analysis. To defend phenomenology from Searle's charge that it is misleading and superficial, I will need to show that Searle's attempt to smuggle in his phenomenological account as part of his logical account is incoherent.

Searle begins his account with a phenomenological description showing that the experience of acting must include an experience of the causal connection between the agent's intention and his movements. He argues persuasively for this by using the work of Wilder Penfield. Penfield claims that when he put an electrode in the brain of a patient that made the patient's arm go up, the patient would feel that he had not performed the movement but that Penfield had "pulled it out of him." What is missing, Searle argues, is the patient's sense of effort, his experience that it was his intention to raise his arm that made his arm go up. Searle concludes, "now this experience with its phenomenal and logical properties I am calling the experience of acting. . . . [T]hat experience has an Intentional content".[34] The experience of acting has the intentional content that the appropriate bodily movement is being caused by the intention to perform the action. Searle calls this intention an intention in action and points out that in normal everyday action "the experience of acting just is the intention in action".[35] The intentional content of an intention in action, its conditions of satisfaction, are that I am causing this bodily movement by way of performing this intention in action. Thus Searle says, "in the case of action my Intentional state causes some movement of my body".[36] For a movement to be an action the movement must be caused and continuously guided by an intention in action. As Searle puts it, "Intentionality reaches down to the bottom level of voluntary actions. . . . Each movement is governed by the Intentionality of the flow."[37]

Given the above claims, I naturally thought of an intention in action as the *experience* of my effort causing my bodily movement. But Searle says I have misrepresented his view by suggesting that Intentional states or mental representations "are a kind of thing." He points out that he explicitly holds that, in the case of unconscious actions, one's intention to perform a certain body movement can cause one to perform it without one's being aware of that intention. He therefore insists that "Representation . . . is not an ontological, much less a phenomenological, category, but a 'functional category'" (74).

I now understand that Searle holds that normally when one acts one's bodily movements are caused by one's experience of acting, so he can use the *phenomenological* contrast between the Penfield case of the patient's arm being made to go up and an experience of acting to get the reader to understand the *logical* conditions for a movement's being an action. The upshot of his logical analysis is that a mental representation of what I am trying to do must accompany and cause my bodily movements whether I am aware of what I am trying to do or not. The minimal logical point is that an action's success conditions must play a causal role in bringing about that action's success conditions. Thus for Searle an intention in action must be causally self-referential, and to speak of causal self-referentiality as he does, he writes, is to talk about "the logical structure of intentional phenomena." So it should be clear that the phenomenology of my *experience* of acting was only an entering wedge, a ladder that has to be cast aside. Searle insists that in the last analysis it is the intentional content itself, not the experience of acting, that causes the bodily movement.

I now see I was wrong in thinking Searle was attributing causal powers to a mental item, namely the experience of acting, but I find Searle's talk of a logical structure having causal powers, hard to understand. For Searle, "the basic notion of causation is the notion of making something happen".[38] Thus, when I have the experience of raising my arm it is that very experience that makes my arm go up. So whenever I perform an action, even an unconscious one, one would think there must be something making my bodily movement happen. Indeed, Searle is emphatic on this point when he says, "We are causal realists if we believe, as I do, that 'cause' names a real relation in the real world".[39] And he goes on to say that, "Actions . . . on my account are causal and intentional transactions between mind and world".[40] But how can an abstract structure exist in the real world and make something happen?

Searle would no doubt reply that intentional content, even though it is only a logical structure, can act causally by being realized in a brain state that can act causally.[41] But even if we grant Searle's mind/brain monism, it does not solve the present problem. Searle holds that brain states that are not correlated with a conscious experience cannot have intentionality. So, even if we grant that a formal logical structure could be realized in the brain as in a computer and thereby have causal power, it does not follow that an intentional structure such as an action's conditions of satisfaction could be realized in the brain apart from consciousness. What could at best be realized without consciousness would be a disposition to realize a conscious intentional state. As Searle says:

Unconscious intentional states, for example, unconscious beliefs, are really just brain states, but they can legitimately be considered mental states because they have the same neural structure as brain states which, if not blocked in some way, would be conscious. They have no intentionality as mere brain states, but they do have latent intentionality.[42]

This is a plausible account of how we can speak of unconscious beliefs, but this view has strange consequences when generalized to unconsciously motivated actions. How can a merely latent intention in action cause a bodily movement to be an action? Searle sees the problem and responds:

Within our current nondualistic conception of reality no sense can be attached to the notion that aspectual shape can be both manifest as aspectual shape and yet totally unconscious. But since unconscious intentional states with aspectual shape exist when unconscious and cause behavior when unconscious, what sense are we attaching to the notion of the unconscious in such cases? I have argued that we can attach to it the following perfectly adequate sense: The attribution of unconscious intentionality to the neurophysiology is the attribution of a capacity to cause that state in a conscious form. This point holds whether or not the unconscious intentionality causes an unconscious action without causing a conscious mental event.[43]

But this will not work. Suppose that at a family dinner Bill "accidentally" spills a glass of water into his brother Bob's lap because, as Bill's therapist tells him later, he has an unconscious desire to annoy Bob. The explanation of this behavior requires not just latent beliefs such as Bill's long-standing belief that Bob stole his mother's affection, but also actually occurring beliefs, such as that the accident will upset Bob, and actually occurring desires, such as the desire that Bob be upset. It also requires what Searle calls a "prior intention"—to upset Bob by means of spilling the water—and an "intention in action" which actually "governs" Bill's bodily movements, so that these movements are a case of spilling water, not of moving H_2O around.

According to Searle, unconscious brain states cannot determine aspectual shape, and yet my example requires that the intention in action that causes the appropriate bodily movements have an actual, not just a potential aspectual shape. Otherwise, one cannot say what Bill is doing or, indeed, that he is doing anything at all. It seems that, for the movements that make up an action to be caused by an intention in action, the intention in action must be more than a logical structure; it must be a mental state.

In "Neither Phenomenological Description Nor Rational Reconstruction: Reply to Dreyfus," a paper appearing soon in *La Revue Internationale de Philosophie,* Searle says of his own work: "I tried to analyze intentionality without using phenomenological methods. One unexpected consequence of the enterprise is that the combination of causal and logical structures my analyses reveal are beyond the reach of phenomenological analysis. The phenomenological tradition, whether in the transcendental form of Husserl or the existential form of Heidegger can't deliver these results." But what we have just seen is that to answer the causal question concerning the production of the bodily movement Searle has to go beyond logical analysis, to phenomenology. So it looks to me like the role of phenomenology in Searle's logical analysis has to be more than merely pedagogical. Whether he likes it or not, Searle seems to be committed to the view that it is part of the logical conditions of a movement's being an action that one experience one's intentional state as that movement's cause. Searle's most important insight may be, in the case of action at least, that phenomenology is not a superficial starting point but a necessary ending point; that logical analysis necessarily leads to phenomenology. That, I suspect, is why we have been talking and giving courses together for thirty years.

One way to think about this is to note that Searle goes beyond Husserl in taking account of the importance of causality in an analysis of action. But it seems to me that, in doing so, he only succeeds in showing that trying to explain perception and action by tracing their possibility back to minds and their intrinsic intentionality is bound to fail. The Cartesian/Husserlian ontology of the brute physical world and the intrinsic intentionality of individual minds just is not rich enough to explain how we are able to act. We may just have to grit our teeth and countenance body-intentionality and being-in-the-world as a third way of being.

In the end, to make sense of what Searle says about me, I have to assume there are really two Searles, the phenomenologist and the analytic philosopher, each of whom holds a powerful and consistent position. The phenomenologist takes the strong view that there are real entities called intentional states and that, for there to be actions, these states have to be the efficient causes of movements, just as, for there to be meaning and functions in the physical world, people have to impose a meaning or function on brute physical stuff.

This view resembles Husserl's and is a true description of certain kinds of human activity that involve language, trying to succeed, and the setting up of new social institutions. But, as an account of *all* human intentional comportment and *all* functional stuff in the world, it is simply false because it ignores a more basic form of intentionality—ongoing coping—that makes this propositional form of intentionality possible, and a kind of comportment—background coping—that enables one to find one's way about in the world.

It seems to me that, when I play Heidegger to his Husserl, Searle sees that his phenomenology cannot be defended. He then retreats to a weaker position and contends he is only doing logical analysis since phenomenology is superficial anyway. For the logical analyst, he points out, there are various types of entities in the world such as actions, speech acts, and social entities like money, and each has a logical structure involving intentional content which Searle analyzes in subtle and convincing detail. Whenever I criticize the phenomenologist I discover the logical analyst, but I soon find phenomenological claims that I cannot accept creeping back in. It is as if the neutral logical analysis solicits the analyst to fill out the causal claims built into the analysis and that Searle cannot resist this challenge. He thus introduces causally efficacious *mental representations* and then claims they need only be logical structures.

I know that Searle does not appreciate the compliment, but I find his attempt to do justice both to the logical and the phenomenological requirements his most impressive achievement and I have learned a huge amount from reading his books and arguing with him. He has an account of action and the social, as well as a Heideggerian sense of the importance of the Background that Husserl lacks. And, unlike Heidegger, he has worked out a convincing account of the propositional contents of linguistic behavior and of the more effortful intentional states. He also has many arresting examples of the phenomenon of skillful coping scattered throughout his books. I do not see why he does not take advantage of these to develop his own version of our everyday, nonpropositional being-in-the-world so as to complete his impressive project. But of course that would mean he would have to adopt a richer ontology than the Cartesian one of brute objects and self-sufficient subjects (minds in brains in vats) he champions.[44]

Reply to Mark Wrathall

I am amazed that Mark Wrathall found time to write a chapter for this collection at all since during the past year he has been spending more than full time editing both these volumes. Furthermore, I am delighted that, in spite of Mark's having to write his chapter while overseeing the birth of these two books and a baby, the paper is a definitive contribution to understanding an issue that has puzzled me for a long time.

The puzzle can be put in several ways. (1) How can the background make intentionality possible? Either the background coping is already a form of intentionality or it is some kind of meaningless movement and so cannot account for intentionality.[45] Or (2) how can Heidegger, after distinguishing intentional comportment from openness or transcendence and saying that "the problem of transcendence is not at all identical with the problem of intentionality"[46] refer to the "the twofold task, *intrinsically one*, of interpreting more radically the phenomena of intentionality and transcendence."[47] How can the job of interpreting these radically different phenomena be one task?

I tried in my *Commentary* to make sense of this strange claim by saying that

originary transcendence is not something radically different from ontic transcending; rather, it is *the same sort of coping* functioning as the holistic background for all purposive comportment.[48]

But, then, that makes background coping just more coping, while for Heidegger it seems to be something more basic than coping that makes coping possible.

In my groping around I tried, in a seminar with John Searle on the background, to use Merleau-Ponty to suggest that the background was a kind of set to respond in an appropriate way to the solicitations of the current situation. I spelled this out in my *Commentary* by glossing Heidegger's notion of familiarity as readiness:

My "set" or "readiness" to cope with chairs by avoiding them or by sitting on them, for example, is "activated" when I enter a room. . . . Thus the sort of background familiarity that functions when I take in a room full of furniture as a whole and deal with it is neither a specific action like sitting in a chair, nor is it merely a capacity in the body or the brain for carrying out specific actions. . . . It is being ready in particular circumstances to respond appropriately to whatever might normally come along.[49]

But I was not at all clear that readiness was not just more coping. As Wrathall points out, in my *Commentary* I claim that coping *discloses* the referential totality whereas Heidegger is clear that even holistic coping is still a kind of *discovering*.[50] Indeed, it is only after reading Wrathall's chapter that I see that the phenomenon of readiness is not just more coping but that it solves the problem of finding something that is not an activity but is more active than a capacity. Our global or circumspective readiness to act appropriately makes intentional comportment possible but it is not itself a kind of comportment. Rather, readiness is the common root of intentional comportment and transcendence.[51]

The point is so basic and subtle that Heidegger himself was not clear on the subject and said both that the "intentional constitution of Dasein's comportment is precisely the ontological condition the possibility of every and any transcendence",[52] and "intentionality is founded in Dasein's transcendence and is possible solely for this reason".[53] Now, thanks to Mark, we can see what Heidegger and I should have said: "Disclosure for Heidegger is meant to point to the . . . [readiness] to activate coping skills. . . . [A readiness] pointed to by . . . noting the way mood 'attunes' or 'disposes' us to certain possibilities for certain possibilities within the world" (109).

Reply to Charles Taylor

Back in 1952 when I visited Oxford, I looked up Ryle in the hope of discussing Heidegger and Merleau-Ponty with him. He, however, found such philosophers far from his current concerns and sent me off to see a Fellow at All Souls with interests as bizarre as mine. Charles Taylor and I have been talking and exchanging papers ever since. In those days we were each criticizing mainstream Anglo-American philosophy and its psychological spin-offs, behaviorism and cognitivism, on the basis of the then highly suspect ideas of Heidegger and Merleau-Ponty. Our interests have changed, but I still find everything Charles writes that touches on Heidegger and Merleau-Ponty so congenial that I can only cheer the clarity and persuasiveness with which he says it.

We differ, however, in our assessment of the generation of "post-modern" thinkers who stand on Heidegger's shoulders and use his insights to criticize both his own work and the current cultural scene. Taylor contends that thinkers like Derrida and Foucault neglect the causal power of the meanings embodied in cultural practices—meanings that are focused in rituals, symbols, narratives, and the writing of philosophers that influence how our culture changes. For the post-moderns, he says, the practices seem to change just by "the contingent flow of events." Our disagreement grows out of an NEH Summer Institute on alternative conceptions of how practices work to produce intelligibility that I codirected and that Taylor and several other contributors to this volume attended. Our discussion there was cut short by the fact that each presenter could stay only one week, so I shall use the limited space I have here to continue our debate by defending Derrida and Foucault.

Taylor is true to Heidegger in holding that all cultural practices have a tendency to gather—they work by what Heidegger calls appropriation (*Ereignis*)—and this tendency solicits people to produce works of art and other "ways truth establishes itself," such as the words of thinkers. These works articulate and hold up to the culture its shared meanings. Early Heidegger may not have thought that such cultural foci were necessary, but by the time he writes "The Origin of the Work of Art" Heidegger explicitly says that "there must be a being in the clearing in which the clearing takes its stand."[54] When I teach this essay I refer to Kuhnian paradigms and to Taylor's account of the necessity and function of "common meanings." Heidegger, who is like Kuhn raised to a cultural scale, thinks that a cultural revolution is produced by a paradigm shift. Also like Kuhn, and unlike Hegel, and perhaps Taylor, Heidegger does not think that such a shift makes rational sense. Rather, he sees the change as a reconfiguration (an *Ur-sprung* or originating leap) brought about when, for all sorts of contingent reasons, some practices that have been marginal become prominent. The work of art and other such media then enable these marginal practices to establish themselves as central.

So Heidegger, like Taylor, argues that practices gather into meaningful wholes and that all sorts of things can and must play an articulating role to transform and preserve cultural meanings. But Heidegger does not seek to offer an explanation of change in terms of the value of the practices made dominant by these meanings. That puts Heidegger one step beyond the Hegelian view that cultural styles or understandings of being supersede each other for good reasons. The thinkers of the next, post-Heidegger, generation, however, are more radical. They do not just ignore or deny the Hegelian and Heideggerian accounts of how cultural practices work by articulating; they offer alternative accounts of the tendencies in the cultural practices.[55] As Taylor says, "historical change is a rich brew," and each of these thinkers focuses on different sorts of cases as the ones most revealing of how we best make things intelligible. Derrida privileges cases where the practices, far from gathering into greater unity and clarity, disperse into greater and greater pluralism as new events occur. To take a simple example, we understand things best when we see that men and women mean different things by "mercy," and that as the term is used again and again greater differences arise, with no overarching conception governing all the meanings. Overarching conceptions are only convenient after-thoughts. Moreover, if we think that such overarching concepts govern intelligibility, such terms as mercy impede our sensitivity to the generation of differences in meaning. Sensitivity to differences and how they arise makes things more intelligible than does trying to understand things in terms of governing or focusing unifying conceptions.

Foucault has a different story. Influenced by Nietzsche, he sees cultural practices as agonistic and thinks that they tend to be focused by specific problematizations that come to occupy some influential group in the culture. For example, in classical Athens things made the most sense in the light of certain problems, one of which was how one could sexually subordinate boys who would later become leaders.

Taylor's example of Carnival gives us a good way of seeing the Foucaultian and Derridian points. Foucault would presumably emphasize how Carnival problematized authority and thereby made more relations among people more intelligible, while Derrida would focus on how disorder native to our ways of making things intelligible was acknowledged in the Carnival, which no one could make sense of but which nearly all respected. So it looks as though order coexists with what Taylor, sounding like Derrida, calls "chaos and contradictory principles." For Derrida, order is always mixed with, and ultimately based on, disorder, but this disorder is more and more suppressed by logocentrism. Foucault would speak of the covering up of problematizations by the techniques of disciplinary power.

As Taylor explains it, hermeneutics must seek a way out of conflict and disorder by putting anomalies in a new context where they will become orderly and clear. Against Taylor, Derrida and Foucault would claim that, because hermeneutics is ultimately committed to the view that practices solicit coherent articulation, it cannot make disorder meaningful without denigrating it. But neither Derrida nor Foucault rejects hermeneutics in favor of cultural drift. Rather, each rejects hermeneutics in claiming that we make the best sense of people and things when we understand how they are shaped by dissemination (Derrida) or problematization (Foucault). Things like Carnival become more intelligible in light of either of these basic tendencies of the practices than when covered up by an exclusive concern with gathering and articulation. Taylor, in opposition, recognizes cultural conflict as, in fact, inevitable, but follows hermeneutics in emphasizing the tendency of cultural practices toward one harmonious order that, while not achievable in this world, must be striven for as an ideal limit. Thus, while acknowledging that hermeneutics misses the inevitability of conflict, Taylor emphasizes the causal power of ideals as they tend to bring out and sustain a unified cultural style. The postmoderns, on the contrary, are suspicious of any ideals, even the most enlightened ones, if they treat disorder as a problem to be overcome and so cover up its positive role in producing intelligibility. But that does not mean that they do not appreciate other kinds of meaningful ideals such as deconstruction or living your life as a work of art. These ideals do imply certain kinds of disorder as crucial to our ways of making things and people intelligible.

None of these thinkers, including Taylor, denies that there is also an element of drift. (Taylor speaks of how the culture "gradually slips over more and more in a secular direction.") And none of these thinkers denies that meanings, among many other reasons, produce cultural change. The real difficulty for Taylor is that it seems the postmodern thinkers deny the causal efficacy of goods. The issue, though, is what counts as goods. It is not that Heidegger and his followers deny the importance of goods in holding up to a culture what it is up to. Heidegger emphasizes that works of art and thinkers hold up meaningful differences. Foucault focuses on the writings of the police commissioners and the social engineers that extol welfare and discipline in order to show the effect of "goods" that totalize. Derrida looks to literary, philosophical texts and, more recently, legal texts to see the terms with which our society defends order and justifies authority and so covers up the disorder that makes order possible.

Thus Foucault and Derrida have their own kinds of goods, which are very different from the kind Taylor's commitment to hermeneutics and gathering leads him to extol. Foucault wants to problematize our current dependence on biopower and make us face the agonism at the basis of society.[56] So for Foucault, problematizations and agonisms are goods. Derrida calls our attention to dissemination and the imposition of order and thereby seeks to combat the logocentrism that is still found in those hermeneutical tendencies that cause us to live intelligibility-impoverished lives. The famous incoherences in literature, philosophy, and law serve as Derrida's goods. Carnival would serve Derrida too.

The real issue for Taylor, then, is not whether postmodern thinkers see the power of an appeal to goods or even whether they are committed to any goods of their own. What Taylor thinks they lack is an understanding of the ultimate causal power of goods and the way that practices get their power from the goods they articulate. The postmoderns, starting already with Heidegger, think that the ultimate causal power lies not in goods, but in the practices themselves *and how they work*. Thus, for Heidegger, the work of art does not so much articulate a good as glamorize the style found in the coordination of the practices. The causal power ultimately comes from the way the practices gather. ("*Ereignis* sends being," to put the case in Heidegger jargon.) In Derrida it is dissemination that does the sending, and in Foucault struggle is at the basis of power. If either Derrida or Foucault is right about how human intelligibility works, then the tendency of articulation to unify a culture's goods weakens the culture by covering up what is really going on. This is why Derrida and Foucault focus on the dark side of the Enlightenment and seem to ignore its ideals.

I am not writing this to attack articulation and defend problematization or dissemination. If there is one dominant tendency in our practices—and this, of course, is itself questionable—these three opposed accounts cannot all be right, and I do not know which one is. I am trying to raise the level of the debate, since I hope that, once Charles takes seriousty the basis of the postmoderns' suspicion of the causal power of our culture's current goods, he will be able to find the flaws in their approach and so supersede them.

Reply to Daniel Andler

In his wonderfully lucid chapter, Daniel has done me a great service by showing to what extent my arguments that go back to the middle sixties[57] are still relevant to cognitive science. In doing so, he has undertaken to illuminate the single most difficult question in the field. What is a context and how do we deal with it? Since this is a question that I have been struggling with from the start, I very much admire and appreciate the clarity with which Daniel has distinguished situation and background as two kinds of context, related these notions to contemporary discussions, and illuminated the issues involved.

Reading Andler's valiant attempt to define the background in the clear, analytical terms that would make the notion relevant to cognitive science, however, makes me realize how hard the job is and how far from helpful my attempts have been. Andler is right that the background is "no thing, not even a set of objective practices, corporal dispositions, acquired skills, or whatever; rather it is what practices, corporal dispositions, acquired skills, etc., jointly secrete in historical time" (147). But what in the world is that? Now, thanks to my co-authors of *Disclosing New Worlds*, I think I can go a little further in spelling out the idea.[58] What is "secreted" by the practices is a style. Each epoch in our culture has a different style, and so, to take a more mundane example, do the driving practices in California and in New York. In terms of a style, certain things and events show up as relevant and others do not. Moreover, what counts as a thing, an event, or a situation depends on the style. Thus Heidegger calls what I am calling the culture's style its understanding of being.

This is a very down-to-earth kind of antinaturalism. The style is obviously not some nonnatural meaning that supervenes on the practices or is secreted by them. It is the way the practices themselves are organized, or, as we put it in *Disclosing New Worlds*, the way they are coordinated. Not that that makes everything clear, but it will, I hope, help Daniel in his worthy project of trying to demystify the idea of the background by keeping close to the phenomenon.

Reply to Harry Collins

Harry Collins has a special flair for giving elegant examples of what computers cannot do. When these examples support my view, like his examples of the need for a particularly trained body to exercise each particular embodied skill, it is my turn to think, "Wow, I wish I had thought of that." However, when he uses his ingenuous examples like the overzealous spell-checker to defend his basic thesis that enculturated skill/knowledge does not require that the person enculturated have a fully functioning human body, I begin to worry. Soon, I fear, we will hear that a suitably enculturated entity will not need a body at all.

I fear what is coming because I have already been through this debate in an exchange about Madeleine, a blind and partially paralyzed woman described by Oliver Sacks, who acquired her understanding of the human world from having books read to her.[59] That debate revealed an ambiguity in my talk of "a body like ours." Thanks to Collins, it became clear to me that insofar as I argued that one needs a body shaped like ours to understand our world, I was wrong. But I tried to show that, nonetheless, to share our form of life an entity would need to share our understanding of self-movement, overcoming obstacles, and so forth. I resisted then, and I resist now, Collins's move from the fact that someone physically handicapped can be socialized into our form of life to the claim that "gray stationary metal boxes" could be socialized and so have intelligence like ours.

Now Collins wants to accept my point that to be acculturated a computer has to be more than a metal box with a floppy drive input, but he only concedes that the box will have to have "some sensory inputs." I do not think that such a box, even with some sensory inputs, could be socialized at all because it would not be able to be in subtle sync with the bodies of its caretakers, and that is where early socialization seems to occur.

It now looks like we have reached agreement that, as Collins puts it, "all an intelligence needs is enough of a body to be potentially socialized" (188), but we differ on how much that is. Collins even admits that "socialization . . . involves far richer mechanisms [than stimulus-response conditioning] that we don't understand" (190). I think that the socializable entity will have to be self-moving, have feelings and emotions, be able to detect and care about approval and disapproval, and a lot more—way beyond the capacities of Collins's gray box.

Oddly enough this abstract and rather dogmatic standoff in which we both appeal to our uninformed intuition on the matter is now being put to an empirical test. Rodney Brooks and his colleagues at MIT have constructed a robot they have named Cog that is a metal torso that can move its arms and has "eyes" and "ears" and a head it can turn in various directions.[60] Cog clearly embodies Collins's vision of a robot with sensory inputs and even has some limited motion thrown in. Indeed, Cog is "designed to go through an embodied infancy and childhood," and the MIT researchers now plan to find a dedicated group of graduate students who, in their spare time, will look at, move around, and say things to this augmented metal box in the expectation that Cog will gradually become socialized and thereby intelligent.[61] All I can say for now is that I am ready to go out on a limb and predict that Cog will not learn a thing, in part because no graduate student will take it to his or her breast; and even if he or she did, Cog would not feel good about it.

Whichever of us turns out to be right in his predictions, I appreciate Harry's challenge because it puts us both back in touch with work on the cutting edge of AI.

Reply to Fernando Flores

It is always a joy to read one of Fernando Flores's papers or to attend one of his workshops because, there more than anywhere else, I see the practical implications of being sensitive to the phenomena Heidegger describes. Fernando's contribution to this volume is a case in point. I am always amazed that Heidegger's seeming abstruse ideas about being and world-disclosing can have such importance for business. I consider it one of my lucky days when Fernando showed up in my office, just out of prison in Chile, and told me that he had been studying Heidegger and thought that his work was a better basis for revolution than Marx and therefore wanted to study with me. I could not have guessed that Fernando's dissertation would give rise to innovations in the use of computers in management and that his interest in later Heidegger would lead to a new understanding of business practice. Nor could I have imagined that we would become close friends and end up collaborating for over a decade, most recently co-authoring (along with Charles Spinosa) a revolutionary manifesto for business and politics.

Not that I thought that Heidegger's ontology was too rarefied to be relevant to the real world. I always believed in applying philosophy to our lives, and I supposed that Heidegger would have agreed. But applying Heidegger ideas to business! That seemed a bit much. I knew that people in business regarded philosophy as impractical because it is too disinterested and that most continental philosophers tended to treat business thinking as crude because business is supposed to be utilitarian. Heidegger himself was fond of pointing out that philosophy never produces any practical results. Nonetheless, his own work shows that he thought it was essential for a philosopher, not just to speculate or do logical analysis, but to show people new ways of looking at their lives and their culture and so to open people up to new possibilities for action.

Only later did I learn that Heidegger himself was practically a business consultant. It started when Heidegger, banned from teaching at the university, was invited to address the Club of Bremen, "an association of prominent representatives of the Hanseatic upper middle class made up of businessmen, particularly, specialists in overseas commerce and directors of shipping lines and dockyards."[62] According to his friend Heinrich Petzet:

Heidegger considered it in many ways a helpful and invigorating experience. . . . This was an audience that was certainly not philosophically trained; but, by the same token, it was less prejudiced and more willing to hear new ideas. . . . It was this that constituted what Heidegger frequently cited as the "clean air" that was very important to him. . . . What he presented in Bremen for the first time were those statements about the metaphysics of technology that became famous and formed the foundation of his entire philosophical work for the last three decades of his life. His presentations at the Club of Bremen constituted a group of four speeches . . . : "Das Ding" (The Thing), "Das Ge-stell" (Enframing), "Die Gefahr" (The Danger), and "Die Kehre" (The Turning).[63]

The businessmen seem to have felt they got something out of their discussions with Heidegger, and Heidegger apparently very much liked the seminars that he led for the Club. Even after he was reinstated at the university, "he returned eight times during the 1950s and used the Club as a testing ground for most of his major papers."[64]

Now, thanks to Flores, businessmen are beginning to realize that, ironically, the largely Cartesian philosophical claims, which non-philosophers have thought too impractical to examine, govern their approach to business. Once business people see this, many of their grounds for prejudice against the relevance of philosophy dissolve. Then Flores and his colleagues can work with people in the business community to find ways to structure organizations, develop strategies, and produce corporate cultures that develop innovations and that operate on the assumption that people are not primarily detached decision makers but rather skillful agents and world disclosers.

Flores seems to me to have developed and applied insights from each stage of Heidegger's development, and his use of Heidegger has in turn illuminated for me the phenomena Heidegger was interpreting at each stage. To begin with, Flores's experience as finance minister in Chile had sensitized him to the importance of language for coordinating action. In his dissertation he therefore used Searle's theory of speech acts to develop the instrumental, pragmatist understanding of language in *Being and Time*. Drawing on John Austin, Flores saw that, as he put it, performatives bring forth commitments by bringing forth conditions of satisfaction. But Flores emphasized the importance of declaratives, arguing that all speech acts were commitments that were not discharged until those to whom the commitment was made declared their satisfaction. Like early Heidegger in his transcendental phase, Flores thought of the requests, offers, promises, orders, and declarations whose structure he analyzed as basic to all activity anywhere anytime.

Flores also saw that speech acts served as more than a tool for tracking the commitments implicit in business activity. He understood that sensitizing people to the speech acts they were engaged in would enable them to develop a more authentic understanding of the everyday situations of their lives. So far as they were bringing forth new or particular conditions of satisfaction through the particular requests they made, people could experience themselves as co-constituters of the situations in which they lived. They could, in short, awaken from the sleep of thinking that they were exchanging information about the world, and take responsibility for the kind of being-with-others they were making for themselves. They could give up the picture of themselves as having to understand the whole of their business and could replace that notion with a sense of themselves as a negotiator working with partners. By developing their sensitivity to their constituting roles, business people, among others, became more entrepreneurial, more flexible, and more innovative. This was Flores's version of the authenticity Heidegger describes in Division II of *Being and Time*.

Finally, Flores found that if you change the coordination of the practices, you change the style or understanding of being of a company. Changing the style or understanding of being in turn opens up new domains of activity and new possibilities for action. As Flores went on applying this philosophy in the business world he saw that language "brings forth reality by bringing forth new worlds." This insight led to our collaboration (with Charles Spinosa) on our book, *Disclosing New Worlds*, which shows the relevance of later Heidegger's thinking for understanding entrepreneurship and political action. I look forward to many more years of collaboration. Heidegger would have been lucky (and I think delighted) to have found among the businessmen in Bremen such a student as Fernando.

Notes

Foreword

1. AI Memo 154, January 1968.

2. Philip E. Agre, *The Dynamic Structure of Everyday Life*, MIT AI Technical Report 1085, October 1988, chapter 1, Section A1a, 9.

3. Terry Winograd and Fernando Flores, *Understanding Computers and Cognition: A New Foundation for Design* (Norwood, N.J.: Ablex, 1986).

4. Hubert L. Dreyfus and Stuart E. Dreyfus, "Making a Mind vs. Modeling the Brain: Artificial Intelligence Back at a Branchpoint," *Daedalus* 117 (Winter 1988): 15–44.

5. Hubert L. Dreyfus, *Being-in-the-World: A Commentary on Heidegger's* Being and Time, *Division I* (Cambridge: MIT Press, 1991).

Chapter 1: Coping and Its Contrasts

1. This chapter is in honor of Hubert Dreyfus, and in memory of my graduate teacher, Samuel Todes. I have benefited from comments by Hubert Dreyfus, Charles Guignon, and Theodore Schatzki on an earlier version.

2. Karen Barad coins this term in her discussion of scientific apparatus and the phenomena it measures, to emphasize that neither measurement apparatus nor objects measured are determinately identifiable prior to or apart from specific forms of encounter "between" them. "Meeting the Universe Halfway: Realism and Social Constructivism without Contradiction," in *Feminism, Science and the Philosophy of Science*, ed. Lynn H. Nelson and Jack Nelson (Dordrecht: Reidel, 1996), 161–194. Similarly here, neither activity nor the world's resistance or accommodation to it are determinate apart from their mutual intra-action.

Notes

3. Hubert L. Dreyfus, "The Hermeneutic Approach to Intentionality," presented to the 18th Annual Meeting of the Society for Philosophy and Psychology, Montreal, Quebec (1992), 3.

4. Hubert L. Dreyfus, *What Computers Can't Do: The Limits of Artificial Intelligence*, rev. ed. (New York: Harper & Row, 1979), 214.

5. Ibid., 266.

6. Dreyfus, *Being-in-the-World*, 96. Dreyfus specifically cites "medical practice" as an exemplary sense in which being a for-the-sake-of-which can be described as "a practice." Ibid.

7. Hubert L. Dreyfus and Paul Rabinow, *Michel Foucault: Beyond Structuralism and Hermeneutics.* 2d ed. (Chicago: University of Chicago Press, 1983), 166.

8. Michel Foucault, *Discipline and Punish: The Birth of the Prison* (New York: Random House, 1977), 153.

9. Dreyfus attributes this distinction to Heidegger, and takes Heidegger's use of *Auslegung* (interpretation) to single out the "contextual explication" involved in noticing, repairing, replacing, adjusting, and otherwise shifting attention from the task at hand to how that task is being performed. I think this attribution is mistaken; *Auslegung* also includes the ways one takes up specific possibilities in Dreyfus's "practical coping." This is not the place to dispute the interpretation of Heidegger, however; both positions are philosophically interesting and worthy of discussion.

10. "The Hermeneutic Approach to Intentionality," 6.

11. *Being-in-the-World*, 211.

12. "The Hermeneutic Approach to Intentionality," 5.

13. Ibid.

14. *Being-in-the-World*, 30.

15. Ibid.

16. Ibid., 203.

17. Dreyfus mentions Tyler Burge, Robert Brandom, and John Haugeland (with Wittgenstein and Sellars in the background) as prominent proponents of intentionality as social-normative. Haugeland's attribution of a strongly social-normative position to Heidegger has undoubtedly been an important spur for Dreyfus to articulate a divergence between them.

18. "The Hermeneutic Approach to Intentionality," 2.

19. Ibid., 8.

20. This specification is much too loose, because to capture Dreyfus's point, it must rule out simulations that reproduce the capacity in a radically different way (e.g.,

chess mastery would not be made explicit by a program that could defeat grand-masters through brute calculational power if, as Hubert Dreyfus argues, grandmas-ters choose moves according to a situational gestalt). See *What Computers Can't Do.* Yet the requisite similarity must not be specified so strictly that the "inexplicable" character of skills becomes trivially true.

21. Aage Peterson, "The Philosophy of Niels Bohr," *Niels Bohr: A Centenary Volume,* ed. A. P. French and P. J. Kennedy (Cambridge: Harvard University Press, 1985), 302. Peterson quotes this remark as Bohr's characteristic response in conversation to those who would claim that reality must be more fundamental than language in guiding our understanding of the world. I owe special thanks to Karen Barad for bringing this passage to my attention. See "Meeting the Universe Halfway," 175.

22. Samuel C. Wheeler III, "True Figures: Metaphor, Social Relations, and the Sorites," in *The Interpretive Turn: Philosophy, Science, Culture,* ed. David Hiley, James Bohman, and Richard Shusterman (Ithaca: Cornell University Press, 1991), 200.

23. Naturalistic accounts of meaning rely upon the causal/functional role of an expression to fix its sense, but such approaches are not open to Dreyfus, and in any case encounter other difficulties in both their mentalist and pragmatist versions.

24. *Being-in-the-World,* 274.

25. Ibid., 215–217.

26. Donald Davidson, *Inquiries into Truth and Interpretation* (Oxford: Oxford Univer-sity Press, 1984); Robert Brandom, *Making it Explicit: Reasoning, Representing, and Dis-cursive Commitment* (Cambridge: Harvard University Press, 1994).

27. This approach suggests an interesting reinterpretation of the famous "Chinese Room" argument against causal/functional role semantics in John R. Searle, *Minds, Brains, and Science* (Cambridge: Harvard University Press, 1984). Searle is correct that someone who merely follows formal rules for manipulating symbols does not thereby understand or speak a language. The reason, however, is not that one's manipula-tions are not "expressed in symbols whose meanings are known to you." Ibid., 33. It is that the practices of a rule-follower isolated in a room are not sufficiently integrated with other practices for coping with her surroundings to sustain their intelligibility.

28. *Being-in-the-World,* 212–214.

29. The classical expositions of this conception of theoretical practice are Nancy Cartwright, *How the Laws of Physics Lie* (New York: Oxford University Press, 1983), and Ronald Giere, *Explaining Science: A Cognitive Approach* (Chicago: University of Chicago Press, 1988), chap. 3. For further discussion of its philosophical significance, see Joseph Rouse, *Engaging Science: How to Understand Its Practices Philosophically* (Ithaca, N.Y.: Cornell University Press, 1996).

30. Nancy Cartwright, "Fundamentalism vs. the Patchwork of Laws," *Proceedings of the Aristotelian Society* 94 (1994): 279–292.

31. Widespread dealings with laboratories as familiar work-sites makes it easy to over-look the extent to which experimentation is a *modeling* practice not so different from

theoretical modeling (the parallel is discussed more extensively in *Engaging Science*, 129–132; 228–229). The emergence of intermediate cases such as thought experiments and computer simulations highlight the parallel.

32. Peter Galison, *Image and Logic: A Material Culture of Microphysics* (Chicago: University of Chicago Press, 1997).

33. *Making it Explicit*, chap. 3, 5–8.

34. Robert Brandom offers perhaps the clearest version of such an approach to the normativity of meaning and action. "Freedom and Constraint by Norms," *American Philosophical Quarterly* 16 (1979): 187–196.

35. See *Engaging Science*.

36. "The Hermeneutic Approach to Intentionality," 2.

37. *Being-in-the-World*, chap. 8.

38. See *Making it Explicit*. Brandom perhaps misleadingly calls such intra-active recognition an "I/Thou" conception of the social, misleading because it suggests an *inter*-action between already intentional agents rather than a constitutively *intra*-active practical "recognition."

39. This distinction of objective accountability from epistemic sovereignty is developed in Joseph Rouse, "Beyond Epistemic Sovereignty," in *The Disunity of Science: Boundaries, Contexts, and Power*, ed. Peter Galison and David Stump (Stanford: Stanford University Press, 1996), 398–416.

Chapter 2: Coping with Others with Folk Psychology

1. See Donald Davidson, *Essays on Actions and Events* (Oxford, Oxford University Press, 1980), and Theodore R. Schatzki, *Social Practices: A Wittgensteinian Approach to Human Activity and the Social* (New York: Cambridge University Press, 1996).

2. Dreyfus, *Being-in-the-World*, 151, 96.

3. Martin Heidegger, *Being and Time*, trans. John Macquarrie and Edward Robinson (New York: Harper & Row, 1962), 163; henceforth cited as *BT*.

4. I should make explicit that in this essay the terms "action" and "activity" are used interchangeably. I use the terms thus: actions are particular doings and activity is the flow of doings that any awake and sentient human performs.

5. The phenomenon of nondeliberate action bears strong resemblance to Ludwig Wittgenstein's notion of a reaction (*Reaktion*). For Wittgenstein, a reaction is a spontaneous behavior, where "spontaneous" means unreflective, or unconsidered. An action is unreflective when it is not preceded or accompanied by explicit reflection or consideration about what to do. Such behavior, Wittgenstein writes, is "next to hand" (*nächstliegenden*); Ludwig Wittgenstein, *Philosophical Investigations*, trans. G. E. M. Anscombe (New York: Macmillan, 1958), 201.

6. Hubert L. Dreyfus, *What Computers* Still *Can't Do: A Critique of Artificial Reason* (Cambridge: MIT Press, 1992), xxviii–xxix.

7. Dreyfus, *Being-in-the-World*, 92.

8. I skip over the contentious interpretive question whether the "for-the-sake-of-whichs" that Heidegger further characterizes as "possibilities of existence" are best understood as ends, self-interpretations, roles, sets of practices, or some combination of these.

9. In this regard, skills resemble Bourdieu's *habitus*; Pierre Bourdieu, *The Logic of Practice*, trans. Richard Nice (Stanford: Stanford University Press, 1990), book 1.

10. Jerome Wakefield and Hubert Dreyfus, "Intentionality and the Phenomenology of Action," in *John Searle and his Critics*, ed. Ernest Lepore and Robert van Gulick (Oxford: Blackwell, 1991), 259.

11. *Being-in-the-World*, 70.

12. Ibid., 69.

13. Ibid., 70.

14. Ibid.

15. Many theorists are suspicious of the notion of an awareness whose object is not there as such for the person aware. Nothing in the following depends, however, on accepting this idea. Those wary of the notion can still capture the phenomenon Dreyfus is pointing at by saying, for example, that even when a person is not paying attention or thinking about her activity, she usually *knows* what she is doing and why. Dreyfus would resist this description and works instead with the notion of nonthematic awareness because for him knowledge is a "mental state" and the objects of "mental states" are thematic.

16. *Being-in-the-World*, 58, 85.

17. Wakefield and Dreyfus, "Intentionality and the Phenomenology of Action," 269.

18. For instance, *Being-in-the-World*, 5.

19. Ibid., 58.

20. See Ibid., 70.

21. See George Downing, *Körper und Wort in der Psychotherapie* (Munich: Kösel, 1996).

22. For the rationale behind this terminology, see my book, *Social Practices*, chap. 2.

23. *Being-in-the-World*, 208; see also 220.

24. Ibid., 86.

25. Ibid., 58.

26. For a book-length treatment, see Paul Johnston, *Wittgenstein: Rethinking the Inner* (London: Routledge, 1993). See also Malcolm Budd, *Wittgenstein's Philosophy of Psychology* (London: Routledge, 1989). In addition, see my review discussion of Johnston's book, "Inside-out?" *Inquiry* 38 (1995): 329–347.

27. This is, I stress, my interpretation of Wittgenstein's remarks. For discussion of this interpretation and of ideas broached in the following two paragraphs, see *Social Practices*, chaps. 2 and 4.

28. Robert Brandom, *Making it Explicit*, 13–18. Brandom, it seems to me, has illicitly transferred Wittgenstein's thoughts about rule following to his remarks on life conditions.

29. In this context, recall Weber's claim that a meaning-adequate attribution of motives need not construe action as rational. Such a construal only enjoys the highest degree of such adequacy. Max Weber, *Basic Concepts of Sociology*, trans. H. P. Secher (New York: Citadel, 1962), 32ff.

30. Analyses that tie such terms essentially to normative structures of reasoning qualify. For two recent examples, see Brandom, *Making it Explicit*, chap. 4, and Jane Heal, "Replication and Functionalism," in *Folk Psychology: The Theory of Mind Debate*, ed. Martin Davies and Tony Stone (Oxford: Blackwell, 1995), 45–59.

31. See Hubert L. Dreyfus and Stuart E. Dreyfus, *Mind Over Machine: The Power of Human Intuition and Expertise in the Era of the Computer* (New York: The Free Press, 1986), chap. 1.

32. See *Being-in-the-World*, 56–59. See also his review of Wittgenstein's *Remarks on the Philosophy of Psychology*, in which he (nondeliberately) attributes the conception of mental states as conscious states, in this case, experiences to Wittgenstein; Hubert L. Dreyfus, "Wittgenstein on Renouncing Theory in Psychology," *Contemporary Psychology* 27 (1982): 940–942. Thanks to David Stern for suggesting that I look at this review.

33. *Being-in-the-World*, 49.

Chapter 3: Practices, Practical Holism, and Background Practices

1. Hubert L. Dreyfus, "Reflections on the Workshop on 'The Self'" *Anthropology and Humanism Quarterly* 16 (1991): 27.

2. Stephen P. Turner, *The Social Theory of Practices: Tradition, Tacit Knowledge, and Presuppositions* (Cambridge: Polity Press, 1994), 1. The first quoted passage is from Wittgenstein, *On Certainty* (New York: J. & J. Harper Editions, 1969), 15; the second is from Hubert L. Dreyfus, "The Mind in Husserl: Intentionality in the Fog," *Times Literary Supplement* (July 12, 1991), 25.

3. *The Social Theory of Practices*, 2.

4. Ibid., 13.

5. Dreyfus, *Being-in-the-World*, 19.

6. Ibid., 22.

Notes

7. Hubert L. Dreyfus, "Holism and Hermeneutics," *Review of Metaphysics* 34 (1980): 7.

8. Ibid., 10–11.

9. Ibid., 12.

10. Wittgenstein, *Philosophical Investigations*, I §241.

11. *Being-in-the-World*, 5–6.

12. "Holism and Hermeneutics," 8.

13. Wittgenstein, *On Certainty*, §204; cited in "Holism and Hermeneutics," 8.

14. Heidegger, *Being and Time*, 122; cited in "Holism and Hermeneutics," 9.

15. "Holism and Hermeneutics," 7.

16. "Reflections on the Workshop on 'The Self,'" 27.

17. Ibid.

18. Ibid., 27–28.

19. See section V.

20. Hubert L. Dreyfus and Stuart Dreyfus, "Why Computers May Never Think Like People," *Technology Review* 89 (1986): 51.

21. *Philosophical Investigations* §§206, 208, 211, 217.

22. "Holism and Hermeneutics," 7. In a footnote attached to reason 2, Dreyfus notes that on his account of cultural practices, they involve a lot more than bodily skills: they incorporate the appropriate equipment, symbols, and general cultural moods. These two reasons are, in effect, restated in the passage from *Being-in-the-World*, 22, quoted at the beginning of section II.

23. "Holism and Hermeneutics," 7.

24. Charles Taylor, *Philosophical Arguments* (Cambridge: Harvard University Press, 1995), 69–70.

25. Hubert L. Dreyfus "Why Expert Systems Don't Exhibit Expertise," *IEEE-Expert* 1 (1986): 86–87.

26. "Holism and Hermeneutics," 8–9.

27. Ibid., 9.

28. Martin Heidegger, *The Basic Problems of Phenomenology*, trans. Albert Hofstadter (Bloomington: Indiana University Press, 1982), 275.

29. Hubert L. Dreyfus, "Heidegger's Critique of the Husserl/Searle Account of Intentionality," *Social Research* 60, no.1 (1993): 17–38.

30. Charles Spinosa, Fernando Flores, and Hubert Dreyfus, *Disclosing New Worlds: Entrepreneurship, Democratic Action, and the Cultivation of Solidarity* (Cambridge: MIT Press, 1997), 189.

31. "Reflections on the Workshop on 'The Self,'" 27.

32. Ibid.

33. The following five points are based on a handout provided by Dreyfus at the NEH Summer Institute on Practices on July 24, 1997, under the title "Conclusion: How background practices and skills work to ground norms and intelligibility: the ethico-political implications."

Chapter 4: The Limits of Phenomenology

1. Unless otherwise noted, parenthetical references are to Hubert L. Dreyfus, *Being-in-the-World*.

2. Hubert L. Dreyfus, "Heidegger's Critique of the Husserl/Searle Account of Intentionality," 34.

3. Ibid., 33.

4. See chapter 3 in John R. Searle, *Intentionality: An Essay in the Philosophy of Mind* (Cambridge: Cambridge University Press, 1983).

5. Ibid., 12.

6. "Heidegger's Critique of the Husserl/Searle Account of Intentionality," 34 (emphasis in the original).

7. Ibid., 28–29 (emphasis in original).

8. See my account of the overflow of consciousness in John R. Searle, *The Rediscovery of the Mind* (Cambridge: MIT Press, 1992).

9. To block two possible misunderstandings: I am not saying that all conscious content is intentional content, nor that all intentional content is conscious.

10. For example, John R. Searle, *The Construction of Social Reality* (New York: The Free Press, 1995).

11. I am indebted to Sean Kelly, Dagmar Searle, and Hubert Dreyfus for comments on this article.

Chapter 5: Background Practices, Capacities, and Heideggerian Disclosure

1. Citations are to the MIT Press edition, Hubert L. Dreyfus, *What Computers Still Can't Do: A Critique of Artificial Reason* (Cambridge: MIT Press, 1992), 233.

2. "Introduction to the Revised Edition," *What Computers Still Can't Do*, 56–57.

3. Hubert L. Dreyfus, *Being-in-the-World*, 7. All parenthetical references in the text are to *Being-in-the-World*.

4. Hubert L. Dreyfus, "Heidegger's Critique of the Husserl/Searle Account of Intentionality," 35–36.

5. John R. Searle, *The Rediscovery of the Mind*, 189.

6. Ibid., 179.

7. John R. Searle, *The Construction of Social Reality*, 131.

8. *The Rediscovery of the Mind*, 180–181.

9. *The Construction of Social Reality*, 129.

10. *The Rediscovery of the Mind*, 192.

11. *The Construction of Social Reality*, 137.

12. John R. Searle, *Intentionality: An Essay in the Philosophy of the Mind*, 154 (emphasis supplied).

13. See Hubert L. Dreyfus, "Phenomenological Description versus Rational Reconstruction," forthcoming in *Revue Internationale de Philosophie*; John R. Searle, "The Limits of Phenomenology," in this volume.

14. *Intentionality*, 154.

15. Heidegger, *Being and Time (BT)*, 115.

16. Ibid., 98.

17. Ibid., 118/85.

18. *Being-in-the-World*, 103. Dreyfus draws a distinction between the local background and the general background, which doesn't change this analysis. Both are viewed as opened up by disclosive activity. See ibid., 189f.

19. *BT*, 232.

20. *The Construction of Social Reality*, 129.

21. See *BT*, 400.

22. Ibid., 416.

23. Ibid., 391.

24. Ibid., 393.

25. *BT*, 393.

26. Ibid., 394.

27. Indeed, it is hard to imagine what the conditions of satisfaction of an anxious state would be since, as Heidegger describes it, "[t]hat in the face of which one has anxiety is not an entity within-the-world," and the way in which it threatens "does not have the character of a definite detrimentality which reaches what is threatened." *BT*, 231. But it doesn't seem right, either, to dismiss the state of anxiety as a non-intentional state (as Searle would, given its lack of conditions of satisfaction), because it is not simply a subjective state—it is, as Searle would put it, "directed at or about or of . . . states of affairs in the world." *Intentionality*, 1.

28. *The Rediscovery of the Mind*, 140.

29. I'm grateful to Sean Kelly for bringing this point home to me.

30. See Dreyfus's excellent discussion of understanding in chapter 11, *Being-in-the-World*.

31. *BT*, 385.

32. *The Construction of Social Reality*, 135.

33. My thinking on these matters has benefited from being able to discuss them with Sean Kelly and James Siebach. This paper, like many others I have written, would not have been possible without Bert Dreyfus's readiness to discuss and entertain challenges to his views, his insightful but kind-hearted criticism, and his steady encouragement. I consider myself fortunate to have had him as a teacher, an advisor, and a friend.

Chapter 6: What's Wrong with Foundationalism?: Knowledge, Agency, and World

1. See Charles Taylor, "Overcoming Epistemology," in *Philosophical Arguments*, 1–19.

2. See Dreyfus, *What Computers Still Can't Do: A Critique of Artificial Reason*.

3. See especially Dreyfus, *Being-in-the-World*.

4. Dreyfus and Dreyfus, *Mind over Machine*.

5. "Se demander si le monde est réel, ce n'est pas entendre ce qu'on dit," Merleau-Ponty, *La Phénoménologie de la Perception* (Paris: Gallimard, 1945), 396.

6. Natalie Zemon Davis, *Society and Culture in Early Modern France: Eight Essays* (Stanford: Stanford University Press, 1975).

7. Quoted in Peter Burke, *Popular Culture in Early Modern Europe* (London: T. Smith 1978), 202.

8. M. M. Bakhtin, *Rabelais and His World*, trans. Helene Iswolsky (Cambridge: MIT Press, 1968).

9. Victor Turner, *Dramas, Fields and Metaphors: Symbolic Action in Human Society* (Ithaca, N.Y.: Cornell University Press, 1978).

10. *Popular Culture in Early Modern Europe*, 209.

11. Ibid., 212.

12. Ibid., 217.

13. Ibid., 270.

14. Ibid., 271.

15. Ibid., 221.

16. Henri Xavier Arquillière, *L'Augustinisme politique* (Paris: Vrin, 1934).

17. Arquillière quotes Isidore of Seville: "Ceterum, intra ecclesiam, potestates necessariae non essent, nisi ut, quod non prevalet sacerdos efficere per doctrine sermonem, potestas hoc imperet per discipline terrorem." Ibid., 142.

18. See Dreyfus and Rabinow, *Michel Foucault: Beyond Structuralism and Hermeneutics*, 245, 251.

19. See Michel Foucault "Politics and Ethics: an Interview," in *The Foucault Reader*, ed. Paul Rabinow (New York: Pantheon Press, 1984), 373–380.

Chapter 7: Context and Background: Dreyfus and Cognitive Science

1. Hubert L. Dreyfus, *What Computers Can't Do* (1972); *What Computers Can't Do* (1979); *What Computers Still Can't Do* (1992). All references are to the 1972 edition unless otherwise noted.

2. In the introduction to the 1979 revised edition of *What Computers Can't Do*, Dreyfus refers to cognitive science (27) and quotes in a footnote (309) the definition given by Allan Collins in the first issue of the journal *Cognitive Science* (1976). Today's cognitive scientist, regardless of persuasion and field, would be quite amazed by Collins's definition: as Dreyfus reports it, it clearly puts GOFAI in the center, with psychology the only other field mentioned as germane, and in a marginal role at that (some "experimental techniques developed by cognitive psychologists in recent years" are included among the "analysis techniques" of the new discipline).

3. A felicitous phrase coined by John Haugeland in *Artificial Intelligence: The Very Idea* (Cambridge: MIT Press, 1985), to refer to the first epoch of artificial intelligence, roughly from its Promethean beginnings in the mid-fifties to the onset of doubt in the late 1970s, which coincided with, and in fact was correlated with, the rebirth of connectionism.

Notes

4. Dreyfus and Dreyfus, *Mind over Machine*.

5. He certainly does say this whenever he comments on Fodor or Chomsky, but of course what he then picks on are "formalist" pronouncements by these authors which reflect but one current within cognitive science, and in somewhat dated terms at that—no criticism of Dreyfus being implied, of course: he rightly dealt with the "best scientific theory" available at the time he wrote. This leaves entirely open the question raised: is Dreyfus willing to say that essentially all of cognitive science today is either neuroscience or glorified AI? What would militate against this interpretation of Dreyfus's attitude is his recourse, especially in and since *Mind over Machine*, to arguments drawn precisely from empirical research in cognitive psychology.

6. "Cognitivism," as it has come to be known since John Haugeland and John Searle (independently?) coined the word.

7. To paraphrase Haugeland's title.

8. I.e., independently of feasibility issues.

9. The context thus appears on this view under the guise of "cognitive environment": it stands to mental happenings in the relation in which physical happenings stand to the physical environment. The use of "environment" in the discussion of context is indicative of a strong naturalistic stance which is of course quite foreign to Dreyfus. Dan Sperber and Deirdre Wilson's Relevance Theory is the most sophisticated research program predicated on the identification of context with cognitive environment. See Dan Sperber and Deirdre Wilson, *Relevance: Communication and Cognition* (Oxford: Blackwell, 1986).

10. To which one might wish to associate the technological problem of simulating the process.

11. PDP stands for Parallel Distributed Processing. See *Parallel Distributed Processing: Explorations in the Microstructure of Cognition*, vol. 1, *Foundations*, ed. David E. Rumelhart, James L. McClelland, and the PDP Research Group (Cambridge: MIT Press, 1986). PDP models are feed-forward neural nets made up of successive layers going from input to output; thus they are generalized perceptrons; see *Neurocomputing: Foundations of Research*, ed. James Anderson and Edward Rosenfeld (Cambridge: MIT Press, 1988), for a history of the neurocomputing tradition, including Rosenblatt's perceptron.

12. John McCarthy's way of putting it. "Programs with Common Sense," in *Semantic Information Processing*, ed. M. Minsky (Cambridge: MIT Press, 1969), 403–418. Dreyfus quotes the passage in *What Computers Can't Do: A Critique of Artificial Reason* (1972), 125.

13. This distinction is proposed by Claudia Bianchi in her dissertation, "Flexibilité Sémantique et Sous-détermination," Ph.D. diss., CREA, École Polytechnique, Paris, 1998.

14. *What Computers Can't Do*, 221.

15. Ibid., 261. Concern should not be too quickly reduced to a goal in the standard (detachable) sense.

16. Searle, *Intentionality*, 143.

17. Searle, *The Rediscovery of the Mind*, 175.

18. Ibid., 129.

19. Ibid.; emphasis in the original.

20. Ibid.

21. Hubert L. Dreyfus, "Phenomenological Description versus Rational Reconstruction," section II, emphasis in the original.

22. Hubert L. Dreyfus, "Introduction" to *Husserl, Intentionality, and Cognitive Science* (Cambridge: MIT Press, 1982).

23. *What Computers Can't Do*, 248.

24. *Mind over Machine*, chap. 1.

25. The other being historical and sociological, a matter of what one has time to read, how much attention one is ready to invest, how generously one acknowledges intellectual debts, and so forth.

26. *Themes from Kaplan*, ed. Joseph Almog, John Perry, and Howard Wettstein (New York: Oxford University Press, 1989).

27. John Perry, *The Problem of the Essential Indexical and Other Essays* (New York: Oxford University Press, 1993), especially the title essay.

28. Ibid., especially "Thought without Representation."

29. Recanati makes extensive use of this case. See, for example, Françoise Recanati, "Déstabiliser le Sens" (forthcoming).

30. Friedrich Waismann coins the expression in relation to empirical predicates. "Verifiability," in *Logic and Language*, ed. Antony Flew (Oxford: Basil Blackwell, 1951), 122–151. His position reflects Wittgenstein's famous remarks on family resemblance in the *Philosophical Investigations*.

31. Charles Travis, *The Uses of Sense: Wittgenstein's Philosophy of Language* (Oxford: Oxford University Press, 1989).

32. I focus here not on "the" in the first and third sentences, but on what counts as water being present in the refrigerator, York lying (exactly?) 25 miles in a (exactly?) north-westerly direction from Leeds, or crumbs (literally?) covering the table (so as to make it invisible?, etc.). Travis invents and examines such examples with exquisite thoroughness.

33. *The Rediscovery of the Mind*, 175.

34. In this area, very few of the examples are important in themselves (X's Y, as in Jim's book above, being one exception). What is needed is the basic intuition which

allows one to manufacture them as the need arises. In his critique of Schank's restaurant script, Dreyfus shows how to do it: the trick is to focus on just about any feature of the situation, examine what commonsense and tacit assumptions about the material or social world make that feature the way it is, and negate any one of these assumptions. A comic touch does no harm. See *What Computers Can't Do*, 41 et seq.

35. Which is, *of course*, not to claim that Searle's and Bourdieu's theories are contained in Dreyfus's! But there is considerable overlap.

36. In conversation, Searle once mentioned to Dreyfus the impact which the reading of Wittgenstein's *On Certainty* had on his thinking.

37. *The Rediscovery of the Mind*, 175.

38. I owe these references to Bianchi's dissertation.

39. In English, and in French even more clearly perhaps. The grammar is of course very dependent on the language; French, for example, has one word ("esprit") for both "mind" and "spirit", a linguistic fact which makes life difficult for a French philosopher of mind.

40. See Daniel Andler, "Turing: Pensée du Calcul, Calcul de la Pensée," in *Les Années 1930: Réaffirmation du Formalisme*, ed. F. Nef and D. Vernant (Paris: Vrin, 1998), 1–41, for preliminaries. Turing himself did not make the move, perhaps only for lack of time, but perhaps also for deeper reasons.

41. The shallow one being the historical situation of the field at the time Dreyfus got involved in it (as the introduction reminds the reader).

42. Non-eliminative mentalistic naturalism, that is (as opposed to Searle's uneasy, or the Churchlands' unabashed, neurobiological naturalism).

43. Sperber and Wilson, *Relevance*.

44. Daniel Andler, "The Normativity of Context," *Philosophical Studies* (forthcoming).

45. Jerry Fodor, *The Modularity of Mind: An Essay on Faculty Psychology*. (Cambridge: MIT Press, 1983), 129.

46. Dan Sperber, "The Modularity of Thought and the Epidemiology of Representations," in *Mapping the Mind: Domain Specificity in Cognition and Culture*, ed. Lawrence A. Hirchfeld and Susan A. Gelman (Cambridge: Cambridge University Press, 1994), 39–67.

47. This can be seen as part of a much broader issue, that of nonconceptual content, which is at present a lively area of research in the philosophy of mind. See Christopher Peacocke, "Nonconceptual Content Defended," *Philosophy and Phenomenological Research* 58 (1998): 381–388.

48. He credits Searle for having brought about this change in his views. See "Phenomenological Description versus Rational Reconstruction."

49. See, for example, Marc Jeannerod, *The Cognitive Neuroscience of Action* (Cambridge: Blackwell, 1997).

50. See, for example, Susan Carey, "Continuity and Discontinuity in Cognitive Development," in *An Invitation to Cognitive Science*, vol. 3 of *Thinking*, 2d ed., ed. E. Smith and D. Osherson (Cambridge: MIT Press, 1995).

Chapter 8: Grasping at Straws: Motor Intentionality and the Cognitive Science of Skilled Behavior

1. Heidegger, *Being and Time*, 59.

2. Ibid., 60.

3. P. F. Strawson, *Individuals: An Essay in Descriptive Metaphysics* (London: Methuen, 1959).

4. Ibid., 9.

5. See Gareth Evans, *Varieties of Reference* (Oxford: Oxford University Press, 1982), esp. chap. 6. Evans may have been influenced indirectly by Merleau-Ponty's views through the work of Charles Taylor.

6. See Sean Kelly, "The Non-conceptual Content of Perceptual Experience and the Possibility of Demonstrative Thought," forthcoming.

7. For an example of this position, see the chapter entitled "The Thing and the Natural World" in Maurice Merleau-Ponty, *Phenomenology of Perception*, trans. Colin Smith (London: Routledge and Kegan Paul, 1962).

8. Dreyfus has not, to my knowledge, published anything on this issue. I attribute to him this position, I hope not unjustly, on the basis of comments he has made both in joint seminars with Freeman and in personal conversations I have had with him myself.

9. *Phenomenology of Perception*, 104.

10. Ibid., 110.

11. Ibid., 5.

12. Ibid., 6.

13. Ibid., 103.

14. Ibid.

15. Goldstein, *Zeigen und Greifen*, 453–466, as quoted in Merleau-Ponty, *Phenomenology of Perception*, 103.

16. *Phenomenology of Perception*, 103.

17. Ibid., 104.

18. Heather Carnahan, "Eye, Head and Hand Coordination during Manual Aiming," in *Vision and Motor Control*, ed. L. Proteau and D. Elliott (Elsevier Science Publishers B. V., 1992), 188.

19. See Meyer et al., "Speed-Accuracy Tradeoffs in Aimed Movements: Toward a Theory of Rapid Voluntary Action," in *Attention and Performance XIII: Motor Representation and Control*, ed. M. Jeannerod (Hillsdale, N.J.: Lawrence Erlbaum Associates, 1990), 173–226.

20. R. S. Woodworth, "The Accuracy of Voluntary Movement," in *Psychological Review* 3, no. 13, (July 1899): 1–114.

21. Paul M. Fitts, "The information capacity of the human motor system in controlling the amplitude of movement," *Journal of Experimental Psychology* 47 (1954): 381–391.

22. It seems to me that it is in general the need to explain behavioral constants that drives psychologists to develop underlying theoretical accounts of behavior that run the risk of being at odds with the phenomenology of that behavior. This is true also, for instance, with the perceptual constants that Merleau-Ponty talks about extensively in the chapter entitled "The Thing and the Natural World," *Phenomenology of Perception*.

23. "Speed-Accuracy Tradeoffs," 180.

24. Woodworth, "The Accuracy of Voluntary Movement," 54.

25. Ibid., 59.

26. "Speed-Accuracy Tradeoffs," 201.

27. E. R. F. W. Crossman and P. J. Goodeve, "Feedback control of hand-movements and Fitts' law," *Quarterly Journal of Experimental Psychology* 35A (1983): 251–278.

28. *Phenomenology of Perception*, 104. Gareth Evans essentially follows Merleau-Ponty on this point, though he is on the face of it describing a different distinction altogether, that between perceptual content and the content of demonstrative thoughts. The relation is that perceptual content, according to Evans, is spelled out in terms of dispositions to act toward the object of perception—i.e., in the most basic cases, to grasp it—while demonstrative thoughts are, in the most basic cases, accompanied by a pointing gesture. Evans follows Merleau-Ponty exactly when he attributes the distinction between perceptual and demonstrative content to a distinction in the understanding of place that underlies the perceptual and the demonstrative acts. In the case of perception he calls this understanding "egocentric," in the case of demonstration he calls it "objective." See *Varieties of Reference*, chap. 6.

29. *Phenomenology of Perception*, 104.

30. Goodale, et al., "A neurological dissociation between perceiving objects and grasping them," *Nature: An International Weekly Journal of Science* 349 (Jan. 10, 1991): 154–156.

31. Ibid., 155.

32. See M. A. Goodale and A. D. Milner, "Separate visual pathways for perception and action," *Trends in Neuroscience* 15, 1 (1992): 20–25.

33. Phenomenologists in general, and Merleau-Ponty in particular, want to make the further claim that grasping behavior is in fact the condition of the possibility of pointing behavior. If this were right, then there ought not to be patients who can point without being able to grasp. The extensive literature on optic ataxia, however, makes this claim difficult to defend. For examples of this literature, see, for instance, Damasio et al., *Neurology* 29 (1979): 170–178, or Perenin et al., *Brain* 111 (1988): 643–674. Optic ataxia, as mentioned above, is a disorder in which, roughly speaking, patients have the capacity to point but not grasp. In order to defend Merleau-Ponty's claim that grasping is the condition of the possibility of pointing, one would have to argue that, despite appearances, optic ataxics are not actually pointing at objects when they appear to be.

34. *Phenomenology of Perception*, 104. In Evans's vocabulary, its place is given in "the objective order."

35. Ibid., 105.

36. Ibid.

37. Ibid., 103–104.

38. Ibid.

39. Goodale, Jakobson, Keillor, "Differences in the visual control of pantomimed and natural grasping movements," *Neuropsychologia* 32, no. 10 (1994): 1159–1178.

40. *Phenomenology of Perception*, 104.

41. Hon C. Kwan, et al., "Network relaxation as biological computation," *Behavioral and Brain Sciences* 14, no. 2 (1991): 354–356.

42. There is feedback during the learning phase of the network, of course, just as there is feedback during the learning phase of any action.

43. This paper has benefited greatly, of course, from discussions with Bert Dreyfus, who has been both my "advisor," in the administrative sense, and also my most helpful philosophical companion. Rarely do these two characteristics co-exist so harmoniously in a single person. I also owe a large debt of gratitude to the neurologist Donald Borrett, with whom I have worked closely on this topic over the course of the last several years. I have also been lucky enough to discuss this material with John Searle and Brendan O'Sullivan. This paper could not have been written without the support and advice of Cheryl Chen.

Chapter 9: Four Kinds of Knowledge, Two (or Maybe Three) Kinds of Embodiment, and the Question of Artificial Intelligence

I am grateful to Gary Wickham for helpful comments on an earlier draft of this text.

1. Hubert L. Dreyfus, *What Computers Can't Do* (1972); Hubert L. Dreyfus, *What Computers Still Can't Do* (1992).

2. Parts of this paper are adapted from H. M. Collins, "The Structure of Knowledge," *Social Research* 60 (1993): 95–116; "Humans, Machines and the Structure of Knowledge," *Stanford Humanities Review* 4, no. 2 (1995): 67–83; and "Embedded or Embodied: A Review of Hubert Dreyfus's *What Computers Still Can't Do*," *Artificial Intelligence* 80, no. 1 (1996): 99–117.

3. The mundane applications of Hollywood's brilliant scientific breakthroughs are depressing.

4. This is not *just* a matter of necessary conditions for tennis playing. We do not want to say that tennis playing knowledge is contained in the blood, even though a person without blood could not play tennis. We do not want to say that the body is like a tool and that tennis playing knowledge is contained in the racket (after all, we can transfer a tennis racket with hardly any transfer of tennis-playing ability).

5. The first phrase is so well embedded in society I need not provide a reference for it; the second is from Anthony Burgess's *A Clockwork Orange* (New York: Norton, 1962).

6. But it is the easiest element to explain so I have stayed with this dimension throughout the chapter. I argue elsewhere that skilled speakers of a language are able to make all kinds of "repairs" to damaged strings of symbols that the Chinese Room would not. For discussion of these other ways in which the social embeddedness of language shows itself, see H. M. Collins, *Artificial Experts: Social Knowledge and Intelligent Machines* (Cambridge: MIT Press, 1990), and H. M. Collins, "Hubert Dreyfus, Forms of Life, and a Simple Test For Machine Intelligence," *Social Studies of Science* 22 (1992): 726–739.

7. I am aware of the arguments that suggest all typed language processing could, in principle, be available to brute strength methods, but have argued against this possibility in the context of a more full analysis of the Turing Test in *Artificial Experts*.

8. See Dreyfus's response to the reviews of his book in "Response to my Critics," *Artificial Intelligence* 80, no. 1 (1996): 171–191.

9. For this argument in the context of the Patriot versus Scud battle in the Gulf War, see H. M. Collins and T. J. Pinch, *The Golem at Large: What You Should Know About Technology* (Cambridge: Cambridge University Press, 1998).

10. H. M. Collins, "Socialness and the Undersocialised Conception of Society," *Science Technology and Human Values* 23, no. 4 (1998): 494–516.

11. This is a strongly anthropocentric view, but I can think of no other way to say sensible things about the issue. It is no good saying that dogs "have their own private social world which is like ours but different" because you might as well say the same of waste-paper bins. The way you know whether or not some entity can acquire a culture is to try to teach it yours and see if it succeeds.

12. These things are by no means exclusive categories though many philosophers of my acquaintance consider that leaving the study would be a dereliction of duty.

13. Kusch and I try to supply such a new theory in H. M. Collins and Martin Kusch, "Two Kinds of Actions: A Phenomenological Study," *Philosophy and Phenomenological Research* 55, no. 4 (1995): 799–819; and H. M. Collins and M. Kusch, *The Shape of Actions: What Humans and Machines Can Do* (Cambridge: MIT Press, 1999).

Chapter 10: Semiartificial Intelligence

1. Hubert L. Dreyfus, *What Computers Still Can't Do*, ix.

2. Sabra Chartand, "A Split in Thinking Among Keepers of Artificial Intelligence," *New York Times* (July 18, 1993), sec. 4, 6.

3. John Horgan, *The End of Science: Facing the Limits of Knowledge in the Twilight of the Scientific Age* (Reading, Mass.: Addison-Wesley Publishing Co., 1996).

4. Sherry Turkle, *Life on the Screen: Identity in the Age of the Internet* (New York: Simon and Schuster, 1995), 88.

5. Ibid.

6. A. M. Turing, "Computing Machinery and Intelligence," *Mind* 59 (1950): 433–460.

7. *Life on the Screen*, 88. Julia's Web page is at http://fuzine.mt.cs.cmu.edu/mlm/julia.html where you can talk to Julia or read the record of one of her (imperfect) conversations.

8. *Life on the Screen*, 91.

9. Atul Gawande, "No Mistake," *New Yorker* (March 30, 1998), 74–81.

10. *Life on the Screen*, 207.

11. William Gibson, *Neuromancer* (New York: Ace Books, 1984).

12. Ibid., 159.

13. Kendall Hamilton and Julie Weingarden, "Lifts, Lasers, and Liposuction: The Cosmetic Surgery Boom," *Newsweek* (June 1998), 14.

14. Tom Kuntz, "A Death on Line Shows a Cyberspace with Heart and Soul," *New York Times* (April 23, 1995), sec. 4, 9.

15. Hans Moravec, *Mind Children: The Future of Robot and Human Intelligence* (Cambridge: Harvard University Press, 1988); Frank Tipler, *The Physics of Immortality: Modern Cosmology, God, and Resurrection* (New York: Doubleday, 1994).

16. Charles Taylor, *Sources of the Self: The Making of the Modern Identity* (Cambridge: Harvard University Press, 1989), 72.

Chapter 11: Heidegger on Living Gods

1. For Heidegger on the divinity of cultural works, see Martin Heidegger, "The Origin of the Work of Art," *Poetry, Language, Thought*, trans. Albert Hofstadter (New York: Harper & Row, 1971) 17–87. For Heidegger on accepting the presence of divinities when falling under the influence of things and locations, see in the same volume, "The Thing," 165–186 and "Building Dwelling Thinking," 145–161.

2. Hubert L. Dreyfus, "Heidegger on the Connection between Nihilism, Art, Technology, and Politics," *The Cambridge Companion to Heidegger*, ed. Charles Guignon (Cambridge: Cambridge University Press, 1993): 289–316.

3. See, for instance, the respect Merold Westphal has for Otto's thematics in *God, Guilt, and Death: An Existential Phenomenology of Religion*, ed. James M. Edie (Bloomington: Indiana University Press, 1984), 37.

4. Rudolf Otto, *The Idea of the Holy*, trans. John W. Harvey (London: Oxford University Press, 1958), 26–27.

5. *The Idea of the Holy*, 41–49.

6. Heidegger, "The Origin of the Work of Art," 42 (translation altered).

7. Martin Heidegger, *Identity and Difference*, trans. Joan Stambaugh (New York: Harper & Row, 1969), 72.

8. William James, *Varieties of Religious Experience: A Study in Human Nature* (New York: Random House-Modern Library, 1902), lectures 2 and 3, 53–76.

9. David Farrell Krell usefully shows that, for Heidegger, the *Theoi*, the gods, and the daimons are the same in their functional relation to the human way of being. See David Farrell Krell, *Daimon Life* (Bloomington: Indiana University Press, 1992), 20.

10. Martin Heidegger, *Parmenides*, trans. André Schuwer and Richard Rojcewicz (Bloomington: Indiana University Press, 1992), 102.

11. Ludwig Wittgenstein, *Philosophical Investigations*, 214–219, where Wittgenstein talks about the feel of words.

12. Ibid., 219.

13. Heidegger, *Parmenides*, 106 (translation slightly altered).

14. Ibid., 110–111.

15. Ibid., 111.

16. Ibid., 104.

17. Heidegger expresses this by saying that gods are "the attuning ones," ibid., 111.

18. I adopt Charles Taylor's formulation here. See Charles Taylor, "Interpretation and the Sciences of Man," *Philosophy and the Human Sciences: Philosophical Papers 2* (Cambridge: Cambridge University Press, 1985), 15–57, esp. 38–40.

19. See Martin Heidegger, *The Fundamental Concepts of Metaphysics: World, Finitude, Solitude*, trans. William McNeill and Nicholas Walker (Bloomington: Indiana University Press, 1995), 66–67. Heidegger uses the example of a person with good humor bringing a lively atmosphere with him.

20. Noting this understanding of the look of a look helps us to understand how Heidegger explains that gods can be seen in both human and animal shape. See *Parmenides*, 109.

21. Heidegger, "The Origin of the Work of Art," 43.

22. We should remember that the strong notion of individual identities, each with an individual fate is an early-modern notion.

23. This account comes from Ronald Spon, an Ohio state judge. I have changed some of the small details, but nothing essential to the account. Seeing this account as an experience of a divinity who comes from a dimension of being that is neither subjective nor objective will be at odds with certain metaphysical claims fundamentalist Christians would be disposed to make about the objectivity of God, angels, heaven, and so forth. There is no little confusion over fundamentalist and scientific usages of "objectivity." Both scientists and fundamentalists claim to be talking about objective stuff, but each means something different. I believe it would be acceptable to many fundamentalists and scientists to allow that scientists describe what is objective but not what is fundamental. Whether and how the domains of the objective and objectively fundamental interact with each other is a subject for another paper. For the beginnings of an answer to that question, see Hubert L. Dreyfus and Charles Spinosa, "Coping with Things-in-Themselves," *Inquiry* 42 (March 1999): 49–78. Also see Charles Spinosa and Hubert L. Dreyfus, "Robust Intelligibility: Response to our Critics," *Inquiry* 42, no. 2 (June 1999): 177–194.

24. To some, there seem to be striking epistemological differences between money and angels. If we see all money that looks like our nation's currency as valuable, we will be misled by counterfeiters. The same is true of angels. If the fundamentalist sees angelic actions as all performed by angels, then he will be subject to various kinds of people counterfeiting angels. Someone might be able to get a fundamentalist attuned to things as though the attuner were an angel only to deceive the fundamentalist. Likewise, the problem posed by tracking the angel down and discovering that he lives in Fort Lee, New Jersey, goes away when we realize that an angel may be on an extended mission as are the angels on today's popular television shows about angels.

25. Patrick Harpur, who finds a similar kind of divinity in alien and fairy sightings, notes how aliens and fairies both tend to address concerns that we all share with claims that we also all share. Like experiences with angels, many of the experiences with aliens that Harpur describes accord with this account of experiences of the holy. Harpur himself uses the Jungian ontology of a collective unconsciousness, as opposed to the more Heideggerian common meanings, to make sense of aliens and fairies. See Patrick Harpur, *Daimonic Reality* (New York: Penguin, 1996).

26. *Parmenides*, 112. Heidegger develops this point later in the same text when he explains that gods do not so much give us information as appear in situations and speak in order to attune us to the situations.

The *daimonion* is the essential character of the *Theion*, which, as the looking one, looks into what is normal and ordinary, i.e., appears in it. This appearing is in itself *daion*, the divine as entering into the unconcealed. What enters into the unconcealed and appears there has as basic modes of appearance looking and saying, whereby we must note that the essence of saying does not consist in vocal sound but in the voice

[*Stimme*] in the sense of soundless attuning [*Stimmenden*], signaling, and bringing the essence of man to itself (ibid., 114).

27. I would like to thank Jeff Malpas, Maria Flores, and Mark Wrathall for their helpful suggestions.

Chapter 12: Trusting

1. C. A. J. Coady, *Testimony: A Philosophical Study* (Oxford: Clarendon Press, 1992); Keith Lehrer, *Self-Trust: A Study of Reason, Knowledge, and Autonomy* (New York: Oxford University Press, 1997).

2. Bernard Barber, *The Logic and Limits of Trust* (New Brunswick, N.J.: Rutgers University Press, 1983); Niklas Luhmann, *Trust and Power: Two Works*, trans. Howard Davis, John Raffan, and Kathryn Rooney (New York: John Wiley and Sons, 1979); Anthony Giddens, *Modernity and Self-Identity: Self and Society in the Late Modern Age* (Stanford: Stanford University Press, 1991); Francis Fukuyama, *Trust: The Social Virtues and the Creation of Prosperity* (New York: Free Press, 1995).

3. Karen Jones, Russell Hardin, and Lawrence C. Becker, "Symposium on Trust," *Ethics* 107, no. 1 (1996): 4–61.

4. Annette C. Baier's recent work on Hume and on trust can be found in her *A Progress of Sentiments: Reflections on Hume's* Treatise (Cambridge: Harvard University Press, 1991) and in *Moral Prejudices: Essays on Ethics* (Cambridge: Harvard University Press, 1994), esp. "Trust and Antitrust," 95–129.

5. See, for example, virtually all of the essays in Diego Gambetta's book *Trust: Making and Breaking Cooperative Relations* (Oxford: Blackwell, 1988), especially the lead-off piece, "Formal Structures and Reality," 3–13, by an uncharacteristically game theoretical Bernard Williams.

6. Fukuyama, *Trust*. See also Sissela Bok, *Lying: Moral Choice in Public and Private Life* (New York: Vintage Books, 1979) for use of the same metaphor.

7. See, for example, very clever treatments of trust by Phillip Pettitt, "The Cunning of Trust," *Philosophy and Public Affairs* 24, no. 3 (1995): 202–225; Richard Horton, "Deciding to Trust, Coming to Believe," *Australasian Journal of Philosophy* 72, no. 1 (1994): 63–76; and Simon Blackburn, "Trust, Cooperation, and Human Psychology," in *Trust and Governance*, ed. Valerie Braithwaite and Margaret Levi (New York: Russell Sage Foundation, 1998), 28–45.

8. Baier, "Trust and Antitrust."

9. See Horton, "Deciding to Trust, Coming to Believe."

10. Baier, "Trust and Antitrust"; Jones, "Symposium on Trust," 14–25.

11. Luhmann, *Trust and Power*; Giddens, *Modernity and Self-Identity*.

12. Fukuyama, *Trust*. But there is no suggestion of any kind how this medium comes to be found in some cultures and not others, and, more urgently, how it can be created or restored in societies that lack it.

13. The concept of the *background* comes from Heidegger's *Being and Time*, and is elaborated by Hubert Dreyfus in his *Being-in-the-World*, 75ff. It has also been analyzed at length by John Searle in his *Intentionality*, 141–159.

14. Becker, "Symposium on Trust," 43–61.

15. Karen Jones, for instance, discusses Othello's trust of Iago at some length ("Symposium on Trust"). Of equal importance and in many ways more instructive, however, is Othello's growing *distrust* of Desdemona. The one is as blind as the other, but the latter might be viewed as a dynamic and unfolding version of distrust, whereas the former is a rather static and unthinking version of trust.

16. My thesis is akin to the thesis that Dostoyevski (and many others) have suggested concerning religious faith, that faith is not *really* faith unless it is punctuated, perhaps even pervaded by doubt. Faith is a form of self-overcoming, not simply a matter of naivete, or "blind" faith.

17. But see Laurence Thomas, "Reasons for Loving," in *The Philosophy of (Erotic) Love*, ed. Kathleen Higgins and Robert Solomon (Lawrence, Kans.: University of Kansas Press, 1991), 467–477.

18. The classic work here is Sigmund Freud, of course, "Psychoanalytic Notes upon an Autobiographical Account of a Case of Paranoia" (The Schreber Case) in *Three Case Histories*. See also Melanie Klein, "The Importance of Symbol Formation in the development of the Ego" and "A Contribution to the Psychogenesis of Manic-Depressive sates" in *Selected Melanie Klein*. For a recent account of paranoia, see Richard Hofstadter, "The Paranoid Style in American Politics," in *The Paranoid Style in American Politics: And Other Essays* (New York: Knopf, 1965).

19. Martin Seligman, *Creating Optimism* (New York: Knopf, 1991).

20. I owe my interest and many of my ideas on this subject to Fernando Flores, co-author with Dreyfus and Charles Spinosa of *Disclosing New Worlds* and my co-author in several recent studies in trust, including *Business Ethics Quarterly* (1998), and *Coming to Trust* (Oxford University Press, forthcoming). Parts of this essay have been adapted from those works.

Chapter 13: Emotion Theory Reconsidered

1. Robert Solomon's *The Passions* (Garden City, N.Y.: Anchor/Doubleday, 1976) for example, is far and away the contemporary philosophic text most cited by experimental psychologists.

2. For example, Leslie Greenberg and Jeremy D. Safran, *Emotion in Psychotherapy: Affect, Cognition, and the Process of Change* (New York: Guilford, 1987) concerning psychotherapy; White, "Emotions Inside Out: The Anthropology of Affect," in Michael Lewis and Jeannette Haviland, *Handbook of Emotions* (New York: Guilford, 1993) concerning anthropology; Theodore D. Kemper "Sociological Models in the Explanation of Emotions" (ibid.) concerning sociology.

3. See John T. Cacioppo et al., "The Psychophysiology of Emotion," in Michael Lewis and Jeannette Haviland, *Handbook of Emotions* (New York: Guilford, 1993), and Robert

Plutchik, *The Psychology and Biology of Emotion* (New York: Harper, 1994), chapters 11 and 12 for recent overviews.

4. Especially to recommend in this regard are Annette C. Baier, *A Progress of Sentiments: Reflections on Hume's Treatise* on Hume, and Jerome Neu, *Emotion, Thought, and Therapy* (London: Routledge and Kegan Paul, 1977) on Spinoza.

5. William Lyons, *Emotion* (Cambridge: Cambridge University Press, 1980).

6. Justin Oakley, *Morality and the Emotions* (London: Routledge, 1992).

7. Robert Solomon, *The Passions.*

8. Nico H. Frijda, *The Emotions* (Cambridge: Cambridge University Press, 1986).

9. Richard S. Lazarus, *Emotion and Adaptation* (New York: Oxford University Press, 1991).

10. *The Nature of Emotion: Fundamental Questions*, ed. Paul Ekman and Richard J. Davidson (New York: Oxford University Press, 1994).

11. A like critique, by the way, could be made of the existent experimental psychology literature on emotion. I will not take that up here, apart from some comments in passing. In general, experimental psychologists tend at least to mention the body more often, and to reflect a little on how it might enter into our emotion experiences. These reflections seldom go far, however. And rarely so far as to confront the fundamental point about the body which I try in these pages to clarify.

12. Anthony Kenny, *Action, Emotion and Will* (Bristol: Thoemmes, 1994); Solomon, *The Passions*; Lyons, *Emotion.*

13. Merleau-Ponty, *Phenomenology of Perception.*

14. Merleau-Ponty's "lived body" concept actually operates at two levels. It refers to both (a) how one experiences her body and (b) the subconscious processes which make such experiencing possible. For a good discussion of this distinction see Shaun Gallagaher, "Body Image and Body Schema: A Conceptual Clarification," *Journal of Mind and Behavior* 7 (1986): 541–554; and "Body Schema and Intentionality," in *The Body and the Self*, ed. José L. Bermúdez et al. (Cambridge: MIT Press, Bradford Books, 1995). Both these levels are critical for the account of emotion I am giving here. See also Richard Shusterman's helpful discussion of the body in chapter 6 of *Practicing Philosophy* (New York: Routledge, 1997).

15. For example, *The Passions*, 157, 159.

16. Jean-Paul Sartre, *Sketch for a Theory of the Emotions*, trans. Philip Maret (London: Methuen, 1962).

17. William James, *The Principles of Psychology*, 2 vols. (New York: H. Holt, 1890).

18. Robert M. Gordon, *The Structure of Emotions: Investigations in Cognitive Philosophy* (Cambridge: Cambridge University Press, 1987).

19. In a series of innovative recent writings on simulation theory, however, Robert M. Gordon (see, for example, his article in Peter Carruthers and Peter Smith, eds., *Theories of Theories of Mind* [Cambridge: Cambridge University Press, 1996]) seems clearly to be moving toward a richer sense of the role of the body.

20. Patricia Greenspan also comes close to dealing with the body (*Emotions and Reasons: An Inquiry into Emotional Justification* [New York: Routledge, 1988]). She elaborates a concept of "discomfort," a kind of push toward action present in many emotional states. Unfortunately she never tries to be more specific about a bodily dimension of this aspect.

21. *Emotion*, 115. One discussion of emotion that does give attention to its subjective bodily component is that of Sue L. Cataldi (*Emotion, Depth, and Flesh: A Study of Sensitive Space* [Albany: State University of New York Press, 1993]), which I came across just as this chapter was heading toward print. Much in Cataldi's position seems compatible with the view I argue for here.

22. Claire Armon-Jones, *Varieties of Affect* (New York: Harvester Wheatsheaf, 1991).

23. E.g., Robert M. Gordon, *The Structure of Emotions: Investigations in Cognitive Philosophy* (Cambridge: Cambridge University Press, 1987); William Lyons, *Emotion*.

24. See George Downing, *Körper und Wort in der Psychotherapie* (Munich: Kösel, 1996).

25. The linguistic research of Lakoff and Kovecses (George Lakoff, *Women, Fire, and Dangerous Things: What Categories Reveal about the Mind* [Chicago: University of Chicago Press, 1987]) provides interesting collaborative evidence. Lakoff and Kovecses, taking anger as an example, demonstrate how thoroughly our habitual language for emotional states is full of metaphors which describe body conditions.

26. For a more extensive discussion see Downing, *Körper und Wort*.

27. E.g., Nico H. Frijda, *The Emotions*, 133–136.

28. Cf. Lakoff and Kovecses's discussion of this point (Lakoff, *Women*).

29. Notably *Emotion in the Human Face*, ed. Paul Ekman (New York: Pergamon, 1972). Occasionally (e.g., Gordon, *The Structure of Emotions*, 93) one finds a passing reference to such phenonema in the philosophic literature, but never with discussion.

30. Ekman, *Emotion in the Human Face*.

31. E.g., Nina Bull, *The Attitude Theory of Emotion* (New York: Johnson Reprint Corp., 1968).

32. Anna Freud, for example, in her classic *The Ego and the Mechanisms of Defense* (trans. Cecil Baines [London: Hogarth Press, 1948]), lists it as one of the major forms of defense. The pervasiveness of the body defenses is one reason some therapists, myself included, at times supplement the traditional verbal therapy dialogue with physical interventions (e.g., work with breathing, movements, physical tensions, and the like). This assists patients in reorganizing micro-level bodily skills and practices (Downing, *Körper und Wort*).

33. George Mandler, *Mind and Body: Psychology of Emotion and Stress* (New York: W.W. Norton, 1984).

34. Keith Oatley, *Best Laid Schemes: The Psychology of Emotions* (Cambridge: Cambridge University Press, 1992). Cf. also Nancy L. Stein, Tom Trabasso, and Maria Liwag, "The Representation and Organization of Emotional Experience: Unfolding the Emotion Episode," in Michael Lewis and Jeannette Haviland, eds., *Handbook of Emotions* (New York: Guilford, 1993) for a good overview of this concept.

35. For more comments on the level of generality question see below.

36. Operating in tandem are therefore (1) my perception of the outer situation, (2) my perception of my changing body state, and (3) the subconscious bodily processes which implement affectmotor schemas and coordinate them with this global field. These distinctions are similar to Gallagaher's (1986, 1995) clarification of the difference between "body image," equivalent to (2), and "body schema," equivalent to (3). Merleau-Ponty's philosophic interest was almost exclusively in (3). An extraordinary fact about *The Phenomenology of Perception* is that Merleau-Ponty only seldom discusses any forms of direct experience of the body. Nevertheless he could have done so at more length without contradicting the main lines of his theory.

37. Cf. Stein, Trabasso, and Liwag, "The Representation and Organization of Emotional Experience" for a good discussion of the need of an adequate concept of duration. They point out how little thinking and research has been addressed to this issue.

38. For twenty minutes an ecstatic joy was my dominant state. Should we call this one continuous feeling, or a series of them? Where, and according to what criteria, should we make the conceptual cut?

39. See Downing, *Körper und Wort.*

40. Theodore R. Schatski, *Social Practices: A Wittgensteinian Approach to Human Activity and the Social.*

41. Schatzki is in agreement with this point (personal communication).

42. Cf. Schatzki's account of what he calls the "teleoaffective structure" of integrative practices.

43. An additional argument could well be made that speech acts too have an "instinctual" element.

44. Downing, *Körper und Wort.*

45. Cf. Pierre Bourdieu, *Outline of a Theory of Practice,* trans. Richard Nice (Cambridge: Cambridge University Press, 1977).

46. E.g., Beatrice Beebe, "Mother-Infant Mutual Influence and Precursors of Self- and Object Representations," in *Empirical Studies of Psychoanalytical Theories, Vol. 2,* ed. Joseph Masling (Hillsdale, N.J.: The Analytic Press, 1986); Beatrice Beebe and Daniel N. Stern, "Engagement-Disengagement and Early Object Experiences," in *Communicative Structures and Psychic Structures,* ed. Norbert Freedman and Stanley Grand (New York: Plenum, 1977); Beatrice Beebe, Frank Lachmann, and Joseph Jaffe,

Notes

"Mother-Infant Interaction Structures and Presymbolic Self- and Object Representations," *Psychoanalytic Dialogues* 7 (1997): 133–182; Daniel N. Stern, *The Interpersonal World of the Infant: A View from Psychoanalysis and Developmental Psychology* (New York: Basic Books, 1985); Edward Z. Tronick, "Affectivity and Sharing," in *Social Interchange in Infancy: Affect, Cognition, and Communication*, ed. Edward Z. Tronick (Baltimore: University Park Press, 1982); "The Transmission of Maternal Disturbance to the Infant," in *Maternal Depression and Infant Disturbance*, ed. Edward Z. Tronick and Tiffany Field (San Francisco: Jossey-Bass, 1986); and "Emotions and Emotional Communication in Infants," *American Psychologist* 44 (1989): 112–119.

47. See Downing, *Körper und Wort.*

48. See ibid.

49. E.g., *Emotion in the Human Face*, ed. Paul Ekman.

50. Needless to say this point has many implications for psychotherapy. For example, the admirable therapeutic techniques of Eugene Gendlin (1978) can be understood as a means of helping a client alter such bodily practices. Gendlin's techniques make more explicit what I have here described as "affective interrogation."

51. Body micropractices appear to be shaped by whoever has frequent regular contact with the infant.

52. Michel Foucault, *Discipline and Punish: The Birth of the Prison*, trans. Alan Sheridan (New York: Pantheon, 1977); *The History of Sexuality.* Volume I, *An Introduction*, trans. Alan Sheridan (New York: Pantheon, 1978); *Power/Knowledge: Selected Interviews and Other Writings 1972–1977*, ed. and trans. Colin Gordon (New York: Pantheon, 1980).

53. Cf. Elaine Hatfield, et al., *Emotional Contagion* (Cambridge: Cambridge University Press, 1994); Brian Parkinson, *Ideas and Realities of Emotion* (London: Routledge, 1995).

54. Downing, *Körper und Wort.* Cf., for example, the landmark research of Michael Heller, e.g., "Posture as an interface between biology and culture," *Nonverbal Communication: Where Nature Meets Culture*, eds. Ullica Segerstråle and Peter Molnár (Mahwah, N.J.: Lawrence Erlbaum Associates, 1997).

55. Jean Paul Sartre, *Being and Nothingness: An Essay on Phenomenological Ontology*, trans. Hazel Barnes (New York: Philosophical Library, 1956).

56. Roy Schafer, *A New Language for Psychoanalysis*, trans. Hazel Barnes (New Haven: Yale University Press, 1976).

57. A curiosity is that Schafer saw himself as building upon the philosophy of Gilbert Ryle (*The Concept of Mind* [New York: Barnes and Noble (1949)]). In actuality the position he developed is the most purely Sartrean to be found in contemporary psychoanalytic theory.

58. There are actually therapists today who, when a patient reports "I feel angry" (or, "I feel sad," etc.), insist that he say instead, "I'm making myself angry" ("I'm making myself sad," etc.). See for example James I. Kepner, *Body Process: A Gestalt Approach to*

Working with the Body in Psychotherapy (New York: Gardner Press: Gestalt Institute of Cleveland, 1987).

59. E.g., Lyons, *Emotion*, 180ff.; Gordon, *The Structure of Emotions*, 110ff.

60. Gordon (*The Structure of Emotions*, 112) points out that most adjectives describing emotions are taken from the participles of verbs: "'amused,' 'annoyed,' 'astonished,' 'depressed,' 'vexed,'" etc. Even our language conveys that emotion is a response to something acting upon us.

61. A point having many consequences for psychotherapy, incidentally. I will not explore this issue here.

62. Cf. Merleau-Ponty's (*Phenomenology of Perception* [New York: Routledge and Kegan Paul, 1962]) criticism of Sartre that by exaggerating the scope of human freedom he ignored the role of habit.

63. More precisely would be that this open-endedness of context belongs to all affective revealing. It simply shows up more dramatically with some emotion episodes.

64. Martin Heidegger, *Being and Time*. See especially sections 29, 30, and 40.

65. I simplify. There is more than just this to Heidegger's *Sein zum Tode*. For an extensive discussion see Hubert L. Dreyfus, *Being-in-the-World*.

66. Heidegger in fact built much of his own thinking about these matters upon that of Kierkegaard. (Cf. Heidegger, *Being and Time*, 338, note iii; Dreyfus, *Being-in-the-World*, 299ff.)

67. Much of what is called cognitive therapy (e.g., Aaron T. Beck, *Depression: Causes and Treatment* [Philadelphia: University of Pennsylvania Press, 1972]) examines and seeks to change the exact details of how a patient may be creating such a prison of self-torment. The escalation of emotion, rather than being a means of productively opening up the future, in this case has gone awry. But cf. footnote 66.

68. E.g., in Søren Kierkegaard, *The Concept of Anxiety: A Simple Psychologically Orienting Deliberation on the Dogmatic Issue of Hereditary Sin*, ed. and trans. Reidar Thomte (Princeton: Princeton University Press, 1987).

69. E.g., in the long passages on despair in Søren Kierkegaard, *Either/Or: A Fragment of Life*, 2 vols, trans. David F. Swenson and Lillian Marrin Swenson (Princeton: Princeton University Press, 1987).

70. Obviously what I am describing here involves *par excellence* both bodily skills and verbal cognitive skills. Compare John D. Teasdale's and Philip J. Barnard's research-based critique of cognitive therapy (*Affect, Cognition and Change: Re-Modelling Depressive Thought* [Hillsdale, N.J.: L. Erlbaum, 1993]). Drawing upon numerous outcome studies as well as related experimental research, they elegantly demonstrate the potential advantages of supplementing purely verbal cognitive work with some form of intervention capable of more directly affecting the body and the emotions. Cf. also John D. Teasdale "Emotion and Two Kinds of Meaning: Cognitive Therapy and Applied Cognitive Science," *Behaviour Research and Therapy* 31 (1993): 351.

71. Donald Davidson, "Paradoxes of Irrationality," in *Philosophical Essays on Freud*, ed. Richard Wollheim and James Hopkins (Cambridge: Cambridge University Press, 1982); "Deception and Division," in *The Multiple Self*, ed. Jon Elster (Cambridge: Cambridge University Press, 1985); David F. Pears, *Motivated Irrationality* (Oxford: Oxford University Press, 1984); Marcia Cavell, "Metaphor, Dreamwork, and Irrationality," in *Truth and Interpretation: Perspectives on the Philosophy of Donald Davidson*, ed. Ernest LePore (Oxford: Blackwell, 1986); *The Psychoanalytic Mind from Freud to Philosophy* (Cambridge: Harvard University Press, 1993); "Triangulation, One's Own Mind and Objectivity," *International Journal of Psycho-analysis* 79 (1998): 449–468.

Chapter 14: Heideggerian Thinking and the Transformation of Business Practice

1. See, for instance, the recent issue of *Information Technology and People* 11.4 (1998) devoted to Heidegger.

2. I learned Bert Dreyfus's interpretation of Heidegger from classroom experience and his attentive personal mentoring. Dreyfus's core interpretation of *Being and Time* may be found in Hubert L. Dreyfus, *Being-in-the-World*.

3. For more on this, see Charles Spinosa, Fernando Flores, and Hubert L. Dreyfus, *Disclosing New Worlds*.

4. Martin Heidegger, *Being and Time*, trans. John Macquarrie and Edward Robinson (New York: Harper & Row, 1962), 341–348, 352–358, 434–439, and 443.

5. Another paper could be written on the indebtedness of my work to the thinking of John Searle and his reformulation of John Austin's account of speech acts. Four of Searle's five basic speech acts constitute the basic commitments of commerce: directives, commissives, declarations, and a particular form of assertive. See my "Information Technology and the Institution of Identity: Reflections since *Understanding Computers and Cognition*," *Information Technology and People* 11.4 (1998): 35–372.

6. Remember pricing changes according to short-term market conditions. The broader economic value used in making strategic evaluations, that is, the value to the customers during the life of the product, is determined independently of current exchange relationships.

7. Here we must thank Charles Taylor for helping us toward this reading of Heidegger. See Charles Taylor, "What Is Human Agency" and "Self-Interpreting Animals," *Human Agency and Language*, Philosophical Papers 1 (Cambridge: Cambridge University Press, 1985), 16–44, 45–76.

8. In saying that organizations have their own ways of being manifested by exemplars, we are drawing first on Dreyfus's interpretation of what Heidegger says about cultures and their exemplars (which Heidegger calls cases of truth establishing itself). We draw later on Heidegger's work on dwelling to see how exemplars of a slightly different kind can focus organizations the size of business enterprises and smaller. See Martin Heidegger, "The Origin of the Work of Art," *Poetry, Language, Thought*, 17–87, and Martin Heidegger, "Building Dwelling Thinking," *Poetry, Language, Thought*, 145–161.

9. See Martin Heidegger on Dasein's falling into idle talk, curiosity, and ambiguity, *Being and Time*, 210–224.

10. For a more complete account of the cultivation of trust, see Fernando Flores and Robert Solomon, *The Cultivation of Trust* (Oxford: Oxford University Press, forthcoming).

11. Hubert L. Dreyfus, "Heidegger on the Connection between Nihilism, Art, Technology, and Politics," *Cambridge Companion to Heidegger*, 289–316.

12. Martin Heidegger, *What Is Called Thinking?* trans. J. Glenn Gray (New York: Harper & Row, 1968), 100–110, esp. 109.

13. I use Hannah Arendt's formulation as one that captures a general attitude. See Hannah Arendt, *The Human Condition* (Chicago: University of Chicago Press, 1970).

14. I would like to thank Chauncey Bell, Maria Flores, Charles Spinosa, and Bud Vieira for their careful and helpful comments.

Chapter 15: The Quest for Control and the Possibilities of Care

1. Martin Heidegger, *Being and Time*, 274.

2. Patricia Benner, "Caring practice," in *Caregiving, Readings in Knowledge, Practice, Ethics and Politics*, eds. Suzanne Gordon, Patricia Benner, and Nel Noddings (Philadelphia: University of Pennsylvania Press, 1996), 40–55.

3. *Being and Time*, 159.

4. See Hubert L. Dreyfus, *Being-in-the-World*.

5. See Hubert L. Dreyfus, *What Computers Can't Do: The Limits of Artificial Intelligence*, rev. ed.

6. See Hubert L. Dreyfus and Stuart E. Dreyfus, *Mind over Machine: The Power of Human Intuition and Expertise in the Era of the Computer*.

7. See Charles Taylor *Philosophical Papers*, vols. 1 and 2 (Cambridge: Cambridge University Press, 1985).

8. See Jane Rubin, "Too much of nothing: Modern culture, the self and salvation in Kierkegaard's thought." (Ph.D. diss., University of California, Berkeley, 1984.)

9. Patricia Benner and Judith Wrubel, "Skilled Clinical Knowledge: The Value of Perceptual Awareness," *Nurse Educator* 7, 3 (1982): 11–17; Patricia Benner, "Discovering Challenges to Ethical Theory in Experience-Based Narratives of Nurses' Everyday Ethical Comportment," in *Health Care Ethics: Critical Issues*, ed. J. F. Monagle and D. C. Thomasma (Gaithersburg, Maryland: Aspen Publishers, 1994), 401–411; Patricia Benner, "The Role of Experience, Narrative, and Community in Skilled Ethical Comportment," *Advances in Nursing Science* 14, 2 (1991): 1–21.

10. Patricia Benner, Christine Tanner, and Catherine Chesla, *Expertise in Nursing Practice: Caring, Clinical Judgment, and Ethics* (New York: Springer, 1996); Patricia

Benner, *From Novice to Expert: Excellence and Power in Clinical Nursing Practice* (Reading, Mass.: Addison-Wesley, 1984).

11. Patricia Benner and Judith Wrubel, *The Primacy of Caring, Stress and Coping in Health and Illness* (Reading, Mass.: Addison-Wesley, 1989); Patricia Benner, *Stress and Satisfaction on the Job: Work Meanings and Coping of Mid-Career Men* (New York: Praeger Scientific Press, 1984).

12. Patricia Benner, *Interpretive Phenomenology: Embodiment, Caring and Ethics in Health and Illness* (Thousand Oaks, Calif.: Sage, 1994).

13. Hubert L. Dreyfus, *What Computers Can't Do: The Limits of Artificial Intelligence*, rev. ed.; Hubert L. Dreyfus and Stuart E. Dreyfus, *Mind over Machine: The Power of Human Intuition and Expertise in the Era of the Computer*.

14. M. J. Dunlop, "Is a Science of Caring Possible?" *Journal of Advanced Nursing* 11 (1986): 661–670.

15. Martin Heidegger, "The question concerning technology," in *Basic Writings*, rev. ed, trans. David F. Krell (San Francisco: Harper, 1993), 323.

16. Renee C. Fox and Judith P. Swazey, "Leaving the field" *Hastings Center Report* 22 (5) (1992): 9–15.

17. Samuel Levey and Douglas D. Hesse, "Sounding board: Bottom-line Health Care?" *New England Journal of Medicine* 312 (10) (1985): 644–647.

18. Martin Heidegger, "The question concerning technology," 326.

19. Martin Heidegger, "Letter on Humanism," in *Basic Writings*, 217.

20. Christine Tanner, et al., "The phenomenology of knowing a patient," *Image, the Journal of Nursing Scholarship* 25(4): 273–280; P. Benner, P. Hooper-Kyriakidis, and D. Stannard, *Clinical Wisdom and Interventions in Critical Care, a Thinking-in-Action Approach* (Philadelphia: Saunders, 1999).

21. Martin Heidegger, *Being and Time*, trans. J. Macquarrie and E. Robinson (New York: Harper & Row, 1962); Patricia Benner, *From Novice to Expert: Excellence and Power in Clinical Nursing Practice*; Patricia Benner, Christine Tanner, and Catherine Chesla, *Expertise in Nursing Practice: Caring, Clinical Judgment, and Ethics* (New York: Springer, 1996).

22. Martin Heidegger, "What Calls for Thinking?" in *Basic Writings*.

23. Jane Rubin, "Impediments to the development of clinical knowledge and ethical judgment in critical care nurses," in Patricia Benner, Christine Tanner, and Catherine Chesla, *Expertise in Nursing Practice: Caring, Clinical Judgment, and Ethics* (New York: Springer, 1996); P. L. Hooper, "Expert Titration of Multiple Vasoactive Drugs in Post-cardiac Surgical Patients: An Interpretive Study of Clinical Judgment and Perceptual Acuity." (Ph.D. diss., University of California, San Francisco, 1995); Patricia Benner, Patricia Hooper-Kyriakidis, and Daphne Stannard, *Clinical Wisdom and Interventions in Critical Care: A Thinking-in-Action Approach*.

24. Martin Heidegger, "The way to language," in *Basic Writings*, 411–413.

25. Patricia Benner and Judith Wrubel, "Skilled Clinical Knowledge"; Patricia Benner, *From Novice to Expert: Excellence and Power in Clinical Nursing Practice.*

26. T. Holden, "Seeing Joan Through," *American Journal of Nursing* 91 (December, 1992): 26–30.

27. Martin Heidegger, *Being and Time*, 159–161.

28. June S. Lowenberg, *Caring and Responsibility* (Philadelphia: University of Pennsylvania Press, 1989).

29. Charles Taylor, *Sources of the Self.*

30. Charles Taylor, "Social theory as practice," in *Philosophy and the Human Sciences: Philosophical Papers*, vol. 2 (Cambridge: Cambridge University Press, 1985), 104.

31. Christine Tanner, et al., "The Phenomenology of Knowing the Patient," *Image, the Journal of Nursing Scholarship* 25 (1993): 273–280.

32. Patricia Benner, "Quality of life: A phenomenological perspective on explanation, prediction, and understanding in nursing science," *Advances in Nursing Science* 8 (1) (1985): 1–14; Hubert L. Dreyfus, Stuart E. Dreyfus, "Towards a Phenomenology of Ethical Expertise," *Human Studies* 14 (1991): 229–250; Patricia Benner, "The Role of Experience, Narrative, and Community in Skilled Ethical Comportment," *Advances in Nursing Science* 14 (2) (1991): 1–21.

33. Patricia Benner and J. Wrubel, *The Primacy of Caring: Stress and Coping in Health and Illness* (Reading, Mass.: Addison-Wesley, 1989).

34. Martin Heidegger, "The question concerning technology," in *Basic Writings*, 333.

35. Patricia Benner, ed., *Interpretive Phenomenology: Embodiment, Caring and Ethics in Health and Illness* (Thousand Oaks, California: Sage, 1994); Charles Taylor, *Sources of the Self* (Cambridge: Harvard University Press, 1989), 159–184.

36. Patricia Benner and Judith Wrubel, *The Primacy of Caring: Stress and Coping in Health and Illness* (Reading, Mass.: Addison-Wesley, 1989).

37. *Sources of the Self*, 495–521.

38. Martin Heidegger, "What calls for thinking?" in *Basic Writings*, 379.

39. Hubert L. Dreyfus, and Stuart E. Dreyfus, *Mind over Machine: The Power of Human Intuition and Expertise in the Era of the Computer*; H. L. Dreyfus, *What Computers Can't Do: The Limits of Artificial Intelligence*, rev. ed.; Patricia Benner, Christine Tanner, and Catherine Chesla, "From Beginner to Expert: Gaining a Differentiated World in Critical Care Nursing," *Advances in Nursing Science 14* (3) (1992): 13–28; Joseph Dunne, *Back to the Rough Ground: "Phronesis" and "Techne" in Modern Philosophy and in Aristotle* (Notre Dame: Notre Dame University Press, 1993).

40. Martin Heidegger, "The question concerning technology," in *Basic Writings*, 318–319.

41. C. Taylor, "Social theory as practice" in *Philosophy and the Human Sciences*, Philosophical Papers, vol. 2, 104.

42. Martin Heidegger, "The question concerning technology"; Hubert L. Dreyfus, *Being-in-the-World*; Patricia Benner, "The Moral Dimensions of Caring," in *Knowledge about Care and Caring: State of the Art and Future Developments*, ed. J. Stephenson (New York: American Academy of Nursing, 1989); June Lowenberg, *Caring and Responsibility*.

43. M. Foucault, *The Birth of the Clinic: An Archeology of Medical Perception* (New York: Vintage Books, 1973).

44. Patricia Benner, "Discovering Challenges to Ethical Theory in Experience-Based Narratives of Nurses' Everyday Ethical Comportment," 401–411.

Chapter 16: Responses

1. I prefer to speak of *transparent* coping rather than *practical* coping since, as Joe rightly argues, all activity can be viewed as some kind of practical coping. Joe, it seems to me, wants to use the fact that all activity is some form of practical coping to level every distinction in sight.

2. Heidegger is not consistent in his use of either of these terms. This follows, I think, from his not being clear about the distinctions themselves, but I don't want to argue with Rouse about the terminology but rather keep focused on the phenomena.

3. See Daniel N. Stern, *The Interpersonal World of the Infant: A View from Psychoanalysis and Developmental Psychology*.

4. See my discussion of Japanese and American babies in my *Being-in-the-World*, 17.

5. (18). It's no accident that the paper Rouse cites where I make these regrettable claims was only read at a meeting in Canada. To paraphrase *Candide*, that was in another country and besides, the paper was never published.

6. As Charles Taylor points out so well in his chapter in this volume, there can be a whole system of norms already effective in the way children are socialized into a deferential way of standing, speaking, and so forth in the presence of adults.

7. No doubt Rouse will say Heidegger did not insist on the distinction for the good reason that it can't be maintained. I think Heidegger, influenced by Aristotle, simply failed to recognize the importance of the new phenomenon of situated action and the aspects it reveals.

8. I discuss the sense in which a skill can and cannot be made explicit in my response to Taylor Carman in *Heidegger, Authenticity, and Modernity*, so I won't go back over that point here.

9. Martin Heidegger, *Being and Time*, 200.

10. See my forthcoming article, "Telepistemology: Descartes' Last Stand" in *The Robot in the Garden: Telerobotics and Telepistemology on the Internet*, ed. Ken Goldberg (forthcoming from MIT Press, 2000).

11. H. Dreyfus and Charles Spinosa, "Coping with Things-in-Themselves."

12. I leave it to Searle and Davidson to debate whether animals have minds or not, and whether their intentional states have propositional content. It's hard for me to imagine a position, however, that denies that even asocial animals have highly developed skills.

13. I unfortunately denied that there was a difference between normative and merely pragmatic success and failure in the same unpublished paper that Rouse likes to quote, but I am happy to have this opportunity to agree with Rouse in insisting, for a change, on maintaining a distinction.

14. John Haugeland, "Heidegger on Being a Person," *Nous* 16 (1982): 6–26.

15. Another way to put my phenomenological point is that we don't *inhabit* the *world* as Joe suggests in his concluding remarks. As Sam Todes, to whom I would like to dedicate this response, used to say, we are in the world only by way of inhabiting a specific situation.

16. For more on this issue, see my response to David Cerbone.

17. John R. Searle, "Response: The Background of Intentionality and Action," in *John Searle and his Critics*, eds. Ernest Lepore and Robert van Gulick (Cambridge: Basil Blackwell, 1991), 291.

18. Martin Heidegger, *History of the Concept of Time*, 189.

19. John R. Searle, *Intentionality*, 150. Searle notes on page 5 that "intending and intentions are just one form of Intentionality among others . . . [50] . . . to keep the distinction clear I will capitalize the technical sense of 'Intentional' and 'Intentionality.' "

20. "Response: The Background of Intentionality and Action," 291.

21. Ibid.

22. See Sean Kelly's paper in this volume.

23. John R. Searle, *The Construction of Social Reality*, 14.

24. Ibid., 73.

25. Ibid., 5.

26. I did in the distant past hold what Searle rightly called my zombie view, viz., that one could act skillfully while being completely unconscious of what one was doing. I thank Searle for arguing me out of this position. I see now that, even when stepping on the clutch while shifting gears, I must have a marginal sense that things are going as they should. Otherwise, I can't explain the fact that, if things start to go wrong, my attention is immediately drawn to the problem.

27. Another mistake I'm glad to correct is my confusion of self-referentiality with self-awareness. I now understand that animals, according to Searle, have self-referential intentional states although they are certainly not reflective. But I still have trouble understanding how dogs, although they don't have language, nonetheless have intentional states with propositional content. If one holds that dogs' actions are caused by the gestalt intentionality described by Merleau-Ponty, one can avoid this dubious claim.

28. John R. Searle, "Response: The Background of Intentionality and Action," 295.

29. To defend the requirement that all actions require a propositional representation of their conditions of satisfaction, Searle needs a strong and weak sense of "propositional content". Such content would have to be abstract, i.e., nonsituational, to account for deliberate action, and concrete, i.e., indexical, to account for absorbed coping. See my article "The Primacy of Phenomenology over Logical Analysis" in *Philosophical Topics* 27 (Fall 1999). From now on in this paper I will use "propositional" in the strong sense.

30. See my paper, cited in 29.

31. See Timothy Gallwey's critique of competitive tennis playing and his discussion of the state of mind of the Zen tennis player in *Inner Tennis: Playing the Game* (New York: Random House, 1976); see also Mihaly Csikszentmilalyi, *Flow: the Psychology of Optimal Experience* (New York: Harper Collins, 1991).

32. (85). Wittgenstein makes a similar point when he says in *The Blue and Brown Books*: "I deliberate whether to lift a certain heavyish weight, decide to do it, I then apply my force to it and lift it. . . . One takes one's ideas, one's language, about volition from this kind of example and thinks that they must apply—if not in such an obvious way—to all cases which one can properly call willing" (150).

33. Maurice Merleau-Ponty, *Phenomenology of Perception*, 153.

34. *Intentionality*, 90.

35. Ibid., 91.

36. Ibid., 119.

37. "Response: The Background of Intentionality and Action", 293. Although Husserl did not have much to say about action it seems his view was very close to Searle's. According to Kevin Mulligan's article, "Perception," in *The Cambridge Companion to Husserl* (Cambridge: Cambridge University Press, 1988), 232 footnote 54, Husserl "rejects the view that trying simply initiates and precedes movement. Rather, trying coexists with and causes movement, an achievement which is made possible by the fact that perception and volition accompany and steer one another"; cf. Husserliana XXVIII, A §§13–16. I certainly don't want to deny that this is sometimes the case.

38. *Intentionality*, 123.

39. Ibid., 120–121.

40. Ibid., 130.

41. See John R. Searle, *Mind, Language, and Society* (New York: Basic Books, 1998), chap. 2.

42. John R. Searle, "Consciousness, Explanatory Inversion, and Cognitive Science," *Behavioral and Brain Sciences*, 13, no. 4 (1990): 603, 604.

43. Ibid., 634.

44. I've reached the limit of the space I've been allowed for responding, but luckily most of the remaining issues Searle raises have been dealt with by my former students in ways I agree with. For a sense in which Searle still accepts the Cartesian internal/external distinction, see David Cerbone's paper in Volume I. On the question of the reality of the Olympian gods, see Charles Spinosa's chapter in this volume. For an important sense in which background is not representable in propositional (or even conceptual) terms, see Sean Kelly's paper. As to my view on realism in physics and how it is compatible with realism concerning noncausal accounts of reality, see my article with Charles Spinosa "Coping with Things-in-Themselves". The problems raised by Searle's claim that brain phenomena *are* mental phenomena have been pointed out by Corbin Collins in his paper, "Searle on Consciousness and Dualism" in *International Journal of Philosophical Studies*, vol. 5 (1), 1–33.

45. This is a version of Barry Stroud's illuminating way of putting the problem in his paper on John Searle's account of the background. See "The Background of Thought," in *John Searle and His Critics*, 245–258.

46. Martin Heidegger, *The Metaphysical Foundations of Logic* (Bloomington: Indiana University Press, 1984).

47. Martin Heidegger, *The Basic Problems of Phenomenology*. Trans. Albert Hofstadter (Bloomington: University of Indiana Press, 1982), 162 (my emphasis).

48. *Being-in-the-World*, 107.

49. Ibid., 103.

50. I'm not convinced by Wrathall's other argument to show that disclosing is not a form of coping. He argues that in anxiety coping ceases and yet Heidegger says "anxiety reveals the world as world." But revealing the world *as* world for Heidegger is a special form of disclosing in which, just because coping breaks down, the world *as such* obtrudes itself. This special kind of disclosing, however, does not show that everyday disclosing is not a form of coping. But Wrathall's first argument is so convincing he does not need a second one.

51. It's better to say that it makes *intentional comportment* possible than, as Wrathall says, that it makes intentional *content* or intentional *states* possible since both of these are Cartesian terms for referring to derivative, propositional forms of intentionality. Likewise, readiness is not quite "disposedness to act in certain kinds of ways" in the world as Wrathall puts it, but a disposedness to act *in an appropriate way* in *the specific situation one is currently in*.

52. *Basic Problems*, 65.

53. Ibid., 162.

54. Martin Heidegger, *Poetry, Language, Thought*, 61.

55. This idea was first suggested in Charles Spinosa's "Derrida and Heidegger: Iterability and *Ereignis*," in *Heidegger: A Critical Reader*, eds. Hubert L. Dreyfus and Harrison Hall (Oxford: Blackwell, 1992), and developed in Spinosa's "Derridian Dispersion and Heideggerian Articulation: General Tendencies in the Practices that Govern Intelligibility," *The Practice Turn in Contemporary Theory*, eds. Ted Schatzki et al. (London: Routledge, forthcoming).

56. Foucault also wants to make his life a work of art although he does not seem to connect this practice with problematization. Perhaps Foucault thinks that making one's life a work of art is the best one can hope to achieve in a welfare society just as it was the favored way of life in late antiquity, an epoch characterized by the administration of everything including the self.

57. See my first paper on AI, *Alchemy and Artificial Intelligence*, published in 1965 by The RAND Corp.

58. See Charles Spinosa, et al., *Disclosing New Worlds*, 17–22.

59. See the issue of *Artificial Intelligence* to which Collins refers and also Hubert Dreyfus, *What Computers Still Can't Do*, xx and xxi.

60. See Daniel Dennett, "The Practical Requirements for Making a Conscious Robot," *Philosophical Transactions of the Royal Society*, 349 (1994): 133–146.

61. Ibid.

62. Heinrich Wiegand Petzet, *Encounters and Dialogues with Martin Heidegger, 1929–1976*, trans. Parvis Emad and Kenneth Maly (Chicago: University of Chicago Press, 1993), 53–56.

63. Ibid.

64. Ibid.

References

Agre, Philip E. *The Dynamic Structure of Everyday Life*. MIT AI Technical Report 1085, October 1988.

Almog, Joseph, John Perry, and Howard Wettstein, eds. *Themes from Kaplan*. New York: Oxford University Press, 1989.

Anderson, James, and Edward Rosenfeld, eds. *Neurocomputing: Foundations of Research*. Cambridge: MIT Press, 1988.

Andler, Daniel. "The Normativity of Context." *Philosophical Studies*. Forthcoming.

Andler, Daniel. "Turing: Pensée du Calcul, Calcul de la Pensée." In *Les Années 1930: Réaffirmation du Formalisme*, edited by F. Nef and D. Vernant, 1–41. Paris: Vrin, 1998.

Arendt, Hannah. *The Human Condition*. Chicago: University of Chicago Press, 1970.

Armon-Jones, Claire. *Varieties of Affect*. New York: Harvester Wheatsheaf, 1991.

Arquillière, Henri Xavier. *L'Augustinisme politique*. Paris: Vrin, 1934.

Baier, Annette C. *Moral Prejudices: Essays on Ethics*. Cambridge: Harvard University Press, 1994.

Baier, Annette C. *A Progress of Sentiments: Reflections on Hume's Treatise*. Cambridge: Harvard University Press, 1991.

Bakhtin, M. M. *Rabelais and his World*. Translated by Helene Iswolsky. Cambridge: MIT Press, 1968.

Barad, Karen. "Meeting the Universe Halfway: Realism and Social Constructivism without Contradiction." In *Feminism, Science and the Philosophy of Science*, edited by Lynn H. Nelson and Jack Nelson, 161–194. Dordrecht: Reidel, 1996.

Barber, Bernard. *The Logic and Limits of Trust*. New Brunswick, N.J.: Rutgers University Press, 1983.

References

Beck, Aaron T. *Depression: Causes and Treatment*. Philadelphia: University of Pennsylvania Press, 1972.

Becker, Lawrence. "Trust as Noncognitive Security about Motives." *Ethics* 107 (1996): 43–61.

Beebe, Beatrice, and Daniel N. Stern. "Engagement-Disengagement and Early Object Experiences." In *Communicative Structures and Psychic Structures*, edited by Norbert Freedman and Stanley Grand, 35–56. New York: Plenum, 1977.

Beebe, Beatrice. "Mother-Infant Mutual Influence and Precursors of Self- and Object Representations." In *Empirical Studies of Psychoanalytical Theories*, vol. 2, edited by Joseph Masling, 27–48. Hillsdale, N.J.: The Analytic Press, 1986.

Beebe, Beatrice, Frank Lachmann, and Joseph Jaffe. "Mother-Infant Interaction Structures and Presymbolic Self- and Object Representations." *Psychoanalytic Dialogues* 7 (1997): 133–182.

Benner, Patricia. *From Novice to Expert: Excellence and Power in Clinical Nursing Practice*. Reading, Mass.: Addison-Wesley, 1984.

Benner, Patricia, ed. *Interpretive Phenomenology: Embodiment, Caring and Ethics in Health and Illness*. Thousand Oaks, Calif.: Sage, 1994.

Benner, Patricia. *Stress and Satisfaction on the Job: Work Meanings and Coping of Mid-Career Men*. New York: Praeger Scientific Press, 1984.

Benner, Patricia, and Suzanne Gordon. "Caring Practice." In *Caregiving: Readings in Knowledge, Practice, Ethics and Politics*, edited by Suzanne Gordon, Patricia Benner, and Nel Noddings, 40–55. Philadelphia: University of Pennsylvania Press, 1996.

Benner, Patricia. "Discovering Challenges to Ethical Theory in Experience-Based Narratives of Nurses' Everyday Ethical Comportment." In *Health Care Ethics: Critical Issues*, edited by J. F. Monagle and D. C. Thomasma, 401–411. Gaithersburg, Md.: Aspen Publishers, 1994.

Benner, Patricia. "The Moral Dimensions of Caring." In *Knowledge about Care and Caring: State of the Art and Future Developments*, edited by J. Stephenson, 5–17. New York: American Academy of Nursing, 1989.

Benner, Patricia. "Quality of Life: A Phenomenological Perspective on Explanation, Prediction, and Understanding in Nursing Science." *Advances in Nursing Science* 8, no. 1 (1985): 1–14.

Benner, Patricia. "The Role of Experience, Narrative, and Community in Skilled Ethical Comportment." *Advances in Nursing Science* 14, no. 2 (1991): 1–21.

Benner, Patricia, Patricia Hooper-Kyriakidis, and Daphne Stannard. *Clinical Wisdom and Interventions in Critical Care: A Thinking-in-Action Approach*. Philadelphia: Saunders, 1999.

Benner, Patricia, Christine Tanner, and Catherine Chesla. *Expertise in Nursing Practice: Caring, Clinical Judgment, and Ethics*. New York: Springer, 1996.

References

Benner, Patricia, Christine Tanner, and Catherine Chesla. "From Beginner to Expert: Gaining a Differentiated World in Critical Care Nursing." *Advances in Nursing Science* 14, no. 3 (1992): 13–28.

Benner, Patricia, and Judith Wrubel. *The Primacy of Caring: Stress and Coping in Health and Illness.* Reading, Mass.: Addison-Wesley, 1989.

Benner, Patricia, and Judith Wrubel. "Skilled Clinical Knowledge: The Value of Perceptual Awareness." *Nurse Educator* 7, no. 3 (1982): 11–17.

Bianchi, Claudia. "Flexibilité Sémantique et Sous-détermination." Ph.D. diss., CREA, École Polytechnique, Paris, 1998.

Blackburn, Simon. "Trust, Cooperation, and Human Psychology." In *Trust and Governance,* edited by Valerie Braithwaite and Margaret Levi, 28–45. New York: Russell Sage Foundation, 1998.

Bok, Sissela. *Lying: Moral Choice in Public and Private Life.* New York: Vintage Books, 1979.

Bourdieu, Pierre. *The Logic of Practice.* Translated by Richard Nice. Stanford: Stanford University Press, 1990.

Bourdieu, Pierre. *Outline of a Theory of Practice.* Translated by Richard Nice. Cambridge: Cambridge University Press, 1977.

Brandom, Robert. *Making it Explicit: Reasoning, Representing, and Discursive Commitment.* Cambridge: Harvard University Press, 1994.

Brandom, Robert. "Freedom and Constraint by Norms." *American Philosophical Quarterly* 16 (1979): 187–196.

Budd, Malcolm. *Wittgenstein's Philosophy of Psychology.* London: Routledge, 1989.

Bull, Nina. *The Attitude Theory of Emotion.* New York: Johnson Reprint Corp., 1968.

Burgess, Anthony. *A Clockwork Orange.* New York: Norton, 1962.

Burke, Peter. *Popular Culture in Early Modern Europe.* London: T. Smith, 1978.

Cacioppo, John T., et al. "The Psychophysiology of Emotion." In *Handbook of Emotions,* edited by Michael Lewis and Jeannette Haviland, 119–142. New York: Guilford, 1993.

Carey, Susan. "Continuity and Discontinuity in Cognitive Development." In *An Invitation to Cognitive Science,* 2d ed., vol. 3 of *Thinking,* edited by E. Smith and D. Osherson, 101–129. Cambridge: MIT Press, 1995.

Carnahan, Heather. "Eye, Head and Hand Coordination during Manual Aiming." In *Vision and Motor Control,* edited by Luc Proteau and Digby Elliott, 179–196. New York: Elsevier, 1992.

Cartwright, Nancy. *How the Laws of Physics Lie.* New York: Oxford University Press, 1983.

References

Cartwright, Nancy. "Fundamentalism vs. the Patchwork of Laws." *Proceedings of the Aristotelian Society* 94 (1994): 279–292.

Cataldi, Sue L. *Emotion, Depth, and Flesh: A Study of Sensitive Space*. Albany: SUNY Press, 1993.

Cavell, Marcia. *The Psychoanalytic Mind From Freud to Philosophy*. Cambridge: Harvard University Press, 1993.

Cavell, Marcia. "Metaphor, Dreamwork, and Irrationality." In *Truth and Interpretation: Perspectives on the Philosophy of Donald Davidson*, edited by Ernest LePore, 495–507. Oxford: Blackwell, 1986.

Cavell, Marcia. "Triangulation, One's Own Mind and Objectivity." *International Journal of Psycho-analysis* 79 (1998): 449–468.

Chartand, Sabra. "A Split in Thinking Among Keepers of Artificial Intelligence." *New York Times*, July 18, 1993.

Coady, C. A. J. *Testimony: A Philosophical Study*. Oxford: Clarendon Press, 1992.

Collins, Corbin. "Searle on Consciousness and Dualism." *International Journal of Philosophical Studies* 5 (1997): 1–33.

Collins, H. M. *Artificial Experts: Social Knowledge and Intelligent Machines*. Cambridge: MIT Press, 1990.

Collins, H. M. "Embedded or Embodied: A Review of Hubert Dreyfus's *What Computers Still Can't Do*." *Artificial Intelligence* 80, no. 1 (1996): 99–117.

Collins, H. M. "Hubert Dreyfus, Forms of Life, and a Simple Test For Machine Intelligence." *Social Studies of Science* 22 (1992): 726–739.

Collins, H. M. "Humans, Machines, and the Structure of Knowledge." *Stanford Humanities Review* 4, no. 2 (1995): 67–83.

Collins, H. M. "Socialness and the Undersocialised Conception of Society." *Science Technology and Human Values* 23, no. 4 (1998): 494–516.

Collins, H. M. "The Structure of Knowledge." *Social Research* 60 (1993): 95–116.

Collins, H. M., and Martin Kusch. *The Shape of Actions: What Humans and Machines Can Do*. Cambridge: MIT Press, 1999.

Collins, H. M., and Martin Kusch. "Two Kinds of Actions: A Phenomenological Study." *Philosophy and Phenomenological Research* 55, no. 4 (1995): 799–819.

Collins, H. M., and Trevor Pinch. *The Golem at Large: What You Should Know About Technology*. Cambridge: Cambridge University Press, 1998.

Crossman, E. R. F. W., and P. J. Goodeve. "Feedback Control of hand-movements and Fitts' Law." *Quarterly Journal of Experimental Psychology* 35A (1983): 251–278.

References

Csikszentmilalyi, Mihaly. *Flow: The Psychology of Optimal Experience.* New York: Harper Collins, 1991.

Damasio, Antonio R., and Arthur L. Benton. "Impairment of Hand Movements under Visual Guidance." *Neurology* 29 (1979): 170–174.

Davidson, Donald. *Essays on Actions and Events.* Oxford: Oxford University Press, 1980.

Davidson, Donald. *Inquiries into Truth and Interpretation:* Oxford: Oxford University Press, 1984.

Davidson, Donald. "Deception and Division." In *The Multiple Self,* edited by Jon Elster, 79–92. Cambridge: Cambridge University Press, 1985.

Davidson, Donald. "Paradoxes of Irrationality." In *Philosophical Essays on Freud,* edited by Richard Wollheim and James Hopkins, 289–305. Cambridge: Cambridge University Press, 1982.

Davis, Natalie Zemon. *Society and Culture in Early Modern France: Eight Essays.* Stanford: Stanford University Press, 1975.

Dennett, Daniel. "The Practical Requirements for Making a Conscious Robot." *Philosophical Transactions of the Royal Society* 349 (1994): 133–146.

Downing, George. *Körper und Wort in der Psychotherapie.* Munich: Kösel, 1996.

Dreyfus, Hubert L. *Being-in-the-World: A Commentary on Heidegger's* Being and Time, *Division I.* Cambridge: MIT Press, 1991.

Dreyfus, Hubert L. *What Computers Can't Do: A Critique of Artificial Intelligence.* New York: Harper & Row, 1972.

Dreyfus, Hubert L. *What Computers Can't Do: The Limits of Artificial Intelligence.* Rev. ed. New York: Harper & Row, 1979.

Dreyfus, Hubert L. *What Computers* Still *Can't Do: A Critique of Artificial Reason.* Cambridge: MIT Press, 1992.

Dreyfus, Hubert L., ed. *Husserl, Intentionality, and Cognitive Science.* Cambridge: MIT Press, 1982.

Dreyfus, Hubert L. "Alchemy and Artificial Intelligence." *RAND* Paper P-3244 (December 1965).

Dreyfus, Hubert L. "Heidegger's Critique of the Husserl/Searle Account of Intentionality." *Social Research* 60, no. 1 (1993): 17–38.

Dreyfus, Hubert L. "Heidegger on the Connection between Nihilism, Art, Technology, and Politics." In *Cambridge Companion to Heidegger,* edited by Charles Guignon, 289–316. Cambridge: Cambridge University Press, 1993.

Dreyfus, Hubert L. "Holism and Hermeneutics." *Review of Metaphysics* 34 (1980): 3–24.

394

References

Dreyfus, Hubert L. "The Mind in Husserl: Intentionality in the Fog." *Times Literary Supplement,* July 12, 1991, 24–250.

Dreyfus, Hubert L. "Phenomenological Description versus Rational Reconstruction." Forthcoming in *La Revue Internationale de Philosophie.*

Dreyfus, Hubert L. "Reflections on the Workshop on 'The Self.'" *Anthropology and Humanism Quarterly* 16 (1991): 27.

Dreyfus, Hubert L. "Response to my Critics." *Artificial Intelligence* 80, no. 1 (1996): 171–191.

Dreyfus, Hubert L. "Searle's Freudian Slip." *Behavioral and Brain Sciences* 13 (1990): 603–604.

Dreyfus, Hubert L. "Telepistemology: Descartes' Last Stand." In *The Robot in the Garden: Telerobotics and Telepistemology on the Internet,* edited by Ken Goldberg. Cambridge: MIT Press, 2000.

Dreyfus, Hubert L. "Why Expert Systems Don't Exhibit Expertise." *IEEE-Expert* 1 (1986): 86–87.

Dreyfus, Hubert L. "Wittgenstein on Renouncing Theory in Psychology." *Contemporary Psychology* 27 (1982): 940–942.

Dreyfus, Hubert L., and Stuart E. Dreyfus. *Mind over Machine: The Power of Human Intuition and Expertise in the Era of the Computer.* New York: Free Press, 1986.

Dreyfus, Hubert L., and Stuart E. Dreyfus. "Making a Mind vs. Modeling the Brain: Artificial Intelligence Back at a Branchpoint." *Daedalus* 117 (Winter 1988): 15–44.

Dreyfus, Hubert L., and Stuart Dreyfus. "Towards a Phenomenology of Ethical Expertise." *Human Studies* 14 (1991): 229–250.

Dreyfus, Hubert L. and Stuart Dreyfus. "Why Computers May Never Think Like People." *Technology Review* 89 (1986): 42–61.

Dreyfus, Hubert L., and Paul Rabinow. *Michel Foucault: Beyond Structuralism and Hermeneutics.* 2nd ed. Chicago: University of Chicago Press, 1983.

Dreyfus, Hubert L. and Charles Spinosa, "Coping with Things-in-Themselves." *Inquiry* 42 (1999): 49–78.

Dunlop, M. J. "Is a Science of Caring Possible?" *Journal of Advanced Nursing* 11 (1986): 661–670.

Dunne, Joseph. *Back to the Rough Ground: "Phronesis" and "Techne" in Modern Philosophy and in Aristotle.* Notre Dame, IN: University of Notre Dame Press, 1993.

Ekman, Paul, ed., *Emotion in the Human Face.* New York: Pergamon, 1972.

Ekman, Paul, and Richard J. Davidson, eds. *The Nature of Emotion: Fundamental Questions.* New York: Oxford University Press, 1994.

Evans, Gareth. *Varieties of Reference*. Oxford: Oxford University Press, 1982.

Fitts, Paul M. "The Information Capacity of the Human Motor System in Controlling the Amplitude of Movement." *Joural of Experimental Psychology: General* 47 (1954): 381–391.

Flores, Fernando. "Information Technology and the Institute of Identity: *Reflections since Understanding Computors and Cognition*. Information Technology and People II, 4 (1998): 35–372.

Flores, Fernando, and Robert Solomon. *Business Ethics Quarterly* (1998).

Flores, Fernando, and Robert Solomon. *Coming to Trust*. Oxford: Oxford University Press, forthcoming.

Flores, Fernando, and Robert Solomon. *The Cultivation of Trust*. Oxford: Oxford University Press, forthcoming.

Fodor, Jerry. *The Modularity of Mind: An Essay on Faculty Psychology*. Cambridge: MIT Press, 1983.

Foucault, Michel. *The Birth of the Clinic: An Archeology of Medical Perception*. New York: Vintage Books, 1973.

Foucault, Michel. *Discipline and Punish: The Birth of the Prison*. New York: Pantheon, 1977.

Foucault, Michel. *The History of Sexuality*, vol. 1. Translated by Alan Sheridan. New York: Pantheon, 1978.

Foucault, Michel. *Power/Knowledge: Selected Interviews and Other Writings 1972–1977*. Edited and translated by Colin Gordon. New York: Pantheon, 1980.

Foucault, Michel. "Politics and Ethics: An Interview." In *The Foucault Reader*, edited by Paul Rabinow, 373–380. New York: Pantheon, 1984.

Fox, Renee C., and Judith P. Swazey. "Leaving the Field." *Hastings Center Report* 22, no. 5 (1992): 9–15.

Freud, Anna. *The Ego and the Mechanisms of Defense*. Translated by Cecil Baines. London: Hogarth Press, 1948.

Freud, Sigmund. "Psychoanalytic Notes upon an Autobiographical Account of a Case of Paranoia." In *Three Case Histories*. New York: Collier Books, 1963.

Frijda, Nico H. *The Emotions*. Cambridge: Cambridge University Press, 1986.

Fukuyama, Francis. *Trust: The Social Virtues and the Creation of Prosperity*. New York: Free Press, 1995.

Galison, Peter. *Image and Logic: A Material Culture of Microphysics*. Chicago: University of Chicago Press, 1997.

References

Gallagaher, Shaun. "Body Image and Body Schema: A Conceptual Clarification." *Journal of Mind and Behavior* 7 (1986): 541–554.

Gallagaher, Shaun. "Body Schema and Intentionality." In *The Body and the Self*, edited by José L. Bermúdez et al., 225–244. Cambridge: MIT Press, Bradford Books, 1995.

Gallwey, W. Timothy. *Inner Tennis: Playing the Game.* New York: Random House, 1976.

Gambetta, Diego. *Trust: Making and Breaking Cooperative Relations.* Oxford: Blackwell, 1988.

Gawande, Atul. "No Mistake." *New Yorker* (March 30, 1998): 74–81.

Gibson, William. *Neuromancer.* New York: Ace Books, 1984.

Giddens, Anthony. *Modernity and Self-Identity: Self and Society in the Late Modern Age.* Stanford: Stanford University Press, 1991.

Giere, Ronald N. *Explaining Science: A Cognitive Approach.* Chicago: University of Chicago Press, 1988.

Goodale, M. A., and A. D. Milner. "Separate visual pathways for perception and action." *Trends in Neuroscience* 15, no. 1 (1992): 20–25.

Goodale, M. A., L. S. Jakobson, and J. M. Keillor. "Differences in the Visual Control of Pantomimed and Natural Grasping Movements." *Neuropsychologia* 32, no. 10 (1994): 1159–1178.

Goodale, M. A., et al. "A Neurological Dissociation between Perceiving Objects and Grasping Them." *Nature: An International Weekly Journal of Science* 349 (1991): 154–156.

Gordon, Robert M. *The Structure of Emotions: Investigations in Cognitive Philosophy.* Cambridge: Cambridge University Press, 1987.

Gordon, Robert M. "Radical Simulations." In *Theories of Theories of Mind*, edited by Peter Carruthers and Peter Smith, 11–21. Cambridge: Cambridge University Press, 1996.

Greenberg, Leslie, and Jeremy D. Safran. *Emotion in Psychotherapy: Affect, Cognition, and the Process of Change.* New York: Guilford, 1987.

Greenspan, Patricia. *Emotions and Reasons: An Inquiry into Emotional Justification.* New York: Routledge, 1988.

Hamilton, Kendal, and Julie Weingarden. "Lifts, Lasers, and Liposuction: The Cosmetic Surgery Boom." *Newsweek* (June 15, 1998): 14.

Hardin, Russell. "Trustworthiness." *Ethics* 107 (1996): 26–42.

Harpur, Patrick. *Daimonic Reality.* New York: Penguin, 1996.

Hatfield, Elaine, John T. Cacioppo, and Richard L. Rapson. *Emotional Contagion.* Cambridge: Cambridge University Press, 1994.

References

Haugeland, John. *Artificial Intelligence: The Very Idea*. Cambridge: MIT Press, 1985.

Haugeland, John. "Heidegger on Being a Person." *Nous* 16 (1982): 15–26.

Heal, Jane. "Replication and Functionalism." In *Folk Psychology: The Theory of Mind Debate*, edited by Martin Davies and Tony Stone, 45–59. Oxford: Blackwell, 1995.

Heidegger, Martin. *Basic Problems of Phenomenology*. Translated by Albert Hofstadter. Bloomington: Indiana University Press, 1982.

Heidegger, Martin. *Basic Writings*, rev. ed. Edited by David F. Krell. New York: Harper & Row, 1993.

Heidegger, Martin. *Being and Time*. Translated by John Macquarrie and Edward Robinson. New York: Harper & Row, 1962.

Heidegger, Martin. *The Fundamental Concepts of Metaphysics: World, Finitude, Solitude*. Translated by William McNeill and Nicholas Walker. Bloomington: Indiana University Press, 1995.

Heidegger, Martin. *History of the Concept of Time*. Translated by Theodore Kisiel. Bloomington: Indiana University Press, 1962.

Heidegger, Martin. *Identity and Difference*. Translated by Joan Stambaugh. New York: Harper & Row, 1969.

Heidegger, Martin. *The Metaphysical Foundations of Logic*. Bloomington: Indiana University Press, 1984.

Heidegger, Martin. *Parmenides*. Translated by André Schuwer and Richard Rojcewicz. Bloomington: Indiana University Press, 1992.

Heidegger, Martin. *Poetry, Language, Thought*. Translated by Albert Hofstadter. New York: Harper & Row, 1971.

Heidegger, Martin. *What Is Called Thinking?* Translated by J. Glenn Gray. New York: Harper & Row, 1968.

Heller, Michael. "Posture as an interface between biology and culture." In *Nonverbal Communication: Where Nature Meets Culture*. Edited by Ullica Segerstråle and Peter Molnár. Mahwah, N. J.: Lawrence Erlbaum Associates, 1997.

Hofstadter, Richard. "The Paranoid Style in American Politics." In *The Paranoid Style in American Politics: And Other Essays*. New York: Knopf, 1965.

Holden, T. "Seeing Joan Through." *American Journal of Nursing* 91 (December 1992): 26–30.

Hooper, P. L. "Expert Titration of Multiple Vasoactive Drugs in Post-cardiac Surgical Patients: An Interpretive Study of Clinical Judgment and Perceptual Acuity." Ph.D. diss., University of California at San Francisco, 1995.

Horgan, John. *The End of Science: Facing the Limits of Knowledge in the Twilight of the Scientific Age*. Reading, Mass.: Addison-Wesley, 1996.

References

Horton, Richard. "Deciding to Trust, Coming to Believe." *Australasian Journal of Philosophy* 72, no. 1 (1994): 63–76.

James, William. *The Principles of Psychology*, 2 vols. New York: H. Holt, 1890.

James, William. *Varieties of Religious Experience: A Study in Human Nature*. New York: Random House-Modern Library, 1902.

Jeannerod, Marc. *The Cognitive Neuroscience of Action*. Cambridge: Blackwell, 1997.

Johnston, Paul. *Wittgenstein: Rethinking the Inner*. London: Routledge, 1993.

Jones, Karen, Russell Hardin, and Lawrence C. Becker. "Symposium on Trust." *Ethics* 107 (1996): 4–61.

Kelly, Sean. "The Non-conceptual Content of Perceptual Experience and the Possibility of Demonstrative Thought." Forthcoming.

Kenny, Anthony. *Action, Emotion, and Will*. Bristol: Thoemmes, 1994.

Kemper, Theodore D. "Sociological Models in the Explanation of Emotions."

Kepner, James I. *Body Process: A Gestalt Approach to Working with the Body in Psychotherapy*. New York: Gardner Press: Gestalt Institute of Cleveland, 1987.

Kierkegaard, Søren. *The Concept of Anxiety: A Simple Psychologically Orienting Deliberation on the Dogmatic Issue of Hereditary Sin*. Edited and translated by Reidar Thomte. Princeton: Princeton University Press, 1980.

Kierkegaard, Søren. *Either/Or: A Fragment of Life*, 2 vols. Translated by David F. Swenson and Lillian Marvin Swenson, vol. 2 translated by Walter Lowrie. Princeton: Princeton University Press, 1944.

Klein, Melanie. *The Selected Melanie Klein*. New York: Free Press, 1987.

Krell, David Farrell. *Daimon Life: Heidegger and Life-Philosophy*. Bloomington: Indiana University Press, 1992.

Kuntz, Tom. "A Death on Line Shows a Cyberspace with Heart and Soul." *New York Times*, 23 April 1995.

Kwan, Hon C., et al. "Network Relaxation as Biological Computation." *Behavioral and Brain Sciences* 14, no. 2 (1991): 354–356.

Lakoff, George. *Women, Fire, and Dangerous Things: What Categories Reveal about the Mind*. Chicago: University of Chicago Press, 1987.

Lazarus, Richard S. *Emotion and Adaptation*. New York: Oxford University Press, 1991.

Lehrer, Keith. *Self-Trust: A Study of Reason, Knowledge, and Autonomy*. New York: Oxford University Press, 1997.

Levey, Samuel, and Donglas D. Hesse, "Sounding Board: Bottom-line Health Care?" *New England Journal of Medicine* 312, no. 10 (1985): 644–647.

References

Lowenberg, June S. *Caring and Responsibility*. Philadelphia: University of Pennsylvania Press, 1989.

Luhmann, Niklas. *Trust and Power: Two Works*. Translated by Howard Davis, John Raffan, and Kathryn Rooney. New York: John Wiley and Sons, 1979.

Lyons, William. *Emotion*. Cambridge: Cambridge University Press, 1980.

Mandler, George. *Mind and Body: Psychology of Emotion and Stress*. New York: W. W. Norton, 1984.

McCarthy, John, "Programs with Common Sense." In *Semantic Information Processing*, edited by M. Minsky. Cambridge: MIT Press, 1969.

Merleau-Ponty, Maurice. *La Phénoménologie de la Perception*. Paris: Gallimard, 1945; *Phenomenology of Perception*. Translated by Colin Smith. New York: Routledge and Kegan Paul, 1962.

Meyer, David, et al. "Speed-Accuracy Tradeoffs in Aimed Movements: Toward a Theory of Rapid Voluntary Action." In *Attention and Performance XIII: Motor Representation and Control*, edited by M. Jeannerod, 173–226. Hillsdale, N.J.: Lawrence Erlbaum Associates, 1990.

Moravec, Hans. *Mind Children: The Future of Robot and Human Intelligence*. Cambridge: Harvard University Press, 1988.

Mulligan, Kevin. "Perception." In *The Cambridge Companion to Husserl*, edited by Barry Smith and David W. Smith, 168–238. Cambridge: Cambridge University Press, 1995.

Neu, Jerome. *Emotion, Thought, and Therapy*. London: Routledge and Kegan Paul, 1977.

Oakley, Justin. *Morality and the Emotions*. London: Routledge, 1992.

Oatley, Keith. *Best Laid Schemes: The Psychology of Emotions*. Cambridge: Cambridge University Press, 1992.

Otto, Rudolf. *The Idea of the Holy: An Inquiry into the Non-rational Factor in the Idea of the Divine and its Relation to the Rational*. Translated by John W. Harvey. London: Oxford University Press, 1958.

Parkinson, Brian. *Ideas and Realities of Emotion*. London: Routledge, 1995.

Peacocke, Christopher. "Nonconceptual Content Defended." *Philosophy and Phenomenological Research* 58 (1998): 381–388.

Pears, David F. *Motivated Irrationality*. Oxford: Oxford University Press, 1984.

Perenin, M. T., and A. Vighetto. "Optic Ataxia: A Specific Disruption in Visuomotor Mechanisms. I. Different Aspects of the Deficit in Reaching for Objects." *Brain: A Journal of Neurology* 111 (1988): 643–674.

Perry, John. *The Problem of the Essential Indexical and Other Essays*. New York: Oxford University Press, 1993.

References

Peterson, Aage. "The Philosophy of Niels Bohr." In *Niels Bohr: A Centenary Volume*, edited by A. P. French and P. J. Kennedy, 299–310. Cambridge: Harvard University Press, 1985.

Pettit, Philip. "The Cunning of Trust." *Philosophy and Public Affairs* 24, no. 3 (1995): 202–225.

Petzet, Heinrich W. *Encounters and Dialogues with Martin Heidegger,1929–1976*. Translated by Parvis Emad and Kenneth Maly. Chicago: University of Chicago Press, 1993.

Plutchik, Robert. *The Psychology and Biology of Emotion*. New York: Harper, 1994.

Recanati, Françoise. "Déstabiliser le Sens." Forthcoming.

Rouse, Joseph. *Engaging Science: How to Understand Its Practices Philosophically*. Ithaca, N.Y.: Cornell University Press, 1996.

Rouse, Joseph. "Beyond Epistemic Sovereignty." In *The Disunity of Science: Boundaries, Contexts, and Power*, edited by Peter Galison and David Stump, 398–416. Stanford: Stanford University Press, 1996.

Rubin, Jane. "Too Much of Nothing: Modern Culture, the Self, and Salvation in Kierkegaard's Thought." Ph.D. diss., University of California, Berkeley, 1984.

Rubin, Jane. "Impediments to the Development of Clinical Knowledge and Ethical Judgment in Critical Care Nurses." In *Expertise in Nursing Practice: Caring, Clinical Judgment, and Ethics*, edited by Patricia Benner, Christine Tanner, and Catherine Chesla, 170–192. New York: Springer, 1996.

Rumelhart, David E., James L. McClelland, and the PDR Research Group. *Parallel Distributed Processing: Explorations in the Microstructure of Cognition*, vol. 1, *Foundations*. Cambridge: MIT Press, 1986.

Ryle, Gilbert. *The Concept of Mind*. New York: Barnes and Noble, 1949.

Sartre, Jean-Paul. *Being and Nothingness: An Essay on Phenomenological Ontology*. Translated by Hazel Barnes. New York: Philosophical Library, 1956.

Sartre, Jean-Paul. *Sketch for a Theory of the Emotions*. Translated by Philip Maret. London: Methuen, 1962.

Schafer, Roy. *A New Language for Psychoanalysis*. New Haven: Yale University Press, 1976.

Schatzki, Theodore R. *Social Practices: A Wittgensteinian Approach to Human Activity and the Social*. New York: Cambridge University Press, 1996.

Schatzki, Theodore R. "Inside-out?" *Inquiry* 38 (1995): 329–347.

Searle, John R. *The Construction of Social Reality*. New York: Free Press, 1995.

Searle, John R. *Intentionality: An Essay in the Philosophy of Mind*. Cambridge: Cambridge University Press, 1983.

References

Searle, John R. *Mind, Language, and Society.* New York: Basic Books, 1998.

Searle, John R. *Minds, Brains, and Science.* Cambridge: Harvard University Press, 1984.

Searle, John R. *The Rediscovery of the Mind.* Cambridge: MIT Press, 1992.

Searle, John R. "Conscionsness, Explanatory Inversion, and Cognitive Science." *Behavioral and Brain Sciences* 13, no. 4 (1990): 603–604.

Searle, John R. "Response: The Background of Intentionality and Action." In *John Searle and His Critics,* edited by Ernest Lepore and Robert van Gulick, 289–299. Cambridge: Basil Blackwell, 1991.

Seligman, Martin. *Creating Optimism.* New York: Knopf, 1991.

Shusterman, Richard. *Practicing Philosophy,* New York: Routledge, 1997.

Solomon, Robert C. *The Passions.* Garden City, N.Y.: Anchor/Doubleday, 1976.

Sperber, Dan. "The Modularity of Thought and the Epidemiology of Representations." In *Mapping the Mind: Domain Specificity in Cognition and Culture,* edited by Lawrence A. Hirchfeld and Susan A. Gelman, 39–67. Cambridge: Cambridge University Press, 1994.

Sperber, Dan, and Deirdre Wilson. *Relevance: Communication and Cognition.* Oxford: Blackwell, 1986.

Spinosa, Charles. "Derrida and Heidegger: Iterability and *Ereignis.*" In *Heidegger: A Critical Reader,* edited by Hubert L. Dreyfus and Harrison Hall, 270–297. Oxford: Blackwell, 1992.

Spinosa, Charles. "Derridian Dispersion and Heideggerian Articulation: General Tendencies in the Practices that Govern Intelligibility." In *The Practice Turn in Contemporary Theory,* edited by Ted Schatzki, et al. London: Routledge, forthcoming.

Spinosa, Charles, and Hubert L. Dreyfus. "Robust Intelligibility: Response to Our Critics." *Inquiry* 42 (March 1999): 49–78.

Spinosa, Charles, Fernando Flores, and Hubert Dreyfus. *Disclosing New Worlds: Entrepreneurship, Democratic Action, and the Cultivation of Solidarity.* Cambridge: MIT Press, 1997.

Stein, Nancy L., Tom Trabasso, and Maria Liwag. "The Representation and Organization of Emotional Experience: Unfolding the Emotion Episode." In *Handbook of Emotions,* edited by Michael Lewis and Jeannette Haviland, 279–300. New York: Guilford, 1993.

Stern, Daniel N. *The Interpersonal World of the Infant: A View from Psychoanalysis and Developmental Psychology.* New York: Basic Books, 1985.

Strawson, P. F. *Individuals: An Essay in Descriptive Metaphysis.* London: Methuen, 1959.

Stroud, Barry. "The Background of Thought." In *John Searle and His Critics,* edited by Ernest Lepore and Robert van Gulick, 245–258. Cambridge: Basil Blackwell, 1991.

References

Tanner, Christine, et al. "The Phenomenology of Knowing the Patient." *Image: The Journal of Nursing Scholarship* 25, no. 4 (1993): 273–280.

Taylor, Charles. *Human Agency and Language*. Philosophical Papers, vol. 1. Cambridge: Cambridge University Press, 1985.

Taylor, Charles. *Philosophical Arguments*. Cambridge: Harvard University Press, 1995.

Taylor, Charles. *Philosophy and the Human Sciences*. Philosophical Papers. vol. 2. Cambridge: Cambridge University Press, 1985.

Taylor, Charles. *Sources of the Self: The Making of Modern Identity*. Cambridge: Harvard University Press, 1989.

Teasdale, John D. "Emotion and Two Kinds of Meaning: Cognitive Therapy and Applied Cognitive Science." *Behaviour Research and Therapy* 31 (1993): 339–354.

Teasdale, John D., and Philip J. Barnard. *Affect, Cognition and Change: Re-Modelling Depressive Thought*. Hillsdale, N.J.: Erlbaum, 1993.

Thomas, Laurence. "Reasons for Loving." In *The Philosophy of (Erotic) Love*, edited by Kathleen Higgins and Robert Solomon, 467–477. Lawrence, Kans.: University of Kansas Press, 1991.

Tipler, Frank. *The Physics of Immortality: Modern Cosmology, God, and Resurrection*. New York: Doubleday, 1994.

Travis, Charles. *The Uses of Sense: Wittgenstein's Philosophy of Language*. Oxford: Oxford University Press, 1989.

Tronick, Edward Z. "Affectivity and Sharing." In *Social Interchange in Infancy: Affect, Cognition, and Communication*, edited by Edward Z. Tronick, 1–6. Baltimore: University Park Press, 1982.

Tronick, Edward Z. "Emotions and Emotional Communication in Infants." *American Psychologist* 44 (1989): 112–119.

Tronick, Edward Z. "The Transmission of Maternal Disturbance to the Infant." In *Maternal Depression and Infant Disturbance*, edited by Edward Z. Tronick and Tiffany Field, 5–11. San Francisco: Jossey-Bass, 1986.

Turing, A. M. "Computing Machinery and Intelligence." *Mind* 59 (1950): 433–460.

Turkle, Sherry. *Life on the Screen: Identity in the Age of the Internet*. New York: Simon and Schuster, 1995.

Turner, Stephen P. *The Social Theory of Practices: Tradition, Tacit Knowledge, and Presuppositions*. Cambridge: Polity Press, 1994.

Turner, Victor. *Dramas, Fields and Metaphors: Symbolic Action in Human Society*. Ithaca, N.Y.: Cornell University Press, 1978.

References

Waismann, Friedrich. "Verifiability." In *Logic and Language*, edited by Antony Flew, 122–151. Oxford: Basil Blackwell, 1951.

Wakefield, Jerome, and Hubert L. Dreyfus. "Intentionality and the Phenomenology of Action." In *John Searle and His Critics*, edited by Ernest Lepore and Robert van Gulick, 259–270. Oxford: Blackwell, 1991.

Weber, Max. *Basic Concepts of Sociology.* Translated by H. P. Secher. New York: Citadel, 1962.

Westphal, Merold. *God, Guilt, and Death: An Existential Phenomenology of Religion.* Edited by James M. Edie. Bloomington: Indiana University Press, 1984.

Wheeler, Samuel C., III. "True Figures: Metaphor, Social Relations, and the Sorites." In *The Interpretive Turn: Philosophy, Science, Culture*, edited by David Hiley, James Bohman, and Richard Shusterman, 197–217. Ithaca, N.Y.: Cornell University Press, 1991.

White, Geoffrey M. "Emotions Inside Out: The Anthropology of Affect." In *Handbook of Emotions*, edited by Michael Lewis and Jeannette Haviland, 29–40. New York: Guilford, 1993.

Winograd, Terry, and Fernando Flores. *Understanding Computers and Cognition: A New Foundation for Design.* Norwood, N.J.: Ablex, 1986.

Wittgenstein, Ludwig. *The Blue and Brown Books.* Oxford: Blackwell, 1958.

Wittgenstein, Ludwig. *On Certainty.* Translated by Dennis Paul and G. E. M. Anscombe. New York: J. & J. Harper Editions, 1969.

Wittgenstein, Ludwig. *Philosophical Investigations.* Translated by G. E. M. Anscombe. New York: Macmillan, 1958.

Woodworth, R. S. "The Accuracy of Voluntary Movement." *Psychological Review* 3, no. 13 (1899): 1–114.

Contributors

Daniel Andler is Professor of Philosophy at the University of Paris X, Nanterre.

Patricia Benner is Professor of Nursing at the University of California at San Francisco.

Albert Borgmann is Professor of Philosophy at the University of Montana.

H. M. Collins is Professor of Sociology at Cardiff University.

George Downing is part of a research and treatment program for infant psychiatry at Salpêtrière Hospital, and Professor of Clinical Psychology at the University of Klagenfurt, Austria.

Fernando Flores is President of Business Design Associates.

Sean D. Kelly is Assistant Professor in Philosophy at Princeton University.

Joseph Rouse is Professor of Philosophy at Wesleyan University.

Theodore R. Schatzki is Associate Professor in Philosophy at the University of Kentucky.

John Searle is Professor of Philosophy at the University of California at Berkeley.

Robert C. Solomon is Professor of Philosophy at the University of Texas at Austin.

Charles Spinosa is Head of Research at Business Design Associates.

David Stern is Assistant Professor in Philosophy at the University of Iowa.

Charles Taylor is Professor of Philosophy at McGill University.

Contributors

Mark A. Wrathall is Assistant Professor in Philosophy at Brigham Young University.

Terry Winograd is Professor of Computer Science at Stanford University, California.

Index